A Special Issue of
Visual Cognition

Independence and integration of perception and action

Edited by

Robert Ward
University of Wales, Bangor, UK

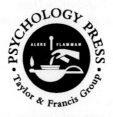

Published in 2002 by Psychology Press Ltd
27 Church Road, Hove, East Sussex BN3 2FA
www.psypress.co.uk

Simultaneously published in the USA and Canada
by Taylor & Francis Inc.
29 West 35th Street, New York, NY 10001

Psychology Press is part of the Taylor & Francis Group

British Library Cataloguing in Publication Data
A catalogue record for this book is available from the British Library

ISBN 1–84169–927–6 (hbk)
ISSN 1350-6285

Cover design by Joyce Chester.
Typeset in the UK by Quorum Technical Services, Cheltenham, Glos.
Printed in the UK by Henry Ling Ltd, Dorchester, Dorset.
Bound in the UK by TJ International Ltd, Padstow, Cornwall.

Contents*

---

* This book is also a special issue of the journal *Visual Cognition* and forms
Issues 4 and 5 of Volume 9 (2002). The page numbers used here are taken from
the journal and so begin on p. 385.

VISUAL COGNITION, 2002, 9 (4/5), 385–391

Independence and integration of perception and action: An introduction

Robert Ward

Centre for Cognitive Neuroscience, University of Wales, Bangor, UK

This special issue examines the relationships between cognitive systems for perception and action. "Action" is meant in a very broad sense, to include processes of selecting, planning, and executing overt responses. Recent interest in the psychology and neuropsychology of action has led to a variety of approaches describing visuomotor systems and the relationship between perception and action. There is at least one basic constraint on this relationship that everyone can agree on: Perceptual systems have evolved to guide action. So although it is at least conceivable that perceptual processing could go on largely independent of concurrent action, a system that planned and executed actions without perceptual guidance would be worse than useless—it would be a complete disaster in anything but the most predictable environment.

ARCHITECTURES FOR PERCEPTION AND ACTION

But even given this fundamental constraint, there are many frameworks for understanding integration and independence of perception and action. One framework deserves special attention, because it is certainly the most widely accepted view of perception-action linkage, and because it carries crucial theoretical and methodological implications. This approach is the hypothesis of *perception independent of action*, hinted at previously. Traditional models of perception and action have assumed a linear, feed-forward sequence of processing, in which the outputs of perception are used to drive a subsequent, terminal stage of response execution (e.g., Sternberg, 1969). The flow of information in such a model allows perceptual analysis to guide action, but does not allow action systems to have reciprocal effects on perception. This does not mean that task demands can not influence perceptual processing. It is

Please address all correspondence to R. Ward, Centre for Cognitive Neuroscience, University of Wales, Bangor LL57 2AS, UK. Email: r.ward@bangor.ac.uk

© 2002 Psychology Press Ltd
http://www.tandf.co.uk/journals/pp/13506285.html   DOI:10.1080/13506280042000502

entirely consistent with the idea of perception independent of action that cognitive systems can be preconfigured to adapt to task demands. So for example, when performing a grasping action, three-dimensional object shape is important and less so colour, when monitoring a traffic signal, the reverse is true. What the hypothesis does mean is that neither action nor preparation for action in themselves can influence ongoing perceptual processing. That is, waving one arm, or planning to wave one arm, should not have any influence on visual perception or attention as long as the movement itself is not seen.

The hypothesis that perception is independent of action is widely accepted in many cognitive theories, usually implicitly. This would include numerous theories of visual attention and object recognition in which action plays no role. It would be difficult and misleading to cite any one theory as a particular example here, since it is a property of so many models. In many cases, it might be argued that the absence of a role for action does not reflect a fundamental claim of the theory, but simply the limited domain which any theory can capably address. However, even this disclaimer would imply that action is seen as irrelevant to many of the fundamental properties of perception and attention addressed by theorists. The important implication is that, since responses cannot directly affect perceptual processing, then perception can be studied independently of response. For example, by this model, target recognition in visual search would proceed in the exact same manner, regardless of whether responses are made verbally, by keypress, by foot switch, by saccade, by pointing to, or by grasping the target.

Conversely, if perception is not independent of action, then perception and action must be considered together rather than separately. A variety of approaches have been developed emphasizing the implications of action on perceptual processing, including: (1) specialized visual streams for action (Milner & Goodale, 1995); (2) the common coding theory for perceptual events and action (Prinz, 1990), which describes mutual influence of perception and action processing at the level of shared codes at their interface; (3) the premotor theory of visual attention, which suggests that spatial maps used for planning and executing action are also used for directing perceptual processing (Rizzolatti, Riggio, & Sheliga, 1994). It's beyond the scope of this introduction to review all these accounts, but they are considered in detail in the papers here, and in reviews elsewhere (e.g., Hommel & Prinz, 1997).

The first papers in this issue look to explicitly demonstrate an influence of action on concurrent perception. Hommel and Schneider adapt the PRP (psychological refractory period) paradigm as used previously by Pashler (1991) to argue against a shared bottleneck for perceptual processing and response selection. Participants in the Hommel and Schneider task made a speeded left or right keypress in response to a tone. Shortly after a visual search array appeared. Hommel and Schneider find evidence of general interference, but also for specific correspondence effects. The keypress made in response to the tone induced a bias in spatial attention, so that the side of the array correspond-ing to the keypress was searched first. Similar to our previous example of arm waving changing perception, this study demonstrates that motor activity in the form of an unseen action can induce a lateralized attention bias.

Müsseler and colleagues have previously identified another way in which action can bias concurrent perception (e.g., Müsseler & Hommel, 1997; Müsseler, Wühr, & Prinz, 2000). In their previous studies of action–effect blindness, they have demonstrated competition for common semantic codes between perceptual and response-related processes. So for example, making a response categorized as "left" interferes with the detection and identification of concurrent stimuli that would also be categorized as "left", e.g., a left- as opposed to right-facing arrow. Wühr and Müsseler examine the time course of this effect in a series of experiments. Among other findings, they show that action–effect blindness is sustained during the delay period in which an action is prepared but not executed. However, after response execution, the semantic code associated with the response is made rapidly available. That is, after exe-cution, response systems "release" their associated semantic codes so they are available to other systems. In addition to these effects tied to the overlap of spe-cific perceptual and response codes, Wühr and Müsseler also find general dual-task interference from maintaining a prepared action on perceptual processing.

The results of Hommel and Schneider and Wühr and Müsseler show that action can produce both spatial and semantic cases, respectively, on concurrent perceptual processing. However, Bonfiglioi et al. have also set out a series of careful studies looking for similar effects. Here they aimed to uncover spatial biases in visual attention evoked by lateralized reaching movements. Their findings were consistently negative: Attention was not biased towards the side of space where reaching movements were occurring, and in fact movement pro-duced no spatial attention bias at all. Given the contrary Hommel and Schneider findings, we are left with the idea that either the effects of action on perception are small, and that there will be frequent issues of experimental power in look-ing for these effects: or that the influence of action on perception is bound to specific task parameters, established on the positive side by Hommel and Schneider, and on the negative side by Bonfiglioi et al. Either way we are left with an important question: Do the current findings establishing effects of action on perception reflect a fundamental and critical property of the visuomotor architecture? The papers here provide theoretical arguments for the necessity of these interactions, and perhaps future research will identify the task conditions that do and do not support biases from action on perception.

The next papers examine the integration of stimulus and response process-ing during the preparation and control of responses. Responses to frequent, predictable stimuli are fast compared to conditions where the correct response cannot be easily prepared. Interestingly, prepared responses are also likely to be more efficient, in that they can be made with less force, and previous accounts have suggested that these benefits of response preparation originate in the motor system (Mattes, Ulrich, & Miller, 1997). However, Mattes, Ulrich, and Miller note here that preparation could also affect stimulus processing, and that previous studies have confounded these possibilities. Mattes et al. dissociate the effect of stimulus and response probability on motor preparation using both response time (RT) and response force measures. They establish that stimulus and response probability have independent effects on response force and RT. These findings demonstrate that effects of motor preparation are best understood by considering both stimulus and response factors, and so argue against the notion of functionally encapsulated modules for stimulus and response. That is, just as studies by Hommel and Schneider, and by Wühr and Müsseler, illustrate situations in which perception cannot be studied independently of action, here motor processing cannot be considered in the absence of related perceptual processing.

An enduring issue concerns the use of perceptual information before and during action, in the control of response. The concept of forward dynamic models of action has been used to describe how plans for action integrate on-line sensory guidance. Forward models describe how the parameters of action (such as limb position and speed) will change over time. Feedback from sensory systems is used to refine these parameters during the course of movement, so that the predicted end-state of movement approximates the desired end-state. Fleming, Klatzky, and Behrmann further develop the concept of forward models by examining sensitivity to parameters for action during the course of manipulatory actions. They find a gradual unfolding of action parameters prior to and during motor execution, so that performance is most sensitive to variables affecting the current phase of action: During transport, sensitivity to object parameters indicating grasp force begins, followed by sensitivity to object weight around the time of contact. Thus, perceptual systems deliver relevant information for response control at the time it is needed.

Dynamic forward models for control require that the consequences of action be continuously predicted and incorporated into current planning. The action–concept view, as developed in the common-coding approach (Prinz, 1990), suggests that predictable consequences of action are integrated at another level as well, into the representation of the action itself. For example, a keypress response with the right hand not only produced predictable limb movements, but tactile, auditory, and possibly visual stimulation from the button click. According to the action–concept view, all these consequences of action are integrated into the representation of the pressing response, even though some are subsequent and are irrelevant to the goal of response. Grosjean and Mordkoff investigate the action–concept view, using a modified Simon task (Hommel, 1993). Lateralized responses triggered task-irrelevant post-response stimulation, appearing predictably in either the same or opposite side of space as the response. Simon effects were reduced by opposite-side and heightened by same-side effects, suggesting that these effects were incorporated into the meaning of the response. These findings suggest an intriguing approach to the fundamental problem of how a single action is selected from innumerable possibilities: By encoding responses in terms of the effects they produce on the environment, responses can then be selected on the relevance of their effect to current goals.

ROUTES TO ACTION

We pay attention to only selected parts of the sensory world. This selection is controlled by both voluntary top-down factors, based on current goals, and involuntary bottom-up factors, based on stimulus properties. Our actions are determined by what may be a similar combination of voluntary and involuntary factors. So although we can control action voluntarily at least to some degree, much of our behaviour results from involuntary responses triggered by the perception of the environment, and the objects within it.

Phillips and Ward investigate the nature of involuntary actions evoked by visual affordances. Object affordances are parts of objects which support or allow particular types of action; in this sense, a handle affords grasping and a button affords pushing. Previous studies have found that object affordances can evoke corresponding actions (Tucker & Ellis, 1998). Phillips and Ward examine the nature of these evoked actions. Do objects trigger only actions specific to their affordances? Phillips and Ward find that they do not. Instead, object affordances activate a range of responses, consistent with an abstract spatial response code. So a pan presented with the handle to one side not only evoked activation of the ipsilateral hand, but also activation of the contralateral hand when the hands were crossed, and activation of the ipsilateral foot. They find gradually developing and long-lasting effects of affordances in all response conditions.

Pavese and Buxbaum examine the interaction of voluntary and involuntary influences on responses to real objects providing different affordances for action. Participants responded to a target object presented with a concurrent distractor. When the response was a keypress to the target, independent of specific object affordances, distractor interference was determined primarily by low-level salience. However, when the task demanded action on the target, such as grasping, interference was a function of the affordances offered by the strength of the distractor's affordances. These results show that involuntary object affordances and their evoked actions can be modulated by task set and intentions.

These two studies show different effects of affordances on action. Phillips and Ward demonstrate that irrelevant affordances can activate a range of potential actions, whereas Pavese and Buxbaum show that task set can eliminate affordance effects when they are irrelevant to action. How can these results be reconciled? This is an issue for subsequent research, but here we can note one possibility is that effective suppression of irrelevant affordances decays with time. For Pavese and Buxbaum, effective suppression may last until response to the target; for Phillips and Ward, the gradual development of affordance effects over enforced delays may reflect a gradual loss of suppression.

The studies mentioned so far have looked at evoked action in simple contexts, when the participant is well positioned for interaction with nearby objects. However, reaching and manipulation actions in the real world are frequently complicated by obstacles in the reach path. Tipper, Meegan, and Howard look at how obstacles for reaching and manipulation affect competition for action selection. Participants reached for a target object in the presence of a competing distractor, within a negative priming paradigm. In baseline conditions, the strength of negative priming was tied to an action-centred frame referenced to the responding hand. In obstacle conditions, the distractor was occluded by a transparent cover, which prevented easy reach but did not obscure vision. Negative priming was reduced in these conditions, suggesting that the obstacle reduced the competitive strength of the action afforded by the distractor. These results raise the possibility that objects evoke responses in a sophisticated manner, as a function of the observer's current capabilities for action.

If objects can evoke action automatically, how are the possible actions to an object determined? Rumiati and Humphreys (1998) have suggested two routes to action: A direct route based on visual structure, and a mediated route based on identification of the object and its semantics. Some of the most compelling evidence for this dual-route model comes from dissociations found between optic aphasic patients (who can gesture appropriately to objects but not name them from visual presentation), and visual apraxics (who can name visual objects but are impaired in making action to them). The Naming and Action Model (NAM) developed by Yoon, Heinke, and Humphreys describes a distributed network for processing objects and their associated actions, consistent with the dual-route model. One processing stream of NAM processes visual structure, and a second lexical inputs; these two routes converge on a shared semantic system. Action outputs are associated directly with the visual structure stream and indirectly with the lexical stream via the semantic system. The model accounts for an impressive variety of data, including dissociations between aphasia and apraxia and normal RT and error performance in action selection to words and pictures. The model also makes a number of interesting predictions describing the integration of these routes during action selection: For example, damage to either route singly slowed processing along the undamaged route.

The neural basis of the dual-route model of action retrieval is investigated in positron emission tomography (PET) imaging experiments by Phillips et al.

Participants made action, semantic, or visual judgements to visually presented objects, words, and novel non-objects. Their results are consistent with several key assumptions of the dual-route model, including NAM (Yoon et al.). Action judgements to pictures and words activated left front and temporal areas, previously identified as components of a general semantic system. However, within this common area for action retrieval, words produced more activity than picture. These findings would be expected if action judgements from words, relative to pictures, place a greater load on a shared semantic system.

The studies in this special issue explore multiple pathways between perception and action, the ways in which vision promotes action, and even the degree to which action and its consequences can influence vision. They are part of a changing emphasis away from the conception of rigidly segmented perception and action systems, and towards the study of integrated visuomotor networks.

REFERENCES

Hommel, B. (1993). Inverting the Simon effect intention: Determinants of direction and extent of effects of irrelevant spatial information. *Psychological Research–Psychologische Forschung*, *55*, 270–279.

Hommel, B., & Prinz, W. (Eds.). (1997). *Theoretical issues in stimulus–response compatibility*. Amsterdam: North-Holland.

Mattes, S., Ulrich, R., & Miller, J. (1997). Effects of response probability on response force in simple RT. *Quarterly Journal of Experimental Psychology*, *50A*, 405–420.

Milner, A.D., & Goodale, M.A. (1995). *The visual brain in action*. Oxford, UK: Oxford University Press.

Müsseler, J., & Hommel, B. (1997). Blindness to response-compatible stimuli. *Journal of Experimental Psychology: Human Perception and Performance*, *23*, 861–872.

Müsseler, J., Wühr, P., & Prinz, W. (2000). Varying the response code in the blindness to response-compatible stimuli. *Visual Cognition*, *7*, 743–767.

Pashler, H. (1991). Shifting visual attention and selecting motor responses: Distinct attentional mechanisms. *Journal of Experimental Psychology: Human Perception and Performance*, *17*, 1023–1040.

Prinz, W. (1990). A common coding approach to perception and action. In O. Neumann & W. Prinz (Eds.), *Relationships between perception and action: Current approaches* (pp. 167–201). New York: Springer.

Rizzolatti, G., Riggio, L., & Sheliga, B.M. (1994). Space and selective attention. In C. Umiltà & M. Moscovitch (Eds.), *Attention and performance XV. Conscious and unconscious information processing* (pp. 232–265). Cambridge, MA: MIT Press.

Rumiati, R.I., & Humphreys, G.W. (1998). Recognition by action: Dissociating visual and semantic routes to actions in normal observers. *Journal of Experimental Psychology: Human Perception and Performance*, *24*, 631–647.

Sternberg, S. (1969). The discovery of processing stages: Extensions of Donders' method. In W.G. Koster (Ed.), *Attention and performance II*. Amsterdam: North-Holland Publishing Company.

Tucker, M., & Ellis, R. (1998). On the relations between seen objects and components of potential actions. *Journal of Experimental Psychology: Human Perception and Performance*, *24*, 830–846.

VISUAL COGNITION, 2002, 9 (4/5), 392–420

Visual attention and manual response selection: Distinct mechanisms operating on the same codes

Bernhard Hommel

*Section of Cognitive Psychology, University of Leiden, The Netherlands
and Max Planck Institute for Psychological Research,
München, Germany*

Werner X. Schneider

*Department of Experimental Psychology, Ludwig-Maximilians-Universität
München, Germany*

In four experiments, participants made a speeded manual response to a tone and concurrently selected a cued visual target from a masked display for later unspeeded report. In contrast to a previous study of H. Pashler (1991), systematic interactions between the two tasks were obtained. First, accuracy in both tasks decreased with decreasing stimulus (tone-display)–onset asynchrony (SOA)— presumably due to a conflict between stimulus and response coding. Second, spatial correspondence between manual response and visual target produced better performance in the visual task and, with short SOAs, in the tone task, too—presumably due to the overlap of the spatial codes used by stimulus- and response-selection processes. Third, manual responding slowed down with increasing SOA—reflecting either a functional bottleneck or strategic queuing of target selection and response selection. Results suggest that visual stimulus selection and manual response selection are distinct mechanisms that operate on common representations.

The present paper deals with the relationship and possible interactions between two human control processes, one concerned with the selection of environ-mental stimulus information and the other with the voluntary selection of

Please address all correspondence to B. Hommel, University of Leiden, Section of Cognitive Psychology, Postbus 9555, 2300 RB Leiden, The Netherlands.
Email: hommel@fsw.leidenuniv.nl

We wish to thank Benjamin Beyer, Irmgard Hagen, Nike Hucke, Nicola Korherr, Albrecht Schnabel, and Alexandra Tins for collecting the data; and John Duncan, Pierre Jolicoeur, Hal Pashler, Mark Van Selst, and Rob Ward for comments on previous versions of this paper.

http://www.tandf.co.uk/journals/pp/13506285.html   DOI:10.1080/13506280143000511

action. The first one, commonly called "attention", has been thoroughly investigated for decades in experimental psychology and, more recently, also in the
neurosciences (for recent overviews, see Allport, 1983; Desimone & Duncan,
1995; Posner & Petersen, 1990). Most research in this area, the present work
included, has been concentrated on visual attention, hence, the selection of
visual stimuli or objects. Although many questions concerning the details of
attentional selection are still unsettled (Allport, 1993), most researchers agree
in that visual attention is in some sense capacity-limited, dealing with only one
object (or few objects) at a time. In the process of selecting a given visual
object, spatial stimulus information seems to play a major role, presumably
because object features are cross-linked and integrated by referencing their
common location in space (e.g., LaBerge & Brown, 1989; Schneider, 1999;
Treisman, 1988; Van der Heijden, 1992; Wolfe, 1994).

The second control process of interest, commonly called "response selection", is assumed to be invoked whenever people are choosing among several
possible actions. The response selection mechanism seems to share some characteristics with visual attention. As with stimulus selection, response-selection
processes are believed to be strictly limited in capacity, dealing with only one
response at a time (for recent overviews, see Pashler, 1993, 1994). Furthermore, studies on phenomena of stimulus–response compatibly (for a recent
overview, see Hommel & Prinz, 1997) have repeatedly shown evidence of
strong, spontaneous interactions between spatial stimulus and response codes,
suggesting that spatial information plays an important role not only in stimulus
selection, but in action control as well (e.g., Hommel, 1993a; Proctor, Reeve, &
Van Zandt, 1992; Wallace, 1971).

How are visual attention and response selection, or the processes subserving
them, related to one another? Despite some obvious similarities and some arguments for a more integrated view (Allport, 1993; Deubel, Schneider, &
Paprotta, 1998; Rizzolatti, Riggio, & Sheliga, 1994; Schneider, 1995), mechanisms of stimulus and response selection have been traditionally treated as
separate and independent—and, in fact, it may not seem obvious why it should
be otherwise. Support for the traditional (although usually implicit) independence assumption comes from a study of Pashler (1991), the first one that tackled
this issue directly. In Experiment 1 of that study, participants were presented
with a visual attention task while performing a manual binary-choice task (see
Figure 1 for our own, somewhat simplified, design version). The manual task
required a speeded left or right keypress response (R1) to the pitch of a tone
(S1). In the visual attention task, a brief masked letter array was presented. One
of the letters was cued as target (S2) that was to be reported at leisure (R2) after
the manual response. The stimulus–onset asynchrony (SOA) between tone and
visual array and, hence, the temporal overlap of the two tasks, varied randomly
between 50, 150, and 650 ms. Pashler reasoned that if both manual response
(R1) selection and visual stimulus (S2) selection would require the same

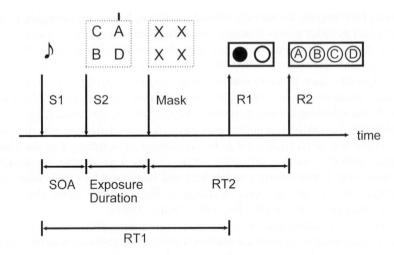

Figure 1. A schematic illustration of the procedure in Experiment 1. Task 1 requires a speeded left–right keypressing response to the pitch of a tone. Task 2 requires an unspeeded judgement of the marked target of a brief, masked four-letter display.

capacity-limited mechanism, then visual stimulus selection should suffer the more the greater the temporal overlap with manual response selection. Hence, the accuracy of S2 report should get worse the shorter the SOA. However, the results did not show any dependence of report accuracy on SOA, which led Pashler to conclude that visual attention and manual response selection do not rely on the same mechanism but are independent.

In our view, this conclusion might be premature for two reasons. The first reason has to do with Pashler's (1991) emphasis on SOA main effects as an indicator of interdependence between stimulus and response selection. Focusing on main effects makes sense from a bottleneck view, hence if we assume that interdependence necessarily shows up as a non-specific queueing of selection processes. However, interdependence may also produce specific interactions between stimulus and response selection, interactions that do not need to express themselves in SOA main effects. As already mentioned, both the selection of visual stimuli and of manual responses can be assumed to rely and operate on spatial representations. If one adds the assumption of a structural overlap between spatial stimulus and response codes (Hommel, 1997; Prinz, 1990) and/or the processes operating on them (Duncan, 1996; Rizzolatti et al., 1994; Schneider, 1995), one might expect rather specific patterns of spatially mediated interactions between stimulus and response selection. If, for instance, a left-hand keypress response is selected in the manual task, this might facilitate shifting attention to, or selecting, a left-side target stimulus in the visual task. As a consequence, one would expect spatial correspondence effects between (manual-)response location and (visual-)target location. Although such a correspondence effect might vary in size with SOA, thus producing a correspondence-by-SOA interaction, it would not yield an SOA main effect.

A second reason for us to hesitate accepting Pashler's (1991) negative conclusion is that it is based on investigating only three particular levels of SOA. If both tasks were processing in parallel, these values may not have produced (sufficient) temporal overlap of stimulus-selection processes in task 2 and response-selection processes in task 1 (cf., Hommel, 1993b). Moreover, both particular SOA values and the range of SOA levels have been shown to affect the strategies subjects employ under dual-task conditions, especially with combinations of an easy, speeded manual-choice task and a difficult, unspeeded visual-attention task (De Jong & Sweet, 1994). Thus, it may be that choosing other SOAs increases the temporal overlap of selection processes and/or induces different strategies in ways that do reveal interactions between stimulus and response selection.

In summary, we feel that Pashler's (1991) evidence for claiming independence of visual attention and response selection is inconclusive and possibly premature. In the present Experiments 1 and 2 we tested whether focusing on non-specific queueing effects in the original study might have concealed the view on specific interactions between stimulus- and response-selection processes. To do so, we replicated Pashler's first experiment and considered in our analyses not only effects of SOA, but also those of the spatial correspondence between R1, the manual response, and S2, the to-be-selected visual target stimulus. In Experiments 3 and 4 we investigated the role of temporal overlap of stimulus and response selection by using SOAs between 200 and 400 ms, a range that might be expected to increase overlap.

EXPERIMENT 1

Experiment 1 had two aims. First, we wished to replicate the most important finding of Pashler (1991, Exp. 1) by using a slightly simplified search task (i.e., four rather than eight letters, see Figure 1), but the same levels of SOA. In the visual attention task, Pashler found no effect of SOA, although he did find one in the manual task, where RTs decreased significantly from 650 to 150 ms SOA. This latter effect was not interpreted as resulting from temporal overlap of stimulus and response selection, but rather as a kind of warning effect—an issue to be treated in more detail in Experiment 4 and in the General Discussion. More relevant for the moment, however, is the question of whether the theoretically important null effect of SOA on the attention task can be reproduced.

Second, we did not only look for main effects of SOA, but also included analyses of the impact of spatial correspondence between visual target and manual response. If our previously mentioned considerations concerning specific interactions between spatial stimulus and response selection were correct, one would expect target–response correspondence to affect performance, whether a main effect of SOA occurs or not.

Method

Participants.   Twenty-four adults were paid to participate in single sessions of about 50 min. They reported having normal or corrected-to-normal vision and audition, and were not familiar with the purpose of the experiment.

Apparatus and stimuli.   The experiment was controlled by a Hewlett Packard Vectra QS20 computer, attached to an Eizo 9070S monitor via an Eizo MD-B11 graphics adaptor for stimulus presentation, and interfaced with a D/A card (Data Translation 2821) for auditory output. Tone judgements in the manual task were given by pressing the left or right of two microswitches mounted side by side on a slightly ascending wooden plate. Letter responses in the visual-attention task were given by pressing one of four horizontally arranged keys of the computer keyboard (function keys F1–F4, accordingly labelled as *A*, *B*, *C*, and *D*). Each participant operated the microswitches with the index and middle finger of the right hand and the computer keys with four fingers of the left hand.

Auditory stimuli (S1) were sinusoidal tones of 200 and 800 Hz. Each tone was presented simultaneously through two loudspeakers located about 50° left and right of the median plane. Visual stimuli were all taken from the standard text mode font and were presented in white on a black screen. A plus sign served as fixation cross, a vertical line as marker, the uppercase letters *A*, *B*, *C*, and *D* as stimuli for the visual task (S2), and four *X*s as mask. From a viewing distance of about 60 cm, each letter measured 0.3° in width and 0.4° in height. The fixation cross always appeared at screen centre. The four stimulus letters, as well as the four *X*s replacing them, were centred at the four stimulus positions 0.6° to the left and right and 0.4° above and below screen centre. The target was indicated by the bar marker appearing 0.3° (edge-to-edge) above the (upper) target or below the (lower) targe (see Figure 1).

Design.   The experiment consisted of five blocks of 96 randomly ordered trials each, preceded by 40 randomly determined practice trials. The trials in each block resulted from the possible combinations of two tone stimuli or responses (left vs right key), three tone-letter SOAs (50, 150, or 650 ms), four letter targets (A, B, C, or D), two vertical target locations (upper vs lower row), and two horizontal target locations (left vs right).

Procedure.   The verbal instruction stressed that tone responses should be speeded (within a reasonable accuracy range), whereas letter responses were to be given at leisure. Following an intertrial interval of 1300 ms, each trial began with the presentation of the fixation mark for 1000 ms and a further blank interval of 500 ms. The tone was then presented for 100 ms and the letter display appeared at a variable time after tone onset (50, 150, or 650 ms, depending on the SOA, see Figure 1). Each letter display consisted of the four letters A, B, C, and D, distributed across the four stimulus positions, with the target indicated by the bar marker. The identity and the location of the target letter depended on the respective condition and were thus balanced across trials, whereas the locations of the remaining three nontarget letters were determined randomly in each trial. After a variable exposure duration (see later), the marker was deleted and the reaction stimuli were replaced by the mask, which stayed on until the letter response was given.

Following tone onset, the program waited 1000 ms for the tone response. In case of a missing or incorrect tone response, or with anticipations (RT < 150 ms), auditory error feedback was given. The respective trial was recorded and repeated at some random position in the remainder of the block. In order to discourage speeded letter responses, the program did not accept those responses earlier than 700 ms after mask onset. There was no upper temporal limit for letter responses.

Exposure duration of the visual display was set to 400 ms during practice trials and then reduced to 200 ms when the first block started. At the end of each block, the duration was individually adjusted according to the error rate in the letter task since the last adjustment: It was reduced by 42 ms (corresponding to three screen-refresh cycles) with an error rate below 20%, but increased by 42 ms with a rate above 30%. After each block, participants were given feedback about their average RT in the tone task and their accuracy in the letter task. On that occasion, they could pause as long as they wished.

Results

Trials with missing tone responses or anticipations accounted for 2.9% and 0.1% of the data, respectively, and were excluded from analyses. For each participant, mean RTs and proportions of (choice) error (PEs) in the manual task, and PEs for letter responses in the visual task were computed as a function of R1–S2 correspondence and SOA.

Tone task. An ANOVA of RTs revealed that reactions were quicker with the two shorter than the longest SOA (462, 461, and 481 ms, respectively), $F(2, 46) = 5.50, p < .01$. For choice errors all three effects were significant. The main effect of SOA, $F(2, 46) = 12.38, p < .001$, indicated a monotonous decrease of error rates with increasing SOA (5.7%, 4.4%, and 2.6%, respectively), and the correspondence effect, $F(1, 23) = 8.85, p < .01$, was due to less errors being made with correspondence (3.5%) as compared with

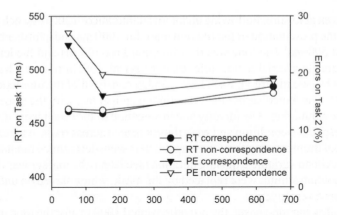

Figure 2. Experiment 1: Reaction times (RTs, in ms) on Task 1 and proportions of errors (PEs, in %) on Task 2 as a function of stimulus–onset asynchrony (SOA) and spatial compatibility between primary response and secondary target stimulus.

non-correspondence (4.9%). As indicated by the interaction, $F(2, 46) = 3.76$, $p < .05$, the correspondence effect was restricted to the two short SOAs (effect sizes: 2.2%, 1.9%, and 0.1%).

Letter task. The result pattern more or less mirrored the pattern of choice errors in the tone task. The SOA effect, $F(2, 46) = 11.50$, $p < .01$, reflected a substantial decrease of error rates from the shortest to the two longer SOAs (26.0%, 18.0%, and 18.9%, respectively), whereas the correspondence effect, $F(1, 23) = 7.05$, $p < .05$, was due to fewer errors with correspondence (20.0%) than non-correspondence (21.8%). Again, however, these two effects interacted, $F(2, 46) = 53.65$, $p < .05$, indicating that reliable correspondence effect were only obtained for the two shorter SOAs (see Figure 2).

Discussion

Experiment 1 yielded three relevant results. First, manual RTs did not increase with increasing task overlap, but there was a positive correlation between RTs and SOA instead (i.e., a decrease with increasing overlap). The finding of a positive relationship replicates the results of Pashler (1991) and will be discussed in more detail in Experiment 4 (along with the accompanying negative relationship in manual PEs). More important for now is the absence of a negative relationship, which indicates that manual response selection was more or less (if we ignore the effect in manual PEs for a moment) unimpaired by task overlap. Hence, if there was queuing of stimulus and response selection, it must have been the former that was delayed until the latter was completed. Indeed, the second important result is that, in contrast to Pashler (1991), we did obtain a main effect of SOA in the visual attention task. Following Pashler's reasoning this might indicate the queuing of (manual) response selection and (visual) stimulus selection. That is, stimulus selection might have had, or was scheduled, to await the completion of response selection. Third, however, the picture is complicated by substantial effects of spatial target–response correspondence on errors in either task, which points to some interaction between stimulus and response selection. In our view, a simple queuing story is insufficient to account for such an outcome pattern, for the following reasons.

One implication of our findings is that subjects seem to have some choice about when to start selecting the visual target. Obviously, correspondence effects on response selection as found in PEs presuppose that the visual target (or its marker) has already been located, which implies that stimulus selection must have at least started in some trials before the manual response was selected. According to the same reasoning, correspondence effects on the visual task indicate that other trials must have been associated with the reverse sequence, that is, target selection must have followed manual response selection. Moreover, correspondence affected manual errors at SOA levels that were not associated with any RT effect. This means that if in some trials target selection did start before the manual response was selected, this occurred without a RT cost. Put differently, working on target selection does not delay response selection. As this also implies the reverse—no delay of target selection by response selection—it raises two questions: First, why then were selection processes sequenced at all and, second, why did task overlap impair visual performance? To address these questions let us consider how and on what kinds of codes stimulus and response selection processes may operate.

A working model

One way to conceive this is illustrated in Figure 3A, where we slightly simplified matters by assuming that only two letters (A and B) appear in each visual display. Before a target is selected, so our explanation goes, its elements are read into and temporarily stored in some kind of working memory (cf., Schneider, 1999). As the target letter is not yet selected (for reasons discussed in Experiment 2), all the elements need to be spatially coded—otherwise later attempts to select the target letter according to a spatial criterion (i.e., whether or not it occupied the location indicated by the marker) would necessarily fail. This means that letter identities are bound to location codes, and vice versa, just as indicated on the left-hand part of Figure 3A. Responses are also spatially coded, which requires the binding of response identities to location codes (Stoet & Hommel, 1999; Wallace, 1971) as illustrated on the right-hand part of Figure 3A. Let us assume that R1 selection typically precedes S2 selection—as suggested by the asymmetry of SOA effects on manual RTs and visual PEs. If in the process of selecting a response one of the spatial codes is activated—the

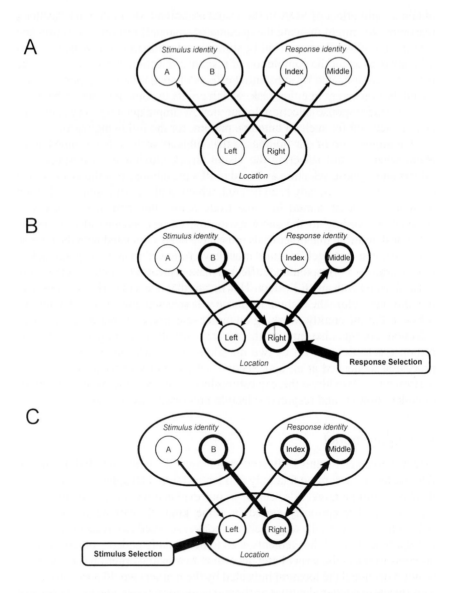

Figure 3. Simplified network of bindings between stimulus-identity (i.e., letter-related) codes and location codes on the one hand, and between response-identity (i.e., finger-related) codes and location codes on the other. The example is based on a two-letter display. Panel A shows the basic architecture, assuming that the letters A and B appear on a left and right location, respectively, and that a left and right response are operated by the index and middle finger of the right hand. Panel B illustrates how selecting a (right) response affects stimulus selection, while Panel C shows how selecting a (right) stimulus affects response selection.

RIGHT code, say—the stored code of the spatially corresponding target (here, the letter B) is also activated via the common link to the RIGHT code (see Figure 3B). Increased activation of a letter representation implies a higher probability of retrieving it from working memory when stimulus selection proper takes place, which supports target selection if this letter actually is the target but makes selection errors more likely if it is not (see the example for non-correspondence in Figure 3C). In other words, selecting a response primes the selection of (codes of) spatially corresponding stimuli.

This model can nicely account for our correspondence effects. As the stronger correspondence effects on the second than the first task suggest, response selection commonly preceded target selection, so that the outcome of the former influenced the latter according to the scenario in Figure 3B–C. However, as soon as the manual response was selected and executed there was no need to maintain the activation of the corresponding response-related codes any further and, in fact, there is evidence for a quick decay of response codes after use (Stoet & Hommel, 1999). Accordingly, correspondence effects only appeared when target selection immediately followed response selection but not at the longest SOA. Yet, even if targets are eventually selected only after response selection is completed, it may be possible to already prepare their selection to some degree by marking the target location (e.g., by activating the spatial code associated with the bar marker, which we have omitted in Figure 3). This would allow for a correspondence effect on manual RTs, which may not have appeared here for reasons addressed in Experiment 2, and on manual choice errors, which we did obtain in Experiment 1.

There are two possibilities to account for the SOA main effects we obtained in the visual task. One is to assume that selecting a response requires the same mechanism or resources needed for stimulus encoding. In a recent series of studies, Jolicoeur, Dell'Acqua, and colleagues (e.g., Jolicoeur & Dell'Acqua, 1998, 1999; for a recent summary, see Jolicoeur, Tombu, Oriet, & Stevanovski, in press) have provided strong evidence for interactions between stimulus encoding and response selection. They argue that processing a stimulus for later report requires consolidation of its code in working memory, a process that is assumed not to allow for concurrent response selection. According to this view, the SOA effects we obtained may reflect the effect of delayed consolidation: Selecting the manual response deferred consolidating the visual stimulus, the more so the greater the task overlap, so that information was lost with short SOA.

Alternatively, not the encoding of the visual items may have been deferred until (or, sometimes, carried out before) manual response selection but only the selection of the target from those encodings. That is, codes of all letter may have been bound to codes of their current location before, or concurrently with, manual response selection, but the actual target selection may have taken place only after response selection was completed. If so, the stored bindings may decay over time, so that increasing task overlap would lead to a loss of information about identity–location relationships. As stimulus selection relies on this information, the quality of its outcome will decrease with decreasing SOA.

Although our data will not allow a final conclusion, we find the latter scenario more plausible than the assumption of delayed consolidation. Consider visual performance with short SOAs: Even though error rates were increased with the shortest SOA, accuracy was relatively good at all SOAs and in no case approached chance level. Although this is partly a consequence of our adaptive presentation procedure, it is difficult to see how that reasonable performance was possible if any encoding had been suspended for several hundred milliseconds after the actual stimuli disappeared. Moreover, if consolidation is as time and resource consuming as the findings of Jolicoeur and colleagues suggest, it would seem odd to consolidate traces of the whole stimulus array before or even instead of selecting the target. Rather, it made more sense either to select the target on presentation—what does not seem to have happened—or to encode the items for later selection. This suggests that storing the whole display is somehow easier and/or goes quicker than selecting the target. Thus, our first guess regarding the impact of SOA on visual search in our design is that task overlap delays target selection, not visual encoding as such.[1]

This leaves open our first question, namely, why was temporal overlap of stimulus and response selection avoided at all? In our view, a possible, though tentative answer to this is suggested by recent observations of Müsseler and Hommel (1997a, b). They found that preparing a left or right keypress *impairs* both detection and identification of a feature-overlapping, masked stimulus, a pattern that Hommel and Müsseler (2002) were able to replicate with combinations of verbal actions and words. As proposed by Hommel, Müsseler, Aschersleben, and Prinz (in press) and Stoet and Hommel (1999), this may be due to that a feature code that is integrated into an action plan is, in a sense, temporarily "occupied" and thus less available for representing a stimulus possessing the same feature. Now, given that in our task the manual response and the

---

[1]Note that our preference, and the arguments supporting it, does not necessarily question the general assumption of Jolicoeur and colleagues that memory consolidation can constitute a real bottleneck. As Jolicoeur and Dell'Acqua (2000) have pointed out, consolidation costs may be much reduced if the display conditions are favourable, stimulus presentation is relatively long, and/or masking is not severe. Given our adaptive timing procedure, such conditions may have been met in our study. Moreover, the tasks employed by Pashler (1991) and us differ from the tasks showing clear demonstrations of consolidation costs. Whereas Jolicoeur and Dell'Acqua (1998, 1999) used tasks combining non-trivial demands on identification (identifying randomly presented, masked letters or symbols) with virtually none on spatial selection, our task had exactly opposite characteristics. Thus, all our subjects had to do when encoding and storing the visual stimulus was to bind known characters to new locations—a process that may not pose severe capacity problems on visual encoding and short-term storage.

visual target were spatially defined, there was always the possibility of feature overlap between response and visual target. To avoid any complication and confusion arising from that and, in particular, to prevent spatial codes needed for target selection from being occupied by manual action planning, any overlap between stimulus and response selection may have been circumvented. Hence, the sequencing of selection processes may have been a strategy to reduce crosstalk between stimulus- and response-feature codes in order to avoid selection errors. We get back to this consideration in Experiment 2.

In sum, Experiment 1 shows that Pashler's (1991, Exp. 1) main finding, the statistical independence between search performance and SOA, did not replicate. Instead, we find a substantial impairment in search performance with increasing task overlap. Moreover, search performance is better with spatial correspondence than non-correspondence between the search target and a concurrently performed manual response, also suggesting that stimulus and response selection processes are interdependent.

EXPERIMENT 2

Although we saw an effect of response–target correspondence in Experiment 1, it was asymmetric and only occurred in task 2. According to our explanation, this was because participants attempted to minimize interference of and from the manual task by merely encoding the visual display upon presentation and delaying target identification until the manual response was selected. Obviously, manual correspondence effects can only be produced by selecting the target, not by merely storing it, because it is the selection process that uses spatial codes to access and determine the target's identity via location-identity bindings (see Figure 3). As target selection followed response selection, it could not affect its outcome. One might object that at least the shorter SOAs in Experiment 1 (50 and 150 ms) should have allowed for selecting the target before the manual response. However, recall that these short SOAs were intermixed with a rather long one (650 ms), so that preparing to select the target before the response would not have paid for about one-third of the trials. Therefore, although participants could have often been able to select the target upon presentation, they may have been reluctant to do so. Instead, they may have favoured an all-purpose "late-selection" strategy they could apply to both short and long SOAs (for similar considerations, cf., De Jong & Sweet, 1994; Rogers & Monsell, 1995).

Admittedly, our story is post hoc, so that we conducted Experiment 2 to seek for independent evidence supporting it. One important and testable implication of our interpretation is that manual correspondence effects should show up if participants would only be given sufficient time to always select the visual target before the manual response. In Experiment 2 we restricted the range of possible SOAs to very small values only by replacing the 650 ms SOA of

Experiment 1 by one of 100 ms. That is, we used SOAs of 50, 100, and 150 ms, intervals that should provide participants with sufficient time to determine the visual target letter before starting to select their manual response. If so, and if participants would accept this offer, response selection would follow target selection and should therefore be affected by spatial target–response correspondence.

Method

Participants. Nineteen adults were paid to participate in single sessions. They fulfilled the same criteria as in Experiment 1.

Apparatus, stimuli, design, and procedure. These were as in Experiment 1, except that the three SOAs were 50, 100, and 150 ms, and that the error feedback was visual.

Results

Trials with missing tone responses (1.4%) and anticipations (0.1%) were excluded from analyses. The remaining data were treated as in Experiment 1.

Tone task. The RT analysis revealed two significant main effects (see Figure 4): RTs increased with SOA (443, 440, and 450 ms, respectively), $F(2, 36) = 3.93$, $p < .05$, and correspondence produced faster responses than

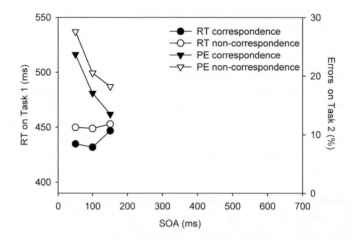

Figure 4. Experiment 2: Reaction times (RTs, in ms) on Task 1 and proportions of errors (PEs, in %) on Task 2 as a function of stimulus–onset asynchrony (SOA) and spatial compatibility between primary response and secondary target stimulus.

non-correspondence (438 vs 451 ms), $F(1, 18) = 19.34, p < .001$. The interaction approached the 10% level. The choice-error analysis yielded a significant main effect of correspondence, $F(2, 18) = 7.91, p < .05$, produced by smaller error rates with correspondence than non-correspondence (3.6% vs 5.2%).

Letter task.   Both main effects were highly significant, SOA, $F(2, 36) = 17.53, p < .001$, and correspondence, $F(1, 18) = 27.82, p < .001$. As shown in Figure 4, error rates decreased with increasing SOA (25.6%, 18.8%, and 15.9%, respectively), and less errors were made with correspondence than with non-correspondence (18.1% vs 22.1%).

Discussion

The most important outcome of Experiment 2 is that, as expected, manual responses were clearly affected by spatial target–response correspondence. This strongly suggests that, in contrast to Experiment 1, the target was selected before manual response selection set in, or at least before it was completed. Selecting the target must have required, or been associated with, the activation of spatial codes representing its location and these codes must have affected the process of selecting the manual response. The interaction of correspondence and SOA fits well into this picture. Because with increasing SOA the likelihood increases that response selection begins before the visual target is identified, correspondence effects on manual responses become less and less likely.

Comparing Experiments 1 and 2 it is interesting to note that, in accordance with our speculation, exchanging just one SOA value (100 for 650 ms) was sufficient to change the whole outcome pattern, at least in the manual task. This is most obvious for the shortest SOA, which was associated with a substantial correspondence effect in Experiment 2 but not in Experiment 1. If the 50 ms SOA allowed for early target selection in Experiment 2 it should have done so in Experiment 1, too, which leads us to conclude that our participants were able to adopt rather different ways to coordinate their two sub-tasks in the two experiments. Hence, if the task context suggests that target selection is manageable before response selection, the visual display is analysed and the target is selected right after presentation. In contrast, the display is merely encoded if the task context suggests that target and response selection might often interfere with each other. That is, people seem to be able to configure their own cognitive system in order to meet external constraints on dual-task performance to quite a remarkable degree, a fact emphasized by De Jong and Sweet (1994) and Meyer and Kieras (1997).

Apart from its expected effect on manual responses, correspondence also affected letter-report performance. If we assume that correspondence effects in the search task reflect the impact of manual response selection on visual target selection, and if it is true that in Experiment 2 target selection took place before the manual response was selected, how can we account for the presence of such an effect? In our view, an effect of correspondence on target selection is surprising only if one assumes that selecting a stimulus object is a discrete, separable processing step of a fixed, short duration. Indeed, if the target letter would have been identified and selectively stored right after letter-display presentation, it would be difficult to see how this process could ever be affected by response-selection processes some 100 ms later. But assume target selection in the present context consisted in only priming the target letter for later report, hence increasing the activation level of the target-letter code to a greater extent than that of its competitors. To take the example from Figure 3, the target letter *A* may be selected by activating its identity code, as well as its associated location code (here: the *left* code), to a larger degree than the competing *B* code. Naturally, this would prime the corresponding manual response (here: the *index* code), thus producing manual correspondence effects of the kind observed in Experiment 2. As soon as the manual response is selected, including the activation of the response-related location code, activation of this latter code would spread to the associated letter-identity code. In the example, selecting the index-finger response would prime the letter code of *A*, whereas selecting the middle-finger response would prime the letter code of *B*. If priming through target selection and priming through response selection converge on the same identity code, the respective letter will be reported with a high likelihood, hence, accuracy will be high. However, if the target is primed by stimulus-selection processes, but one of its competitors is primed by response-selection processes, participants may sometimes erroneously report the competing letter, which impairs report performance. In other words, response–target correspondence can well affect target report even if target selection takes place before the manual response is selected.

The observation of a higher degree of interaction between the two tasks in the context of a rather small SOA range may suggest that these conditions tempted subjects to conjoin tasks, that is, to effectively transform the two tasks into one. Accordingly, one may doubt whether the outcome of Experiment 2 allows for conclusions that are applicable to standard dual-task situations. On the one hand, it is clear that blocking short SOAs did affect the way subjects scheduled stimulus- and response-related processes, thereby allowing more crosstalk between the tasks. On the other hand, though, there is no evidence for a strict temporal locking of processes across the two tasks. For instance, consider RTs and PEs for the two shortest SOAs in Figure 4. If the two tasks were really treated as one we would expect that manual response selection awaits stimulus processing in the visual task, which should delay RT with increasing SOA. Yet, there is not the slightest increase from 50 ms to 100 ms SOA, hence, no evidence of any grouping or synchronization of selection or other processes. For the same SOAs strong correspondence effects were observed in both tasks, which suggests that the underlying processes do not depend on task conjoining.

In sum, Experiment 2 shows that correspondence effects in manual responses, which were absent in Experiment 1, can be obtained if both the length and the range of tone-display SOAs is chosen to allow for selecting the visual target before manual response selection begins. This demonstrates that manual response selection can be affected by visual target selection in very much the same way as target selection is influenced by response selection, which provides further support for our assumption that stimulus and response selection are not entirely independent.

EXPERIMENT 3

Experiment 3 focused on a possible role of the degree of temporal overlap between stimulus and response selection. As the hitherto used SOA levels of 50, 150, and 650 ms do not fully cover the temporal range of possible interactions between the two selection processes, we chose to investigate SOAs of 200, 300, and 400 ms in Experiment 3, which in all other respects replicated Experiments 1 and 2. If Pashler's (1991) claim of independence between stimulus and response selection is correct, this modification should have no effects on the results, which amounts to predicting a null effect of SOA in either task. If, however, the degree of temporal overlap of the selection processes does play a critical role, an SOA main effect might show up in at least one of the two tasks.

Method

Participants.   Twenty-four adults were paid to participate in single sessions. They fulfilled the same criteria as in Experiment 1.

Apparatus, stimuli, design, and procedure.   These were as in Experiment 1, except that the three SOAs were 200, 300, and 400 ms.

Results

Anticipations (0.1%) and trials with missing tone responses (2.0%) were excluded from analyses. The remaining data were treated as in Experiment 1.

Tone task.   In the RT analysis, only the main effect of SOA was significant, $F(2, 46) = 31.16, p < .001$, due to an increase of RTs with SOA (483, 501, and 530 ms, respectively). An SOA main effect was also obtained in the choice error analysis, $F(2, 46) = 5.55, p < .01$, but here performance was worse with the shortest than the longer SOAs (2.9%, 2.0%, and 2.4%, respectively).

Letter task.   The main effect of correspondence was significant, $F(1, 23) = 7.47, p < .05$, as was the interaction of correspondence and SOA, $F(2, 46) =$

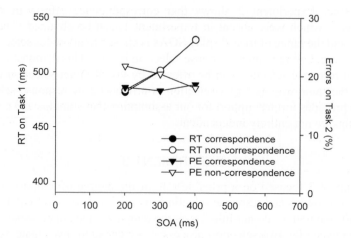

Figure 5.   Experiment 3: Reaction times (RTs, in ms) on Task 1 and proportions of errors (PEs, in %) on Task 2 as a function of stimulus–onset asynchrony (SOA) and spatial compatibility between primary response and secondary target stimulus.

3.91, $p < .05$, whereas the SOA effect was not reliable ($p = .13$). As shown in Figure 5, substantial (and significant) correspondence effects were obtained with SOAs of 200 and 300 ms but not with 400 ms.

Discussion

First of all, we were able to replicate the correspondence effects on search performance for the two shorter SOAs. This completes the picture from Experiments 1 and 2 in indicating continuous decrease of correspondence effects with increasing SOA. According to the model sketched in Figure 3, such effects represent the impact of preceding response selection processes on target selection. And, indeed, this impact should get weaker as the delay of target selection to response selection gets longer.

Even more important in the present context, comparing the results of Experiments 1–3 reveals that our variation of the temporal overlap between manual response selection and visual stimulus processing led to a considerable change in the data pattern of Experiment 3. In particular, the effect of SOA on performance in the tone task became more pronounced with longer SOAs. Considering that increasing the SOA (within the range of manual RTs) is likely to increase the to-be-expected (but obviously avoided) temporal overlap of manual response selection and visual stimulus selection, this may be another indication of the strategic queuing of stimulus- and response-selection processes. However, there are three problems with this interpretation: (1) An easy one that can be rejected on grounds of the present data, (2) a not so easy one that we tested in Experiment 4, and (3) a crucial one that we will address in the General Discussion.

The easy problem is that the increase of RTs with SOA was accompanied by a decrease of choice errors, which might indicate a speed–accuracy tradeoff. Yet, there are two reasons to doubt that such a tradeoff was responsible for the SOA effect on RTs. One is, that choice errors in the tone task decreased with SOA in all four experiments of the present study—often to a larger extent than in Experiment 3, whatever SOA values were used and whether an SOA effect on RTs was obtained or not (see Figure 7). This mirrors the similar findings of Pashler (1991), who consistently observed negative correlations between choice errors and SOA across a number of task variations. Obviously, the error effect does not go with the RT effect but seems to be a standard byproduct of the basic task design used here (see General Discussion for some consider-ations on underlying causes). Another reason to doubt that our RT effect was due to a speed–accuracy tradeoff becomes evident if we compare the tone-task data from the two longest SOAs only (i.e., 300 and 400 ms). Here, RTs increased markedly from 501 to 530 ms, and so did the error rates (2.0% and 2.4%, respectively). Hence, a positive SOA effect on RTs can be obtained in the absence of a negative effect on errors, a finding that runs counter to a tradeoff account.

A perhaps more serious objection to interpret the SOA effect on RTs as a queuing effect has already been considered by Pashler (1991). The original idea of varying the SOA between the tone and the visual display was to manipulate the onset of stimulus-selection processes in the search task relative to response-selection processes in the tone task. If SOA has an effect, so the reasoning goes, this can be attributed to the varying degree of temporal overlap between stimulus- and response-related processes. However, note that this kind of manipulation confounds the variation of the onset of stimulus-directed processes with the variation of the onset of the visual stimulus itself. Therefore, we cannot be sure whether an effect of SOA really reflects characteristics of the attentional process we wish to index or only those of the attention-drawing visual stimuli. In fact, from studies on sensory facilitation we know that RT to a stimulus in one modality can be reduced by presenting a stimulus in another modality, even if this latter stimulus is irrelevant to the task (see Nickerson, 1973, for an overview). That is, responses in our tone task may have been quicker with short than with long SOAs not because visual stimulus processing hampered manual response selection with long SOAs, but because the mere presence of the visual stimulus display facilitated the manual response with short SOAs. As the validity of this interpretation cannot be evaluated on the basis of the present data, we conducted Experiment 4 to provide an empirical test.

EXPERIMENT 4

The aim of Experiment 4 was to find out whether the positive correlation between manual RT and SOA observed in Experiments 1–3 might have been due to sensory facilitation, hence, to an unspecific facilitation effect of the visual display. We tested the sensory-facilitation account by comparing the effect of the mere presentation of a letter-task display with the effect of requiring active processing of the display. We did that by using the same task and SOA range as in Experiment 3, but in addition to the *search blocks*, where participants again searched for a cued letter target, we also ran a *non-search block*, where the search display was presented but no search was to be performed. The predictions were straightforward. Clearly, we expected to replicate the increase of manual RT with SOA in the search block (apart from the correspondence effect on search performance). According to the sensory-facilitation hypothesis, the non-search block should give rise to the same positive relationship between RT and SOA—after all, the stimulus conditions were virtually identical in search and non-search blocks. In contrast, if visual-attentional processes were responsible for the increase of manual RT with SOA in Experiment 3, no such an effect should occur in the non-search block.

Method

Participants.   Twenty adults were paid to participate in single sessions. They fulfilled the same criteria as in Experiment 1.

Apparatus, stimuli, design, and procedure.   These were as in Experiment 3, with the following exceptions. One of the five experimental 96-trial blocks was replaced by a non-search block of about the same length (96 plus 9 additional catch trials, see later). During this block, the display conditions were basically the same as in the search blocks, including the presentation of the briefly masked four-letter displays at the three SOAs. However, the participants performed the tone task only but did not search for target letters. Accordingly, no target marker was presented and no letter was to be reported. In order to require the participants to monitor the visual events none the less, nine catch trials were randomly distributed across the block. In these catch trials a bright yellow frame appeared for 300 ms, which was to be responded to by pressing the space bar with 2000 ms after the tone response. Each frame appeared with one of nine randomly ordered frame–tone onset asynchronies, ranging from –200 ms (frame before tone) to 600 ms (frame after tone), in steps of 100 ms. The frame outline measured $3.3° \times 3.6°$ with an edge-to-edge distance between frame and (area of) letter display of $0.3°$ horizontally and $0.4°$ vertically. The non-search block was run after the first, second, third, or fourth (i.e., last) search block. Its position was balanced across participants, so that each of the four possible positions was realized with two participants.

Results

Each participant responded correctly to all catch trials with no exception. Trials with missing tone responses (1.3%) and anticipations (0.02%) were excluded from analyses. The remaining data from the standard search blocks were treated as in Experiment 1. From non-search blocks, the data from catch trial were excluded and mean RTs and PEs for tone responses were computed as a function of SOA.

Tone task in search vs non-search blocks.   A 2×3 (Task context × SOA) ANOVA was run on the RTs to tones from search and non-search blocks. Apart from a significant effect of SOA, $F(2, 38) = 9.05$, $p < .001$, responses were quicker in the non-search block than in search blocks (397 vs 497 ms), $F(1, 19) = 61.56$, $p < .001$. More important, the interaction was significant, $F(2, 38) = 16.67$, $p < .001$. As shown in Figure 6 and confirmed by separate analysis, this was due to that RT increased with SOA in the search blocks, but not in the non-search block. The errors analysis did not produce significant results. The SOA main effect approached the significance criterion ($p = .051$), but the underlying pattern was opposite to the RT pattern (5.3%, 3.6%, and 3.8% in search blocks, and 3.9%, 3.8%, and 2.8% in non-search blocks).

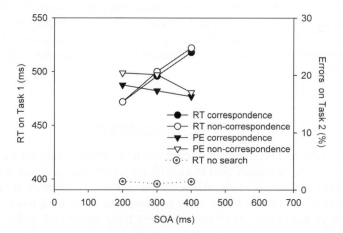

Figure 6.   Experiment 4: Reaction times (RTs, in ms) for search blocks (straight lines) and non-search blocks (dotted line) on Task 1 and proportions of errors (PEs, in %) on Task 2 as a function of stimulus–onset asynchrony (SOA) and spatial compatibility between primary response and secondary target stimulus.

Tone task in search blocks.   In the RT analysis (Correspondence × SOA), only the main effect of SOA was significant, $F(2, 38) = 16.92, p < .001$, reflecting an increase of RTs with SOA (472, 498, and 520 ms, respectively). An SOA main effect was also obtained in choice errors, $F(2, 38) = 6.65, p < .005$, again indicating that the shortest SOA was associated with an increased error rate (5.3%, 3.6%, and 3.8%). Interestingly, the main effect of correspondence was also significant, $F(1, 19) = 10.30, p < .005$, indicating less errors with correspondence (3.6%) than non-correspondence (4.9%), whereas the interaction missed the 5% level ($p = .072$).

Letter task.   Both main effects were significant. The effect of SOA, $F(2, 38) = 7.74, p < .005$, indicated that errors decreased with increased SOA (19.3%, 18.7%, and 16.6%) and the effect of correspondence, $F(1, 19) = 7.53$, $p < .05$, showed that less errors were made with correspondence (17.3%) than with non-correspondence (19.2%).

Discussion

The results are clear-cut. In all relevant aspects the findings from Experiment 3 were replicated. In particular, when participants searched through the visual display their manual RT increased again as a function of SOA—in fact, the RT slopes in the two experiments are virtually identical. However, when the display was just presented with no search being required, RT was no longer positively correlated with SOA. This is strong evident against the idea that the SOA effects on manual performance in search blocks might reflect sensory facilitation by the mere presence of a visual stimulus. Obviously, the SOA effect is related to perceiving and processing a visual display, not just to watching it. Taken altogether, then, the present data allow us to reject both the speed–accuracy and the sensory-facilitation account of the effect of SOA on manual RT.

GENERAL DISCUSSION

Our goal was to investigate the relationship between visual attention and manual response selection, and to identify possible interactions of processes subserving the selection of visual objects and of manual responses. We did that by using Pashler's (1991) technique of pairing a speeded manual binary-choice task with an unspeeded attention-demanding letter-report task under varying degrees of temporal task overlap. Although Pashler found no indications for a dependence of letter-report performance on task overlap, we had two reasons to object his conclusion from this finding on the independence between visual attention and response selection. First, we argued that the interdependence between stimulus and response selection need not necessarily express itself as non-specific interference on secondary-task performance, but may produce specific effects of spatial correspondence between the manual response and the to-be-attended letter target. In fact, we were able to find such specific effects in each of our four experiments. Second, we pointed out that Pasher (1991) used only a limited set of SOAs, which may have concealed or prevented possible interactions of the critical selection processes. Indeed, we found an increase of dual-task costs under conditions that can be expected to increase temporal overlap of target processing and response selection. Summing up, the present findings do not support the assumption that visual attention and manual response selection are entirely independent, but rather suggest the existence of both non-specific and specific interactions, which we will now discuss in turn.

Non-specific interference between tasks

In all four experiments of this study, the accuracy of both manual choices and letter reports varied systematically as a function of SOA, that is, of the temporal overlap between the tasks. Interestingly, the two effect patterns are very similar, as is obvious from Figure 7. The error rates in the manual task

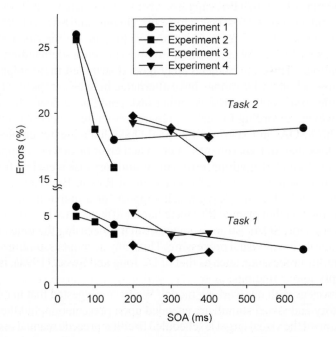

Figure 7.   Overview of the proportions of choice errors made on Task 1 and search errors made on Task 2 of Experiments 1–4 as a function of stimulus–onset asynchrony (SOA).

consistently decreased with SOA in all four experiments and so did the error rates in the search task. The first part of this pattern, the SOA dependency of the manual errors, is consistent with the results of Pashler (1991), and other authors have reported similar findings. For instance, De Jong and Sweet (1994) and Pashler (1989) obtained SOA-dependent error rates in either task with combinations of speeded manual responses to auditory pitch and unspeeded reporting the highest digit in a briefly masked visual display. Apparently, then, presenting a tone and a visual search display in close succession impairs either task and the question is "why?".

One possibility is that switching between stimulus modalities takes time (e.g., Cohen & Rist, 1992). If so, switching from primary- to secondary-task modality may not have been completed with short SOAs, which would have impaired the processing of the second stimulus. However, a modality-switching account would suggest that the SOA effect is only, or at least much more, observed in the secondary task, which is inconsistent with our findings. Moreover, recent findings suggest that attending to targets appearing in fact succession is easier, rather than more difficult, if they differ in modality (e.g., Duncan, Martens, & Ward, 1997).

Another possible account may assume that identifying a stimulus requires explicit preparation, as proposed by De Jong (1993; De Jong & Sweet, 1994). Again, one may object that this suggests error rates to increase at short SOAs for the second, but not the first task. However, De Jong and Sweet (1994) have provided evidence that subjects do not always prepare for the first task first (or most), especially if the second task involves attention-demanding visual discriminations. Thus, our subjects may have distributed their preparatory capacity across both tasks, or may have alternated between preparing for one and the other task, so that errors in either task could have been affected by SOA. However, according to such a preparation-strategy account blocking the very short SOAs in Experiment 2 should have led a greater emphasis on the visual task than in Experiment 1. Yet, visual error rates were comparable with 50 ms SOA and, if anything, errors in the auditory task were less frequent than in Experiment 1. In view of faster manual RTs in Experiment 2 than Experiment 1 this does not leave much support for a preparation account. Moreover, the fact that manual RTs were hardly affected at all by SOA, especially at very short SOAs, strongly suggests that processing the tone had not to await completion of visual processing. Thus, any account assuming strictly serial stimulus processing, such as that of De Jong and Sweet (1994), is difficult to apply to our findings.

This leaves us with our working model. We have suggested that in our task both auditory and visual stimuli are encoded upon presentation, but the eventual selection of the visual target is scheduled to either precede manual response selection (e.g., when SOAs are all short enough) or to wait until the manual response is selected. Accordingly, one problem for a delayed visual stimulus selection is the possible loss of stimulus information and, in particular, of information about letter–location relationships. As this kind of loss is likely to increase over time, increasing task overlap should lead to an increase in search errors, just as observed. Moreover, encoding the visual stimuli immediately on presentation increases the competition with codes of the auditory stimulus and, perhaps, of its assigned action. Consider, for instance, coding of the tone, the search-display items, and the manual response take place in the same capacity-limited coding system (i.e., working memory; as sketched in Figure 3), in which activating and maintaining a code or a code compound directly leads to a decrease of other codes' activation levels (cf., Schneider, 1999). If so, coding and maintaining the search items in this system would interfere with the coding of any other event, be it the tone or the manual response, and vice versa. Accordingly, the coding of stimuli (and, perhaps, responses) gets more difficult and error-prone the greater the temporal overlap of the two tasks, hence the SOA effects on even the auditory task.

A further, also non-specific interaction between the two tasks refers to the manual RTs and their increase as a monotonous function of SOA. We have argued that, although the errors do show an opposite tendency as the RTs, the particular result pattern does not suggest a speed–accuracy tradeoff. Moreover, the observation from Experiment 4 that the RT effect disappears if participants no longer search through the visual display, rules out Pashler's (1991) account in terms of sensory facilitation. Instead, it seems that participants were reluctant to schedule their selection processes in a way that would produce temporal processing overlap, possibly because overlap would have resulted in coding or selection conflicts of the sort demonstrated by Müsseler and Hommel (1997a; Hommel & Müsseler, 2002). This is apparent from the SOA main effects on RTs in Experiments 3 and 4, which suggest that response selection was sometimes delayed until the search display was presented (and encoded). Possibly, these cases reflect trials in which the processes preceding response selection took relatively long, so that temporal overlap of target and response selection was expected. Avoidance of temporal processing overlap is also suggested by the different manual correspondence-effect patterns in Experiments 1 and 2. When only short SOAs were used, as in Experiment 2, some indications for the preparation of target selection were obtained (i.e., the manual correspondence effect); yet, no evidence for target-related processing before response selection was found if a long SOA was included, as in Experiment 1. According to our interpretation, this is because target selection was immediately prepared (but not yet completed) only if and when no temporal overlap with response selection is to be expected—such as when the visual display always appeared before response selection was initiated. Here we assume that in performing one or more tasks, people are not bound to work through a fixed chain of cognitive processes, as assumed by stage models of information processing, but are able to flexibly tailor the temporal order of those processes to the task demands at hand (Meyer & Kieras, 1997). In our task, subjects employed this ability to keep stimulus and response selection separate. However, whether they did so by necessity or preference we are unable to tell—after all, avoiding concurrent selection does not mean that it cannot be done in principle. In cases of no code overlap and overlearned associations between the features of a given stimulus and response, it may well be that both can be selected at the same time. Thus, it still needs to be determined whether the bottleneck our findings point at is of functional or strategic nature.

Code sharing between stimulus and response selection

We consistently obtained effects of spatial correspondence between visual target and manual response, which demonstrates that stimulus and response selection can affect each other. However, these correspondence effects were asymmetric, with response selection always affecting stimulus selection, but stimulus selection affecting response selection only in Experiment 2. As already pointed out, the mere presence of this asymmetry suggests that correspondence effects do not reflect the *direct* interaction of concurrent selection processes but, rather, aftereffects of one selection process on the other due to the sharing of cognitive codes. According to our interpretation, the visual target was not determined on the basis of the sensory information presented on the screen, but selected from a transient (working) memory representation of the letter-display elements. Presumably, this selection took place during the interval between the manual response and the letter report, so that it was open to aftereffects of response selection. Even in Experiment 2, where there was some time to process the visual target before the manual response, target selection was only prepared but was not yet completed before the manual response was carried out—otherwise response–target correspondence could not have affected report accuracy of that short SOAs. From this follows that target selection should not be envisioned as a discrete act of transforming the status of an object from mere input to target once for all. Instead, selection may simply mean marking or priming (i.e., increasing the activation level of) the target representation for later use, as assumed, for instance, in the attentional models of Bundesen (1990) or Van der Heijden (1992). This marking or priming operation should greatly increase the chances of an item to affect later action (e.g., letter report), but it does not seem to shield the selected target from competition with other items as long as that action is not underway (Schneider, 1999). Interestingly, the same can be said of response selection: Even if, for instance, a left- or right-hand response is validly precued, so that it can be selected long before its execution is signaled, it is still affected by its spatial compatibility with the go signal, hence, sensitive to conflict with a competing response (Hommel, 1996).

A rough but plausible sketch of the how of specific interactions between stimulus and response selection has already been laid down in Figure 3. Basically, we assume that both stimulus and response representations are made up of identity-specific codes and location codes. For our argument it is not essential exactly how stimulus and response identity are represented—whether by single, integrated "integrated" codes, as our (in this respect too) simplified figure might suggest, or by more complex clusters of stimulus-feature codes, as claimed by Hommel (1998b), Kahneman, Treisman, and Gibbs (1992), and others. But it is important that these identity representations are temporarily associated with codes that refer to their (presumably allocentric-relative) location. Because both stimulus and response are thus spatially coded, their representations overlap (i.e., are shared) to a degree that depends on their spatial correspondence. Code overlap, however, is well known to produce compatibility effects (Hommel, 1997; Kornblum, Hasbroucq, & Osman, 1990; Prinz, 1990) and, in a way, this is what we obtained.

In fact, the correspondence effect of target marking on response selection shows obvious parallels to the Simon effect (Simon & Rudell, 1967; see Lu & Proctor, 1995, for an overview), which refers to the finding that spatially defined responses are faster to spatially corresponding than non-corresponding stimuli, even if the location of that stimulus is not relevant. As in a Simon task, we found that the location of the target stimulus affected the selection of the manual response, even though this stimulus and this response, as well as their locations, did not depend on each other. It is true that in standard Simon tasks only a single stimulus is presented, not an array from which the target is to be selected. However, previous demonstrations of Simon effects with multiple-item displays (e.g., Grice, Boroughs, & Canham, 1984; Hommel, 1993c; Proctor & Lu, 1994) have already shown that this is not an essential task feature, so that the present observation of correspondence effects is not too surprising—if one only allows for crosstalk between the manual and the search task (or outcome conflict in the sense of Navon & Miller, 1987).

More surprising—and theoretically interesting—from a compatibility point of view are the "backward" correspondence effects of manual response selection on visual target selection. To our knowledge, this is the first demonstration of an action-induced biasing of visual search, although it is not the first observation of action effects on perception. Apart from the already mentioned studies of Müsseler and Hommel (1997a, b; Hommel & Müsseler, 2002), there is also evidence for backward effects under more standard dual-task conditions. Hommel (1998a) showed that in a dual-task design the congruence between a secondary-task colour–word response and a primary-task colour stimulus facilitates processing of the latter, hence, there is a colour-related backward compatibility effect of verbal response selection on a visual target identification. In the present experiment, compatibility referred to the location, not to the direction, meaning, or colour of the stimuli, and what was affected was (presumably) the selection, not the identification, of the target. Nevertheless, the evidence available so far does converge to indicate that code sharing between stimuli and responses not only affects response selection, as has been commonly assumed (e.g., Kornblum et al., 1990), but stimulus processing as well (Hommel, 1997; Hommel et al., in press; Müsseler & Hommel, 1997a; Prinz, 1990). That is, stimulus–response interactions can go either way.

REFERENCES

Allport, D.A. (1993). Attention and control: Have we been asking the wrong questions? A critical review of twenty-five years. In D.E. Meyer & S. Kornblum (Eds.), *Attention and performance XIV: Synergies in experimental psychology, artificial intelligence, and cognitive neuroscience* (pp. 183–218). Cambridge, MA: MIT Press.

Bundesen, C. (1990). A theory of visual attention. *Psychological Review, 97*, 523–547.

Cohen, R., & Rist, F. (1992). The modality shift effect: Further explorations at the crossroads. *Annals of the New York Academy of Sciences, 658*, 163–181.

De Jong, R. (1993). Multiple bottlenecks in overlapping task performance. *Journal of Experimental Psychology: Human Perception and Performance, 19*, 965–980.

De Jong, R., & Sweet, J.B. (1994). Preparatory strategies in overlapping-task performance. *Perception and Psychophysics, 55*, 142–151.

Desimone, R., & Duncan, J. (1995). Neural mechanisms of selective visual attention. *Annual Review of Neurosciences, 18*, 193–222.

Deubel, H., Schneider, W.X., & Paprotta, I. (1998). Selective dorsal and ventral processing: Evidence for a common attentional mechanism in reaching and perception. *Visual Cognition, 5*, 81–107.

Duncan, J. (1996). Cooperating brain systems in selective perception and action. In T. Inui & J.J. McClelland (Eds.), *Attention and performance XVI: Information integration in perception and communication* (pp. 549–578). Cambridge, MA: MIT Press.

Duncan, J., Martens, S., & Ward, R. (1997). Restricted attentional capacity within but not between sensory modalities. *Nature, 387*, 808–810.

Grice, G.R., Boroughs, J.M., & Canham, L. (1984). Temporal dynamics of associative interference and facilitation produced by visual context. *Perception and Psychophysics, 36*, 499–507.

Hommel, B. (1993a). Inverting the Simon effect by intention: Determinants of direction and extent of effects of irrelevant spatial information. *Psychological Research, 55*, 270–279.

Hommel, B. (1993b). The relationship between stimulus processing and response selection in the Simon task: Evidence for a temporal overlap. *Psychological Research, 55*, 280–290.

Hommel, B. (1993c). The role of attention for the Simon effect. *Psychological Research, 55*, 208–222.

Hommel, B. (1996). S–R compatibility effects without response uncertainty. *Quarterly Journal of Experimental Psychology, 49A*, 546–571.

Hommel, B. (1997). Toward an action–concept model of stimulus–response compatibility. In B. Hommel & W. Prinz (Eds.), *Theoretical issues in stimulus–response compatibility* (pp. 281–320). Amsterdam: North-Holland.

Hommel, B. (1998a). Automatic stimulus–response translation in dual-task performance. *Journal of Experimental Psychology: Human Perception and Performance, 24*, 1368–1384.

Hommel, B. (1998b). Event files: Evidence for automatic integration of stimulus–response episodes. *Visual Cognition, 5*, 183–216.

Hommel, B., & Müsseler, J. (2002). Action-feature integration blinds to feature-overlapping perceptual events. *Manuscript submitted for publication*.

Hommel, B., Müsseler, J., Aschersleben, G., & Prinz, W. (in press). The theory of event coding (TEC): A framework for perception and action planning. *Behavioral and Brain Sciences*.

Hommel, B., & Prinz, W. (Eds.). (1997). *Theoretical issues in stimulus–response compatibility*. Amsterdam: North-Holland.

Jolicoeur, P., & Dell'Acqua, R. (1998). The demonstration of short-term consolidation. *Cognitive Psychology, 36*, 139–202.

Jolicoeur, P., & Dell'Acqua, R. (1999). Attentional and structural constraints on visual encoding. *Psychological Research, 62*, 154–164.

Jolicoeur, P., & Dell'Acqua, R. (2000). *From the attentional blink to the psychological refractory period: Empirical and theoretical unification of two paradigms*. Unpublished manuscript.

Jolicoeur, P., Tombu, M., Oriet, C., & Stevanovski, B. (in press). From perception to action: Making the connection. In W. Prinz & B. Hommel (Eds.), *Common mechanisms in perception and action: Attention & performance XIX*. Oxford: Oxford University Press.

Kahneman, D., Treisman, A., & Gibbs, B.J. (1992). The reviewing of object files: Object-specific integration of information. *Cognitive Psychology, 24*, 175–219.

Kornblum, S., Hasbroucq, T., & Osman, A. (1990). Dimensional overlap: Cognitive basis for stimulus–response compatibility—a model and taxonomy. *Psychological Review, 97*, 253–270.

LaBerge, D., & Brown, V. (1989). Theory of attentional operations in shape identification. *Psychological Review, 96*, 101–124.

Lu, C.-H., & Proctor, R.W. (1995). The influence of irrelevant location information on performance: A review of the Simon and spatial Stroop effects. *Psychonomic Bulletin and Review, 2*, 174–207.

Meyer, D.E., & Kieras, E.D. (1997). A computational theory of executive cognitive processes and multiple task performance: Part 1. Basic mechanisms. *Psychological Review, 104*, 3–75.

Müsseler, J., & Hommel, B. (1997a). Blindness to response-compatible stimuli. *Journal of Experimental Psychology: Human Perception and Performance, 23*, 861–872.

Müsseler, J., & Hommel, B. (1997b). Detecting and identifying response-compatible stimuli. *Psychonomic Bulletin and Review, 4*, 125–129.

Navon, D., & Miller, J. (1987). Role of outcome conflict in dual-task interference. *Journal of Experimental Psychology: Human Perception and Performance, 13*, 435–448.

Nickerson, R.S. (1973). Intersensory facilitation of reaction time: Energy summation or preparation enhancement? *Psychological Review, 80*, 489–509.

Pashler, H. (1989). Dissociations and contingencies between speed and accuracy: Evidence for a two-component theory of divided attention in simple tasks. *Cognitive Psychology, 21*, 469–514.

Pashler, H. (1991). Shifting visual attention and selecting motor responses: Distinct attentional mechanisms. *Journal of Experimental Psychology: Human Perception and Performance, 17*, 1023–1040.

Pashler, H. (1993). Dual-task interference and elementary mental mechanisms. In D.E. Meyer & S. Kornblum (Eds.), *Attention and performance XIV: Synergies in experimental psychology, artificial intelligence, and cognitive neuroscience* (pp. 245–264). Cambridge, MA: MIT Press.

Pashler, H. (1994). Dual-task interference in simple tasks: Data and theory. *Psychological Bulletin, 116*, 220–244.

Posner, M.I., & Petersen, S.E. (1990). The attention system of the human brain. *Annual Review of Neuroscience, 13*, 25–42.

Prinz, W. (1990). A common coding approach to perception and action. In O. Neumann & W. Prinz (Eds.), *Relationships between perception and action* (pp. 167–201). Berlin, Germany: Springer-Verlag.

Proctor, R.W., & Lu, C.-H. (1994). Referential coding and attention shifting accounts of the Simon effect. *Psychological Research, 56*, 185–195.

Proctor, R.W., Reeve, T.G., & Van Zandt, T. (1992). Salient-features coding in response selection. In G.E. Stelmach & J. Requin (Eds.), *Tutorials in motor behavior* (Vol. 2, pp. 727–741). Amsterdam: North-Holland/Elsevier.

Rizzolatti, G., Riggio, L., & Sheliga, B.M. (1994). Space and selective attention. In C. Umiltà & M. Moscovitch (Eds.), *Attention and performance XV: Conscious and unconscious information processing* (pp. 232–265). Cambridge, MA: MIT Press.

Rogers, R.D., & Monsell, S. (1995). Costs of a predictable switch between simple cognitive tasks. *Journal of Experimental Psychology: General, 124*, 207–231.

Schneider, W.X. (1995). A neuro-cognitive model for visual attention control of segmentation, object recognition, and space-based motor action. *Visual Cognition, 2*, 331–375.

Schneider, W.X. (1999). Visual-spatial working memory, attention, and scene representation: A neuro-cognitive theory. *Psychological Research, 62*, 220–236.

Simon, J.R., & Rudell, A.P. (1967). Auditory S–R compatibility: The effect of an irrelevant cue on information processing. *Journal of Applied Psychology, 51*, 300–304.

Stoet, G., & Hommel, B. (1999). Action planning and the temporal binding of response codes. *Journal of Experimental Psychology: Human Perception and Performance, 25*, 1625–1640.

Treisman, A. (1988). Features and objects: The fourteenth Bartlett memorial lecture. *Quarterly Journal of Experimental Psychology, 40*, 201–237.

Van der Heijden, A.H.C. (1992). *Selective attention in vision*. London: Routledge.

Wallace, R.J. (1971). Stimulus–response compatibility and the idea of response codes. *Journal of Experimental Psychology, 88*, 354–360.

Wolfe, J.M. (1994). Guided Search 2.0: A revised model of visual search. *Psychonomic Bulletin and Review, 1*, 202–238.

VISUAL COGNITION, 2002, 9 (4/5), 421–457

Blindness to response-compatible stimuli in the psychological refractory period paradigm

Peter Wühr and Jochen Müsseler

*Max Planck Institute for Psychological Research,
Munich, Germany*

This study investigated the conditions under which the processing in a speeded response task interferes with concurrent processing in a visual encoding task. Three experiments used a dual-task paradigm, in which a speeded left or right response to a tone was combined with the identification of a masked left- or right-pointing arrow following the tone with variable SOA. Two additional experiments tested the impact of the presentation of pure tone on visual encoding. There were four major findings. First, an unspecific decrease in identification accuracy was observed with decreasing SOA. Second, a blindness to response-compatible stimuli was observed with speeded responses. Third, a specific interference was found between low- and high-pitched tones and left- or right-pointing arrows. Fourth, the specific tone-arrow interference modulated the specific response-arrow interference when the task allowed both to occur simultaneously. The present findings, which suggest both procedural and structural interference between response preparation and stimulus encoding, are discussed in terms of a two-stage model of action planning.

Most studies of the relationship between perception and action have been concerned with the impact of stimulus information on response selection. Only recently has there been an increase of interest in the reversed question of whether and how action-control processes are able to affect perceptual processing. One reason for this reversal can be found in a recent shift towards

---

Please address all correspondence to P. Wühr, who is now at the Institute for Psychology I, University of Erlangen, Kochstrasse 4, D-91054 Erlangen, Germany.
Email: prwuehr@phil.uni-erlangen.de

This research was supported by a grant from the Deutsche Forschungsgemeinschaft (Mu 1298/2). We thank Michael Blum-Kalagin, Sven Garbade, and Albert-Georg Lang for collecting parts of the data, and Megan Otermat for stylistic suggestions. In addition, we are grateful to Shai Danziger and an anonymous reviewer for their comments on an earlier version of this paper.

http://www.tandf.co.uk/journals/pp/13506285.html   DOI:10.1080/13506280143000520

theoretical frameworks of action planning in which voluntary actions are seen to be cognitively evoked by the anticipations of their sensory effects. Thus, the assumption is that movements are cognitively represented by their external effects and, thus, could be initiated by the activation of the corresponding *effect codes* (Greenwald, 1970; Hoffmann, 1993; Hommel, Müsseler, Aschersleben, & Prinz, in press; MacKay, 1987; Prinz, 1990, 1997; for early versions of this idea see James, 1890; Lotze, 1852). This view implies that not only stimulus codes (i.e., codes of perceived events), but also response codes represent external events (i.e., codes of yet to-be-produced events). Accordingly, cognitive codes common to perception and action constitute the interface between these domains. Another consequence of this notion is that stimulus processing and response preparation can overlap both in time and in structure and, thus, are able to affect each other in a specific manner (Hommel, 1997; Hommel et al., in press; Müsseler, 1999).

The question of whether action–control processes are able to affect perceptual processing can be put to an empirical test by using a dual-task paradigm; that is, observers' ability to identify a stimulus should be studied in situations in which they are engaged in an unrelated motor task. In the most established experimental dual task, the so-called paradigm of the psychological refactory period (PRP), individuals have to perform two speeded responses to different stimuli presented in close succession. In the case of a short stimulus onset asynchrony (SOA), processing on the two tasks overlaps in time, and the second response slows down (see Pashler, 1994, for an overview). Most authors attributed this latency increase of the second response during the preparation and execution of the first response to a "bottleneck" in cognitive processing. In other words, when the system is occupied with processing in one task, processing in a second task must be postponed when it requires the same cognitive operations (e.g., Pashler, 1994; Welford, 1952, 1980) or cognitive resources (e.g., Kahneman, 1973; Wickens, 1980).

Many studies investigated dual-task interference between two speeded response tasks. The observed costs were assumed to originate from a bottleneck at the response selection stage, that is, from the inability simultaneously to select (e.g., Pashler, 1984, 1989; Welford, 1952, 1980) and/or to execute (e.g., De Jong, 1993; Karlin & Kestenbaum, 1968; Keele & Neill, 1978) two motor responses. Only a few authors were interested in the question of whether the processing of a response task also affects the processing of a perceptual task; and, indeed, they found perceptual impairments (Arnell & Duncan, 1998; De Jong, 1993; De Jong & Sweet, 1994; Jolicoeur, 1999a). For example, Jolicoeur (1999a) reported that the identification of a foveally presented, pattern-masked letter is impaired when the observer is simultaneously engaged in responding to an auditory stimulus. Jolicoeur (1999a) suggested that the "short-term consolidation" of visual information in short-term memory is disturbed by the concurrent processing of the response task. However, it remained unclear which of the processes in the response task was responsible for this disturbance.

Indeed, most of the studies showing unspecific impairments in perceptual performance when the participants are simultaneously engaged in a response task are not able to unequivocally localize the source of interference. For example, De Jong and Sweet (1994) found a decline in accuracy in a visual encoding task when the SOA was shortened between a tone calling for a manual response and the visual stimulus. Additionally, they observed that the size of the decline in perceptual accuracy varied substantially, depending on which task had been emphasized in the instruction. From this observation, the authors concluded that there are at least two factors limiting perceptual performance under dual-task conditions: The inability to fully prepare two tasks simultaneously and the interference between these two tasks. Thus, both the source and the relative contributions of (unspecific) interference and preparatory limitations remain vague.

A different strategy in the investigation of whether the processing in a motor task can actually affect the concurrent processing in a perceptual task is to look for specific interferences between a motor task and a perceptual task. Specific interferences are observed when the performance in the perceptual task varies as a function of the degree of *feature overlap* between the to-be-identified stimulus and the concurrent response. Because the feature overlap between a response task and a perceptual task can be varied while holding the preparation for the perceptual task constant, the observation of specific interference would indicate a structural crosstalk between response preparation and stimulus encoding.

Recent experiments in our lab revealed such specific interferences. The assumption was that the initiation of an action leads to a temporary insensitivity to a stimulus that shares common codes with the response within the same cognitive system. More concretely, such a code was considered to be used when a right (left) keypress (indicated by a response cue) was generated as well as when an arrow pointing to the right (left) was encoded (Müsseler, 1995; Müsseler & Prinz, 1996). Accordingly, the observer's sensitivity to stimulus events that share features with a response was assumed to decrease during the execution of this response. In other words, the perceptual and the motor event codes come into conflict with respect to the overlapping feature code in the compatible condition, whereas they can coexist without any conflict in the incompatible condition. And, indeed, this was observed in our experiments: The identification of a right arrow was reduced when presented during the execution of a right response as compared to during the execution of a left response and vice versa ("blindness to response-compatible stimuli"; Müsseler & Hommel, 1997a, b; Müsseler, Steininger, & Wühr, 2001; Müsseler, Wühr, & Prinz, 2000; Wühr & Müsseler, 2001; for overviews see Müsseler, 1999; Wühr, 2000).

When these experiments were designed, the main interest was to determine the influence of a pure motor response on the perceptual encoding of visual stimuli. Consequently, the aim was to minimize the contribution of the response-inducing stimulus (i.e., of the response cue). Therefore, participants were instructed to perform the response at leisure after the presentation of the response cue in order to ensure that an already selected and prepared response would be executed when the masked stimulus was presented. Accordingly, the perceptual impairment still occurred when the response cue was omitted from the procedure and participants were instructed to generate the response endogenously (Müsseler et al., 2000). Thus, in contrast to the PRP experiments mentioned earlier (e.g., De Jong & Sweet, 1994; Jolicoeur, 1999a), the encoding of the response cue and the preparation of the corresponding response were not speeded.

The aim of the present study was to further investigate the blindness to response-compatible stimuli with speeded responses; that is, with a PRP-like paradigm. Therefore, an experimental set-up was used similar to that used by Jolicoeur (1999a). He combined a speeded manual keypress to a tone with the visual identification of a briefly presented, pattern-masked stimulus; and he varied the SOA between the tone and the stimulus. As previously mentioned, the observed decrease in identification accuracy with decreasing SOA between tone and stimulus has been taken as evidence for an unspecific dual-task interference. In contrast to Jolicoeur (1999a), the main interest of the present study was to identify specific interferences between these tasks. Therefore, not only was the temporal relationship between the response task and the identification task varied, but also the amount of feature overlap between responses and visual stimuli.

We expected further theoretical insights from the extension of the blindness paradigm to a PRP task. In the previous studies, the response had never been executed immediately. Instead, the execution of the response had to be postponed (suppressed) either until a neutral response had been performed (e.g., Müsseler & Hommel, 1997a) or until a "go" signal had occurred (e.g., Wühr & Müsseler, 2001). Thus, one might argue that the blindness effect was caused by this temporary withholding of the response; and it is unclear whether the blindness effect would occur in a PRP situation at all.

Furthermore, in a PRP situation, the masked stimulus can be presented in all processing phases of the response task. When the stimulus is presented with varying SOAs in regard to the response-cue tone, the encoding of the visual stimulus can coincide with the encoding of the tone, with the selection of the response, or with the initiation and execution of the response. Thus, the question is: In which of these phases does the blindness effect start to emerge? Consequently, the SOA variation in a PRP paradigm can contribute to a better understanding of the nature of the blindness effect.

GENERAL PROCEDURE

In the present task, participants performed a left or a right keypress in response to a tone and identified a briefly presented and masked left- or right-pointing arrowhead, which followed the tone with a variable SOA (Figure 1). Correspondingly, in half of the trials, responses and visual stimuli were symbolically compatible (i.e., left response and left-pointing arrow, right response and right-pointing arrow); whereas in the other half of the trials, responses and visual stimuli were symbolically incompatible (i.e., left response and right-pointing arrow, right response and left-pointing arrow). Five different SOAs (50, 150, 300, 500, and 1000 ms) were used. The main questions to be examined were whether and when a speeded left or right response specifically affected the accuracy of the participants' identification of a symbolically compatible stimulus as compared to the participants' identification of an incompatible stimulus.

In Experiments 1 and 2, the auditory choice task involved a low- or high-pitched tone and a left or right keypress. In Experiment 5, the auditory choice task involved one long tone or two short tones (with the same pitch) and a left or right response. In these dual-task experiments, the auditory choice task was combined with the visual identification of a masked stimulus, which was a

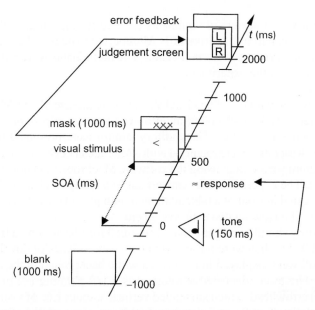

Figure 1.   Schematic illustration of the displays and the timing of events (here with an SOA of 500 ms) in Experiments 1, 2, and 5.

left- or a right-pointing arrowhead. Experiments 3 and 4 were control experiments in which the visual stimulus had to be identified simultaneously with or after the presentation of the—now task irrelevant—tones, which had been used as response cues in the dual-task experiments.

EXPERIMENT 1

The main purpose of the first experiment was to examine whether a speeded motor task specifically affects the encoding of a visual stimulus. Following the procedure of Jolicoeur (1999a), a low- or high-pitched tone was used to indicate a speeded left or right keypress. However, in order to introduce a feature overlap between responses and stimuli, masked left- or right-pointing arrowheads were presented with various SOAs. The expectation was that a common LEFT or RIGHT code has to be accessed when a response is generated and when the compatible stimulus is encoded (Hommel et al., 2001). Accordingly, in addition to unspecific interferences, specific interferences were expected between the speeded left and right motor task and the encoding of the left and right stimuli.

Method

Participants.   Sixteen paid volunteers (twelve females, four males; aged 20–31 years) took part in Experiment 1. All reported to be right handed and to have normal or corrected-to-normal vision. The participants were not familiar with the purpose of the experiment.

Apparatus and stimuli.   The visual stimuli were presented on a Macintosh IIci Computer and a 17-inch colour monitor with a screen refresh rate of 75 Hz and a luminance of 35 cd/m. The auditory stimuli were presented by stereo headphones. Responses were recorded with a Macintosh keyboard. The experimental program was written using the software MacProbe (Version 1.8.1; cf., Hunt, 1994). The experiment was carried out in a dimly lit chamber. Participants were seated in front of a table with their chin placed on a chin rest with a fixed height. The viewing distance was 50 cm.

The auditory stimuli were pure tones presented for 150 ms with a frequency of 300 or 900 Hz. They were presented to both ears well above threshold. All visual stimuli were displayed in black on a white background in the centre of the screen. The to-be-identified stimulus was a left-pointing (<) or a right-pointing (>) arrowhead, which subtended vertically about 1.6° of visual angle, and horizontally about 0.8° of visual angle. The mask consisted of randomly arranged lines, which had the same left or right orientation as the components of the arrowheads and which subtended about 1.0° × 2.0° of visual angle.

Procedure and design.   Each trial started with the presentation of a blank screen for 1000 ms (Figure 1). Then, one of the tones was presented as a response cue for 150 ms. The task was to press as quickly as possible either the left key with the left index finger or the right key with the right index finger according to the pitch of the tone, while making as few errors as possible. Half of the participants had to press the left key if the tone had a low pitch and the right key if the tone had a high pitch, whereas the mapping rule was inverted for the other half of the participants. The instructions stressed the importance of responding quickly to the tone and urged participants not to wait for the visual stimulus to appear before the response is executed.

At an SOA of either 50, 150, 300, 500, or 1000 ms after the tone, the left- or right-pointing stimulus was presented for a brief period of time (see later) and then replaced by the mask, which stayed on the screen for 1000 ms. Half a second after the offset of the mask, the letters "L" and "R", framed by squares, appeared one above the other in the right half of the screen. These letters changed their relative positions randomly from trial to trial. The participants had to report the identity of the visual stimulus in the last trial by clicking on the corresponding letter ("L" for "<" and "R" for ">") with the computer mouse. The instructions for this part of the task stressed the fact that there was no systematic relationship between responses and visual stimuli, and participants were told to guess if uncertain about the identity of the stimulus.

An interval of 2 s followed an error-free trial, then the next trial began. If participant had performed the wrong response and/or reported the wrong stimulus, a corresponding error message occurred for an additional 1 s during the inter-trial interval. If participant did not perform the response within 1 s from the onset of the tone, they received no feedback, but the corresponding trial was repeated at the end of the block. If the reaction time exceeded 1 s in an already repeated trial, this trial was not repeated again. After each block, the participants received feedback about the percentage of trials with wrong responses and/or false stimulus identifications.

To avoid ceiling or floor effects in the identification task, the presentation time for visual stimuli was adjusted to achieve 75% performance accuracy across all SOA conditions. The following staircase procedure was used: After each experimental block, the presentation time was decreased by one screen refresh (13.33 ms) if the error rate in the last block was lower than 10%. It was increased by one refresh if the error rate was above 40%.

The compatibility relationships between the response and the visual stimulus (compatible vs incompatible) were crossed with the five SOAs between the tone and the visual stimulus. Two repetitions of each combination of these factors were presented in each block, which consisted of 20 experimental trials. Each participant completed a total of 30 blocks of experimental trials on 2 different days within 1 week, for a total of 600 trials. On the first day, the experimental phase was preceded by a practice phase consisting of eight blocks of eight trials. In these practice trials, a constant SOA of 250 ms was used. In the first practice block, the visual stimulus was always presented for 70 ms. For the following practice blocks, the presentation time was adjusted, using the same staircase procedure as in the experimental phase. The mean presentation time of visual stimuli in the last three practice blocks were used for the first block of the experimental phase. The whole experiment lasted about 2 hours, including short breaks between blocks.

The compatibility factor and the SOA factor were varied within participants. Additionally, the mapping between the low-pitched or high-pitched tone and the left or right response was varied between participants. Thus, the experiment was based on a $2 \times 2 \times 5$ mixed design. The performance in the response task and the performance in the identification task were analysed independently.

Results

Response task.   Across all conditions and participants, less than 3% of the reaction times exceeded the criterion of 1000 ms. These trials were excluded from analysis. For the remaining data, mean percentages of the false responses (error percentage) and mean correct reaction times were calculated as a function of all possible combinations of the different levels of the factors mapping, compatibility, and SOA (see Table 1).

Across all conditions, the mean error percentage was 1.5% (SD = 1.5). The error percentages were subjected to $2 \times 2 \times 5$ analyses of variance (ANOVA) with the between-participants factor mapping (two levels), and the within-participant factors compatibility (two levels), and SOA (five levels). The only

TABLE 1
Means of correct reaction times (RT; in ms) and percentages of errors (PE)
for the responses in Experiment 1 as a function of the mapping between a tone
and the response, the compatibility between the response and a visual stimulus,
and the SOA between tone and visual stimulus

	SOA									
	50		150		300		500		1000	
Compatibility	*RT*	*PE*	*RT*	*PE*	*RT*	*PE*	*RT*	*PE*	*RT*	*PE*
Mapping low–left, high–right:										
Incompatible	468	1.5	464	1.9	473	1.0	480	0.8	472	0.8
Compatible	469	1.0	456	1.3	474	1.3	476	0.6	473	0.4
Mapping low–right, high–left:										
Incompatible	464	2.3	467	1.3	453	2.1	455	1.9	473	0.8
Compatible	467	3.5	467	1.7	446	1.9	469	0.8	453	2.1

significant effect was the main effect of SOA, $F(4, 56) = 2.75$, $p < .05$, where error percentage increased with decreasing SOA (all other $p > .10$). The mean correct reaction time across all conditions was 466 ms (SD = 92). In an ANOVA with the same factors as in the error analysis, none of the main effects or interactions were significant (all $p > .15$).

Identification task. The mean presentation time for visual stimuli was 51 ms in both groups of participants with the two different tone-response mappings. To compute the mean proportions of correctly identified stimuli (identification accuracy), only those trials were considered in which the response had been correct and reaction time had been less than 1000 ms. Across all conditions, identification accuracy was 0.72 (SD = 0.19). The mean identification accuracy as a function of all possible combinations of the different levels of the factors mapping, compatibility, and SOA can be seen in Figure 2.

Identification accuracy was also analysed in an ANOVA with the between-participant factor mapping (two levels), and the within-participant factors compatibility (two levels), and SOA (five levels). The main effect of mapping was not significant, $F(1, 14) = 1.72$, $p < .211$. However, the main effects of SOA, $F(4, 56) = 50.29$, $p < .001$, and of compatibility, $F(1, 14) = 8.12$, $p < .013$, were significant. The SOA effect reflects the observation that identification accuracy increased when the SOA between the tone and the visual stimulus increased. There was a difference of 0.25 between the accuracy for the shortest SOA of 50 ms ($M = 0.54$) and accuracy for the longest SOA of 1000 ms ($M = 0.79$).[1] The effect of compatibility is due to the fact that response-compatible stimuli ($M = 0.70$) were identified less accurately than response-incompatible stimuli ($M = 0.74$).

The two-way interactions between mapping and SOA and between compatibility and SOA, both $F(4, 56) < 1$, as well as the three-way interaction $F(4, 56) = 1.82$, $p = .138$, were not significant. However, the two-way interaction between

---

[1]Note that in the present series of experiments, the proportions of correctly identified visual stimuli at each SOA should be only interpreted in respect to the values at the other SOAs. The reason is that the presentation time of visual stimuli was adjusted to 75% accuracy across SOAs. The consequence is that accuracy at one SOA is affected by the other SOAs. For example, at first glance, Figure 2 (upper panel) depicts four "easy" levels of SOA (150 to 1000 ms) and one "difficult" level (50 ms). Thus, the majority of "easy" levels has had a greater impact on the mean presentation time to achieve the 75% accuracy level. The consequence is that the adjusted presentation time makes the "difficult" SOA level even more difficult and, therefore, might additionally decrease accuracy at that level. In other words, the absolute accuracy values are affected by the proportion of "easy" and "difficult" SOAs in an experiment. Additionally, it is unlikely that identification accuracy and presentation time constitute a linear relationship. Thus, any *quantitative* conclusions from the accuracy values should be taken with caution.

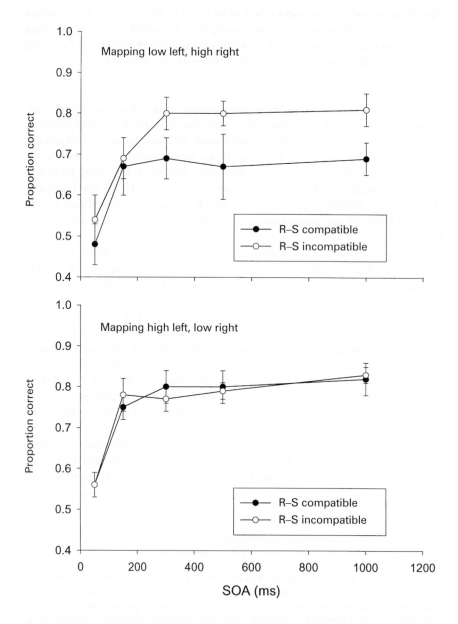

Figure 2. Results from the visual encoding task in Experiment 1. Mean proportion of correctly identified visual stimuli (with standard errors between participants) as a function of the tone–response mapping (upper panel: low–left vs high–right; lower panel: low–right vs high–left), the response-arrow compatibility (compatible vs incompatible), and the tone–arrow SOA. Each data point is based on about 480 observations.

mapping and compatibility was significant, $F(1, 14) = 7.40, p = .016$. This interaction means that—in fact—only that group of participants who had responded according to the tone-response mapping "low–left vs high–right", was less accurate in identifying response-compatible stimuli ($M = 0.64$) than response-incompatible stimuli ($M = 0.73$). In contrast, the other group of participants, who had responded according to the reversed tone-response mapping, showed equal identification accuracy for response-compatible and response-incompatible stimuli ($M = 0.75$ in both cases).

In order to qualify the observed interaction between the factors mapping and compatibility, two-way ANOVAs with the within-participant factors SOA and compatibility were conducted on the identification rates of both groups (i.e., mappings), separately. For the first group that had followed the tone-response mapping "low–left vs high–right", the main effect of SOA, $F(4, 28) = 21.32, p < .001$, and the main effect of compatibility, $F(1, 7) = 15.11, p = .006$, were significant. The interaction was not significant, $F(4, 28) = 1.39, p = .263$. For the second group, which had followed the tone-response mapping "low–right vs high–left", only the main effect of SOA, $F(4, 28) = 30.79$, $p < .001$, was significant (other $F < 1$).

Discussion

In the response task, the increase of falsely executed responses with decreasing SOA indicates an unspecific effect between both tasks. Correspondingly, in the identification task the SOA effect reflects an unspecific interference in visual encoding, similar to the results observed previously by Arnell and Duncan (1998) and by Jolicoeur (1999a). Identification accuracy for visual stimuli decreased with decreasing SOA between the visual stimulus and the response-cue tone. However, the present unspecific effect probably did not only originate from an overlap of the response-generation phase with visual encoding. Instead, the observed accuracy decrements at the very early SOAs of 50 and 150 ms indicates that the interference was also caused—at least in part—by an overlap in the encoding of the tone and the visual stimulus.

More importantly, identification accuracy depended systematically on which response was performed in a trial. When a left response was required, the identification of a left-pointing stimulus was impaired compared to the identification of a right-pointing stimulus (and vice versa). This finding demonstrates the blindness effect to response-compatible stimuli in a PRP paradigm (Müsseler & Hommel, 1997a). Most surprisingly, however, this effect was only observed with a low–left and high–right mapping in the response task. Before explaining this effect, more empirical evidence is needed. Because the tone-response mapping was varied between participants, it is possible that the different results originated from a pure sample bias. Therefore, the subsequent experiment was designed to replicate the present findings.

EXPERIMENT 2

The present experiment aimed to replicate the findings of Experiment 1. Instead of a between-participants design, a within-participants design was applied to further examine the unexpected influence of the mapping in the response task on the blindness to response-compatible stimuli.

Method

Participants.   Eighteen paid volunteers (nine females and nine males; aged 18–32 years) participated in Experiment 2. All of them declared to have normal or corrected-to-normal vision; two participants reported to be left handed. None had participated in Experiment 1.

Apparatus and stimuli.   The apparatus and the stimuli were the same as those used in Experiment 1.

Procedure and design.   The design was the same as in Experiment 1, except that the factor mapping was now varied within participants. This caused the following changes in the procedure. Participants responded either with the low–left and high–right tone-response mapping in the first experimental session, and with the low–right and high–left response mapping in the second experimental session or vice versa (15 blocks per session). This sequence was balanced across participants.

The first session in Experiment 2 was identical to the first session in Experiment 1. However, at the beginning of the second session in Experiment 2, the participants were told that the mapping rule had changed. Then, participants were given one practice block of 20 trials to become familiar with the new mapping.

Results

One participant exceeded the reaction time criterion of 1000 ms in 25% of the trials, whereas the average value for the whole sample was 5% (SD = 7). Another participant achieved 13% of trials with false responses, compared to 5% (SD = 3) of the whole sample. Both participants were excluded from the analysis.

Response task.   Across all conditions and participants, less than 4% of the reaction times exceeded the criterion of 1000 ms. These trials were excluded from further analyses. Across all conditions, the mean error percentage was 4.4% (SD = 2.3). The error percentages were subjected to a $2 \times 2 \times 5$ ANOVA with the within-participants factors mapping, compatibility, and SOA. The main effects for mapping and compatibility were not significant, both $F < 1$, but the error percentage increased again with decreasing SOA, $F(4, 60) = 8.68$,

$p < .001$. The mean correct reaction time was 474 ms (SD = 95). An ANOVA of the reaction times showed no significant effect.

Identification task.   The mean presentation time for visual stimuli was 37 ms for the low–left and high–right tone-response mapping, and 35 ms for the low–right and high–left mapping. The difference was not significant, $t(15) = 1.23$, $p < .20$, two-tailed. Across all conditions, identification accuracy for visual stimuli was 0.74 (SD = 0.07).

The proportions of correctly identified visual stimuli were analysed in an ANOVA with mapping, compatibility, and SOA as within-participants factors. The only significant result was the increase of accuracy with increasing SOA, $F(4, 60) = 45.65$, $p < .001$. However, neither the main effect of compatibility, $F(1, 15) = 1.88$, $p = .191$, nor the two-way interaction between mapping and compatibility, $F(1, 15) = 1.96$, $p = .182$, was significant (all other $p > .10$).

It is possible, however, that the expected two-way interaction between mapping and compatibility failed to reach significance because it occurred in the first session only. In the second session, when the participants had to invert the mappings, carry-over effects from the first session might have diminished or even eliminated mapping effects on the blindness effect. Accordingly, identification accuracy was analysed for each session separately in ANOVAs with the between-participant factor mapping and the within-participant factors compatibility and SOA. The main effect of SOA was significant for the first session, $F(4, 56) = 33.75$, $p < .001$, and for the second session, $F(4, 56) = 30.27$, $p < .001$. The main effects of compatibility and of mapping were not significant in both sessions (all $p > .20$). The two-way interaction of compatibility and mapping approached significance for the first session, $F(1, 14) = 4.02$, $p < .065$, but it was far from significance for the second session ($F < 1$; all remaining interactions: $p > .25$). Figure 3 shows the mean identification accuracy values from the first session in Experiment 2, as a function of the factors mapping, compatibility, and SOA. For the second session in Experiment 2, both groups showed slightly lower identification accuracy for response-compatible stimuli than for response-incompatible stimuli.

In order to qualify the interaction between the factors mapping and compatibility for the first session of Experiment 2, two-way ANOVAs with the within-participant factors SOA and compatibility were conducted on the identification rates of both groups (i.e., mappings), separately. For the first group, with the tone-response mapping "low–left vs high–right", the main effect of SOA, $F(4, 28) = 15.31$, $p < .001$, and the main effect of compatibility, $F(1, 7) = 5.97$, $p < .045$, were significant. The main effect of compatibility means that response-compatible stimuli ($M = 0.71$) were identified less accurately than incompatible stimuli ($M = 0.76$). The interaction between compatibility and SOA was not significant, $F(4, 28) = 1.56$, $p < .211$. For the second group, with the tone-response mapping "low–right vs high–left", only the main effect of

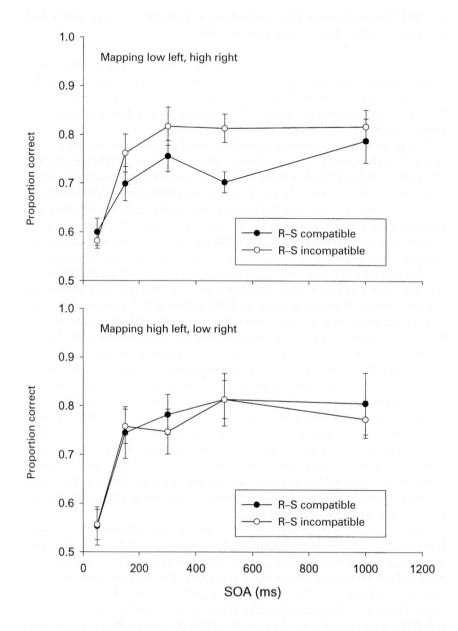

Figure 3. Results from the visual encoding task in the first session of Experiment 2. Mean proportion of correctly identified visual stimuli (with standard errors between participants) as a function of the tone–response mapping (upper panel: low–left vs high–right; lower panel: low–right vs high–left), the response–arrow compatibility (compatible vs incompatible), and the tone–arrow SOA. Each data point is based on about 240 observations.

SOA, $F(4, 28) = 19.45, p < .001$, was significant (other $F < 1$). Thus, the pattern of results observed in the first session of Experiment 2 is exactly the same as that observed in Experiment 1 across both sessions.

Discussion

The present experiment replicates the main findings of Experiment 1. The blindness effect was again observed in a PRP task, but only with a low–left and high–right tone-response mapping and not with the low–right and high–left mapping. However, this pattern of results was only observed in the first session of Experiment 2, when the mapping had been manipulated between participants, as in Experiment 1. When the participants had to invert the tone-response mapping in the second session of Experiment 2, the influence of the mapping on the blindness effect disappeared. This suggests that carry-over effects from the first session eliminated both the blindness effect and the influence of the tone-response mapping on the blindness effect. It seems that in the second session each response-cue tone activated both responses: The response that had to be made to the tone in the first session, and the response that had to be made to the tone in the second session. This interpretation is supported by the observation of a significantly higher percentage of false responses in the second session, $t(15) = 2.22, p = .042$, two-tailed, whereas the reaction times did not differ between sessions (478 vs 471 ms), $t(15) = 0.38, p = .712$, two-tailed. The simultaneous activation of both responses, however, could have led to impairments in the encoding of stimuli that were compatible and of stimuli that were incompatible to the actually performed response and, thus, could have eliminated the blindness effect.

Now, let us turn to the interaction between the tone-response mapping and the blindness to response-compatible stimuli. Why did the blindness effect exclusively occur with the low–left/high–right mapping? At first sight, this observation points to similar effects already known from compatibility research. In several studies on orthogonal compatibility effects, advantages in accuracy and in reaction time were observed when participants were required to press a left button in response to a visual stimulus appearing below a fixation point and to press a right button in response to a stimulus appearing above the fixation point, as compared to the reversed mapping (e.g., Lippa, 1996a, b; Weeks & Proctor, 1990). From these observations, it was concluded that "below" (or "down") is more strongly associated with "left" than with "right", whereas "above" (or "up") is more strongly associated with "right" than with "left" (Lippa, 1996a, b). This kind of preference was observed not only between orthogonal spatial dimensions but also between tone pitch and spatial position. In a preferred matching task, Mudd (1963) found that low tones were preferably associated with left positions, whereas high tones were preferably associated with right positions.

Thus, it is possible that the present impact of the tone-response mapping on the blindness effect originated either from a preferred mapping between tones and responses or from a preference to associate a low (high) tone preferably with a left (right) stimulus. With respect to the first possibility, Simon and co-workers did not find any performance differences in response latencies and errors when comparing the possible mappings of low and high tones to left and right responses (cf., Simon, Meewaldt, Acosta, & Hu, 1976). We were able to confirm these results (Wühr, 2000). In addition, in an experiment on the blindness to response-compatible stimuli, a variation of the strength of association between the response cue and the response did not lead to any observable effects on identification performance (Müsseler et al., 2000). Thus, it is not likely that the present modification of the blindness effect originated from the tone-response mappings being different in their stimulus–response compatibility.

Another way to explain the present blindness effect and its dependence on the tone-response mapping is to assume two different kinds of interference. The first interference might originate from the preparation and the generation of a left (right) response, which impairs the visual encoding of a left (right) arrow, but not that of a right (left) arrow. This is the response-arrow interference that has been assumed in the previous studies (Müsseler & Hommel, 1997a; Müsseler et al., 2000). The second interference might be that the encoding of a low (high) tone impairs the encoding of a left (right) arrow, but not that of a right (left) arrow. This possible tone-arrow interference between the encoding of a frequency-coded tone and the encoding of an arrow is the subject of the next experiment.

Given these two kinds of interference, the present pattern of results could have emerged as follows: In the low–left and high–right mapping, the two kinds of interference may have worked in the same direction and their effects may have added up. In this case, for example, the encoding of a low tone and the subsequent execution of a left response both impaired the identification of a left stimulus, whereas neither the encoding of a low tone nor the execution of a left response interfered with the identification of a right stimulus. In contrast, in the low–right and high–left mapping, the two kinds of interference may have worked in opposite directions and their effects may have nullified each other. In this case, for example, the encoding of a high tone impaired the identification of a right stimulus; but the subsequent execution of a left response impaired the identification of a left stimulus.

If these considerations are correct, it should be possible to demonstrate both interferences independently. Experiment 3 attempted to show that the tone-arrow interference occurs without manual responses. Experiment 4 was a control for Experiments 3 and 5. Finally, Experiment 5 attempted to demonstrate the response-arrow interference without a modulation by frequency-coded tones.

EXPERIMENT 3

A possible interpretation of Experiments 1 and 2 rests on the assumption that the present blindness effect originated from two independent sources of interference: The tone-arrow interference and the response-arrow interference. Both interferences converge in the low–left and high–right tone-response mapping; but they nullify each other with the low–right and high–left mapping. Accordingly, the blindness effect occurred in the low–left and high–right mapping but not in the low–right and high–left mapping.

In this experiment, the implication of this interpretation was examined, which states that the tone-arrow interference should also occur in the absence of the primary response task. In other words, it was examined whether the pure presentation of a low (high) tone specifically impairs the encoding of a left (right) arrow, but not so much the encoding of a right (left) arrow. Thus, in contrast to the previous experiments, the tone did not serve as a response cue. Instead, the tone could be ignored. In order to also examine the unspecific effects of tone presentation on identification, additional trials were introduced, in which no tone was presented.

Method

Participants.   Twelve paid volunteers (six females and six males; aged 21–32 years) took part in Experiment 3. All of them reported to be right handed and to have normal or corrected-to-normal vision. None had participated in Experiments 1 and 2.

Apparatus and stimuli.   The same apparatus and stimuli as in Experiments 1 and 2 were used.

Procedure and design.   Each trial started with the presentation of a blank screen for 1000 ms. Then—with equal probability—either the low-pitched tone, the high-pitched tone, or no tone was presented for 150 ms. There were two differences between the procedure of the present experiment and the procedures of Experiments 1 and 2. First, participants did not have to perform any response to the tones. On the contrary, participants were told that the tones were completely irrelevant for the task and, thus, could be ignored. Second, the five SOAs between the tone and the visual stimulus were changed to 0, 50, 150, 300, and 500 ms. Due to technical difficulties, the SOA of 0 ms was dropped from the analysis, and only the results for the remaining four SOAs are reported. In all other respects, the procedure was identical to the previous experiments.

Two independent variables were crossed in a 3×4 within-participants design. The first factor was the relationship between the three tone conditions and the two visual stimuli. The six possible combinations formed three levels: The first level consisted of the two combinations of no tone and the presentation of a left- or a right-pointing arrow. The second level consisted of the two combinations of a low-pitched tone with a left-pointing arrow and of a high-pitched tone with a right-pointing arrow. The third level consisted of the two combinations of a low-pitched tone with a right-pointing arrow and of a high-pitched tone with a left-pointing arrow. The second factor was the SOA between the tone and the visual stimulus, with the four levels 50, 150, 300, and 500 ms. The intention was to separately test for the unspecific effects and for the specific effects of the presentation of a low- or high-pitched tone on the identification of a left- or right-pointing arrow.

The experimental phase was preceded by a practice phase of 8 block of 12 trials each (3 tone conditions × 2 visual stimuli; fixed SOA of 250 ms). The whole experiment consisted of one session that lasted approximately 1 hour and 15 minutes.

Results

The mean presentation time for visual stimuli was 33 ms. Across all conditions, the proportion of correctly identified stimuli was 0.80 (SD = 0.04). First, the specific effects of the presentation of a low- or high-pitched tone on the identification of a left- or right-pointing arrow were analysed. The identification accuracy was computed for the two combinations of a low-pitched tone with a left-pointing arrow, and of a high-pitched tone with a right-pointing arrow. Additionally, the identification rates for the visual stimuli were computed for the remaining two combinations of a low-pitched tone with a right-pointing arrow, and of a high-pitched tone with a left-pointing arrow. The resulting proportions of correct judgements, which are depicted in Figure 4, were analysed as a function of these two tone–arrow relationships and of the SOA. The ANOVA revealed a significant main effect of SOA, $F(3, 33) = 33.73$, $p < .001$. Furthermore, the main effect of tone–arrow relationship was also significant, $F(1, 11) = 7.51$, $p = .019$. The latter result means that the combinations of a low-pitched tone with a left-pointing arrow and of a high-pitched tone with a right-pointing arrow led to significantly inferior identification performance ($M = 0.77$) than did the two alternative combinations ($M = 0.81$). The two-way interaction was not significant ($F < 1$).

In a second analysis, the unspecific effects were examined for the presence or absence of a low- or high-pitched tone on the identification of a left- or right-pointing arrow. The identification rates for the visual stimuli were computed for all possible combinations of a low- and high-pitched tone with a left- or right-pointing arrow (the filled and unfilled circles in Figure 4), and they were compared with identification performance in the absence of a tone (the filled triangles in Figure 4). This was done in a two-factorial ANOVA with tone (present or absent) and SOA (50, 150, 300, or 500 ms). The main effect of SOA, $F(3, 33) = 19.36$, $p < .001$, was significant, whereas the main effect of tone was

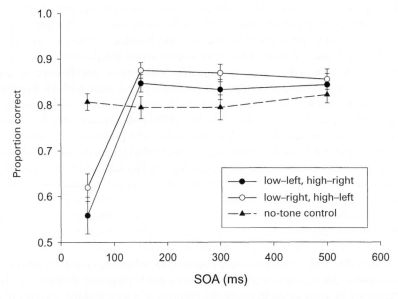

Figure 4. Results from Experiment 3. Mean proportion of correctly identified visual stimuli (with standard errors between participants) as a function of three combinations between the presence or absence of irrelevant tones and the visual stimuli (low-pitched tone/left-pointing arrow and high-pitched tone/right-pointing arrow; low-pitched tone/right-pointing arrow and high-pitched tone/left-pointing arrow; left- and right-pointing arrow without tone), and the tone–arrow SOA. Each data point is based on 360 observations.

not ($F < 1$). The main effect of SOA means that—across all tone conditions— identification accuracy for the SOA of 50 ms ($M = 0.70$) was worse than for the remaining three SOAs of 150 ms ($M = 0.83$), 300 ms ($M = 0.82$), and 500 ms ($M = 0.84$). The interaction between tone and SOA, $F(3, 33) = 23.51, p < .001$, was also significant, which reflects the significant effect of SOA on identification performance when a tone had been presented (see earlier). The SOA had, however, no effect on identification performance when no tone had been presented.

Discussion

The most important finding was the specific interference effect between the presentation of a tone and the identification of a visual stimulus. A left arrow was identified less frequently when it was presented with a low tone than when it was paired with a high tone. In contrast, a right arrow was identified less frequently when it was presented with a high tone than when it was paired with a low tone. In contrast to the previous experiments, this effect was observed with task-irrelevant tones. Thus, the pure presentation of the low–high tone seems to be sufficient to specifically affect the encoding of a left–right arrow-head. This finding presents evidence that the blindness effect observed in Experiments 1 and 2 was modulated by a tone–arrow interference.

A possible interpretation of the specific tone–arrow interference is that when a low (high) tone is presented, it is preferably associated with a left (right) spatial orientation and this affects the identification of a left (right) stimulus. These preferences are in line with Mudd's (1963) observation that low tones were preferably associated with left than with right positions, and that high tones were preferably associated with right than with left positions. In addition, these preferences are similar to the results reported by Lippa (1996a, b) and by Weeks and Proctor (1990), who found that in choice reaction-time tasks observers prefer to associate visual stimuli presented below a fixation point with left responses and stimuli presented above a fixation point with right responses. The specific tone–arrow interference effect observed in the present experiment suggests that not only a feature overlap between a response and a visual stimulus leads to performance decrements, when the visual stimulus has to be encoded during the execution of the compatible response. Rather, also the existence of an association between the features of a tone and the features of a visual stimulus seems to be able to create similar performance decrements. We return to this point in the General Discussion.

In addition to producing the specific effect, the presentation of a low or a high tone seemed to produce both an unspecific impairment in identification performance at the 50 ms SOA and an unspecific facilitation at the remaining SOAs. This conclusion should, however, be examined carefully. Any propor-tion correct value above or below the no-tone control cannot be unequivocally interpreted as impairment or as facilitation. For example, if the tone served as a warning signal for all SOAs of 150 ms and longer (cf., Bertelson, 1967; Bertelson & Tisseyre, 1968), and thus improved visual identification generally, then the identification rate at the 50 ms SOA had to be below the no-tone control due to the adjustment procedure of presentation time (cf., Footnote 1). So it is unclear whether there was an improvement at the longer SOAs, or an impairment at the shorter SOA, or both.

Given that the encoding of visual stimuli at the 50 ms SOA was actually impaired, such an impairment seems to be inconsistent with recent observa-tions by Jolicoeur (1999b). This author had his participants to monitor a stream of briefly presented visual stimuli (letters) for the presence of a target stimulus. The visual target letter followed a low or a high tone with a variable SOA. When the tones required a speeded left or right keypress, the accuracy in letter detection suffered markedly, showing unspecific response–arrow interference. When the tones required no response, no deficit was observed in the visual task. Thus, whereas to-be-ignored low or high tones did not affect concurrent visual encoding in Jolicoeur's (1999b) study, we found such an unspecific impairment in the present experiment. There are two possible explanations for this discrepancy. First, different temporal relationships between the to-be-ignored tones and the visual stimuli in the two studies might account for the different results. In Jolicoeur's (1999b) study, the tones were presented for 100 ms and the shortest SOA was 100 ms. Thus, even for the shortest SOA, there was no concurrent presentation of tones and visual stimuli. In the present experiment, the tones were presented for 150 ms and outlasted the presentation of the visual stimuli at the shortest SOA of 50 ms. Thus, the early impairment of visual encoding in our experiments might be due to the concurrent presentation of a tone (via headphones), whereas there was no concurrent presentation of tones and visual stimuli in Jolicoeur's (1999b) experiment. Second, the existence or non-existence of associations between the to-be-ignored tones and the visual stimuli might also account for the discrepant results. The observation of the specific tone–arrow interference in the present experiment was explained by automatically associating "low" with "left" and "high" with "right" (see previously). It is possible that the association process, which led to the specific interference effect, also caused the (short-lasting) unspecific interference effect. In contrast, there are most likely no associations between low and high tones and the letters "X" and "Y", which were the target letters in Jolicoeur's (1999b) study. Thus, the lack of associations between the tones and the letters might explain the absence of an unspecific interference effect. Experiment 4 examined the question, whether the unspecific interference effect observed in the present experiment is more likely due to the concurrent presentation of tone and visual stimuli or to the existence of associations between features of the tones and features of the visual stimuli.

EXPERIMENT 4

The major aim of the present experiment was to test, whether the to-be-ignored tones in Experiment 3 caused unspecific impairments in the encoding of simultaneously presented visual stimuli because of their simultaneous presentation or because of associations between tones and visual stimuli. Therefore, in Experiment 4, two short tones and one long tone of the same frequency were used as the to-be-ignored auditory stimuli, which were presented before the presentation of a to-be-identified left- or right-pointing arrowhead. We assumed that there were no preferred associations between two short tones or one long tone with either "left" or "right". Accordingly, no specific tone–arrow interference was expected in Experiment 4. If the tones in Experiment 4 caused unspecific impairments in the concurrent processing of visual stimuli without causing specific interference, then the unspecific impairments observed in Experiment 3 can be mainly attributed to their simultaneous presentation, and not to the activation of specific associations. The opposite interpretation would be suggested, however, if the tones in Experiment 4 caused neither specific impairments, nor unspecific impairments on the concurrent processing of visual stimuli. In addition, the demonstration that two short tones and one long tone do not specifically affect the encoding of left- and right-pointing arrows is important for the use of these tones as response cues in Experiment 5.

Method

Participants.   Twelve paid volunteers (five females, seven males; aged 21–28 years) took part in the experiment. All of them reported to be right handed and to have normal or corrected-to-normal vision. None had partici-pated in Experiments 1–3.

Apparatus and stimuli.   The apparatus and the visual stimuli were the same as in Experiment 3, except that now a Macintosh Quadra was used to control the experiment. The major difference between the present experiment and Experi-ment 3 was that the low-pitched and the high-pitched tone, used as auditory stimuli in Experiments 1–3, were replaced by one long tone presented for 150 ms and two short tones presented for 50 ms each with an inter-stimulus interval of 50 ms. These tones had an equal pitch of 600 Hz and were again presented concurrently to both ears.

Procedure and design.   The procedure was the same as in Experiment 3, except that different auditory stimuli were used as distracters. In the present experiment, after a blank interval of 1000 ms either a long tone of 600 Hz, two short tones of 600 Hz, or no tone was presented with equal probability. As in Experiment 3, participants did not have to respond to the tones and were told that these tones were task-irrelevant.

Two independent variables were crossed in a 3 × 4 within-participants design. The first factor was the relationship between the three tone conditions and the two visual stimuli. The six possible combinations were grouped to form three levels of this factor in the following way. The first level consisted of the two combinations of no tone and the presentation of a left- or right-pointing arrowhead. The second level consisted of the two combinations of a long tone with a left-pointing arrow and of two short tones with a right-pointing arrow. The third level consisted of the two combinations of a long tone with a right-pointing arrow and of two short tones with a left-pointing arrow. The second factor was the SOA between the tone and the visual stimulus, with the four levels 50, 150, 300, and 500 ms. As in Experiment 3, it was planned to separately test for the unspecific effects and for the specific effects of the presentation of one long tone or two short tones on the identification of a left- or right-pointing arrow.

Results

The mean presentation time for visual stimuli was 34 ms. Across all conditions, the proportion of correctly identified visual stimuli was 0.80 (SD = 0.05). In a first analysis, the specific effects of the presentation of a long tone or two short tones on the identification of a left- or right-pointing arrow were examined. Therefore, visual identification accuracy was computed for the two combinations of one long tone with a left-pointing arrow and of two short tones with a right-pointing arrow. In addition, visual identification accuracy was computed for the remaining two combinations of one long tone with a right-pointing arrow and of two short tones with a left-pointing arrow. The resulting proportions of correctly identified visual stimuli, which are depicted in Figure 5, were analysed as a function of the two tone–arrow relationships and of the four SOAs. An ANOVA revealed a significant main effect of SOA, $F(3, 33) = 2.93$, $p = .048$, which reflects lower identification accuracy for the SOAs of 50 and 150 ms (both $M = 0.82$) than for the SOAs of 300 ($M = 0.86$) and 500 ms ($M = 0.84$). This effect can be explained by assuming that the tone served as

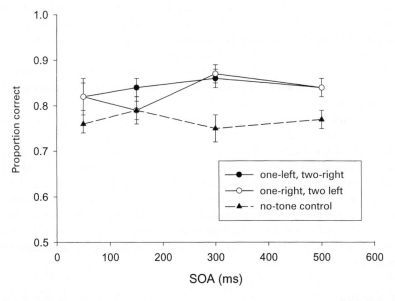

Figure 5. Results from Experiment 4. Mean proportion of correctly identified visual stimuli (with standard errors between participants) as a function of three combinations between the presence or absence of irrelevant tones and the visual stimuli (one long tone/left-pointing arrow and two short tones/right-pointing arrow; one long tone/right-pointing arrow and two short tones/left-pointing arrow; left- and right-pointing arrow without tone), and the tone–arrow SOA. Each data point is based on 360 observations.

warning signal for the occurrence of the visual stimulus, but that participants needed more than 150 ms to effectively use this information (cf., Bertelson, 1967; Bertelson & Tisseyre, 1968). More important, however, neither a main effect of the tone–arrow relationship nor an interaction of this factor with SOA was observed (both $F < 1$). Thus, these results confirmed the prediction that the pure presentation of a long tone or of two short tones can not specifically affect the identification of the arrows.

In the second part of the analysis, the unspecific effects of the presence or absence of a long tone or of two short tones on the identification of a left- or right-pointing arrow were analysed. Therefore, the proportions of correctly identified visual stimuli were computed across all possible combinations of a long tone or two short tones with a left- or right-pointing arrow (the filled and unfilled circles in Figure 5) and compared with the identification rates of visual stimuli when no tone had been presented (the filled triangles in Figure 5). This was done in a two-factorial ANOVA with tone (present or absent) and SOA (50, 150, 300, or 500 ms) as within-participant factors. The main effect of SOA was not significant ($F < 1$), but there was a significant main effect of tone, $F(1, 11) = 28.20, p < .001$. The presentation of a tone improved visual identification accuracy ($M = 0.84$), as compared to the performance in the absence of a tone ($M = 0.77$). The two-way interaction between tone and SOA was also significant, $F(3, 33) = 3.12, p = .039$. This interaction is due to a significant effect of SOA on identification performance when a tone had been presented (see earlier), whereas the SOA had no effect on identification performance in the absence of a tone, $F(3, 33) = 1.14, p = .348$. In other words, the positive effect of tone presentation on visual encoding increases with increasing SOA, as compared to the no-tone condition.

To examine the possibility that the absence of a specific tone–arrow interference in the present experiment would also reduce the unspecific effect as compared to Experiment 3, the identification rates from trials with tone presentation entered into a two-way ANOVA with the factors experiment and SOA. This analysis revealed significant main effects of experiment, $F(1, 22) = 5.76$, $p = .025$, and SOA, $F(3, 66) = 30.82, p < .001$, and—more important—a significant interaction between both factors, $F(3, 66) = 22.69, p < .001$. For the 50 ms SOA, the identification rate was higher in the present experiment ($M = 0.82$) than in Experiment 3 ($M = 0.60$), whereas the identification rates were very similar for the other SOAs.

Discussion

The mere presentation of one long tone or two short tones exerted neither a specific nor an unspecific (negative) effect on the visual encoding of left- or right-pointing arrowheads, even when the tones and the visual stimuli overlapped in time. This result suggests that the early deficit in visual encoding in

Experiment 3 was not due to the concurrent presentation of low or high tones and left- or right-pointing arrowheads. Instead, it suggests that specific associations between these tones and these visual stimuli were also responsible for the unspecific interference effect. These associations are automatically activated by the presentation of a tone (e.g., a low tone), and affect both the encoding of the associated stimulus (left-pointing arrow), as well as the encoding of the non-associated stimulus (right-pointing arrow). A more detailed account is presented in the General Discussion.

The results of Experiment 4 are consistent with the findings of Jolicoeur (1999b), who also observed no (negative) effect from to-be-ignored low or high tones on visual encoding of letters. Together, the findings suggest that there is no unspecific cross-modal interference effect when there are no specific associations between the to-be-ignored tones and the to-be-encoded visual stimuli. We conclude that there are no specific associations between long or short tones with "left" or "right", because no specific interference was observed in the present experiment. In addition, it is very unlikely that there are specific associations between low or high tones and the letters "X" or "Y" (Jolicoeur, 1999b).

The finding that the tones used in the present experiment were unable to specifically affect visual encoding of left- or right-pointing arrowheads was important for the next experiment. In Experiment 5, one long tone and two short tones were used as cues in the response task, in order to demonstrate the blindness effect without modulations through a tone–arrow interference.

EXPERIMENT 5

After the successful demonstration of the tone–arrow interference in the absence of a response task in Experiment 3, the present experiment aimed to isolate the response–arrow interference (i.e., the "original" blindness effect) in the absence of a modulation by a tone–arrow interference. Therefore, the response cues used in Experiments 1 and 2 were replaced by one long tone and two short tones. On the basis of the results of Experiment 4, it was assumed that these response cues do not differ in their relationship to the spatial left/right dimension of the arrows.

Method

Participants.   Sixteen paid volunteers (nine females, seven males; aged 19–34 years) took part in the experiment. All participants reported to have normal or corrected-to-normal vision; only one declared to be left handed. None had participated in Experiments 1–4.

Apparatus and stimuli.   The apparatus and the visual stimuli were the same as in Experiment 1, except that now a Macintosh Quadra was used to control the experiment. The major difference between the present experiment and Experiment 1 was that the low-pitched and the high-pitched tone, used as auditory stimuli in Experiment 1, were replaced by one long tone presented for 150 ms and two short tones presented for 50 ms each with an inter-stimulus interval of 50 ms. These tones had an equal pitch of 600 Hz and were again presented concurrently to both ears via headphones.

Procedure and design.   The procedure of Experiment 5 was identical to the procedure of Experiment 1, except that one half of the participants had to press the left key to one long tone and the right key to the short tones. For the other half of the participants, the mapping rule was inverted. As in Experiment 1, the compatibility between the responses and the visual stimuli, as well as the SOA between the tones and the visual stimuli, were varied within participants, whereas the mapping between tones and responses was varied between participants. Thus, the present experiment was based on a $2 \times 2 \times 5$ mixed design.

Results

Response task.   Across all conditions and participants, less than 4% of the reaction times exceeded the criterion of 1000 ms. The error percentage had a grand mean of 5.3% (SD = 2.8). The error percentages were analysed in an ANOVA with the between-participants factor mapping (two levels), the within-participant factors compatibility (two levels), and SOA (five levels). As in Experiment 1, the only significant effect was the main effect of SOA, $F(4, 56) = 2.95$, $p = .028$, according to which the percentage of false responses increased with decreasing SOA.

The mean correct reaction time across all conditions was 491 ms (SD = 79). A corresponding ANOVA revealed no significant effect.

Identification task.   The mean presentation time for the visual stimuli was 44 ms in the group with the tone–response mapping "one tone–left" and "two tones–right"; and it was 34 ms in the group with the mapping "one tone–right" and "two tones–left". The difference of 10 ms was not significant, $t(14) = 1.37$, $p > .10$ (two-tailed). Across all conditions, the proportion of correctly identified visual stimuli was 0.76 (SD = 0.05). Figure 6 depicts these proportions as a function of all possible combinations of the different levels of the factors compatibility and SOA.

The proportions of correctly identified visual stimuli were analysed in an ANOVA with the between-participant factor mapping (two levels), the within-participant factors compatibility (two levels), and SOA (five levels). This ANOVA revealed the same pattern of main effects as did the ANOVA in Experiment 1. The main effect of mapping was not significant, $F(1, 14) = 2.96$, $p = .108$. However, the main effects of SOA, $F(4, 56) = 7.37$, $p < .001$, and of

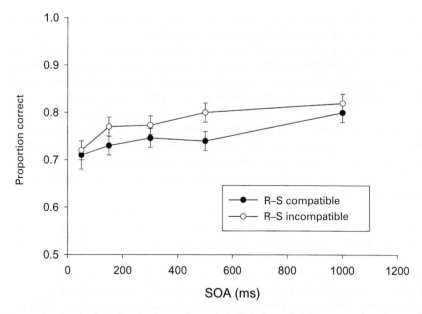

Figure 6. Results from the visual encoding task in Experiment 5. Mean proportion of correctly identified visual stimuli (with standard errors between participants) as a function of the response–arrow compatibility (compatible vs incompatible), and the tone–arrow SOA. Each data point is based on about 950 observations.

compatibility, $F(1, 14) = 8.79$, $p = .010$, were significant. The effect of SOA reflects the observation that identification accuracy increased when the SOA increased: There was a difference of 0.10 between the identification accuracy for the shortest SOA of 50 ms ($M = 0.71$) and the identification accuracy for the longest SOA of 1000 ms ($M = 0.81$). The effect of compatibility was due to the fact that response-compatible stimuli ($M = 0.75$) were identified less accurately than response-incompatible stimuli ($M = 0.78$). Importantly, and in contrast to the results of Experiment 1, none of the interactions between the factors mapping, compatibility, and SOA was significant (all $F < 1$).

Discussion

In line with our original expectations, the blindness to response-compatible stimuli was observed in the present experiment in the absence of the modulation by the tone–arrow interference in Experiments 1 and 2. Therefore, the present finding is highly similar to the response–arrow interference already observed with previous—non PRP—tasks (e.g., Müsseler & Hommel, 1997a). However, in contrast to the previous studies, the present finding demonstrates that the blindness effect is not restricted to situations in which the response has to be withheld before or during stimulus encoding.

Moreover, Experiments 3 and 5 provide indirect evidence for our interpretation of why the blindness effect occurred only for one of the two alternative tone–response mappings in Experiments 1 and 2. The assumption was that in these experiments two different kinds of interference had converged in the low–left and high–right tone–response mapping, but had nullified each other in the low–right and high–left mapping. Experiments 3 and 5 demonstrated the tone–arrow interference and the response–arrow interference independently from each other; thus, these two interferences could have interacted in Experiments 1 and 2. We present an account for these interference effects in the General Discussion.

Finally, Experiment 5 revealed evidence for an unspecific response–arrow interference effect: The greater the temporal overlap between the speeded response task and the visual encoding task, the worse was overall performance in the encoding task. We found a performance decrement of 6% between the SOAs of 50 and 500 ms, which is very similar to the performance decrement that Jolicoeur (1999a, Exp. 2) has observed (about 5% between the SOAs of 50 and 600 ms). But because there was no neutral condition in Experiment 5, it is not for sure that this unspecific effect actually represents costs. Experiment 4 showed that the presentation of short or long tones can improve performance in a concurrent visual encoding task, compared to visual encoding in the absence of a tone, and that this improvement increased with the SOA. Our interpretation of this result was that the tone served as a warning signal for the occurrence of the visual stimulus. It is unlikely, however, that the tones could be used as warning signals in Experiment 5, when the participants had to respond as quickly as possible to the tones. Moreover, Experiment 4 showed no evidence that the mere presentation of short or long tones can impair concurrent visual encoding. Thus, the decrease in visual performance with decreasing SOA in the present experiment is most likely a cost at short SOAs that is caused by the concurrent preparation of a motor response.

GENERAL DISCUSSION

The major aim of the present study was to investigate the conditions under which processing in a motor (response) task specifically interferes with concurrent processing in a visual encoding (identification) task. From such studies it may be possible to learn more about the representations and/or processes in which response preparation and perception overlap.

Such previous studies have demonstrated unspecific impairment of visual encoding when the participants were simultaneously engaged in a speeded choice–response task (e.g., Jolicoeur, 1999a; De Jong & Sweet, 1994). From these studies, however, it remained unclear to which degree the inability to fully prepare for two tasks at the same time has contributed to the observed unspecific impairment. Instead of an interference at the visual encoding phase, the impairment could also have originated from a procedural interference, due to some limited multi-purpose capacity.

Other studies have demonstrated specific impairment of visual encoding when the participants were simultaneously engaged in an unspeeded choice–response task. The finding was that the preparedness to execute a left or right keypress or the execution itself impaired the concurrent encoding of a response-compatible visual stimulus. In these studies, however, the execution of the response had to be postponed (suppressed) either until a neutral response had been performed (e.g., Müsseler & Hommel, 1997a) or until a "go" signal had occurred (e.g., Wühr & Müsseler, 2001). Thus, it was unclear whether the blindness effect originated from the preparation of the response, or from the withholding of the response. In order to test this issue in the present experiments, the participants performed keypresses to a tone as quickly as possible and identified left- or right-pointing arrowheads presented in between. In addition to the compatibility between the response and the visual stimulus, the SOA between the tone and the visual stimulus was systematically varied in order to investigate when—if at all—the blindness effect emerges in respect to the processing in the response task.

There were four major findings. The first finding was that speeded left or right keypresses unspecifically interfered with the encoding of briefly presented visual stimuli (Experiments 1, 2, and 5). The identification of stimuli presented during the preparation and execution of the responses was worse compared to the identification of stimuli after the execution of the responses, irrespective of the compatibility between responses and visual stimuli. This unspecific response–stimulus interference was even observed at SOAs between tones and visual stimuli, at which possible (direct) stimulus–stimulus interferences were unlikely to play a role (SOAs ≥150 ms). This finding replicates the earlier findings reported by De Jong and Sweet (1994) and Jolicoeur (1999a).

Second, a speeded left or right keypress did also specifically interfere with the encoding of the briefly presented visual stimuli (Experiments 1, 2, and 5). The speeded preparation and execution of responses caused inferior identification performance for response-compatible stimuli compared to response-incompatible stimuli. This finding shows that the blindness effect is not restricted to situations in which the response has to be withheld before or during stimulus encoding. In the present experiments, in which the response had to be performed as quickly as possible to the tones, the blindness effect seemed to grow during the processing of the response task and to peak around response execution. Thus, neither an abrupt onset of the blindness effect was observed nor was the blindness effect preceded by a brief period of superior identification of response-compatible stimuli. However, superior identification could be expected under certain assumptions, which are discussed later.

Third, a particular set of auditory stimuli was able to specifically interfere with the encoding of briefly presented visual stimuli (Experiment 3). In particular, the encoding of a left-pointing arrow was inferior when it followed a low-pitched tone than when it followed a high-pitched tone, whereas the encoding of a right-pointing arrow was inferior when it followed a high-pitched tone than when it followed a low-pitched tone. In contrast to this specific tone–arrow interference, the identification of a left- or right-pointing arrow was not differentially affected by the presentation of a long tone or two short tones, with equal pitch (Experiment 4).

Fourth, the specific tone–arow interference modulated the specific response–arrow interference when the task allowed both interferences to occur simultaneously (Experiments 1 and 2). That is, a (response-compatible) left-pointing arrow was identified less well than a (response-incompatible) right-pointing arrow when a left key was pressed to a low-pitched tone, but not when the left key was pressed to a high-pitched tone. Correspondingly, a (response-compatible) right-pointing arrow was identified less well than a (response-incompatible) left-pointing arrow when a right key was pressed to a high-pitched tone, but not when the right key was pressed to a low-pitched tone.

Before we turn to our explanation of these findings, a few comments on the time course of the blindness effect observed in the present experiments seem to be appropriate. Of course, these comments are only based on qualitative observations because we never found a significant two-way interaction between compatibility and SOA, and—therefore—did not perform post hoc comparisons on the data. However, it may be interesting to note that in all of the present dual-task experiments, the blindness effect was numerically greatest for the SOA of 500 ms, when the visual stimulus was presented most closely to response execution (mean reaction times of the Experiments 1, 2, and 5 were 466 ms, 474 ms, and 491 ms, respectively). This observation suggests that the better prepared the response the stronger the blindness to response-compatible stimuli. This suggestion is supported by the results of more recent experiments, in which the participants identified left- and right-pointing arrows while they performed a compatible or an incompatible response, or while they performed one of two neutral responses. We observed a significant disadvantage to identifying response-compatible stimuli compared to the neutral conditions only for the medium SOA of 400 ms, which again was closest to response execution (Müsseler & Wühr, 2001). Thus, the preparation and execution of a speeded response produces costs in the encoding of compatible stimuli that peak around response execution. By contrast, the blindness effect was clearly diminished at the 1000 ms SOA in two out of three of the present dual-task experiments. Only in Experiment 1, the blindness effect seemed to be still large for the 1000 ms

SOA. However, this might be due to the possible additivity of the two specific interference effects, the tone–arrow and the response–arrow interference, in this experiment.

In the following section, it is discussed how well the two-stage model of action planning, proposed by Stoet and Hommel (1999; see also Hommel et al., in press; Müsseler, 1999), is able to account for the different findings of the present study.

The two-stage account of action planning

The two-stage model of action planning (Stoet & Hommel, 1999) has been proposed to explain specific interference effects between different sets of concurrently performed tasks. The model rests on two basic assumptions. The first assumption is that features of to-be-perceived stimuli and features of to-be-performed responses are represented by the same cognitive codes (cf., Hommel, 1997; MacKay, 1987; Müsseler & Prinz, 1996). For example, the identity of a to-be-perceived left-pointing arrow and the position of a to-be-performed left keypress are represented by accessing the same cognitive LEFT code. This common-coding assumption (Prinz, 1990, 1997) allows the model not only to account for specific interference effects between the processing of two different stimuli or between the processing of two different responses (Stoet & Hommel, 1999), but also to account for specific interference effects between the processing of a response and the processing of a stimulus. Any of these interference effects is interpreted as a crosstalk due to structural overlap.

The second basic assumption of the two-stage model is that the formation of any cognitive representation of a stimulus or of a response takes place in two successive steps. During the first stage, the features of a perceived stimulus or of a to-be-performed response are *activated*. However, if more than one stimulus is simultaneously present or if more than one response is to be performed, the activation of feature codes does not allow to distinguish between different stimuli and/or responses. This fact is known as the "binding problem" (cf., Treisman, 1996). Therefore, the already activated feature codes that belong to one and the same stimulus or response are *bound* together, that is, during the second stage of processing, these codes are integrated into an event file. Stoet and Hommel (1999) claimed that if the contents of two tasks, which have to be processed in parallel, overlap in at least one of their features, the performance in the second task critically depends on the temporal relationship between the processing in both tasks. If the overlapping feature code is just activated by the processing in the first task, then processing (of that feature) in the second task should be facilitated. If, however, the overlapping feature code is already bound by the processing in the first task, then processing (of that feature) in the second task should be hampered.

Originally, the two-stage model was applied to account for specific response–response interference effects (cf., Stoet, 1998; Stoet & Hommel, 1999). However, this model can also be applied to account for the blindness effect, a case of specific response–stimulus interference. The explanation is, for example, that when the LEFT feature code is already bound into the plan for a left response, this feature code is not available for the encoding and representation of a left stimulus (cf., Hommel et al., in press; Müsseler, 1999; Stoet & Hommel, 1999). Correspondingly, the blindness effect should emerge as soon as the preparation of the response has begun and should continue until this response is finally executed.

A very similar explanation can account for the specific tone–arrow interference, as it was observed in Experiment 3. Because there is no direct feature overlap between a low-pitched tone and a left response, or between a high-pitched tone and a right response, it has to be assumed that the feature codes of LOW and LEFT, as well as the feature codes of HIGH and RIGHT, are more strongly *associated* than the feature codes of LOW and RIGHT, or the feature codes of HIGH and LEFT. This assumption is supported by observations of corresponding spatial stereotypes associated with the pitch of tones (Mudd, 1963), and by observations of orthogonal stimulus–response compatibility effects between visual stimuli that varied in their vertical positions (up vs down) and left or right keypresses (e.g., Lippa, 1996a, b; Weeks & Proctor, 1990). If, for example, a low-pitched tone is presented, the LOW code and the associated LEFT code are both activated and—at least sometimes—are bound together automatically. As a consequence, the encoding and representation of a left stimulus, presented after the low-pitched tone, is impaired because the LEFT feature code is already bound into a representation of the tone. This explanation implies that not only the feature codes of physical properties of a stimulus are bound into its representation (an event file), but also the feature codes of *semantic* properties of that particular stimulus.

Now, let us turn to the interaction between the specific tone–arrow interference and the specific response–arrow interference, as observed in Experiments 1 and 2. In these experiments, the participants performed a left or right response to the low-pitched or the high-pitched tone, while a visual stimulus had to be identified. In such a situation, one can assume that the low-pitched or the high-pitched tone is processed on two different routes, one route being automatic and (mainly) instruction-independent, and the other route being controlled and instruction-dependent (cf., De Jong, Liang, & Lauber, 1994; Eimer, Hommel, & Prinz, 1995; Kornblum, Hasbroucq, & Osman, 1990).

The consequences for the mapping "low tone–left response vs high tone–right response" are the following. When, for example, a low tone is presented, the feature code LOW activates the feature code for LEFT automatically, because LOW and LEFT are associated (see earlier), but simultaneously the code LEFT is activated on a second, controlled route, because the instruction demands for a left response. Thus, in this case, the activation via two (parallel) routes converges on the same (LEFT) code, which results in a fast and strong binding of this code into the representation of the response, which means that the encoding of the response-compatible (left) stimulus is impaired, whereas the encoding of the response-incompatible (right) stimulus is not affected. As a result, a strong blindness effect can be observed.

A different situation emerges for the mapping "low tone–right response vs high tone–left response". When, for example, a low tone is presented, the feature code LOW again activates the associated feature code for LEFT automatically, but now—according to the instruction—the code RIGHT is activated on the second, controlled route. The result of this divergent activation of both the LEFT and the RIGHT code is that the LEFT code is—at least sometimes—integrated (bound) into a representation of the tone and that the RIGHT code is always integrated (bound) into a representation of the response. The consequence is that this tone–response mapping leads not only to an impairment of encoding the response-compatible (right) stimulus but also to an impairment of encoding the response-incompatible—but tone-associated— (left) stimulus. As a result, the blindness effect is diminished.

Finally, the two-stage model is also able to account for the effects of unspecific response–stimulus interference (e.g., Experiment 5; Jolicoeur, 1999a). The explanation would be that the process of binding feature codes in one task unspecifically interferes with the concurrent binding of different feature codes in a second task. That is, the preparation of a left response, for example, would also interfere with the encoding of a right stimulus, because in both tasks binding processes have to take place which unspecifically interfere with each other. This explanation is in accordance with the observation that not only the preparation of responses impaired the encoding of visual stimuli, but also the other way round, that is, the encoding of stimuli also impaired the prep- aration of responses. This was indicated by the increasing error rates in the response task with decreasing SOA, a finding also reported by Jolicoeur (1999a). The present explanation of unspecific response–stimulus interference is similar to that proposed by Jolicoeur (1999a), because both accounts claim that some process of consolidation of visual stimulus information is impaired by concurrent processing. However, the present account is more precise in localizing the source of that interference. This source is seen in the binding of feature codes in the course of preparing a response, whereas Jolicoeur (1999a, p. 608) localizes this source in "central processing requiring to perform Task$_1$, perhaps response selection".

However, there is one feature of the present data, which is—at first glance— at odds with the predictions of the two-stage model. The two-stage model predicts that during the first stage of processing, that is the activation of feature codes, the processing in a concurrent task should benefit, if there is feature overlap between the contents of both tasks. Accordingly, the observed impairment in the identification of response-compatible stimuli at intermediate SOAs should have been preceded by an early facilitation in the identification of response-compatible stimuli at short SOAs. This, however, was never observed, even not in Experiment 5, in which early tone–arrow interference should not have played a role.

There is one possible explanation for this failure to find early facilitation in the identification of response-compatible stimuli, as predicted by the two-stage model. This explanation localizes the source of this failure in the fact that only auditory stimuli were used as response cues in the response task. It is well known, however, that auditory stimuli are processed significantly faster than visual stimuli (cf., Welch & Warren, 1986, for an overview on this topic). This means that the actual tone–arrow SOAs in the present experiments rather underestimate the lead in the processing of tones compared to the processing of visual stimuli. As a consequence, even for an SOA of 50 ms between tones and visual stimuli, binding could already have begun in the response task when the processing of the visual stimulus is starting. One implication of this post hoc explanation is that early facilitation in the identification of response-compatible stimuli should be observed in a situation, in which the processing of the response cues is slowed down, for example by using visual response cues. In a recent series of experiments, we obtained evidence for this hypothesis to be correct (Müsseler & Wühr, in press).

The present findings and the relationship between perception and action

The findings of the present study suggest not only that perception and action might (partially) operate on common cognitive representations but also that some similarities might exist between perceptual encoding and response preparation. It was not only found that the preparation of a (manual) response can affect the visual encoding of a response-compatible stimulus in a specific way, but also that the processing of an auditory stimulus can affect the visual encoding of a tone-associated visual stimulus in a similar way. In addition, it was observed that the processing of a tone and the preparation of a response interacted in their specific influence on the encoding of a visual stimulus. That is, the impairment in encoding a tone-associated visual stimulus and the impairment in encoding a response-compatible stimulus could either amplify or nullify each other, depending on the tone–response mapping in the response task that had to be performed simultaneously with the visual encoding task.

In particular, the interaction between the specific tone–arrow interference effect and the specific response–arrow interference effect supports the notion of a cognitive domain in which the features of stimuli and the features of responses are represented in a supramodal format (cf., MacKay, 1987; Prinz, 1990). Moreover, the similarity between the ways in which the processing of a tone can affect the encoding of a tone-associated visual stimulus and in which the preparation of a response can affect the encoding of a response-compatible visual stimulus suggests that similar processes might be involved in perception and in response preparation. In particular, it was assumed that the processes of activating and binding cognitive representations (feature codes) were involved in stimulus encoding and in response preparation (cf., Hommel et al., in press; Stoet & Hommel, 1999). The binding of feature codes associated with a tone and the binding of a feature codes associated with a response both lead to similar impairments in encoding a visual stimulus that possesses a feature, whose code is already bound. Thus, perception and action might have more in common than has often been assumed.

REFERENCES

Arnell, K., & Duncan, J. (1998). *Substantial interference between response selection and stimulus encoding*. Poster presented at the 39th annual meeting of the Psychonomic Society, Dallas, TX, USA, November.

Bertelson, P. (1967). The time course of preparation. *Quarterly Journal of Experimental Psychology, 19*, 272–279.

Bertelson, P., & Tisseyre, F. (1968). The time course of preparation with regular and irregular foreperiods. *Quarterly Journal of Experimental Psychology, 20*, 297–300.

De Jong, R. (1993). Multiple bottlenecks in overlapping task performance. *Journal of Experimental Psychology: Human Perception and Performance, 19*, 965–980.

De Jong, R., Liang, C.C., & Lauber, E. (1994). Conditional and unconditional automaticity: A dual-process model of effects of spatial stimulus–response correspondence. *Journal of Experimental Psychology: Human Perception and Performance, 20*, 731–750.

De Jong, R., & Sweet, J.B. (1994). Preparatory strategies in overlapping-task performance. *Perception and Psychophysics, 55*, 142–151.

Eimer, M., Hommel, B., & Prinz, W. (1995). S–R compatibility and response selection. *Acta Psychologica, 90*, 301–313.

Greenwald, A.G. (1970). Sensory feedback mechanisms in performance control: With special reference to the ideo-motor mechanism. *Psychological Review, 77*, 73–99.

Hoffmann, J. (1993). *Vorhersage und Erkenntnis* [Prediction and knowledge]. Göttingen, Germany: Hogrefe.

Hommel, B. (1997). Toward an action–concept model of stimulus–response compatibility. In B. Hommel & W. Prinz (Eds.), *Theoretical issues in stimulus–response compatibility* (pp. 281–320). Amsterdam: Elsevier Science.

Hommel, B., Müsseler, J., Aschersleben, G., & Prinz, W. (in press). The theory of event coding (TEC): A framework for perception and action. *Behavioral and Brain Sciences*.

Hunt, S.M.J. (1994). MacProbe: A MacIntosh based experimenter's workstation for the cognitive sciences. *Behavior Research Methods, Instruments and Computers, 26*, 345–351.

James, W. (1890). *The principles of psychology*. New York: Holt.

Jolicoeur, P. (1999a). Dual-task interference and visual encoding. *Journal of Experimental Psychology: Human Perception and Performance, 25*, 596–616.

Jolicoeur, P. (1999b). Restricted attention capacity between sensory modalities. *Psychonomic Bulletin and Review, 6*, 87–92.

Kahneman, D. (1973). *Attention and effort*. Englewood Cliffs, NJ: Prentice-Hall.

Karlin, L., & Kestenbaum, R. (1968). Effects of number of alternatives on the psychological refractory period. *Quarterly Journal of Psychology, 20*, 167–178.

Keele, S.W., & Neill, W.T. (1978). Mechanisms of attention. In E.C. Carterette & M.P. Friedman (Eds.), *Handbook of perception IX: Perceptual processing* (pp. 3–47). New York: Academic Press.

Kornblum, S., Hasbroucq, T., & Osman, A. (1990). Dimensional overlap: Cognitive basis for stimulus–response compatibility: A model and taxonomy. *Psychological Review, 97,* 253–270.

Lippa, Y. (1996a). A referential-coding explanation for compatibility effects of physically orthogonal stimulus and response dimensions. *Quarterly Journal of Experimental Psychology: Human Experimental Psychology, 49A,* 950–971.

Lippa (1996b). *Über die Vermittlung von Wahrnehmung und Handlung, Kompatibilitätseffekte physikalisch orthogonaler Reiz- und Handlungsdimensionen* [On the mediation of perception and action: Compatibility effects of physically orthogonal stimulus and action dimensions]. Aachen, Germany: Shaker.

Lotze, H. (1852). *Medicinische Psychologie oder Physiologie der Seele* [Medical psychology or physiology of the soul]. Leipzig, Germany: Weidmann.

MacKay, D.G. (1987). *The organization of perception and action.* New York: Springer.

Mudd, S.A. (1963). Spatial stereotypes of four dimensions of pure tone. *Journal of Experimental Psychology, 66,* 347–352.

Müsseler, J. (1995). *Wahrnehmung und Handlungsplanung* [Perception and action planning]. Aachen, Germany: Shaker.

Müsseler, J. (1999). How independent from action control is perception? An event-coding account for more equally-ranked crosstalks. In G. Aschersleben, T. Bachmann, & J. Müsseler (Eds.), *Cognitive contributions to the perception of spatial and temporal events* (pp. 121–147). Amsterdam: Elsevier Science.

Müsseler, J., & Hommel, B. (1997a). Blindness to response-compatible stimuli. *Journal of Experimental Psychology: Human Perception and Performance, 23,* 861–872.

Müsseler, J., & Hommel, B. (1997b). Detecting and identifying response-compatible stimuli. *Psychonomic Bulletin and Review, 4,* 125–129.

Müsseler, J., & Prinz, W. (1996). Action planning during the presentation of stimulus sequences: Effects of compatible and incompatible stimuli. *Psychological Research, 59,* 48–63.

Müsseler, J., Steininger, S., & Wühr, P. (2001). Can actions affect perceptual processing. *Quarterly Journal of Experimental Psychology, 54A,* 137–154.

Müsseler, J., & Wühr, P. (in press). Motor-evoked interference in visual encoding. In W. Prinz & B. Hommel (Eds.), *Attention and performance XIX: Perceptual processing.* Oxford, UK: Oxford University Press.

Müsseler, J., Wühr, P., & Prinz, W. (2000). Varying the response code in the blindness to response-compatible stimuli. *Visual Cognition, 7,* 743–767.

Pashler, H. (1984). Processing stages in overlapping tasks Evidence for a central bottleneck. *Journal of Experimental Psychology: Human Perception and Performance, 10,* 358–377.

Pashler, H. (1989). Dissociations and dependencies between speed and accuracy: Evidence for a two-component theory of divided attention in simple tasks. *Cognitive Psychology, 21,* 469–514.

Pashler, H. (1994). Dual-task interference in simple tasks: Data and theory. *Psychological Bulletin, 116,* 220–244.

Prinz, W. (1990). A common-coding approach to perception and action. In O. Neumann & W. Prinz (Eds.), *Relationships between perception and action* (pp. 167–201). Berlin, Germany: Springer.

Prinz, W. (1997). Perception and action planning. *European Journal of Cognitive Psychology, 9,* 129–154.

Simon, J.R., Mewaldt, S.P., Acosta, E., & Hu, J.M. (1976). Processing auditory information: Interaction of two population stereotypes. *Journal of Applied Psychology, 61,* 354–358.

Stoet, G. (1998). *The role of feature integration in action planning*. Unpublished doctoral thesis, University of Munich, Germany.

Stoet, G., & Hommel, B. (1999). Action planning and the temporal binding of response codes. *Journal of Experimental Psychology: Human Perception and Performance, 25*, 1625–1640.

Treisman, A. (1996). The binding problem. *Current Opinion in Neurobiology, 6*, 171–178.

Weeks, D.J., & Proctor, R.W. (1990). Salient-features coding in the translation between orthogonal stimulus and response dimensions. *Journal of Experimental Psychology: General, 119*, 355–366.

Welch, R.B., & Warren, D.H. (1986). Intersensory interactions. In J.R. Boff, L. Kaufman, & J.P. Thomas (Eds.), *Handbook of perception and human performance: Vol. I—Sensory processes and perception*. New York: John Wiley & Sons.

Welford, A.T. (1952). The "psychological refractory period" and the timing of high-speed performance—a review and a theory. *British Journal of Psychology, 43*, 2–19.

Welford, A.T. (1980). The single-channel hypothesis. In A.T. Welford (Ed.), *Reaction times* (pp. 215–252). London: Academic Press.

Wickens, C.D. (1980). The structure of attentional resources. In R.S. Nickerson (Ed.), *Attention and performance VIII* (pp. 239–257). Hillsdale, NJ: Lawrence Erlbaum Associates, Inc.

Wühr, P. (2000). *Sieht man inumer was man tut? Wie sich Handlungen auf die visuelle Wahrnehmung auswirken* [Do we always see what we are doing? How actions affect visual perception]. Berlin, Germany: Logos.

Wühr, P., & Müsseler, J. (2001). Time course of the blindness to response-compatible stimuli. *Journal of Experimental Psychology: Human Perception and Performance, 27*, 1260–1270.

VISUAL COGNITION, 2002, 9 (4/5), 458–476

Action and perception: Evidence against converging selection processes

Claudia Bonfiglioli

*MRC Cognition and Brain Sciences Unit, Cambridge, UK, and
Dipartimento di Psicologia, Università degli Studi di Bologna, Italy*

John Duncan

MRC Cognition and Brain Sciences Unit, Cambridge, UK

Chris Rorden

*MRC Cognition and Brain Sciences Unit, Cambridge, UK,
and Institute of Cognitive Neuroscience, Department of Psychology,
University College London, UK*

Steffan Kennett

*Institute of Cognitive Neuroscience, Department of Psychology,
University College London, UK*

In a series of experiments we investigated whether identification of a lateralized visual target would benefit from concurrent execution of a reaching movement on the same side of space. Participants were tested in a dual-task paradigm. In one task, they performed a speeded reach movement towards a lateralized target button. The reach was cued by an auditory stimulus, and performed out of the participant's sight. In the other task, participants identified one of two simultaneous visual stimuli presented to the left and right visual fields, close to movement target locations. If motor activity were effective in modulating

Please address all correspondence to C. Bonfiglioli, Department of Psychology, Royal Holloway, University of London, Egham, Surrey TW20 0EX, UK.
Email: claudia.bonfiglioli@rhul.ac.uk
We would like to thank Jon Driver and Rob Ward for useful suggestions and discussions throughout the project. This work was supported by the Medical Research Council (UK).

http://www.tandf.co.uk/journals/pp/13506285.html   DOI:10.1080/13506280143000539

perceptual processes via a visuo-attentional shift, identification performance should have improved when the visual stimulus appeared at the movement target location. In fact, identification was not affected by the side of reach. Such results suggest substantially independent selection processes in motor and visual domains.

One aspect of visual attention is the ability to focus processing on a selected region of space. What factors influence such selection? Recently, many studies have suggested links between the motor and perceptual systems. These studies suggest that spatially directed motor activity could be one of the factors influencing the spatial focus of visual attention.

An influential model of this sort has been proposed by Rizzolatti and co-workers (Rizzolatti, Riggio, Dascola, & Umiltà, 1987). According to this "premotor" model, programming of a movement determines a shift of visual attention towards the region of space where the target for the movement is located. Although premotor effects were originally proposed for the programming of oculomotor responses (see also Deubel & Schneider, 1996), the theory has subsequently been generalized to include movements requiring different effectors (Rizzolatti, Riggio, & Sheliga, 1994), with the idea that attentional shifts depend on the facilitation of neurons within any "pragmatic map" (effector-specific representation of space) that is activated whenever a goal-directed movement is programmed. A similar proposal has been made in the context of Duncan's (1996) "integrated competition hypothesis" (see also Desimone & Duncan, 1995; Duncan, Humphreys, & Ward, 1997). According to this hypothesis, different objects in the environment compete for processing in multiple brain systems, including those representing different object properties and their implications for action. As an object assumes dominance within any one system, this dominance has a tendency to spread both to other representations of the same object (Duncan, 1984) and to related objects (Duncan & Humphreys, 1989), allowing integrated processing of related information across multiple components of the sensorimotor network. Again, selecting a particular region of space as the target for motor activity should produce a general enhancement of that region's processing.

Several studies have investigated interactions between motor activity and perceptual performance in brain-damaged patients. In particular, studies have focused on two disorders relating to lateral attentional bias: Unilateral neglect, manifest as a tendency to disregard the side of space opposite to a brain lesion in a wide range of activities including, for example, drawing, navigation, or eating from a plate; and sensory extinction, manifest as a failure to detect or identify contralesional inputs in the presence of simultaneous, competing inputs on the unimpaired or ipsilesional side. Halligan, Manning, and Marshall (1991), for example, investigated line bisection in a single left neglect patient. Bisection was carried out with the right hand, which was moved from either a left or a right starting position; rightward bias was reduced when movement started from the left. In a series of experiments, Robertson and North (1992, 1993, 1994) required a left neglect patient to perform letter cancellation and reading tasks while simultaneously executing irrelevant movements with different effectors (left/right hand, left leg) in different hemispaces (on the left or on the right of his body midline). For this patient, visual task performance was dramatically improved while moving a left effector in left hemispace. In a similar study, Mattingley, Robertson, and Driver (1998) investigated a patient showing left visual field extinction. The task was to detect briefly presented targets appearing either on the left, on the right, or on both sides of a computer screen. The patient had to trigger each trial herself by pressing a start key that was placed either on the left or on the right, using either her left or right hand. The number of left-sided targets omitted in the bilateral condition was clearly reduced by use of the left hand in left space.

A number of contradictory findings should also be noted. In a group study on patients suffering from left neglect, for example, Cubelli, Paganelli, Achilli, and Pedrizzi (1999) failed to replicate the results obtained by Robertson and North in their patient TD, and Brown, Walker, Gray, and Findlay (1999) reported that limb activation did not reduce the number of left-sided stimuli omitted by left neglect patients in a simple digit detection task. At least in some cases, however, it seems that patients suffering from unilateral neglect or extinction can show a substantial interaction between movement and visual attention, contralesional movements shifting attention towards that side. In this group, the data further suggest that both the hand used and the side of the body on which this hand is placed are important considerations.

For various reasons, we should be cautious in generalizing from a patient group of this sort to the normal case. It has often been suggested, for example, that neglect patients may partly overcome their lateral bias by strategic or top-down direction of attention towards the contralateral field (e.g., Humphreys, Boucart, Datar, & Riddoch, 1996). A requirement to direct movements into that field could plausibly act as a "reminder" or stimulus to such strategic efforts; a form of apparently "motor" effect, which would not be relevant to the normal case. For reasons like this it is important to complement the study of patients with corresponding investigations of normal participants.

One important study of such participants was reported by Deubel, Schneider, and Paprotta (1998). Each trial began with presentation of two horizontal strings of five place-markers, one to the left and one to the right of fixation. Positions 2–4 on each side were potential movement targets; these were marked by coloured ellipses, with a different colour for each position. There followed two events. First, the movement was cued by having the central fixation point turn into a coloured arrow. The direction of the arrow indicated whether to move left or right; the colour indicated which of the three possible target locations on that side to choose. Then, either 150 ms later (Experiment 1) or at movement onset (Experiment 2), an array of ten alphanumeric characters was presented, one at each location. The task was to identify the middle character (position 3) on one side, this attended position (middle position on left or right) being fixed throughout a trial block. The results suggested tight coupling between movement and identification tasks; identification accuracy was substantially increased when the location to be attended for the identification task was also cued as the movement target.

However, it could be argued that the better perceptual performance for targets appearing at movement target location is independent from factors relating to motor preparation and/or execution *per se*. Rather, it could be due to the fact that, in order to identify the correct movement target, subjects had to perform a visual selection prior to any motor process. Selection of the movement target was based on visual identification of which location contained the appropriately coloured ellipse. Thus, it is likely that better performance in the discrimination task when the visual target appeared in the same position as the movement target simply reflected the fact that visual attention was already allocated to that position, because that position had to be selected as movement target to plan the required action accordingly. In other words, what was supposed to be only a movement cue ended up cueing also a specific visual target location.

In the present study, our aim was to extend the work of Deubel et al. (1998) while avoiding such visual factors in the motor task. Participants were tested in a dual-task paradigm. The first, speeded task was to perform a reach movement towards a lateralized target button. The movement was cued by a centrally presented acoustic stimulus, and was made out of the participant's view under a board forming a raised table-top. The second, unspeeded task was visual discrimination of a single, briefly flashed letter. This visual stimulus target was presented either in the left or right visual field, immediately above the board but otherwise close to movement target locations. However, visual stimulation was always bilateral, that is, target appearance on one side was accompanied by the simultaneous appearance of a distractor on the opposite side. In this way, lateral attentional capture due to the abrupt onset of a single bright visual stimulus was prevented. Our simple prediction was that letter identification would be better when movement and visual targets were on the same side (corresponding condition), compared to when they were on different sides (noncorresponding condition). To examine possible evolution of this effect over time, we manipulated the interval between the acoustic movement cue and the subsequent visual target.

It is worth mentioning at least two factors, besides motor preparation itself, that may often be associated with lateralized movements. One is proprioceptive input from the moving limb, a potential influence on visual attention through cross-modal integration (Driver & Spence, 1998; Làdavas, Berti, Ruozzi, & Barboni, 1997). A second is generalized activation of the contralateral hemisphere, sometimes proposed to give a lateralized attentional shift (Reuter-Lorenz, Kinsbourne, & Moscovitch, 1990). In previous work, these potential effects of motor preparation, proprioception, and hemispheric activation have sometimes been confounded (e.g., Halligan et al., 1991), or sometimes clearly separated (e.g., Deubel et al., 1998). Our strategy was to begin by combining all these potential lateral biases, with the view that, if any effect on visual attention was detected, the exact cause could be isolated in subsequent experiments.

EXPERIMENT 1

In the first experiment, the manual task called for a simple, hidden reach from an approximately central start position to a lateralized target. The left hand was used for reaches in left space, while the right hand was used for reaches in right space. Potentially, motor preparation, proprioceptive feedback and hemispheric activation were all possible influences on bias in the visual task.

In this and subsequent experiments, participants were sampled from an elderly population. Most of the studies that reported enhanced perceptual processes as a function of motor activity were carried out on brain-damaged patients, whose ages varied roughly between 50 and 80 years. Elderly healthy subjects were then chosen, in order to determine whether the same beneficial effect of movement on visual performance described in patients could be found in healthy individuals of a comparable age group.

Method

Participants.   Five paid participants (three men and two women, aged between 60 and 69 years) were recruited from the panel of the MRC Cognition and Brain Sciences Unit. Four were right handed, and all had normal or corrected to normal vision and were naive as to the purpose of the experiment. They attended one experimental session of approximately an hour and a half.

Apparatus and materials.   Figure 1 shows the experimental set-up for Experiment 1. The experiment took place in a dimly lit, anechoic room. Participants were seated at a table with the head positioned on a chin rest. The chin rest was fixed on the edge of a wooden board that was mounted 24 cm above the table, completely obscuring the table-top from view. The hands were placed in the space beneath this board, so that they were at all times out of view. Two LED displays (7 cm horizontal × 4.8 cm vertical) were placed on the board with their centres 28 cm on either side of fixation, 39 cm in front of the chin rest. Each LED consisted of seven segments configured as a rectangular figure of

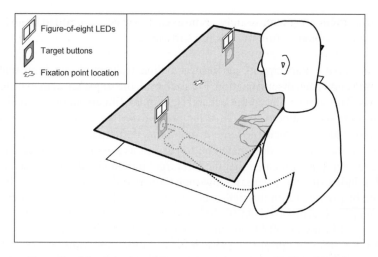

Figure 1.   Schematic view of the experimental set-up used in Experiment 1.

eight lying on its side. Different segments could be independently illuminated to form targets, distractors, and masks.

Two boxes each containing a movement target button were mounted underneath the board, exactly under the corresponding LED, so that the distance between the centre of the button and the board was 9 cm. The buttons (2.5 cm in diameter) were facing towards the front of the table, and participants could reach them quickly and directly without visual feedback about either their moving arm or target location, and usually without "hunting" for the final position. Two origin buttons, one for the left and one for the right index finger, were placed immediately in front of the participant, out of sight on the table-top. They were approximately 2.5 cm apart, centred on the participants' midline, and 25 cm from the edge of the table.

Two tones (high tone: 3000 Hz; low tone: 400 Hz) were used to cue movement direction. These tones were emitted simultaneously by two loud-speakers placed 19 cm on the left and on the right of participants' midline, 45 cm from the edge of the table.

Horizontal eye movement was assessed on each trial, with the intention of excluding any trial with a movement above 7° (note that the centre of the LEDs was 36° away from fixation). Eye movements were recorded with an ASL 504 remote eye tracker (sampling frequency 60 Hz). The spatial error between true eye position and computed measurement was less than 1°. A grid consisting of 3 × 3 positions was laid directly on the board in front of the participants and was used to calibrate visual space. The central position was on participants' midline, aligned with the two LEDs, and was used as a fixation point throughout the experiment.

All stimulus presentation and response recording was controlled by an IBM-compatible computer running custom software.

Procedure. Participants performed a dual task involving both manual reaching and visual discrimination. For each trial, the sequence of events was as follows. The subject placed the left and right index fingers on the left and right origin buttons, respectively. On a keypress from the experimenter, a tone (duration 200 ms) cued movement direction. Participants were required to reach for and press the designated button as fast as possible. For three participants, a high tone indicated that the left target button should be pressed (with the left index finger), whereas a low tone indicated that the right target button should be pressed (with the right index finger). For the remaining participants the mapping was reversed. At 50, 200, 400, or 600 ms after tone onset (stimulus onset asynchrony or SOA), one of the two LEDs (the target LED on this trial) displayed either an upright or an inverted T. At the same time, the other LED (non-target) displayed a distractor stimulus, a single central vertical line. Following a predetermined exposure duration, a backward mask consisting of two vertical lines, the leftmost and rightmost display segments, replaced the upright or inverted T on the target LED. This mask, along with the continuing distractor stimulus (single vertical line) on the non-target LED, remained present until the end of the trial. The task was to report, without time pressure, whether the target T had been upright or inverted. The trial ended when the experimenter typed this response into the computer.

Each participant was tested individually in one experimental session, which comprised 240 trials divided into three blocks. Each combination of reach side, target side for the visual task, and SOA occurred equally often in each block, in an otherwise random order.

Before data acquisition participants were trained for the reaching and the visual discrimination tasks separately (20 trials for each single task), then for the two tasks simultaneously. Dual-task practice was used to establish a suitable exposure duration for the visual task, aiming for accuracy in the region of 70% correct; there were a minimum of 100 dual-task practice trials, with more as needed. Target exposure duration was fixed for the remainder of the experiment; it ranged from 49 to 319 ms.

Data analysis. Trials where horizontal eye movements were detected were discarded. Trials where errors occurred in the motor task (i.e., release of the origin button faster than 100 ms or slower than 2000 ms, wrong origin button released, wrong target button pressed) were excluded from the analysis of visual performance, though their number was analysed.

The aim of the experiment was to compare performance on the visual discrimination task in the "corresponding" situation, when the target of the movement and the target of the discrimination were located in the same spatial hemispace, with the "non-corresponding" situation, where the target of the movement and the target of the discrimination were located in opposite hemispaces. Data for corresponding and non-corresponding trials were collapsed across target sides (left or right).

Results and discussion

For each condition, the following dependent variables were considered: Performance on the visual task (% error), response time (time from onset of the acoustic cue to target button press), reaching errors (% summed anticipatory/delayed releases, releases of wrong origin button, and presses of wrong target button). For the purpose of statistical analysis, values expressed as percentages were arcsine transformed. Analysis of variance (ANOVA) on each variable had the within-subjects factors correspondence (two levels: corresponding, non-corresponding) and SOA (four levels: 50, 200, 400, 600 ms). No trial was excluded because of eye movements.

Results for the visual task appear in Figure 2A. Across SOAs, there was no evident difference between corresponding and non-corresponding trials. The ANOVA showed no effect of correspondence, $F(1, 4) = 0.05$, n.s., SOA, $F(3, 12) = 0.46$, n.s., or their interaction, $F(3, 12) = 0.89$, n.s.

As far as motor performance is concerned, response time was almost homogeneous in all conditions. It ranged between 901 and 1000 ms, with no significant differences as a function of either SOA or correspondence. The only significant difference in motor performance concerned reaching errors, with participants being less accurate in non-corresponding (17% errors) than corresponding trials (11% errors; $F(1, 4)=10.06$, $p < .04$). Although the interaction SOA × Correspondence was not statistically significant, $F(3, 12) = 1.33$, most of the errors were made in the non-corresponding trials at the 50 ms SOA. The result suggests a form of stimulus–response compatibility effect, whereby the onset of a lateralized visual target facilitates an ipsilateral motor response, which is incorrect on non-corresponding trials.

The findings of this first experiment provide no support for the notion that motor processes can affect performance in an independent perceptual task. In particular, similar visual accuracy in corresponding and non-corresponding trials suggests that no attentional shift occurred as a consequence of movement programming and/or execution. In principle, corresponding trials could have yielded a better visual identification for a number of reasons. First, as the premotor theory of attention suggests, pragmatic maps representing the left- or the right-reaching space should have been active, given that the motor response was executed either in the left or in the right hemispace, and was directed towards a lateralized target. Second, given that throughout the experiment participants had to move their left or right hand in a random order, each single trial required the selective activation of a specific cerebral hemisphere to

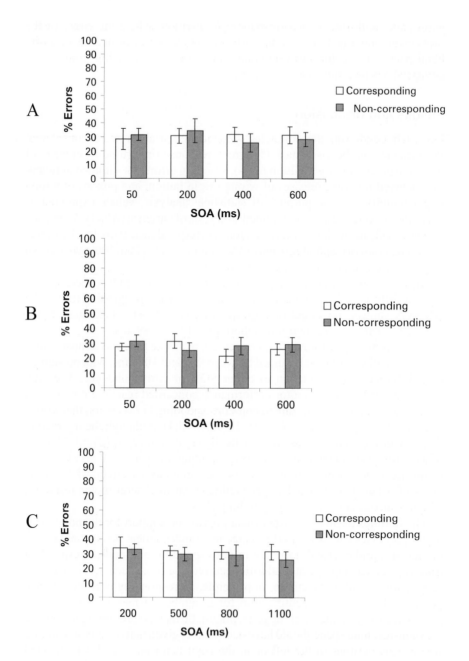

Figure 2. Mean percentage errors as a function of correspondence and SOA in (A) Experiment 1; (B) Experiment 2; (C) Experiment 3. Please note that in Experiment 3 SOAs were different from Experiment 1 and 2. Bars indicate standard error.

programme and execute the reach. Being asymmetrical, such an activation could have induced an attentional shift towards the contralateral visual field. Finally, the proprioceptive feedback arising from the moving limb could have attracted attention to the area of space where the movement was taking place. All the previously mentioned elements might be supposed to enhance selective attention to the general region of the visual stimulus on corresponding trials. Despite this number of potentially contributing factors, however, the data suggested no such spatial enhancement of visual processing.

EXPERIMENT 2

The motor task used in Experiment 1 failed to induce any lateralized attentional shift. Experiment 2 was designed to test whether a motor task more spatially segregated could be more effective in determining such a shift. To that end, two major modifications with respect to Experiment 1 were introduced. First, the origin buttons were moved from their central position to the left and right, in order to stress potential effects of starting position. Second, the experiment was divided into two parts, in each of which motor activity was confined to one hemispace. That is to say, in one half of the experiment the right hand (RH) moved in right space (RS) towards one of two buttons, both located in right hemispace, from a right starting position (RSP). The reverse happened in the other half of the experiment, where the left hand (LH) moved in left space (LS) towards one of two buttons, both located in left hemispace, from a left starting position (LSP). This modification was introduced to test the possibility that movement related enhancement of spatial areas needs time to build up. Specifically, if facilitation induced by a movement towards a lateralized target is to some extent offset by recent movements on the opposite side, then enhancement could be easier to observe when the spatial features of the movement (i.e., effector, starting position, end position, and hemispace where the action takes place) are kept constant across a whole trial block.

As in Experiment 1, the visual target could appear either in the left or in the right visual field. For the left visual target, performance at the discrimination task should be better in LH-LS-LSP blocks, whereas for the right visual target it should be better in RH-RS-RSP blocks.

Method

Participants.   Six right-handed men aged 60–69 years were recruited as before. Three had taken part in the previous experiment.

Apparatus and materials.   Figure 3 shows the experimental set-up for Experiment 2. The visual task was much as before, with a slight change to

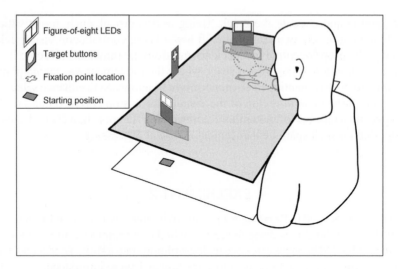

Figure 3.   Schematic view of the experimental set-up used in Experiment 2.

the positioning of LEDs. This time, LEDs were mounted on a raised support on the board covering the table-top, with their centres 25 cm on either side of fixation, 25 cm in front of the chin rest (i.e., 45° away from fixation), and 8.5 cm above the level of the board. They were turned somewhat to face the partici-pant, at an angle of 65° to the frontoparallel plane. For the motor task, two boxes each containing two target buttons were mounted underneath the board, each box centred exactly 11.5 cm under the corresponding LED and aligned per-pendicular to the front edge of the table. The two buttons in each box were positioned 15 cm apart, on the inner vertical face of the box, i.e., facing towards the participant. Again, participants could reach these targets without visual feedback about either their moving arm or target location, and usually without "hunting" for the final position. Two origin buttons were placed on the table, each one below one of the two boxes, 25 cm on either side of participant's midline, and 25 cm in front of the chin rest. In this way, the two target buttons on each side were equidistant from the starting position on that side. Tone cues for the motor task were as before.

Eye movements were recorded much as before, except that the 3 × 3 calibra-tion grid stood upright on the board. The middle position on the bottom row was used as fixation point throughout the experiment. It was at the same height as the centre of the two LEDs, but displaced towards the rear of the table so that it did not interfere with the eye movement recording.

Procedure.   The experiment was divided into two parts. In each part the motor performance was confined to one side of space, that is, it involved only one effector (for example, the left hand), with start- and end-points of all reaches on the side of that effector. Each trial began with the participant placing the index finger of the designated hand on the designated origin button. Tones as before were used to cue speeded reaches: If the tone was high the participant had to press the button further away from himself, whereas if the tone was low the participant had to press the button closer to himself. In other respects, details of procedure for each trial were unchanged from Experiment 1. In particular, visual targets again appeared randomly to left and right within each block, resulting in half corresponding and half non-corresponding trials.

Each participant was tested individually in one experimental session, which comprised 256 trials divided into four blocks, two of LH-LS-LSP followed by two of RH-RS-RSP, or vice versa (counterbalanced across participants). Practice was given as before at the start of each half of the experiment. Target exposure duration was based on performance in the first set of dual-task practice trials, i.e., those preceding the first condition, then fixed for the remainder of the experiment. It ranged from 21 to 350 ms.

Results and discussion

Data were analysed as before, again collapsing over left and right sides. No trial was excluded because of eye movements. Once again, visual performance was not affected by the concurrent execution of lateralized reaching movements (Figure 2B). ANOVA showed no significant effect of correspondence, $F(1, 5)$ = 0.17, n.s., SOA, $F(3, 15)$ = 0.71, n.s., or their interaction, $F(3, 15)$ = 0.52, n.s.

Similarly, motor responses were highly homogeneous; response times ranged from 1224 to 1294 ms, reaching error percentages from 3 to 6%, and ANOVA showed no significant effects for either measure.

As described for Experiment 1, several factors could have contributed to a better performance in the corresponding conditions in the present experiment, namely movement planning, proprioceptive cues, and hemispheric activation. It should be pointed out that in this case any premotor facilitation would have depended not on planning of movement direction, but on the hemispace within which the action was taking place (and within which the movement target was located). In fact, the direction of reaches was neither towards the left nor towards the right with respect to starting position; instead, the paradigm adopted in this experiment stressed the potential effects of hand starting, movement, and ending position. Dividing the experiment into two parts, in each of which the motor task was confined to one hemispace, might in principle have enhanced any visual bias effect. Again, however, there was no suggestion of such a bias in the data.

EXPERIMENT 3

One possible reason why the paradigm adopted in Experiment 1 did not evidence any attentional shift is that having only two targets for the reach could result in movements that are relatively automatic. If the planning of an action (particularly of its direction) plays a crucial role in determining a shift of attention, it could be argued that the more a movement becomes automatic, the less planning is required, with a correspondingly reduced attentional shift.

In Experiment 3 we tested the hypothesis that visual bias might accompany a more difficult motor choice. Difficulty was increased by increasing the number of movement targets on each side.

Method

Participants.   Five right-handed participants (two men, three women, aged 62–68 years) were recruited as before. None had taken part in the previous experiments.

Apparatus and materials.   Figure 4 shows the experimental set-up for Experiment 3. For this experiment, LEDs were placed with their centres 15 cm on either side of fixation, 30 cm in front of the chin rest (i.e., 27° away from fixation), centres raised 8.5 cm above the board covering the table-top. As in Experiment 2, each LED was turned somewhat to face the participant, but this time at an angle of 45° to the frontoparallel plane. Instead of an upright or

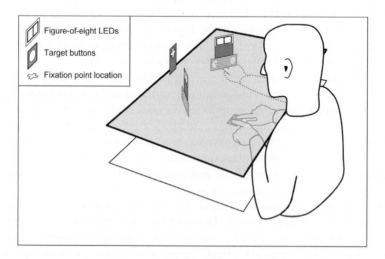

Figure 4.   Schematic view of the experimental set-up used in Experiment 3.

inverted T, visual targets were a schematic S (bottom left horizontal segment; central vertical segment; top right horizontal segment) or Z (the mirror image). Backward masks and distractors were as before.

Two boxes each containing two target buttons were mounted underneath the table, one centred 11.5 cm under each LED. The two buttons on each box were 8 cm apart, mounted on the inner vertical face of the box. The whole box was fixed under the board at 45° to the frontoparallel plane, like the LED above it. Again, participants could reach bottons without visual feedback about either their moving arm or target location, and usually without "hunting" for the final position. Two origin buttons, one for each index finger, were placed side by side on the table at the participant's midline, 19 cm in front of the chin rest and approximately 2.5 cm apart. In this way, the four target buttons were almost equidistant from the starting position.

Four different tones were used to cue movement direction. These were the four combinations of two pitches (high tone: 3000 Hz; low tone: 400 Hz) and two sound qualities (pure tone or rattle). Eye movements were recorded as before, with the same calibration as in Experiment 2.

Procedure.   Trials proceeded as in previous experiments. For the motor task, a high tone cued "left", whereas a low tone cued "right". Within each side, a rattling tone indicated that the more peripheral button was the target, whereas a continuous tone indicated the more central button. In this way, the four possible combinations of pitch and sound quality defined which of the four buttons the participant had to reach for. Given the increased complexity of the required motor response, movement planning was likely to take longer than in previous experiments, resulting in an overall longer response time. Because we were interested in probing visual performance at different phases of motor planning and execution, and because reach times were expected to be longer in this experiment, the SOA between tone and visual target was increased; the four possible SOAs were 200, 500, 800, and 1100 ms.

Each participant was tested individually in one experimental session, which comprised 320 trials divided into four blocks. Before data acquisition, participants were trained as before, and target exposure duration then fixed for the remainder of the experiment. It ranged between 56 and 163 ms.

Results and discussion

Data were analysed as before, again collapsing over left and right sides, and now also across more peripheral and more central reach targets on each side. Eye movements never occurred. Despite its increased complexity, the motor task did not induce any attentional shift. Once again, participants' performance at the discrimination task was not better when the visual target and the movement target were located in the same hemispace (Figure 2C). ANOVA showed no significant effect of correspondence, $F(1, 4) = 3.21$, n.s., SOA, $F(3, 12) = 1.35$, n.s., or their interaction, $F(3, 12) = 0.24$, n.s.

Motor performance was extremely homogeneous across conditions; response times ranged from 1545 to 1667 ms, reaching error percentages from 8 to 19%, and ANOVA showed no significant effects for either measure. To confirm that increasing the number of reach targets was effective in making the motor task more complex, an additional analysis of variance was performed. Response time in this experiment was compared to that of Experiment 1, where only two reach targets were used. Although the two experiments are not completely comparable, given that both visual targets and SOAs were different, a longer average movement duration in Experiment 3 (1582 ms) compared to Experiment 1 (956 ms), $F(1, 8) = 16.04$, $p < .004$, strongly suggests that the manipulation effectively increased movement complexity.

EXPERIMENT 4

A final experiment was designed to ensure that the visual task used in these studies was indeed sensitive to attentional manipulation. In this experiment, attention was oriented by means of an exogenous informative peripheral visual cue towards one of the two LEDs. Once again, participants were required to report the identity of a letter, and accuracy of their performance was taken as a measure of attentional allocation. On the basis of previously reported results (Posner, 1980), performance was expected to improve when the visual target appeared in the same location as the cue.

Method

Participants.   Six right-handed participants (one man, five women, aged 58–67 years) were recruited as before. None had taken part in the previous experiments.

Apparatus and materials.   Materials for the visual task were as described for Experiment 3. Given that no movement was required, the loudspeakers and boxes containing reach buttons were removed.

Procedure.   As before, each trial was initiated by a keypress from the experimenter. After a delay of 500 ms a visual cue, consisting of the lightening of the vertical middle bar of one of the two LEDs, flashed for 100 ms. At an SOA of 600 ms following cue onset, the target S or Z was shown on one LED, then masked as before, while the usual distractor was shown on the other LED. The target appeared on the cued side on 70% of trials ("valid"), and on the other side on the remaining 30% ("invalid"). Other details, including eye monitoring, were as before.

Each participant was tested individually in one experimental session, which comprised 320 trials divided into four blocks. Before data acquisition, participants were trained in the discrimination task (minimum 60 trials), with more as required to establish a suitable target exposure duration. Exposure duration was fixed for the remainder of the experiment, ranging between 25 and 160 ms.

Results and discussion

No trial was discarded because of eye movements. The experiment confirmed an effect of attentional cueing. There were a mean of 23% errors on valid trials, as compared to 35% on invalid trials, $F(1, 5) = 10.36, p < .03$.

GENERAL DISCUSSION

A number of studies have suggested that lateralized motor activity can induce a shift of visual attention towards movement target location or, more generally, towards the side of space where the action is taking place (Halligan et al., 1991; Mattingley et al., 1998; Robertson & North, 1992, 1993, 1994). As we pointed out, however, the majority of these studies have involved patients with unilateral neglect or extinction, raising the possibility of influences not relevant to the normal case. The present study aimed to replicate the same findings in a normal population. In particular, we addressed the issue of whether the identification of a lateralized visual target would benefit from the concurrent execution of a reaching movement in the same side of space, when all aspects of reach cueing and execution were outside visual control. Across three experiments, the results show that participants' performance in the identification task did not differ in the corresponding condition, where the reach target was located in the same hemispace as the visual target, compared to the non-corresponding condition, where reach target and visual target were located in different hemispaces.

As already pointed out in the introduction, different factors associated with motor activity could contribute to induce a shift of visual attention, including proprioceptive cues, movement starting position, planning the direction of the forthcoming movement, and hemispheric activation. Our results are particularly striking because they suggest that none of these factors produces a strong visual bias. The approach we followed was to design an initial task in which all factors were present at once, giving maximum sensitivity for detecting any visual effect. In the subsequent experiments the effects of starting position (Experiment 2) and movement planning (Experiment 3) were emphasized. However, despite the different experimental manipulations, we did not obtain any result in favour of the notion that motor activity can exert facilitatory effects on visual identification.

From a theoretical point of view, it is particularly worth noting that our data do not support the premotor theory of attention, according to which spatial attention results from the activation of a set of neurons in the pragmatic map involved in the planning of a specific goal-directed movement. In its original version, the theory stated that planning a directional movement should shift attention towards the area of space where a movement target is located. We also did not find support for a weaker version of the theory (supported by Mattingley et al., 1998), according to which the crucial aspect of motor planning is not only the direction of the forthcoming movement, but the general area of space within which action occurs. Neither do our data support the general proposal that different components of the sensorimotor network have a strong tendency to converge and work on the same, selected spatial region (Duncan, 1996). In the present experiments, the motor system was favouring a particular side of space (i.e., left vs right hemispace), yet no corresponding visual bias was observed.

One obvious reason why our study did not evidence any improvement in the corresponding versus the non-corresponding conditions could be that the visual task adopted was not sufficiently sensitive to attentional bias. However, the results of Experiment 4 argue strongly against this possibility. When a visual cue was used to orient attention, performance in the letter identification task changed according to whether the cue was valid or invalid. These results confirm that the consequences of an effective cueing mechanism could be detected in the visual task we adopted.

In our experiments we have investigated the possibility of a simple, general bias of visual attention towards the spatial region of motor activity. Of course, there are many other possibilities for interaction between motor and visual processes. According to the integrated competition hypothesis (Duncan, 1996), for example, convergence on the same dominant location is just one aspect of integration between different parts of the sensorimotor network; as for other object-based models, it is all those grouping cues combining the parts and properties of one object that cause them to be attended together (Duncan, 1984). One important possibility, correspondingly, is that crosstalk may be stronger when action is directed not just to the same spatial region as visual input, but to exactly the same object.[1] Another possibility derives from our use of a strict dual-task format. Possibly, crosstalk between motor and visual processes might be stronger when the visual input is relevant to the same task as motor output, as in a recent study suggesting crosstalk between prepared grip orientation and visual detection of an oriented bar (Craighero, Fadiga, Rizzolatti, & Umiltà, 1999). Finally we might consider interactions beyond a simple attentional bias towards the region of motor activity. In another paper in this issue, Hommel and

---

[1] We thank Steve Tipper for this suggestion.

Schneider (this issue) used a design in some ways similar to ours, but with rather different results. A tone cued a speeded keypress response with index or middle fingers of the right hand; during this auditory-manual response, a rectangular array of four letters was briefly presented, with a bar-marker adjacent to one letter indicating that it should be attended and identified. Though the lateralization of the response was far more modest than in our experiments, the results showed clear evidence of spatial crosstalk: When the tone required an index finger response (relatively leftward), visual performance was better if the cued letter was to the left of the array, whereas if the tone required a middle finger response (relatively rightward), visual performance was better if the cued letter was to the right. Contrasting these results with ours, the likely conclusion is that their crosstalk arose directly in the process of identifying and using the bar-marker to direct attention to the specified location; in other words, in an explicitly spatial control process not required in our tasks.

Meanwhile, our data suggest that, at least in the absence of brain damage, a simple bias of visual attention towards the region of motor activity is surprisingly hard to find. To this degree, the results suggest relative encapsulation of selection processes in the two domains.

REFERENCES

Brown, V., Walker, R., Gray, C., & Findlay, J.M. (1999). Limb activation and the rehabilitation of unilateral neglect: Evidence of task specific effects. *Neurocase, 5,* 129–142.

Craighero, L., Fadiga, L., Rizzolatti, G., & Umiltà, C. (1999). Action for perception: A motor-visual attentional effect. *Journal of Experimental Psychology: Human Perception and Performance, 25,* 1673–1692.

Cubelli, R., Paganelli, N., Achilli, D., & Pedrizzi, S. (1999). Is one hand always better than two? A replication study. *Neurocase, 5,* 143–151.

Desimone, R., & Duncan, J. (1995). Neural mechanisms of selective visual attention. *Annual Review of Neuroscience, 18,* 193–222.

Deubel, H., & Schneider, W.X. (1996). Saccade target selection and object recognition: Evidence for a common attentional mechanism. *Vision Research, 36,* 1827–1837.

Deubel, H., Schneider, W.X., & Paprotta, I. (1998). Selective dorsal and ventral processing: Evidence for a common attentional mechanism in reaching and perception. *Visual Cognition, 5,* 81–107.

Driver, J., & Spence, C. (1998). Crossmodal attention. *Current Opinion in Neurobiology, 8,* 245–253.

Duncan, J. (1984). Selective attention and the organization of visual information. *Journal of Experimental Psychology: General, 113,* 501–517.

Duncan, J. (1996). Cooperating brain systems in selective perception and action. In T. Inui & J.L. McClelland (Eds.), *Attention and performance XVI. Information integration in perception and communication* (pp. 549–578). Cambridge, MA: MIT Press.

Duncan, J., & Humphreys, G. (1989). Visual search and stimulus similarity. *Psychological Review, 96,* 433–458.

Duncan, J., Humphreys, G., & Ward, R. (1997). Competitive brain activity in visual attention. *Current Opinion in Neurobiology, 7,* 255–261.

Halligan, P.W., Manning, L., & Marshall, J.C. (1991). Hemispheric activation vs. spatio-motor cueing in visual neglect: A case study. *Neuropsychologia, 29*, 165–176.

Hommel, B., & Schneider, W.X. (this issue). Visual attention and manual response selection: Distinct mechanisms operating on the same codes. *Visual Cognition, 9*, 392–420.

Humphreys, G.W., Boucart, M., Datar, V., & Riddoch, M.J. (1996). Processing fragmented forms and strategic control of orienting in visual neglect. *Cognitive Neuropsychology, 13*, 177–203.

Làdavas, E., Berti, A., Ruozzi, F., & Barboni, F. (1997). Neglect as a deficit determined by an imbalance between multiple spatial representations. *Experimental Brain Research, 116*, 493–500.

Mattingley, J.B., Robertson, I.H., & Driver, J. (1998). Modulation of covert visual attention by hand movement: Evidence from parietal extinction after right-hemisphere damage. *Neurocase, 4*, 245–253.

Posner, M.I. (1980). Orienting of attention. *Quarterly Journal of Experimental Psychology, 32*, 3–25.

Reuter-Lorenz, P., Kinsbourne, M., & Moscovitch, M. (1990). Hemispheric control of spatial attention. *Brain and Cognition, 12*, 240–266.

Rizzolatti, G., Riggio, L., Dascola, I., & Umiltà, C. (1987). Reorienting attention across the horizontal and vertical meridians: Evidence in favor of a premotor theory of attention. *Neuropsychologia, 25*, 31–40.

Rizzolatti, G., Riggio, L., & Sheliga, B.M. (1994). Space and selective attention. In C. Umiltà & M. Moscovitch (Eds.), *Attention and performance XV: Conscious and unconscious information processing* (pp. 231–265). Cambridge, MA: MIT Press.

Robertson, I.H., & North, N. (1992). Spatio-motor cueing in unilateral neglect: The role of hemispace, hand and motor activation. *Neuropsychologia, 30*, 553–563.

Robertson, I.H., & North, N. (1993). Active and passive activation of left limbs: Influence on visual and sensory neglect. *Neuropsychologia, 31*, 293-300.

Robertson, I.H., & North, N. (1994). One hand is better than two: Motor extinction of left hand advantage in unilateral neglect. *Neuropsychologia, 32*, 1–11.

VISUAL COGNITION, 2002, 9 (4/5), 477–501

Response force in RT tasks: Isolating effects of stimulus probability and response probability

Stefan Mattes and Rolf Ulrich

University of Tübingen, Germany

Jeff Miller

University of Otago, New Zealand

Mattes, Ulrich, and Miller (1997) found that as response probability decreases in a simple reaction time (RT) task, participants produce more forceful responses as well as longer RTs, suggesting a direct influence of preparatory processes on the motor system. In this previous study, however, response probability was confounded with stimulus probability, leaving open the possibility that response force was sensitive to stimulus- rather than response-related preparation. The present study was conducted to unravel the effects of stimulus and response probability. Experiment 1 manipulated stimulus probability and revealed that responses to a more probable stimulus are less forceful than responses to a less probable stimulus even when both stimuli require the same response. Experiment 2 demonstrated that this stimulus probability effect does not depend on the overall level of response probability. Experiment 3 showed an analogous effect for response probability when stimulus probability is kept constant. The complete pattern of results suggests that both stimulus probability and response probability affect the forcefulness of a response. It is argued that response probability exerts a direct influence on the motor system, whereas stimulus probability influences the motor system indirectly via premotoric adjustments.

Preparatory processes play a fundamental role in human performance, and the study of these covert processes is therefore essential for understanding human cognition. Preparatory adjustments seem to operate at various levels within the

Please address all correspondence to Rolf Ulrich, Psychologisches Institut, Universität Tübingen, Friedrichstr. 21, D-72072 Tübingen, Germany.

Email: rolf.ulrich@uni-tuebingen.de

This research was supported by the Deutsche Forschungsgemeinschaft (UL 116/3-2). Parts of this paper were presented at the "Tagung experimentell arbeitender Psychologen", 1998 (Marburg, Germany). We thank Raymond Klein for helpful comments and Frauke Becker, Hiltraut Müller-Gethmann, and Jutta Stahl for assistance in data collection.

© 2002 Psychology Press Ltd

http://www.tandf.co.uk/journals/pp/13506285.html   DOI:10.1080/13506280143000548

CNS. For example, attention researchers have shown that advance information about stimulus location prepares the perceptual system leading to improved detection and identification of stimuli that appear within the expected location (e.g., Downing, 1988). Psychophysiological studies support the view that selective attention induces preparatory processes that have influences at very early perceptual levels (Luck, 1998). At the other end of the information processing chain, preparatory processes also influence the motoric level (Requin, Brener, & Ring, 1991). For example, Leuthold, Sommer, and Ulrich (1996) provided evidence from the analysis of the event-related brain potentials that advance information about a response speeds up the motoric portion in a choice reaction time (RT) task. Reflexogenic and magnetic stimulation studies have shown that preparation even extends to quite distal motor levels (Brunia & Boelhouwer, 1988; Hasbroucq, Kaneko, Akamatsu, & Possamaï, 1997)

Because preparatory processes have influences at various levels within the CNS, it is often difficult to find out whether a change in overt behaviour is caused by early or late preparatory processes (Gehring, Gratton, Coles, & Donchin, 1992). To promote the understanding of human performance, however, it is theoretically desirable to determine the preparatory properties of each level and how these properties are related to certain aspects of overt behaviour. The present study contributes to this research area by investigating the influences of stimulus probability and response probability on the motor system. Whereas studies of preparation usually focus on measures of speed and accuracy, the present research emphasizes a different aspect, namely the forcefulness of prepared and unprepared responses. Recent studies suggest that participants exert less response force when they are highly prepared for making a response (Jaśkowski & Verleger, 1993; Mattes et al., 1997; Mattes & Ulrich, 1997; Wascher et al., 1997). For example, in the study of Mattes et al. (1997) participants were to press a force sensitive key with the index finger of their preferred hand as soon as a response signal appeared. At the beginning of each trial a precue indicated the probability that the response signal would occur, with probabilities ranging from .1 to 1.0. As expected, participants produced shorter RTs when response probability was high than when it was low, indicating that preparation increased with response probability. However, preparation influenced not only the speed of the response but also how the response was performed. Surprisingly, participants produced less forceful responses when they were highly prepared to respond.[1] In line with this finding are the results from recent studies which reported that response force was increased in

---

[1]Interestingly, participants were not aware of this effect. A post-experimental interview revealed that most participants misjudged the relation between response probability and force output. Although these participants correctly recognized that preparation shortens RT, they incorrectly believed that preparation would increase response force.

go/nogo tasks when compared to simple and choice RT tasks (Miller, Franz, & Ulrich, 1999; Ulrich, Mattes, & Miller, 1999). Since the probability to respond was lower in the go/nogo tasks (due to inclusion of nogo-trials) than in the two other tasks, this increase of response force in the go/nogo task can be seen as further evidence for the conjecture that response force decreases with response probability.

To account for their findings, Mattes et al. (1997) suggested that the prepara-tory effects reflected adjustments within the motor system. Specifically, a motor preparation hypothesis based on Näätänen's (1972) motor readiness model was advanced to account for the results. According to this model, the level of motor readiness prior to stimulus onset reflects the amount of prepara-tion. Low response probability was assumed to result in poor motor preparation and, consequently, in a low level of motor readiness; conversely, high response probability would result in a prepared motor system. When the response signal is presented, motor activation increases toward a certain threshold value (namely, action limit) to elicit a response. According to this modified model, higher response force on low probability trials could be due to a greater over-shoot of motor activation when the motor system was unprepared. In an unpre-pared state the difference between the momentary level of activation (i.e., motor readiness) and the action limit is relatively large. Because a relatively large activation increment is needed, the motor system is unable to produce a well-calibrated portion of activation just sufficient to produce the manual response. Instead, activation overshoots the action limit by an unnecessarily large amount, resulting in an especially forceful response. In a prepared state, by contrast, motor readiness is already close to the action limit, and the required increment of activation can be calibrated well, producing only a small activa-tion overshoot and consequently a less forceful response. Thus, this elaborated motor-readiness model provides a possible explanation of why responses are both more forceful and slower when they are unprepared.

The elaborated motor-readiness model of Mattes et al. (1997) gains some plausibility of its obvious efficiency. At the functional level, the observed relation of response probability and force might reflect an economical principle of the motor system that evolved during phylogenesis. Optimizing a response might not only mean executing the response as quickly and accurately as possible but also executing it with the smallest amount of energy. In a recent review of movement economy, Sparrow and Newell (1998) proposed that metabolic energy regulation is a fundamental principle underlying the learning and control of motor skills. Assuming that response preparation is a function-ally well-adapted principle in motor behaviour, it is not surprising that well-prepared responses are carried out with less force. The effort to prepare a response pays out in less effort to execute it. This functional view also suggests that the effect on response force should be caused by motor preparation but not by preparation at a premotoric level.

According to this motor readiness model the probability effect on response force originates within the motor system. However, as mentioned previously, advance information should also cause preparatory adjustments at early levels within the stimulus–response (S–R) processing chain. This is because a manipulation of response probability in a go/nogo task changes not only the probability of performing the motor act but also the probability of detecting and encoding the stimulus; thus stimulus-probability and response-probability were confounded in our previous study (Mattes et al.,1997). Hence, one might question whether the effect on response force is caused specifically by motor preparation or might instead be caused by preparation of premotoric processes. For example, it has been repeatedly shown in RT research that premotoric processing links are susceptible to probability manipulations (e.g., Pashler & Baylis, 1991). If similar premotoric effects can be proved for response force, this would clearly suggest that preparatory adjustments at premotoric levels can modulate the processing stream downwards through the motor system and ultimately modulate the strength of a response. To find out whether such downstream effects are possible, the present experiments examined effects of stimulus probability on response force. If response force depends on stimulus probability with response probability held constant, then the motoric interpretation of the stimulus/response probability effect must be reevaluated. Such a finding would also have implications for models of the interface between premotoric and motoric processes (cf., Ulrich, Rinkenauer, & Miller, 1998). By contrast, if preparatory processes at premotoric levels do not affect the force output of a response, this would strengthen the idea of functionally encapsulated modules according to which each module operates in isolation (Fodor, 1983). In such a modular system it seems plausible to assume that preparatory effects operating at premotoric levels should not influence the strength of a response.

The general method we chose was to map two stimuli with unequal probabilities onto the same response. This is a common approach in RT research allowing the manipulation of stimulus probability while keeping response probability constant (Bertelson & Tisseyre, 1966; Biederman & Zachary, 1970; Dillon, 1966; LaBerge, Legrand, & Hobbie, 1969; LeBerge & Tweedy, 1964; Rabbitt, 1959; Spector & Lyons, 1976). For example, LaBerge and Tweedy (1964) assigned two out of three stimuli to one response and the other stimulus to a different response. Thus, stimulus probability as well as response probability could be changed by varying the relative frequencies of the two stimuli that were both assigned to the same response. These authors reported that stimulus probability exerted a larger effect on RT than did response probability. This technique has recently been applied to localize sequential effects in choice RT (Campbell & Proctor, 1993; Pashler & Baylis, 1991; Soetens, 1998). In general, the bulk of research clearly indicates that not only the probability of the response but also the probability of the stimulus affects the processing speed (for a review, see Gehring et al., 1992).

In summary, then, the following experiments were designed to assess whether stimulus probability exerts effects on response force. If changes in stimulus probability do affect response force, this would argue against Mattes et al.'s (1997) motor readiness explanation of the response probability effect and strengthen the view that force is partially or completely determined by the probability of the stimulus rather than the probability of the response. In contrast, if response force is not affected by stimulus probability, then it becomes more likely that the preparatory motor adjustment model is an accurate description of the mechanisms responsible for the effect of probability on response force.

In Experiment 1 three letters were employed as stimuli. The participants were instructed to press the same key when either of two letters appeared but to withhold the response when the third letter was presented. Table 1 shows the stimulus probabilities for the three stimuli. The letters A, B, and C exemplify the stimulus letters. The two stimuli that required a response (A or B) had different probabilities (.64 vs .16). If the dynamics of the responses do not depend on stimulus probability, then response force should not differ between the two stimuli. Experiment 2 in addition varied response probability, which was announced by a precue as in the study of Mattes et al. (1997) (Table 2).

TABLE 1
Stimulus probabilities employed in Experiment 1

	Go[a]		Nogo
	A	B	C
Probability	.64	.16	.20
RT (ms)	327	369	—
Force (cN)	686	704	—

[a]Response: Keypress with index finger to any go-stimulus.

TABLE 2
Stimulus probabilities employed in Experiment 2

	Go		Nogo
	A	B	C
Probability:			
Precue 20%	.16	.04	.80
RT (ms)	363	387	—
Force (cN)	628	640	—
Precue 80%	.64	.16	.20
RT (ms)	350	391	—
Force (cN)	619	640	—

TABLE 3
Stimulus probabilities employed in Experiment 3

	Go			Nogo
	A	B	C	D
Probability:				
Precue 20%	.04	.16	.00	.80
RT (ms)	413	406	—	—
Force (cN)	719	724	—	—
Precue 80%	.64	.00	.16	.20
RT (ms)	362	—	387	—
Force (cN)	664	—	685	—

Experiment 3 was designed to investigate the influence of response probability when stimulus probability is held constant (Table 3).

EXPERIMENT 1

This experiment tested if mere stimulus probability affects the force output of a response. Three different letters, one of which was presented in each trial, served as stimuli. The participants were instructed to respond to two letters (response letters) with the same keypress, but to withhold the response to the third letter (no-response letter). Most important, the two response letters appeared with unequal frequencies. One was presented four times as often as the other, resulting in stimulus probabilities of .16 and .64 for the two response letters, while the sum of both stimulus probabilities constitutes the response probability .8. If these two response letters produce different response force, we can conclude that response force is sensitive to stimulus probability.

After the experiment a questionnaire was given to the participants as in our previous study (see Appendix). This questionnaire assessed whether participants were aware of the effects of probability on RT and response force. In our previous study participants correctly predicted that response probability shortens RT; however, interestingly enough, participants were unaware of the influence of response probability on response force. Specifically, participants incorrectly believed that response force would increase with response probability. Therefore, it seems interesting to know whether the same misconception applies to stimulus probability.

Method

Participants.   Nineteen male and 17 female students (mean age: 25.7 years) took part in a single session. Two of them claimed to be left handed. They were paid for their co-operation and were naive about the purpose of the experiment.

Apparatus and stimuli.   The experiment was carried out in a dimly illuminated room. A microcomputer controlled signal presentation and recorded response force. All signals were presented in the middle of a computer screen. A grey cross (1.1°) served as warning signal and fixation cross. The stimuli were the capital letters X, S, and G. They were light grey, subtended a visual angle of 0.6° horizontally and 1° vertically and their intensity was 41 cd/m^2 against a background intensity of about 0.25 cd/m^2.

Responses were measured means of a force sensitive key, which consisted of a leaf spring (110 × 19 mm) with strain gauges attached on it. The leaf spring was fixed at one end and any force applied to the free end was registered with a rate of 500 Hz throughout the whole trial. The participant pressed this key with the index finger of his or her preferred hand while the forearm rested comfortably on the table. The average response force of 695 cN that was registered in this experiment bent the spring approximately 0.7 mm. The resolution of this device was about 2 cN. RT was measured as the interval between the onset of the response signal and the point in time when response force attained the criterion force of 50 cN. A chin rest was used to maintain a constant posture and viewing distance of 60 cm.

Procedure.   A session lasted about 50 min and consisted of 550 trials. The first 50 trials were considered practice and excluded from data analysis. The whole set of 500 experimental trials was randomized and partitioned into blocks of 50 trials each. At the end of each block participants received feedback about mean RT and response errors for their performance in this block. Participants were encouraged to respond quickly but to avoid errors. They initiated each block with a keypress on the computer keyboard with their non-responding hand.

Participants responded to two letters with their dominant hand but had to withhold the response when the no-response letter was presented. They were told which of the two response letters would be presented four times as often as the other response letter. The assignment of the three letters as frequent response letter, infrequent response letter, and no-response letter was balanced over participants.

A trial started with the presentation of the warning signal (fixation cross) for 300 ms. The interval between the offset of the warning signal and the onset of the letter was 1750 ms. The letter was presented for 150 ms. The computer displayed an error message if the participant failed to respond to a response letter within 1000 ms or if he or she responded to the no-response letter. Other appropriate error messages, for example if participants pressed the key before stimulus onset, were given as well. The next trial started 2 s later.

Design.   The session was split into two halves to assess potential practice effects. Thus, there were two within-subjects factors stimulus probability (.64 vs .16) and practice (first vs second half of session). The dependent variables were mean RT, mean response force, and error rates. As in previous studies (e.g., Mattes et al., 1997) the maximum force level (peak force) of each trial was determined as an index of response strength.

Questionnaire.   The participants completed a questionnaire when they had finished the experiment. The questions assessed whether the participants could predict the results of the experiment. The complete questionnaire along with the results is provided in the Appendix.

Results

A separate ANOVA was conducted for each dependent variable. Table 1 shows data for stimulus A and B.

Response errors.   Anticipations (RT < 100 ms) and misses (RT > 1000 ms) occurred in 0.3% and 0.5% of the trials, respectively. These figures were too low to permit a meaningful statistical analysis. There were 2.4% false alarms, that is, responses to the no-response letter. Only trials without errors were included in the following analyses.

Reaction time.   Participants responded faster to the more frequent stimulus (327 ms) than to the less frequent stimulus (369 ms), $F(1, 35) = 61.9, p < .001$. Practice yielded a main effect, with mean RTs being 358 ms in the first half of the experiment and 338 ms in the second half, $F(1, 35) = 24.7, p < .001$. However, practice did not modulate the effect of stimulus probability on RT, $F(1, 35) = 1.6, p > .2$.

Response force.   More interestingly for the purposes of this paper, response force was influenced by stimulus probability, $F(1, 35) = 7.0, p = .012$. The mean response force was 704 cN for the infrequent letter and 686 cN for the frequent one. Although response force decreased from the first to the second half of the experiment from 750 cN to 640 cN, $F(1, 35) = 7.2, p = .011$, practice did not modulate the effect of stimulus probability ($F < 1$).

Questionnaire.   The Appendix provides the results of the questionnaire. Participants correctly judged how stimulus probability would influence RT and response force, although there was less agreement on the effect of response force than on RT.

Discussion

This experiment showed that with a high probability stimulus RTs become faster and responses are performed with less force. The first finding was of course expected on the basis of earlier studies that varied stimulus probability (e.g., Bertelson & Tisseyre, 1966; LaBerge & Tweedy, 1964), but the evidence concerning response force is new. In particular, the finding that response force depends on stimulus probability shows that the motor-readiness model of Mattes et al. (1997) outlined in the introduction is at best an incomplete account of the effect of stimulus–response probability on response force. Before considering alternative explanations for the effects of stimulus and response probability on force, we first sought to examine the combined effects of stimulus and response probability in Experiment 2.

EXPERIMENT 2

Experiment 2 was designed to test whether the stimulus probability effect found in Experiment 1 is modulated by response probability. To this end, the paradigm of Experiment 1 was supplemented by a condition with low response probability. In each trial a precue announced the probability to respond (.2 or .8). The stimulus set and the response instructions were identical to Experiment 1, that is, one response letter was presented four times as often as the other response letter, resulting in conditional stimulus probabilities of .2 and .8 for the infrequent and frequent response letter, respectively.

Method

The method was identical to Experiment 1 except some modifications as indicated in the following.

Participants.   Thirty-six students (18 male, 18 female; mean age: 26.2 years) took part in a single session. Three of them claimed to be left handed. They were paid for their co-operation and were naive about the purpose of the experiment. None of them had participated in Experiment 1.

Procedure.   As in our previous study (Mattes et al., 1997), response probability was announced at the beginning of each trial. One of two percentages (20% or 80%, visual angle of 4.5° horizontally and 1.6° vertically) was presented in red or green, respectively. In addition to Experiment 1, the participants were told that the percentage number at the beginning of each trial represented the probability that they would have to respond at all. Participants were again told which of the two response letters would be presented four times as often as the other response letter. Table 2 provides the stimulus probabilities for both response probability conditions.

A trial started with the presentation of the response probability cue for a duration of 500 ms. After a blank period of 800 ms a warning signal (fixation cross) of 300 ms duration followed. The interval between the offset of the warning signal and the onset of the letter was 1750 ms. The letter was presented for 150 ms. Each response probability was employed in half of the trials in random order.

Design.   Crossing of the within-subject factors of conditional stimulus probability[2] and response probability (.2 vs .8, due to the advance cue) resulted in four experimental conditions. As in Experiment 1, practice (first vs second half of experiment) was included as an additional factor to assess whether potential probability effects are modulated by practice.

Questionnaire.   Again a questionnaire was given at the end of the session to find out whether the participants could predict the results of the experiment (see Appendix). In comparison to Experiment 1 this questionnaire contained additional questions concerning the response probability precue.

Results

A repeated measures ANOVA was conducted for each dependent variable. Table 2 shows data for stimulus A and B for both levels of response probability.

Response errors.   The percentages of anticipations (RT < 100 ms) and misses (RT > 1000 ms) were 0.01 and 0.6%, respectively. These trials were excluded from further data analysis. As one might expect, responses to the no-response letter were more frequent in trials with high response probability (5.0%) than in trials with low response probability (2.8%), $F(1, 35) = 6.3$, $p < .05$.

Reaction time.   Mean RT was 380 and 370 ms for response probabilities .2 and .8, respectively, $F(1, 35) = 8.8, p < .01$. Stimulus probability also revealed a highly significant main effect, $F(1, 35) = 61.1, p < .001$, with mean RTs of 357 ms for the frequent response letter and 393 ms for the infrequent one. The interaction of the two factors did not reach statistical significance, $F(1, 35) = 1.8, p < .2$, indicating that the effect of stimulus probability on RT does not depend on the absolute level of response probability. The practice factor revealed the expected learning effect with mean RTs declining from 383 ms to 367 ms between the first and the second half of the experiment, $F(1, 35) = 18.9$, $p < .001$, but showed no interaction with either probability factor. The three-way interaction was also not significant ($F < 1$).

----

[2] In trials with response probability .2 the unconditioned stimulus probabilities were now .16 and .04, and in trials with response probability .8 these figures changed to .64 and .16 for the frequent and the infrequent response letter, respectively.

Response force. As response probability increased, response force decreased from 647 to 628 cN, $F(1, 35) = 10.9$, $p < .01$. In agreement with Experiment 1, response force was also strongly influenced by stimulus probability. Mean force was 653 cN for the infrequent letter and 623 cN for the frequent letter, $F(1, 35) = 11.7$, $p < .01$. The interaction between the two probability factors was not significant, $F(1, 35) = 2.4$, $p < .2$. As in Experiment 1, responses were more forceful in the first half of the experiment (704 cN) than in the second half (571 cN), $F(1, 35) = 17.8$, $p < .001$. However, practice did not modulate either the effects of stimulus or response probability ($Fs < 1$) or the interaction between them ($F = 1.1$).

Questionnaire. The results of the questionnaire are provided in the Appendix. Generally, the participants were quite accurate in their predictions for RTs but not for response force. As in our previous study (Mattes et al., 1997) participants believed incorrectly that an increase of response probability would increase response force. However, there was less agreement on how stimulus probability would affect response force.

Discussion

This experiment replicates the findings of Experiment 1 that stimulus probability affects both RT and response force. In addition, the size of the effect on response force was not modulated by response probability. The participants again responded faster and less forcefully to the more frequent stimulus as compared to the less frequent one.

Surprisingly, the effect of stimulus probability on response force was even larger than that of response probability. Unfortunately, we cannot derive accurate measures for the relative contributions of stimulus and response probability from these data. The factor of response probability, despite its interpretative labelling, is still confounded with stimulus probability. This is because the advance probability cue changes not only the probability of responding but of course also the probability of each stimulus. As can be seen from Table 2, stimulus probabilities of .16 and .04 for the 20% precue change to .64 and .16 when the 80% precue announces a higher response probability. Thus, in view of the effects of stimulus probability on response force and the confounding of response probability with stimulus probability, it remains unclear whether response probability actually plays any role at all in the present designs.

This question of a possible effect of response probability on force is of considerable importance since the explanation in terms of the motor readiness model outlined in the introduction was entirely based on the assumption that different levels of response probability result in corresponding adjustments of the motor system. Although Experiment 1 clearly shows that stimulus probability affects response force, it is still possible that response probability also does so. For example, it is conceivable that a manipulation of response probability exerts a specific effect on motor preparation (e.g., as assumed by the motor-readiness model), whereas a manipulation of stimulus probability exerts an indirect effect on response force that is mediated by non-motoric processes. Hence, if both factors produce relatively separable effects on response force, a significant main effect of response probability would still support the motor readiness model as a partial explanation of the S–R probability effect.

Although it appeared that response probability played a minor role in Experiment 2, there is nevertheless some evidence that it did have some effect. False alarm responses to the no-go letters occurred more frequently when response probability was high, in accordance with the idea that motor readiness was closer to the motor action limit when response probability was high. Thus, this aspect of the results is consistent with Mattes et al.'s (1997) motor-readiness model. This evidence is indirect, however, and it would be more convincing to demonstrate an effect of response probability in a design where response probability was not confounded with stimulus probability. Experiment 3 was designed to tackle this matter.

EXPERIMENT 3

Experiments 1 and 2 provided evidence that stimulus probability exerts an effect on response force. The question arises whether response probability has any influence at all on response force, because response probability was confounded with stimulus probability both in our earlier study (Mattes et al., 1997) and in Experiment 2 of the present study. Experiment 3 was designed to test the effects of response probability on RT and response force for constant levels of stimulus probability. To achieve this, the design of Experiment 2 was slightly changed. This experiment employed four stimuli, three of which were response letters and the fourth of which was the no-response letter (see Table 3). One response letter could be presented in both response probability conditions, and the other two response letters were each assigned to just one of the two response probability conditions.

For example, assume that the response letters were A, B, and C and the no-response letter was D. As in Experiment 2 each trial was preceded by a precue "20%" or "80%" that announced the response probability for that trial. Then the precue "20%" would be followed either by the response letter A with $p = .04$, by B with $p = .16$, or by the no-response letter D with $p = .80$. The precue "80%" would either be followed by the response letter A with $p = .64$, by the third response letter C with $p = .16$, or by the no-response letter D with $p = .20$. Only the responses to B and C are of theoretical interest and thus will be analysed further. These stimuli have identical conditional occurrence probabilities (.16) as well as identical overall presentation frequencies (8% of all trials each). However, the response to the letter B has an a priori probability of .2, whereas response probability for C is .8. If response probability has the expected effect on response force, then response force should be higher for stimulus B than for stimulus C. In contrast, if response probability does not affect response force, then response force should be identical for these two letters because they have identical stimulus probabilities.

Method

Participants.   Thirty-six students (sixteen male, twenty female; mean age: 26.7 years) took part in a single session. Three of them claimed to be left handed. They were paid for their co-operation and were naive about the purpose of the experiment. None of them had participated in Experiment 1 or 2.

Apparatus and stimuli.   This was identical to the previous experiment with the following exceptions. The letters G, H, M, and S served as stimuli. Assignment of stimuli to conditions was balanced over participants. A frame centred around the position of stimulus presentation was visible throughout the trial. The frame had the same colour as the precue to enhance its efficiency. The outer border of the frame was 9.9° wide, 7.2° high, and the line had a thickness of 0.7°. The colours of the precues were changed to brown and blue, because the colours of the previous experiment produced undesirable after-effects in the area of the frame when they were changed at the beginning of a trial.

Procedure.   The course of a trial was identical to Experiment 2, except for the coloured frame, which was visible during the whole trial. It changed its colour when the response probability changed. Participants were told that they should respond to three letters but withhold the response when the fourth letter was presented. They were further told that one response letter would be presented more often than the others and that the other two response letters would be presented with equal frequency. The resulting probabilities are provided in Table 3.

Design.   Only the factor response probability (.2 vs .8) was of interest in this experiment. As in the previous experiments a practice factor (first vs second half of experiment) was included to take practice effects into account.

Questionnaire.   The questionnaire of Experiment 2 was only slightly changed in wording to account for the frame that accompanied the precue (see Appendix). All other questions were identical.

Results

Separate repeated measures ANOVAs were conducted for each dependent variable. The analysis only included the responses to the stimuli B and C because this comparison is critical for isolating the effect of response probability on response force. Table 3 shows data for stimulus B and C and, for completeness, also the data for stimulus A.

Response errors.   There were 0.2% anticipations (RT < 100 ms) and 0.3% misses (RT > 1000 ms). These trials were excluded from further analysis. Responses to the no-response letter were more frequent in trials with high response probability (18.1%) than in trials with low response probability (4.1%), $F(1, 35) = 33.1, p < .001$.

Reaction time.   RT analyses revealed a significant main effect of response probability, $F(1, 35) = 10.9, p = .002$. Mean RT was 406 ms for response probability .2 and 387 ms for response probability .8. RT decreased with practice from 402 ms in the first half of the session to 391 ms in the second half, $F(1, 35) = 5.0, p = .031$. The difference between the two response probability conditions was 13 ms in the first half and 24 ms in the second half, but this interaction was not significant, $F(1, 35) = 2.3, p = .139$.

Response force.   Most important, there was a highly significant main effect of response probability on force, $F(1, 35) = 21.8, p < .001$. Mean peak force was 724 cN when response probability was .2 and 685 cN when response probability was .8. Peak force decreased from the first to the second half of the experiment but this practice effect was not significant, $F(1, 35) = 1.9, p = .17$. The interaction of both factors was also not significant ($F < 1$).

Questionnaire.   The results of the questionnaire are provided in the Appendix. Note that the participants predicted fast but weak reactions for high stimulus probability, whereas they expected fast and strong reactions for high response probability. This suggests that the predictions on force are not simply guided by the beliefs about RT but are rather generated independently. In sum, the predictions about RT were again correct, whereas the predictions about response force were correct for stimulus probability but incorrect for response probability.

Discussion

In this experiment different levels of response probability were announced by a precue. Two stimuli of equal frequency were assigned to the two response probability conditions to avoid a confound with stimulus probability. The results demonstrate that response probability affects RT and response force even when stimulus probability is held constant.[3]

One might object that stimulus expectancy for stimuli B and C differs despite the identical stimulus probability. When the precue had announced low response probability, stimulus B was the more expected stimulus of the two possible stimuli (B vs A). In contrast, when the precue had announced high response probability, stimulus C was the less expected one (C vs A). Such a potential influence of stimulus expectancy, however, is not crucial for the main conclusion of this experiment. First, a comparison of stimulus A and B reveals only a small and insignificant RT effect, $t(35) = 0.77$, $p > .4$, suggesting that stimulus expectancy has little effect in this situation. Second, and more important, a potential stimulus expectancy effect would tend to counteract the response probability effect, because participants tend to respond more quickly and less forcefully to expected stimuli than to unexpected ones. Therefore, at the worst, the effect of response probability could be somewhat underestimated in the present experiment and the conclusion that response probability exerts an effect on RT and response force would still be warranted.

GENERAL DISCUSSION

Human performance benefits greatly from preparation. Covert preparation is assumed to increase both the speed and the accuracy of various information processing mechanisms, as demonstrated by the measurement of RT and response errors. Recent research has revealed that preparation even affects the force output involved in performing a response—responses in a simple RT task to stimuli with low occurrence probability are relatively forceful (Jaśkowski & Verleger, 1993; Mattes et al., 1997). As mentioned in the introduction this probability effect may reflect response preparation at a motoric level producing not only short RTs but also a moderate force output that is appropriate to perform the task.

The primary question in the present study was whether the effects of probability on response force generally reflect response preparation at a motoric level or might even be caused by preparation at preceding levels. To answer this question we manipulated stimulus probability while keeping response probability constant, and vice versa. As argued in the introduction, the effects of probability on force in designs confounding stimulus probability with response probability may actually have been due to stimulus probability rather than response probability.

---

[3]Note that the effect of response probability in Experiment 3 was even somewhat larger than in Experiment 2 (39 cN vs 19 cN) despite the confound with stimulus probability in Experiment 2, which should have exaggerated the effect.

Experiment 1 and 2 evaluated the effects of stimulus probability while keeping response probability constant. Participants pressed a key when one of two response letters appeared but refrained from responding when the no-response letter was presented. One of the response letters appeared more often than the other. Participants responded faster and less forcefully to the more probable of the two response letters. Experiment 2 showed that this stimulus probability effect is obtained whether the probability of responding is low or high. Experiment 3 made it plain that a manipulation of response probability affects response force. Although stimulus probability was constant, responses were faster and less forceful when response probability was high than when it was low. Thus, the conclusion that emerges from the results of all three experiments is that both stimulus probability and response probability affect response force in the absence of variations in the other factor.

A noteworthy difference between the present study and our earlier one is that in the earlier one response probability was given by the frequency of stimulus trials among blank trials, whereas in the present study a stimulus was presented in every trial and the participants had to decide whether or not the stimulus was a response letter. Thus, the response probability effect could be demonstrated for a task when stimulus detection is sufficient to trigger a response and also for a task that requires identification of the stimulus.

A post-experimental questionnaire revealed that the participants were not fully aware of the directions of the effect of stimulus and response probability on force. Although most participants correctly recognized that faster RTs are associated with higher stimulus and response probabilities, there was somewhat less agreement on how the two types of probabilities affect response force. Generally, participants tend to presume correctly a decrease of response force when stimulus probability increases. By contrast, they incorrectly believe that increasing response probability yielded more forceful responses. This differential suggests that the participants' judgements about response force are not merely the counterpart of their beliefs about RT.

The main conclusion from the present study is that an interpretation of probability-related changes in motor performance requires consideration of pre-motoric stages of stimulus processing. The increase of response force relatively unlikely stimuli–response pairs cannot solely be attributed to processes that operate at a muscular level, because stimulus specific preparation also affects response force. More generally, this finding sheds some light on the structure of cognitive processes. The demonstration that stimulus probability affects response force appears to be in conflict with the notion of functionally encapsulated modules. In such a modular system it is difficult to see how preparatory effects operating at a premotoric level can influence the strength of a response. However, it is not entirely clear whether this preparatory effect reflects structural processing features or stems from non-specific activation processes that bypass the computational processing route. These and further interpretations are discussed next.

Motor-readiness model

An extended version of Näätänen's (1971) motor-readiness model can account for response probability effects on response force, although it cannot account in its present formulation for the stimulus probability effects on response force. As we outlined in the introduction, this model assumes that poor motor prepara-tion results in a high activation overshoot. Because low response probability is thought to result in poor motor preparation, it follows that manual responses should be executed with more force when response probability was low. This extended motor readiness model can explain the effects of response probability in the present study and our previous study (Mattes et al., 1997).

According to the model, probability effects are due to motor adjustments that take place prior to the onset of the response signal. However, in the case of stimulus probability effects, the level of readiness at the moment of stimulus presentation should always be the same, because response probability was controlled. Therefore, the model in its present formulation cannot explain the observed force effects associated with the manipulation of stimulus proba-bility. One might speculate whether a principle similar to the one assumed in the motor-readiness model might operate at an earlier level. For example, the probability effect on response force could arise in the response selection stage where stimuli are assigned to their associated responses. When the link between a stimulus and its associated response is weak more activation might be necessary to trigger the response. For example, more activation could be needed to overcome competition with more probable links. As in the original formulation of the model, this would imply a response production mechanism which inherently produces more motoric activation whenever a weak stimulus–response link must be processed.

In the remainder of this discussion, we will consider some further possible interpretations of the present results. The next two subsections consider alter-native accounts for the stimulus probability effect and compare these to the modified motor-readiness model. The third section considers recent neuro-physiological findings that might be important for localizing the effects on force within the CNS.

Compensation hypothesis

One alternative explanation for the force effects obtained in this study comes from a compensation hypothesis that was suggested by Jaśkowski and Verleger (1993). According to this hypothesis, participants want to compensate poor preparation at the moment of stimulus detection by activating more motor neurons. These authors observed that participants produce more forceful responses under speed stress and thus concluded that participants increase the force output to generate shorter RTs (Jaśkowski, Verleger, & Wascher, 1994). Although the authors did not further specify this hypothesized compensation process, there are at least two versions conceivable. First, one may assume an automatic mechanism that times the response and if the predicted RT turns out to be slow, this mechanism increases the force level of the response output. This version suggests a positive correlation between RT and force; slow responses should be generally associated with higher response force due to the compensatory mechanism. Several studies, however, reported correlations for RT and response force that were calculated across trials within each experimental condition, so that the correlation was not influenced by the experimental manipulation (Giray, 1990; Giray & Ulrich, 1993; Mattes et al., 1997; Miller et al., 1999; Mordkoff, Miller, & Roch, 1996; Ulrich & Mattes, 1996; Ulrich et al., 1998). The finding that the average correlation has always been close to zero is difficult to explain within the latter version of the compensation hypothesis.

The second version presumes that the compensation tendency is strategically employed rather than an automatic process. Accordingly, the compensation process is not based on online information about the predicted slowness of the forthcoming response. Instead, the participants decide in advance to respond with more force to a stimulus which they suspect produces slower reactions, e.g., one with low probability. However, the results of the questionnaire provide evidence against this version of the compensation hypothesis. If the participants employed such a compensation strategy, they should have been able to predict correctly how probability influences response force, just as they were for RT. However, they tended to expect increased response force only for low stimulus probability, and not for low response probability.

Finally, and probably more crucial for the compensation hypothesis, both versions imply that every factor which shortens RT should also produce less forceful responses. Therefore, it is difficult to see how the compensation hypothesis can explain why RT decreases yet response force increases with stimulus intensity (Angel, 1973; Jaśkowski, Rybarczyk, Jaroszyk, & Lemanski, 1995; Miller et al., 1999), stimulus duration (Ulrich et al., 1998), the number of stimuli (Giray & Ulrich, 1993; Mordkoff et al., 1996), word frequency in a lexical decision task (Abrams & Balota, 1991; Balota & Abrams, 1995), and with the set size in a memory scanning task (Abrams & Balota, 1991).

Arousal effects

A third possible explanation of the stimulus probability effect proceeds from the well-established fact that unlikely events produce a non-specific arousal effect. For example, infrequent events are known to elicit certain neuronal activity patterns, as documented for an event-related potential component known as the mismatch negativity (Näätänen, 1995). Another component that is also sensitive to the probability of stimulus events is the P300. The amplitude of this positive deflection increases as the probability of a rare event decreases. For example, Gehring et al. (1992) found a larger P300 for target letters that were not predicted. These findings demonstrate that deviant or rare events seem to elicit certain activity patterns in the brain. If an infrequent stimulus generally elicits some non-specific arousal effects, this activation could result in a higher response force (Miller et al., 1999; Ulrich & Mattes, 1996). This activation might even exert an indirect influence on the motor system, which is mediated by a route that bypasses the information processing channel (Giray, 1990; Kramer & Spinks, 1991; Miller et al., 1999; Öhman, 1987).

At present, the arousal explanation of stimulus probability effects on force must be regarded as at least as plausible as the modified motor-readiness model, because of the clear-cut evidence that low probability stimuli increase arousal (Sokolov, 1963) and that increases in arousal tend to increase response force (Jaśkowski, Wroblewski, & Hojan-Jezierska, 1994; Miller et al., 1999; Ulrich & Mattes, 1996).

Response force and cortico-spinal excitability

Finally, reflexogenic studies and studies that have employed transcranial magnetic stimulation provide some suggestive hints to localize force effects within the CNS. These studies probe spinal and cortico-spinal excitability, respectively. Reflexogenic studies (Brunia & Boelhouwer, 1998; Requin, Bonnet, & Semjen, 1977) examined spinal reflex pathway activity during the foreperiod between a warning signal and the response signal. Monosynaptic reflexes were evoked during this interval, and the sizes of the evoked reflexes were unrelated to response probability. This result suggests that the probability effect on response force does not reflect changes in spinal excitability and is thus not a peripheral motor phenomenon.

However, as Hasbroucq et al. (1997) pointed out, the use of reflexogenic techniques is restricted to lower limbs, and functional differences of the upper and lower limbs in humans might render a generalization of reflexogenic studies unwarranted. Therefore, these authors probed the motor excitability of the upper limbs during the foreperiod in a RT task by employing transcranial magnetic stimulation. Their study revealed a decrement of cortico-spinal excitability—presumably due to cortical modulations (Hasbroucq, Kaneko, Akamatsu, & Possamaï, 1999a)—when the foreperiod condition facilitated response preparation. Hasbroucq et al. suggested that this decrement reflects an adaptive mechanism increasing the sensitivity of the motor structures to the forthcoming voluntary command. They further speculated that such a mechanism could consist of the active filtering of task-unrelated afferents to the motor structures, which would facilitate the interpretation of the voluntary command by reducing its signal-to-noise ratio. In a further study, Hasbroucq, Osman, et al. (1999b) additionally manipulated event preparation. Surprisingly, they did not find an effect of event preparation on the amplitude of the evoked motor potentials. Thus, it is not yet clearly established whether changes in excitability of cortico-spinal motor system contribute to the probability effect on force. However, the negative findings from reflex studies and the failure to find effects for event preparation in the study of Hasbroucq, Osman, et al. (1999b) presently suggest that probability effects do not operate at this level.

Future research is necessary to clarify whether stimulus and response probability effects share a common underlying principle or whether different mechanisms must be assumed. In either case, the present results challenge the traditional view in information processing research that motoric processes are uninfluenced by premotoric processes and thus may be investigated in isolation. Instead, the present findings support the notion that premotoric processes need to be considered even when one is primarily interested in understanding motor performance. The repeated demonstration of stable effects encourages one to expect that response force can be developed into a useful tool that helps to disclose the preparatory processes taking place at the interface of perception and action.

REFERENCES

Abrams, R.A., & Balota, D.A. (1991). Mental chronometry: Beyond reaction time. *Psychological Science, 2*, 153–157.

Angel, A. (1973). Input–output relations in simple reaction time experiments. *Quarterly Journal of Experimental Psychology, 25*, 193–200.

Balota, D.A., & Abrams, A. (1995). Mental chronometry: Beyond onset latencies in the lexical decision task. *Journal of Experimental Psychology: Learning, Memory, and Cognition, 21*, 1289–1302.

Bertelson, P., & Tisseyre, F. (1966). Choice reaction time as a function of stimulus versus response relative frequency of occurrence. *Nature, 212*, 1069–1070.

Biederman, I., & Zachary, R.A. (1970). Stimulus versus response probability effects in choice reaction time. *Perception and Psychophysics, 3*, 121–130.

Brunia, C.H.M., & Boelhouwer, A.H.W. (1988). Reflexes as a tool: A window in the central nervous system. In P.K. Ackles, J.R. Jennings, & M.G.H. Coles (Eds.), *Advances in psychophysiology* (Vol. 3, pp. 1–67). Greenwich, CT: JAI Press.

Campbell, K.C., & Proctor, R.W. (1993). Repetition effects with categorizable stimulus and response sets. *Journal of Experimental Psychology: Learning, Memory, and Cognition, 19*, 1345–1362.

Dillon, P.J. (1966). Stimulus versus response decisions as determinants of the relative frequency effect in disjunctive reaction time performance. *Journal of Experimental Psychology, 71*, 321–330.

Downing, C.J. (1988). Expectancy and visual-spatial attention: Effects on perceptual quality. *Journal of Experimental Psychology: Human Perception and Performance, 14*, 188–202.

Fodor, J.A. (1983). *The modularity of mind.* Cambridge, MA: MIT Press.

Gehring, W.J., Gratton, G., Coles, M.G., & Donchin, E. (1992). Probability effects on stimulus evaluation and response processes. *Journal of Experimental Psychology: Human Perception and Performance, 18*, 198–216.

Giray, M. (1990) *Über die Aktivierung der menschlichen Motorik: Theoretische und experimentelle Analysen bei Reaktionsaufgaben.* [On the activation of the human motor system: Theoretical and experimental analysis of reaction time tasks.] Unpublished dissertation, Eberhard-Karls-Universität, Tübingen, Germany.

Giray, M., & Ulrich, R. (1993). Motor coactivation revealed by response force in divided and focused attention. *Journal of Experimental Psychology: Human Perception and Performance, 19*, 1278–1291.

Hasbroucq, T., Kaneko, H., Akamatsu, M., & Possamaï C.-A. (1997). Perparatory inhibition of cortico-spinal excitability: A transcranial magnetic stimulation study in man. *Cognitive Brain Research, 5*, 185–192.

Hasbroucq, T., Kaneko, H., Akamatsu, M., & Possamaï, C.-A. (1999a). The time-course of preparatory spinal and cortico-spinal inhibition: An H-reflex and transcranial magnetic stimulation study in man. *Experimental Brain Research, 124*, 33–41.

Hasbroucq, T., Osman, A., Possamaï, C.-A., Burle, B., Carron, S., Depy, D., Latour, S., & Mouret, I. (1999b). Cortico-spinal inhibition reflects time but not event preparation: Neural mechanisms of preparation dissociated by transcranial magnetic stimulation. *Acta Psychologica, 101*, 243–266.

Jaśkowski, P., Rybarczyk, K., Jaroszyk, F., & Lemanski, D. (1995). The effect of stimulus intensity on force output in simple reaction time task in humans. *Acta Neurobiologiae Experimentalis, 55*, 57–64.

Jaśkowski, P., & Verleger, R. (1993). A clock paradigm to study the relationship between expectancy and response force. *Perceptual and Motor Skills, 77*, 163–174.

Jaśkowski, P., Verleger, R., & Wascher, E. (1994). Response force and reaction time in a simple reaction task under time pressure. *Zeitschrift für Psychologie, 202*, 405–413.

Jaśkowski, P., Wroblewski, M., & Hojan-Jezierska, D. (1994). Impending electrical shock can affect response force in a simple reaction task. *Perceptual and Motor Skills, 79*, 995–1002.

Kramer, A., & Spinks, J. (1991). Capacity views of human information processing. In J.R. Jennings & M.G.H. Coles (Eds.), *Handbook of cognitive psychophysiology: Central and autonomic nervous system approaches* (pp. 179–249). Chichester, UK: Wiley.

LaBerge, D., Legrand, R., & Hobbie, R.K. (1969). Functional identification of perceptual and response biases in choice reaction time. *Journal of Experimental Psychology, 79*, 295–299.

LaBerge, D., & Tweedy, J.R. (1964). Presentation probability and choice time. *Journal of Experimental Psychology, 68*, 477–481.

Leuthold, H., Sommer, W., & Ulrich, R. (1996). Partial advance information and response preparation: Inferences from the lateralized readiness potential. *Journal of Experimental Psychology: General, 125*, 307–323.

Luck, S.J. (1998). Neurophysiology of selective attention. In H. Pashler (Ed.), *Attention* (pp. 257–295). Hove, UK: Psychology Press.

Mattes, S., & Ulrich, R. (1997). Response force is sensitive to the temporal uncertainty of response stimuli. *Perception and Psychophysics, 59*, 1089–1097.

Mattes, S., Ulrich, R., & Miller, J.O. (1997). Effects of response probability on response force in simple RT. *Quarterly Journal of Experimental Psychology, 50A*, 405–420.

Miller, J., Franz, V., & Ulrich, R. (1999). Effects of auditory stimulus intensity on response force in simple, go/no-go, and choice RT tasks. *Perception and Psychophysics, 61*, 107–119.

Mordkoff, J.T., Miller, J.O., & Roch, A.C. (1996). Absence of coactivation in the motor component: Evidence from psychophysiological measures of target detection. *Journal of Experimental Psychology: Human Perception and Performance, 22*, 25–41.

Näätänen, R. (1971). Non-aging fore-periods and simple reaction time. *Acta Psychologica, 35*, 316–327.

Näätänen, R. (1995). The mismatch negativity: A powerful tool for cognitive neuroscience. *Ear and Hearing, 16*, 6–18.

Öhman, A. (1987). The psychophysiology of emotion: An evolutionary cognitive perspective. In P.K. Akles, J.R. Jennings, & M.G.H. Coles (Eds.), *Advances in psychophysiology* (Vol. 2, pp. 79–127). Greenwich, CT: JAI Press.

Pashler, H., & Baylis, G.C. (1991). Procedural learning: I. Locus of practice effects in speeded choice tasks. *Journal of Experimental Psychology: Learning, Memory, and Cognition, 17*, 20–32.

Rabbitt, P.M.A. (1959). Effects of independent variations in stimulus and response probability. *Nature, 183*, 1212.

Requin, J., Bonnet, M., & Semjen, A. (1977). Is there a specificity in the supraspinal control of motor structures during preparation? In S. Dornič (Ed.), *Attention and performance VI* (pp. 139–174). Hillsdale, NJ: Lawrence Erlbaum Associates Inc.

Requin, J., Brener, J., & Ring, C. (1991). Preparation for action. In J.R. Jennings & M.G.H. Coles (Eds.), *Handbook of cognitive psychophysiology: Central and autonomic nervous system approaches* (pp. 357–448). New York: Wiley.

Soeten, E. (1998). Localizing sequential effects in serial choice reaction time with the information reduction procedure. *Journal of Experimental Psychology: Human Perception and Performance, 24*, 547–568.

Sokolov, E.N. (1963). *Perception and the conditioned reflex.* Oxford, UK: Pergamon Press.

Sparrow, W.A., & Newell, K.M. (1998). Metabolic energy expenditure and the regulation of movement economy. *Psychonomic Bulletin and Review, 5*, 173–196.

Spector, A., & Lyons, R.D. (1976). The locus of stimulus probability effect in choice reaction time. *Bulletin of the Psychonomic Society, 7*, 519–521.

Ulrich, R., & Mattes, S. (1996). Does immediate arousal enhance response force in simple reaction time? *Quarterly Journal of Experimental Psychology, 49A*, 972–990.

Ulrich, R., Mattes, S., & Miller, J. (1999). Donders's assumption of pure insertion: An evaluation on the basis of response dynamics. *Acta Psychologica, 102*, 43–75.

Ulrich, R., Rinkenauer, G., & Miller, J.O. (1998). Effects of stimulus duration and intensity on simple reaction time and response force. *Journal of Experimental Psychology: Human Perception and Performance, 24*, 915–928.

Wascher, E., Verleger, R., Vieregge, P., Jaśkowski, P., Koch, S., & Kömpf, D. (1997). Responses to cued signal in Parkinson's disease: Distinguishing between disorders of cognition and of activation. *Brain, 120*, 1355–1375.

APPENDIX

This Appendix provides the questionnaires employed in Experiments 1, 2, and 3 along with the observed response frequencies for each item and the two-sided probability from a binomial test in the right-most column. Sums of answers below 36 for some questions are due to participants who felt unable to answer that question.

Questionnaire Experiment 1

1.	Do you think that the frequency of the letter influences reaction time?	*Yes* 26	*No* 10	*p* .01
2.	Given that the frequency of the letter influences reaction time, how would one respond to the less frequent letter?	*Especially fast* 6	*Especially slow* 30	*p* < .0001
3.	Did you notice such an influence for yourself?	*Yes* 27	*No* 9	*p* < .01
4.	Do you think that the frequency of the letter influences the force level of the response?	*Yes* 23	*No* 13	*p* .13
5.	Given that the frequency of the letter influences the force level of the response, how would one respond to the less frequent letter?	*More forceful* 27	*Less forceful* 6	*p* < .001
6.	Did you notice such an influence?	*Yes* 24	*No* 12	*p* .07

Questionnaire Experiment 2

		Yes	No	p
1.	Did you pay attention to the probability cue?	*Yes* 19	*No* 17	p > .2
2.	Do you think that the probability cue influences reaction time?	*Yes* 23	*No* 13	p .13
3.	Given that the probability cue influences reaction time, how would one respond at 80%?	*Especially fast* 30	*Especially slow* 6	p < .0001
4.	Did you notice such an influence for yourself?	*Yes* 14	*No* 22	p > .2
5.	Do you think that the probability cue influences the force level of the response?	*Yes* 13	*No* 23	p .13
6.	Given that the probability cue influences the force level of the response, how would one respond at 80%?	*More forceful* 25	*Less forceful* 10	p .02
7.	Did you notice such an influence?	*Yes* 10	*No* 26	p .01
8.	Do you think that the frequency of the letter influences reaction time?	*Yes* 26	*No* 10	p .01
9.	Given that the frequency of the letter influences reaction time, how would one respond to the less frequent letter?	*Especially fast* 1	*Especially slow* 35	p < .0001
10.	Did you notice such an influence for yourself?	*Yes* 22	*No* 14	p > .2
11.	Do you think that the frequency of the letter influences the force level of the response?	*Yes* 23	*No* 13	p .13
12.	Given that the frequency of the letter influences the force level of the response, how would one respond to the less frequent letter?	*More forceful* 21	*Less forceful* 15	p > .2
13.	Did you notice such an influence?	*Yes* 18	*No* 18	p > .2

Questionnaire Experiment 3

1.	Did you pay attention to the probability cue (respectively the coloured frame, blue, brown)?	*Yes* 33	*No* 3	*p* < .0001
2.	Do you think that the probability cue influences reaction time?	*Yes* 32	*No* 4	*p* < .0001
3.	Given that the probability cue influences reaction time, how would one respond at 80%?	*Especially fast* 34	*Especially slow* 2	*p* < .0001
4.	Did you notice such an influence for yourself?	*Yes* 24	*No* 12	*p* .07
5.	Do you think that the probability cue influences the force level of the response?	*Yes* 15	*No* 21	*p* > .2
6.	Given that the probability cue influences the force level of the response, how would one respond at 80%?	*More forceful* 23	*Less forceful* 12	*p* .09
7.	Did you notice such an influence?	*Yes* 12	*No* 24	*p* .07
8.	Do you think that the frequency of the letter influences reaction time?	*Yes* 31	*No* 5	*p* < .0001
9.	Given that the frequency of the letter influences reaction time, how would one respond to the less frequent letter?	*Especially fast* 10	*Especially slow* 26	*p* .01
10.	Did you notice such an influence for yourself?	*Yes* 28	*No* 8	*p* < .01
11.	Do you think that the frequency of the letter influences the force level of the response?	*Yes* 23	*No* 13	*p* .13
12.	Given that the frequency of the letter influences the force level of the response, how would one respond to the less frequent letter?	*More forceful* 29	*Less forceful* 7	*p* < .001
13.	Did you notice such an influence?	*Yes* 18	*No* 18	*p* > .2

VISUAL COGNITION, 2002, 9 (4/5), 502–527

Time course of planning for object and action parameters in visually guided manipulation

James Fleming

University of Pittsburgh, USA

Roberta L. Klatzky and Marlene Behrmann

Carnegie Mellon University, Pittsburgh, USA

Under visual guidance, subjects reached for and manipulated an object that varied in weight and surface texture (slipperiness). The manipulatory action was either grasping, lifting, or posting in a slot. The task was constrained or unconstrained with respect to speed, grasp pattern, and contact force. Initiation time (pre-reach), movement time (reach), and post-contact errors were measured, to examine planning for task performance at three points in time. Results indicate that in the constrained task, the manipulatory action was planned during the initiation time, but planning for object parameters was deferred until the reach interval. With relaxed task constraints, initiation times increased, and texture and manipulatory action had independent effects on premovement planning. Errors were affected interactively by all variables. The results suggest a planning process that unfolds over time, incorporating in turn the manipulatory action, object texture, and object weight. This unfolding accommodates variables proximate to the time where they will affect physical action.

People act on the world of objects for functional purposes. Functional acts are generally planned in advance, using sensory guidance along with cognitive intention and memory for past actions. Generally, we know what action we intend to perform with an object well before we reach for it—whether we want to push it or lift it, for example. Vision provides us with immediate and ongoing

Please address all correspondence to R.L. Klatzky, Department of Psychology, Carnegie Mellon University, Pittsburgh, PA 15213, USA. Email: klatzky@cmu.edu

This work was supported by a grant from the National Institute of Mental Health, NIMH MH 54246, to Marlene Behrmann. The authors thank Thomas McKeeff for assistance with data analysis.

http://www.tandf.co.uk/journals/pp/13506285.html   DOI:10.1080/13506280143000557

information about the geometry of action space: Where the object is and how its points of contact are oriented with respect to our body. Vision may indicate attributes of the object such as its weight and texture—although these can also be specified from memory, and some attributes may be available only after contact. If we are surprised by any of these parameters, the result can be an action slip: The milk spills; the plate is dropped.

Purposive interactions with objects require that parameters relating to functional action, spatial geometry, and object properties, like those listed earlier, be converted into motor parameters, such as arm velocity, reach direction and extent, hand shape, wrist orientation, grip force, and lift force. When they are planned in advance (cf., reflexive actions), these motor parameters constitute a *forward model* of the action, designating how it will unfold over time. The present paper is concerned with the construction of such a forward model after visual exposure to an object, in response to various action and object constraints. The general issue is how the model is influenced by these constraints at different points in time.

The concept of a forward model has been used extensively in the domain of motor control. Recently, it has been articulated by Wolpert and Ghahramani (2000) as an internalized system that predicts the consequences of action. The model arises from sensorimotor knowledge to predict particular motor events. During such an event, the model predicts values for a set of parameters that describe the continuously changing *state* of the sensorimotor system, for example, the active muscles, the positions of limbs, and so on. The event also takes place in a *context* consisting of parameters that change more slowly, if at all—for example, the identity of the target object or task constraints. Although the context constrains the predicted states, its parameters are not directly incorporated into the forward model.

During the course of any one movement, multiple models are formulated: A forward dynamic model predicts how the state of the system will change as a consequence of a motor command, given the context. A forward sensory model specifies the sensory feedback that will result from the change in state. Feedback from the sensory system can be used to update the models on-line, improving their prediction. For example, the trajectory of a ball can be estimated from its changing retinal position and used to update predictions about its future path. Feedback can also produce long-term sensorimotor learning that changes the predictive models that are formed.

The essence, then, of a forward model is that it predicts the consequences of motor commands for the unfolding states of the sensorimotor system, given motor commands and context. Here, we address the issue of which contextual parameters influence the model, and at what points in time. This issue has received attention in previous research on action planning and execution. Our general approach is to vary contextual parameters that should strongly constrain how an object is manipulated, and hence should alter the states predicted by the forward models. We examine the time course of movement prior to object contact, to determine whether variations in levels of the parameter affect performance. If so, it indicates that the parameter influenced the preparation for the ultimate manipulatory act at that point in time.

Several time periods that might be the locus of action planning and preparation have generally been distinguished. One period is prior to initiating movement. Another is during the reach. Yet another is after contact. The first two of these periods have frequently been differentiated in response-time studies, by partitioning the total pre-contact time into initiation time (from go signal to start of reach) and movement (reaching) time. Although it has sometimes been assumed that movement preparation and planning occur entirely within the initiation time (e.g., Pratt & Abrams, 1994; Rosenbaum, 1980), this assumption is unlikely to hold in general. People may begin reaching before they have entirely planned the action, especially when there is an imperative go signal and no penalty is associated with the action, and some actions must be adjusted while ongoing, in response to sensory input (e.g., Bootsma & Van Wieringen, 1990). Planning seems more likely to be completed prior to movement when there are discrete response alternatives, and less likely to be completed when there is target uncertainty (see Meegan & Tipper, 1998, regarding location uncertainty). Without necessarily assuming that planning is generally completed before movement, research on simple arm movements reveals contexts in which the separation of initiation and movement times provides insights into the planning process.

Klatzky, Fikes, and Pellegrino (1995) found effects of two variables on initiation time in a reach-to-contact task. They had subjects reach for and make contact with an object, using a hand shape (e.g., poking or grasping) that was cued by the object's colour. Movement of the object was to be avoided. The time prior to reaching was affected both by the stimulus–response compatibility—the perceptual affordance of the object for the colour-cued hand shape—and the stability of the object's support, as manipulated by whether the base of the object was on a sliding or stable surface. These effects were attributed to planning for two components of the action, respectively: The hand configuration used at contact, and the reach. Evidence for parallel, independent planning of these components was obtained. In other studies, another variable that has been found to affect pre-movement initiation time is the required spatial precision of an aimed movement (Sidaway, 1991; Spijkers, 1987).

Planning for an action can also occur during the reaching movement itself, prior to contact. Purdy, Lederman, and Klatzky (1999) compared performance in a peg-in-hole task with and without visual guidance. Although vision led to faster movement initiation, grasping, and manipulation, subjects were actually faster to reach when denied vision, indicating that the movement interval was used to plan visually guided action. In particular, the late acceleration phase of reaching has been implicated as a point when people accommodate the force precision required by the action. Marteniuk, MacKenzie, Jeannerod, Athenes, and Dugas (1987) found that the fragility of the object (ball vs light bulb) and the target movement (place vs throw) affected the movement time, particularly the later stages. Klatzky et al. (1995) found that in addition to affecting initiation time, the stability of the object's support plane also affected movement time.

Fikes, Klatzky, and Lederman (1994) found that object texture, in the form of coefficient of friction, affected movement time when subjects grasped and lifted a dowel. (This was in contrast to a null finding of Weir, MacKenzie, Marteniuk, & Cargoe, 1991; however, that study did not have a contact sensor to differentiate between pre-contact and post-contact effects, and those observed were attributed to the post-contact phase.) Based on a model of Fearing (1986), Fikes et al. showed that object slipperiness determines the tolerance for placement of the fingers so as to prevent the object from slipping. Presumably, people were anticipating the greater precision demands of a slippery object while they reached for it, slowing their reaching time. This slowness with the slippery dowel was not observed with the initiation time, indicating that consideration of these constraints was delayed until the hand approached the dowel.

A third point in time at which action and object parameters can affect motor planning and preparation is after contact, but prior to manipulation. Johansson and Westling (1984) found that subjects who were grasping and lifting an object without vision adjusted their grip force according to the coefficient of friction and weight, after the object was contacted. Heavier or slippery objects require greater grip forces than do lighter or less slippery objects. However, the time required to attain a suitable grip force remained invariant across surface textures. This constancy was maintained by increasing the rate of grip force adjustment when the object was slippery.

Weir, MacKenzie, Marteniuk, Cargoe, and Frazer (1991) also found that an object's weight affected the contact time prior to lifting, but not the reaching time. Four visibly distinct dowels, ranging in weight from 20 to 410 g, were reached for, grasped, and lifted in a sequence of either blocked or random trials. The kinematics of movement were measured with a tracking system, and contact was sensed (in Experiment 2 only) with an electrical sensor. This allowed the authors to parse the response interval into two components, pre-contact arm movement and pre-lift contact. The second of these intervals, between initial contact and lift, was greater for the 410 g dowel than for those ranging from 20 to 150 g; however, the free phase of movement was unaffected by weight.

Planning and preparation do not stop, of course, once a manipulatory action—even a simple ballistic action like lifting—has begun. People adjust their grip force on an object that is perturbed during the act of lifting, whether from adding an external force (e.g., Johansson & Westling, 1988) or from changes in the movement itself (e.g., Flanagan & Wing, 1995; Witney, Goodbody, & Wolpert, 1999). Witney, Goodbody, and Wolpert (2000) suggested that the latency to adjust the grip given a change in movement (e.g., one hand pushes on an object being lifted with the other) is so short that it points to predictive adjustment using a forward model (feedforward), rather than a closed-loop correction (feedback).

In the present experiments, variations in object parameters—texture, as used by Fikes et al. (1994), and weight, as investigated by Weir, MacKenzie, Marteniuk, Cargoe, and Frazer (1991) and Johannson and Westling (1984)—was incorporated into multiple task contexts involving grasping and/or lifting an object. One was a highly constrained context, in which the task was speeded, terminal contact force was required to be low so that the object did not slide on a slippery support plane, and the object was to be grasped in a difficult-to-maintain posture (side to side). This was compared to an unconstrained context, in which the task was performed at a comfortable rate, sliding of the object on the support plane was tolerated, and a natural, front-to-back grasp was allowed. Moreover, these contraints were introduced or relaxed in the context of three actions, which varied in the movement trajectory imposed subsequent to object contact: The object was grasped without lifting, lifted above the table, or lifted so as to contact a slot in an upper surface. These actions are ordered in increasing complexity with respect to the movement required.

Our general interest was in how contextual parameters related to object and action would influence the forward model, by their effects on the states that the model predicts. The scope of the forward model is, in these experiments, equivalent to motor planning that takes place prior to object manipulation. As was noted previously, one should not assume that planning is exhausted prior to arm movement; on the contrary, the process extends in time into the reach and even after contact with an object has been made. We examined the planning process at three points in time, using temporal and error measures. Two temporal measures were used: Pre-movement initiation time and pre-contact movement time. Differences between levels of a variable with respect to these measures were taken as evidence that the impact of the variable was incorporated into the forward model at that time. Although we recognize that the locus of planning is to some extent under the subject's control, potentially muddying the initiation/movement time distinction, premature initiation of reaching was discouraged both by instruction and by the inclusion of catch trials, in which no object appeared. Moreover, rather than assuming discrete planning intervals prior and subsequent to movement, we treat the two temporal measures as accessing, at different points in time, a more continuous process of constructing and modifying a forward model.

In addition to the temporal measures, we examined effects of manipulated parameters on post-contact errors. Such errors can be taken as failures of planning, either because the process was incomplete by volition before the manipulation was attempted, or because some motor demands simply cannot be fully assimilated prior to or during initial contact. In either case, to the extent that errors are affected by characteristics of the object or by the action complexity, they indicate that accommodation of these variables is deferred, in whole or part, until the action itself.

Given these assumptions, the following questions were pursued: (1) Would object parameters of weight and texture influence the forward model, that is, would variations in the object affect initiation and/or movement time? Previously these effects were elusive. Texture has been found not to affect initiation time (Fikes et al., 1994), and weight has been found only to affect post-movement, contact time (Weir, MacKenzie, Marteniuk, Cargoe, & Frazer, 1991). However, such effects may be found when different levels of task constraints and action complexity are considered. (2) Would action parameters influence the forward model? Whereas effects of object parameters on initiation time have proved elusive, and effects on movement time have been mixed, complexity of the ultimately required action might be more powerful in affecting temporal planning measures. (3) Would task constraints and object parameters interact? In particular, would object parameters such as texture be incorporated earlier into the forward model when the task was highly constrained (with respect to speed, grasp, and force), or would task constraints dominate motor preparation, precluding object-related planning? (4) Would action complexity and object parameters interact? That is, would more complex actions introduce more or less planning for object parameters? (5) Would the object parameters of weight and texture have equivalent effects on the forward model? These parameters act together to influence the grip force that must be imposed to lift an object. Accordingly, it seems plausible to assume that they would either jointly be included or excluded from the planning process. On other hand, texture has been found to affect movement time, and weight has not. (6) Would some combinations of object, action, and task constraint prove sufficiently demanding that action errors would ensue, and how would these conditions relate to the planning process as revealed by temporal measures?

The experiments addressing these issues proceeded as follows. Experiment 1 manipulated object weight and texture, along with the required manipulatory action, in a highly constrained task (speeded, with grasp and contact-force constraints). Subjects appeared to plan the action during the initiation time, but to defer or fail to consider planning for object parameters. Experiment 2 addressed the same variables, but in an unconstrained environment. Initiation times increased relative to the constrained task, and pre-movement planning for object texture was evidenced as well as for manipulatory action. Experiment 3 examined the effects of texture and action when both varied randomly from trial to trial, placing greater load on the early planning process.

EXPERIMENT 1

Method

Subjects. Thirty-nine right-handed University students participated as part of an optional course requirement. Twenty-four took part with the light dowel, and fifteen with the heavy dowel. An additional eleven subjects were excluded because they could not maintain the required grasp (two subjects in the light group, nine in the heavy); this could potentially bias the heavy condition toward stronger individuals and reduce effects of weight. All subjects had normal vision without glasses. Wearing glasses was not permitted because of potential reflections of the glass lenses onto the Plato spectacle lenses described below.

Stimuli. The stimuli were two wooden dowels, each weighing 127 g, and two steel dowels, each weighing 681 g. Each dowel was 2.9 cm diameter × 15.2 cm long and was mounted to the centre of a 6.4 cm × 6.4 cm wood base. The dowels were painted red. A green slippery coating, consisting of water-soluble lubricating jelly and a few drops of washable green finger-paint, was thinly applied to the entire surface of one wood and one steel dowel. Each coated dowel was recoated immediately following a trial in which it was grasped.

Friction coefficients for the dowels were estimated by having a subject rest the right forearm and hand (cleaned of dirt or oils) on a horizontal platform, palm up with the index and middle fingers extended. The dowel was positioned on its side, perpendicularly across the middle and distal phalanges of the fingers. The base of the dowel did not contact the hand and was suspended over the edge of the platform. The experimenter then slowly tilted the platform until the dowel began to slip across the surface of the fingers. The angle at which the slip occurred was recorded, and the tangent of this slip angle was taken as the friction coefficient. Five observations were taken from each of four partici-pants with each dowel. The average coefficients were as follows: uncoated wooden dowel, .50; coated wooden dowel, .19; uncoated steel dowel, .32; coated steel dowel, .12.

Apparatus and procedure. The apparatus is illustrated in Figure 1. Prior to the start of each trial, the base of one of the two dowels was fitted onto a square with the same dimensions, which had a wood upper surface contacting the dowel's base, bonded to an underside made of plexiglass. Two pegs at opposite corners of the upper surface of the square were aligned with matching holes in the base of the dowel, in order to secure their attachment. The dowel and fitted square were then positioned on the centre of a wooden platform with raised edges that rested on the table, so that there was a distance of 1.9 cm from each edge of the dowel's base to each inner edge of the platform. A plexiglass sheet

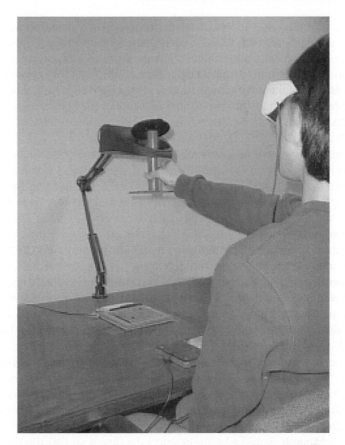

Figure 1. The experimental apparatus. The start key is immediately in front of the subject. The dowel is shown as having been lifted from the home platform through the slot for the posting action.

(10.2 cm × 10.2 cm) was centred on the floor of the platform in order to create a slippery interface between the dowel base and the platform. Using a similar technique as for the dowels, the coefficient of friction between the plexiglass square attached to the dowel and the plexiglass sheet on the platform was found to be 0.42 (averaged over heavy and light dowels).

Finally, a black circular disk was suspended directly above the platform. There was a circular slot (7.3 cm in diameter) in the centre of the disk, and a black, light-weight plastic hinged flap covered the slot from the top. The entire assembly (disk + flap) was supported by a spring-loaded adjustable arm mounted to the back edge of the table. This arm, and thus the disk height, was adjusted relative to the height of each subject while seated at the table, so that the disk could be reached at a distance of 80–90% of the total length of the subject's fully extended arm as measured from the shoulder.

To control the onset of visual input and to prevent vision between trials, subjects wore glasses with liquid-crystal shutters (Translucent Technologies). Under computer control, the shutters change from translucent to transparent within 10 ms and return to translucent in 2 ms. Cardboard barriers were placed on the sides and bottom of the lenses to prevent visual cues from those angles. The subject was seated with the sagittal mid-line of the body aligned with the dowel. A start key was located 9.5 cm from the proximal edge of the table, aligned with the subject's sagittal mid-line.

The spectacles were programmed to occlude the subject's vision between trials. While waiting for the start of each trial, each subject was instructed to gently rest the index, middle finger, and thumb of the right hand on the start key. A radio played between trials, to mask any potential auditory cues that could indicate which of the two dowels (uncoated or coated) was being positioned on the platform.

The start of each trial was indicated by the radio being turned off. After a random interval, ranging approximately from 1 to 3 s, the spectacles became transparent so that the subject could see the dowel. Immediately upon seeing the dowel, the subject was to reach out and perform the correct action with it. To prevent premature lift-off from the start key, instructions were to make the entire movement as smooth and as continuous as possible, without hesitation after lift-off or during the course of the movement.

Subjects performed three manipulatory actions, called grasping, lifting, and posting. In all three actions, the following three constraints were introduced. (1) The reach constraint was to reach as quickly as possible without making errors (described later). (2) The grasp constraint was to grasp the vertical centre of the dowel using a side-to-side pinch grasp involving the index, middle finger, and thumb. Subjects were to grasp the dowel so that the fingers and thumb either contacted or wrapped around the sides of the dowel, rather than simply pinching the front and back surfaces of it. (3) The contact force constraint was to contact the dowel with sufficiently low force that its base did not move and hit the surrounding edges of the platform.

During the grasping action, subjects simply had to observe these constraints and grasp the dowel firmly enough so that it could be lifted—even though it was not to be moved physically. The spectacles were programmed to become translucent to prevent vision 3 s after the initial contact of the hand with the dowel, and subjects were required to maintain the grasp until vision was occluded. This requirement was introduced to approximately equate the total time during which the hand was in contact with the dowel across the three actions.

For the lifting action, subjects were required to reach out, grasp the dowel, lift it and place it on the table to the right of the platform, while following each of the general constraints listed earlier. Importantly, the trajectory of the lift was not specified, and thus subjects usually combined the vertical lift and lateral trajectory to place it on the table into one continuous smooth movement.

For the posting action, subjects were to reach out, grasp the dowel, lift it, "post" it through a slot suspended directly above the dowel, and then put it down to the right of the platform on the table. Since the action required only a vertical post-contact movement, and the ratio of slot diameter to dowel diameter was was 2.5:1, the posting movement could presumably be performed ballistically and with minimal if any visual guidance. However, subjects had to maintain post-contact control by keeping the dowel in a vertical orientation and by preventing it from slipping from the hand during posting.

After receiving the instructions for the first action, subjects practised lifting the dowels. They practised the requisite side-to-side grasp with the uncoated dowel three times, then the coated dowel three times. Subjects were initially instructed to use only the distal phalanges of the index and middle fingers. However, because holding the heavy dowel in this way proved difficult, we allowed subjects in the heavy condition to grip with the middle as well as the distal phalanges of the fingers, if the practice grasps showed they could not lift the dowel with the distal phalanges alone. Seven subjects used only the distal phalanges and eight added the middle phalanges.

Dependent measures.   The *initiation time* was recorded as the time from when the spectacles switched to a transparent state to the time when the hand was released from the start key. To record the *movement time*, the platform for the dowel rested on a piezoelectric force-sensitive plate. The movement time was the interval between release of the start key and triggering of this plate when the dowel was touched. Errors were of two types: *Base move errors* (the base of the dowel slid and contacted an edge of the platform) and *grasp slip errors* (the dowel slipped from the hand either prior to, during, or after lift-off). All errors were recorded by experimenter observation.

Design.   The experiment combined the within-subject factors of surface texture (coated and uncoated) and action (grasping, lifting, and posting), and the between-subjects factor of dowel weight. It lasted approximately 1 h. Each action was performed over a single block of 22–38 trials—as many as permitted in the time allotted for the block (variations in trial N reflected differences across subjects in the time required for instructions and practice lifting, and the time to clean hands after trials with the coated dowel). The order with which each action was performed was counter-balanced across subjects. The texture of the dowel varied randomly within each block, with the constraint that each texture was sampled with approximately equal frequency (with slight departures from equal N due to truncation of blocks). In addition to the texture conditions, 10% of the trials within each block consisted of catch trials in which the dowel was absent, and the subject was instructed not to release the start key. These trials were included to motivate the subjects to wait until they viewed the dowel before initiating movement.

Results

The principal dependent measures were initiation time, movement time, and the two categories of error. Pairwise comparisons between texture and weight levels were performed, where appropriate, as a priori contrasts. Because action effects were not as predicted, we treated comparisons among action levels as post hoc, using a Bonferroni correction with alpha set at 0.05. Figure 2 shows the mean initiation time and movement time across conditions for all experiments, with standard errors of the mean.

To summarize the results, texture and weight affected movement time interactively, but initiation time was affected only by the required action. The coated dowel led to slower movements, particularly when it was heavier. Somewhat surprisingly, the posting action led to the fastest initiation and movement times.

Initiation time. The ANOVA showed only effects of action, $F(2, 74) =$ 3.94, $p = .0237$. Post hoc tests revealed that grasping and lifting were significantly slower than posting, but did not differ from each other. The texture effect did not reach significance ($.15 > p > .10$), although the trend was toward a longer initiation time (by 11 ms) for the coated dowel. Also, the effect of weight was not significant ($.15 > p > .10$), although the trend was toward a longer initiation time (by 48 ms) for the heavier dowel.

Movement time. The ANOVA showed effects of action similar to those found in initiation time, $F(2, 74) = 4.86, p = .0104$. In contrast to the null effect of texture on initiation time, texture significantly affected movement time, $F(1, 37) = 34.78$, $p < .0001$. Both of these variables interacted with weight: for action by weight, $F(2, 74) = 8.19$, $p = .0006$; for texture by weight, $F(1, 37) = 4.88, p = .0334$. The movement time was significantly greater for the coated dowel than the uncoated dowel at both levels of weight, but this difference was enhanced when the dowels were heavy (33 ms for the light object vs 73 ms for the heavy). Conversely, the heavier object led to longer movement time, more so when it was coated (56 ms difference, contrast marginally significant, $p = .0705$) than when it was not (16 ms, non-significant difference). For the heavy objects, the lifting action produced significantly slower reaches than grasping and posting, which did not differ, whereas for the light objects, all means differed significantly, with grasping slowest and posting fastest.

Errors. Figure 3 shows the mean base-move and grasp-slip outcomes for all experiments reported here, along with standard errors of the mean. As all the error data tended to show higher-order interactions as well as main effects, the ANOVAs are summarized in the Appendix. In this and subsequent experiments, errors with the grasping action were low. In the lifting and posting actions, errors were substantial when the dowel was coated; slips rarely

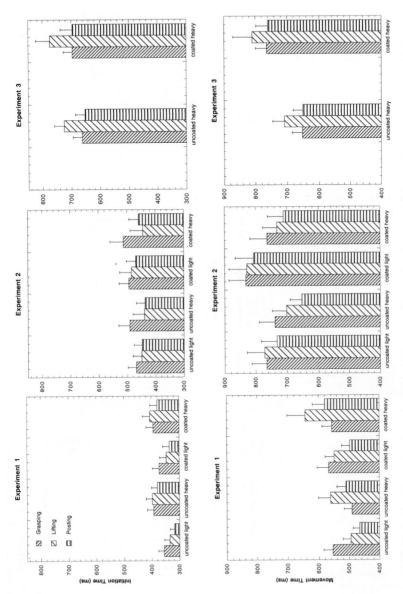

Figure 2. Average initiation time (top row) and movement time (bottom row) for each experiment, by combination of object texture and weight. Bars show standard error of the mean.

513

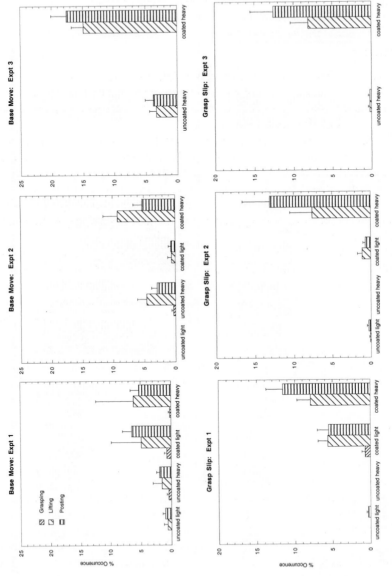

Figure 3. Percentage of trials in each experiment on which base moves (top row) and grasp slips (bottom row) occurred, by combination of object texture and weight. Bars show standard error of the mean.

occurred with the uncoated dowel. In addition, grasp-slip errors, but not base moves, showed an effect of weight. Subjects clearly had difficulty complying fully with the task constraints when the dowels were coated. Grasp slips occurred on a substantial percentage of trials when the coated dowel had to be lifted, principally when it was heavy, but to a lesser extent when it was light.

Discussion

The failure to find effects of texture and weight on initiation time is consistent with previous findings, described in the introduction. The fast initiation and movement times for posting are not what would be expected from movement complexity, and we have no explanation.

A principal finding of this experiment is that texture and weight interacted to affect movement time. The interaction can be understood from the joint effects of these variables on the required grip force. More grip force must be used with a heavier object and with a slippery object. Accordingly, the movement time was slower for the slippery dowel, particularly when it was heavy. Thus the data replicate previous findings indicating that movement time is affected by the force demands of grasping and lifting an object.

The action by weight interaction on movement time is also predicted by the action constraints and their implications for grip force. In the lifting and posting actions, lifting a heavier object requires more grip force, anticipation of which could produce increased movement time. The data show, accordingly, that the heavy dowels led to significantly longer movement times in the lifting and posting action, but not in the grasping action. Since the grasp terminates before the object is lifted, a greater mass could actually be beneficial, if the contact-force constraint (do not move the base upon contact) was easier to satisfy. (However, the trend in this direction was not significant.)

EXPERIMENT 2

The finding that initiation time was unaffected by either weight or texture is consistent with data of Fikes et al. (1994). It suggests that early in its progress, the forward model does not take into account the constraints on action that arise from properties of the object. The model does, however, take into account differences in the actions required, though not as ordered by complexity.

It may be that object-based constraints are not being considered early in planning because task constraints are being given a higher priority. In particular, in Experiment 1 subjects were asked to reach as quickly and as accurately as possible. This instruction may have led subjects to initiate the reach quickly and delay the considerations of object properties until movement onset. Moreover, subjects were required to plan for a somewhat awkward grasp posture and a low terminal force at contact, to avoid sliding the base of the object.

Experiment 2 tested the hypothesis that the consideration of object properties such as texture and weight, which would primarily affect the forces required at lifting, was given a low priority in the context of the multiple pre-lift constraints on performance. The experiment paralleled Experiment 1, but it differed in that the overall task constraints were relaxed: Subjects self-controlled the movement speed, they adopted a more natural, front-to-back grasp, and they were allowed to move the base of the dowel within the frame of the platform. These relaxed constraints may open up the window for subjects to consider action and object properties in the initiation period, anticipating post-contact forces and movement complexity. In support of this prediction, a pilot study with the heavy dowel, in which subjects were told to move at a comfortable rate, showed a significant (61 ms) effect of texture on initiation time, with more rapid initiation for the uncoated dowel.

Method

This experiment was identical to Experiment 1, except that the constraints of reach, grasp, and contact force were relaxed: Subjects were instructed to reach comfortably and naturally rather than as quickly as possible, they were asked to grasp the dowel in a more natural three-finger posture—front-to-back rather than side-to-side, without restriction as to which phalanges contacted the object, and the base of the dowel was allowed to make contact with the inner edges of the platform. Thirty-eight right-handed subjects from the same pool as before participated, twenty-four in a light-dowel group and fourteen in a heavy-dowel group. Four others were excluded by the accuracy constraints described above, and ten others in the heavy condition were excluded because they could not maintain a three-finger grasp, even with the more natural posture allowed; presumably even this posture did not uniformly generate sufficient grip force to counteract the load of the heavy dowel. Again, this could have skewed the pool toward stronger subjects in the heavy condition, but robust weight effects in Experiment 1 indicate this is not critical.

Results

To summarize the findings, the effect of texture now was apparent in both initiation time and movement time. Weight did not affect either temporal measure, but heavier objects produced substantially greater errors.

Initiation time.   The effect of action was again significant, $F(2, 2) = 6.02$, $p = .0038$. The grasping time was greater than lifting and posting, which did not differ significantly. More importantly, the effect of texture was now significant, $F(1, 36) = 5.39, p = .0260$, with the coated dowel leading to slower responses by an average of 24 ms. The texture by action interaction did not approach significance ($F < 1$). The main effect of weight and the interaction between texture and weight did not approach significance, $p > .90$ and $p > .50$, respectively. The effect of weight was only 1 ms in the uncoated-dowel condition and a non-significant -11 ms (faster initiation for the heavy object) in the coated condition.

Movement time.   The effect of action was only marginal ($.10 > p > .05$), although the trend was again for the posting action to be relatively fast. The effect of texture was significant, $F(1, 36) = 18.55$, $p = .0001$. Somewhat surprisingly, no main effect of weight or interactions involving weight approached significance (all $ps > .25$). Indeed, in direct contrast to Experiment 1, the trend was for the difference between coated and uncoated dowels to be greater for the light dowels (65 ms vs 38 ms), and the heavier dowels led to shorter movement times (by 74 ms overall). However, the error pattern suggests that the failure to take weight into account while reaching led to errors.

Errors.   As before, the grasping action showed negligible errors. With the other actions, the heavy dowels led to both more base moves and grasp slips, and the combination of heavy weight and a slippery coating particularly increased errors—grasp slips rarely occurred when the dowels were uncoated or light. Note that base-move outcomes were not errors, strictly speaking, given the relaxation of the contact-force constraint.

Comparison of Experiments 1 and 2.   The two experiments were compared in ANOVAs that added the factor of constraint level (Experiment 1: High; Experiment 2: Low) to those of texture, weight, and action. Here we consider only main effects and interactions involving the constraint factor.

The initiation time ANOVA showed a main effect of constraint, $F(1, 73) = 11.94, p = .0009$, reflecting the slower times in Experiment 2. There was also an Action × Weight × Constraint interaction, $F(2, 146) = 33.29$, $p = .0402$, which was unexpected given that neither experiment showed any effect involving weight. It appeared to reflect a slightly elevated initiation time in Experiment 2 for the grasp/heavy combination, whether or not the dowel was coated. It is unclear why the grasp should be singled out for slower initiation, since the object need not be lifted.

The movement time analysis again showed a main effect of constraint, $F(1, 73) = 25.30$, $p = .0001$, an Action × Weight × Constraint interaction, $F(2, 146) = 5.33, p = .0058$, and a Texture × Weight × Constraint interaction, $F(2, 146) = 5.09, p = .0270$. These interactions reflect the fact that Experiment

1 produced interactions between weight and action, and between weight and texture, whereas Experiment 2 did not.

The ANOVA on base move errors produced interactions between constraint and weight, $F(1, 73) = 15.98$, $p = .0002$; constraint and texture, $F(1, 73) = 6.14$, $p = .0156$; and Constraint × Action × Weight, $F(2, 146) = 6.53$, $p = .0019$. The rate of base moves in Experiment 2 was not systematically higher than in Experiment 1, but the pattern differed: There was a drop in base moves with the light, coated dowel, particularly with the lifting and posting actions, but there was an increase in errors with the heavy, coated dowel. The ANOVA on grasp slip errors produced interactions between constraint and weight, $F(1, 73) = 4.27$, $p = .0424$, and Constraint × Weight × Texture, $F(1, 73) = 4.35$, $p = .0405$. Grasp slips with the light, coated dowel appear to have been reduced by replacing the side-to-side grasp of Experiment 1 with a more natural grasp configuration; on the other hand, errors with the coated, heavy dowel increased somewhat.

Discussion

With the greater tolerance for reaching speed, grasping, and contact force in Experiment 2, initiation time reflected the demands on load force imposed by slipperiness. This is in contrast to the null effect of Experiment 1. However, Experiments 1 and 2 agreed with respect to the null effect of weight on initiation time. In another departure from Experiment 1, the movement time in Experiment 2 was unaffected by weight. However, there was apparently a speed/accuracy tradeoff, since errors in the most difficult condition—lifting a coated, heavy dowel—increased. In the absence of a tradeoff, one would expect errors to *decrease* given a more relaxed speed constraint, as was found for the light, coated dowel.

The initial hypothesis for Experiment 2 was that more relaxed constraints might increase the set of variables incorporated into the forward model during the initiation time. Indeed, the finding that texture had an effect here, but not previously, confirms that hypothesis. It is then particularly interesting that weight still remained without a systematic effect (although there was an elevated initiation time for one condition with the heavy dowel). One possible explanation for the difference between texture and weight is that the latter is more perceptually salient. Our between-subject design, which gave subjects experience with only one weight, should have motivated them to consider it, because they could retain a memory trace of the previous trial and did not have to discern weight perceptually. Nonetheless, they largely did not. The null result agrees with others' findings that weight takes effect late in the course of manipulation (see introduction). Below, we consider a more general hypothesis, namely, that perceptual salience influences the stage at which variables are incorporated into the forward model.

EXPERIMENT 3

In Experiments 1 and 2, the actions were not ordered as predicted, in terms of motor complexity, with respect to initiation or movement time. However, the actions were performed in blocks of trials. Thus, after a few trials of practice, subjects may have no longer needed to consider action constraints on a trial-by-trial basis. Fikes et al. (1994) found stronger effects of texture on movement time in a randomized than in a blocked texture condition, supporting the idea that blocking reduces the effects of variables that enter the planning process. Hence, the main goal of this experiment was to investigate whether action-complexity effects would be observed in initiation and/or movement time if subjects were required to consider action parameters with the onset of each trial. Accordingly, action as well as texture was manipulated randomly rather than blocked.

An additional interest was in whether texture and action would interact in their temporal effects. The observed independence of these variables in the first two studies indicates separate planning processes.

Method

Twenty-two right-handed subjects from the same pool as before participated. Another five subjects were excluded from the analyses due to errors, and two were eliminated because they could not maintain a three-finger grasp. The stimuli and procedures were identical to the heavy-dowel condition of Experiment 2, with the exception that both the action and the texture were randomly varied from trial to trial, within the constraint of approximately equal Ns for each level of the variables. In order to vary the action from trial to trial, subjects had a training session prior to the start of the experiment, during which they learned a correspondence between a tone and each action. Subjects listened to a tape of three 500 ms tones (low 250 Hz, middle 650 Hz, and high 1050 Hz). The ascending sequence of tones was presented three times, while the experimenter indicated which action corresponded to each tone. Then the tones were presented four times in random order, and upon hearing each tone, the subject had to verbally indicate which action to perform while simultaneously mimicking that action. The experiment proceeded once the subject had learned the tone/action correspondence, which was counterbalanced across subjects.

The experimental procedure was identical to those of the previous experiments, except that one of the three tones sounded at the same time as the spectacles cleared. At that point, the subject had to decide which action needed to be performed and to assimilate the surface texture of the dowel.

Results and discusion

Experiment 3 is a parallel experiment to the heavy-dowel condition of Experiment 2. Accordingly, we report an ANOVA that treats the Experiment 3 (random) and Experiment 2 (blocked), heavy-dowel data as two levels of a new factor: Action expectancy. Note that ANOVAs on Experiment 3 alone revealed significant effects of action and texture on both initiation and movement time, and no interactions ($Fs < 1$). To summarize the results of the combined analyses, the blocked actions of Experiment 2 led to shorter initiation times than the randomized actions of Experiment 3, but yielded no overall advantage in movement time. Most importantly, the study replicated the finding that texture could affect pre-movement planning time, and the texture effect (32 ms overall) was not significantly altered by action expectancy. Texture also affected movement time, more so with randomized than blocked actions. Although action effects were obtained with respect to both initiation and movement times, the actions were again not ordered as predicted by movement complexity.

Initiation time.   There were main effects of action expectancy, $F(1, 34) = 22.05$, $p < .0001$, action, $F(2, 68) = 3.20$, $p = .0469$, and texture, $F(1, 34) = 5.82$, $p = .0213$. There was also an action by action-expectancy interaction, $F(2, 68) = 10.28$, $p < .0001$. No other effects approached significance.

The action-expectancy effect reflects the finding that subjects were 237 ms slower to initiate the movement when the action was not known beforehand. Moreover, the order of action initiation times was quite different between the two conditions. In the blocked condition, as described previously, the grasping action was significantly slower than lifting and posting, which did not differ, whereas in the random condition, the lifting action was slower than grasping and posting, which did not differ. The slowing of the lifting action indicates that in a randomized condition, some aspect of this action requires planning that is not present with the other actions. One possibility is that there is uncertainty from trial to trial as to what constitutes an adequate lift distance. Whereas the target movements in the grasping and place actions are fully constrained (i.e., requiring no movement and movement up to the slot, respectively), the lift can be to an arbitrary height. Possibly, the lift must be replanned from trial to trial when the action is random, and memory for immediately prior movement cannot be relied on.

Movement time.   The effects of action and action by action-expectancy interaction were marginal, $.10 > ps > .05$; as with the initiation time, the tendency was for the lifting action to be slowest in the randomized condition. There were significant effects of texture (81 ms overall), $F(1, 34) = 18.46$,

$p < .0001$, and a texture by expectancy interaction, $F(1, 34) = 4.21, p = .0479$. Subjects moved more slowly toward the coated dowel, significantly so at both levels of expectancy, but the difference was substantially greater when the action was random than when it was blocked.

Errors.   Again, only the lifting and posting actions produced base moves and grasp slips. The pattern was much like that observed with the heavy objects in Experiment 2: Grasp slips were found primarily with the coated objects, and base moves were far more common with the coated dowel than the uncoated. The Appendix shows the ANOVA combining Experiment 3 with the heavy-dowel group of Experiment 2; note that ANOVAS on Experiment 3 alone showed significant effects of texture, action, and the interaction, for both base-move and grasp-slip errors.

GENERAL DISCUSSION

The present studies provide a view of the temporal unfolding of a plan for visually guided action on an object, or in other words, they indicate the construction of a forward model. The studies do so by partitioning the response into pre-movement initiation time, movement time, and post-contact errors. In the introduction, we raised a number of questions in regard to the construction of the model. Addressing those questions in turn, we found: (1) With respect to planning for object attributes, texture, but not weight, was incorporated early into the forward model. Weight appeared to enter the planning process only under the most constrained conditions, and then it affected movement time rather than initiation time. (2) Parameters differentiating the action to be performed on the object were incorporated into the model at the earliest stage, and had less effect later, during the reach. The reverse was true for object parameters. (3) When the task was highly constrained with respect to speed, hand posture, and force, planning for object parameters was reduced, suggesting competition between accommodating general task constraints and planning for object contact. (4) Action complexity and object parameters had independent effects when both were present, suggesting that planning based on the object does not change according to the complexity of the act to be performed. (5) The object parameters were themselves prioritized rather than equated in planning; an effect of texture did not guarantee an effect of weight. (6) Error data indicated that action and object parameters, as well as task constraints, interacted during physical contact and action, and certain combinations of those variables led to substantial levels of error.

We draw these conclusions by examining the effects of the various manipulations on our three dependent measures. Consider first the effects on initiation time. The nature of the action that was demanded after contact—grasping, posting, or lifting—affected initiation time across all studies. However, the ordering among actions was not constant: When actions were blocked, the posting initiation was relatively fast, especially in relation to initiation for grasping, with lifting initiation more variable relative to the others. When actions were randomized, lifting became the slowest action to be initiated, possibly because it is the least constrained with respect to final position of the limbs. In a blocked sequence of lifting trials, subjects may have relied on memory for the previous terminal position to determine the current one, which would not be possible in the randomized condition.

Whereas initiation time was consistently affected by action, it was not invariably affected by object texture. Across the studies, and within each weight category, there was a tendency for the slipperiness of the object to affect initiation time more, the longer the baseline initiation time (i.e., the time for the uncoated object). This pattern is shown in Table 1, along with comparable data for movement time. The slowing of initation time reflected two different causes. Initiation time increased from Experiment 1 to Experiment 2 because the speed constraint was relaxed, whereas it increased from Experiment 2 to Experiment 3 because the action variable was randomized. Notwithstanding these variations in the causal manipulation, the increased allocation for pre-movement planning appears to have allowed the texture of the object to be incorporated into the plan. Moreover, the independence of the texture and action variables on initiation time suggests that the nature of the action that is to be performed does not alter the preparation for the object's surface and weight.

Finally, the task parameter of weight failed to show a systematic effect on initiation time in any experiment. This null effect, in contrast to that of texture, indicates that object attributes enter into the planning process differentially.

Next consider the effects of the experimental manipulations on movement time. The action effect on movement time was relatively strong in Experiment 1, but it weakened and became non-significant in Experiments 2 and 3, when the speed constraint was relaxed. In contrast, texture effects were found in all three experiments. Thus the relative importance of these two variables seems to

TABLE 1

Relation of texture effects (coated minus uncoated dowel) to the baseline initiation time (IT) and movement time (MT) with the uncoated dowel

Dowel	Uncoated IT (ms)	Texture effect IT (ms)	% increase IT	Uncoated MT (ms)	Texture effect MT (ms)	% increase MT
Light:						
Experiment 1	336	16	4.76%	505	33	6.53%
Experiment 2	455	28	6.15%	757	65	8.59%
Heavy:						
Experiment 1	390	3	0.77%	521	73	14.01%
Experiment 2	456	16	3.51%	697	38	5.45%
Experiment 3	680	42	6.18%	671	107	15.95%

have shifted between the initiation and movement periods, action being more consequential prior to movement, and texture being more important after the reach onset. When speed was not imposed as a constraint, subjects appeared to have given sufficient time to pre-planning the actions, that additional planning (at least, differential planning across the three actions) during the movement period was not needed. Those action effects that were obtained in movement time mimicked the trends in initiation time, suggesting that the differential planning demands were carried over to the movement phase, if planning was not completed beforehand. This was most likely in the speeded condition of Experiment 1.

It should also be noted that there is some ambiguity about the effects of action on movement time that were obtained. The pattern of base moves, described later, suggests that the actions of grasping, lifting, or posting may actually have led to differential reaching trajectories. In this case, action effects on movement time could be interpreted as arising during movement execution rather than planning. Kinematic data are needed to settle this issue, which we discuss in a more general context later.

Weight effects on movement time were found only with the most constrained condition: The coated object in Experiment 1, where there were task constraints of speed, side-to-side grasp, and low contact force. In this case, the heavy dowel slowed movement time relative to the light object, for those actions where the dowel had to be lifted. This contrasts with the findings of Weir, MacKenzie, Marteniuk, Cargoe, and Frazer (1991) that there were no weight effects in the free movement phase of reaching. However, that study used lighter dowels and did not have the present constraints. It appears that weight affects movement time only under particularly demanding conditions for action.

Finally, considering the error data, which refer to post-contact effects, there were strong and interactive effects of task and object properties. The general error pattern was to find few errors with the grasping action. With the other actions, grasp slips occurred only with coated objects, and far more when they were heavy. Base moves were found with coated objects in Experiment 1 regardless of weight, whereas in subsequent studies, the pattern was to find base moves with heavy objects, more so when they were coated.

It appears that when the base move was no longer treated as an error (i.e., Experiments 2 and 3), the subjects treated the reach, grasp, and lift more as a unit. They tolerated more contact force with the heavy object, moving it within the frame of the base as they grasped and lifted it. When the heavy object was also slippery, the push would last longer, and be more likely to move the dowel within the frame of the base, before it could be adequately grasped for lifting— as is indicated by the prevalence of grasp slips with coated, heavy dowels.

On the whole, these trends suggest that instructions to grasp, lift, or post are incorporated early into the forward model. Object texture is planned for during the reach, and prior to reach onset only if the action is unspeeded and initiation time is relatively slow. In contrast, the accommodation for weight is largely left to the post-contact phase of the action.

This temporal pattern of planning may reflect the point during action at which the planned-for variable takes effect. That is, planning for a parameter may tend to occur in temporal proximity to the point where the parameter directly affects motor output. The action variable may be assimilated earliest, texture next, and weight last, because the points in the action that they influence unfold in this order. Different actions, for example, lifting versus posting, require different post-contact trajectories. As was noted earlier, these different terminal acts may produce variations in the spatial position of the arm throughout reaching, especially when the action is unitized (i.e., the reach does not come to a stop before the grasp and lift). In contrast, manipulations that increase requirements for force precision—which is one effect of slipperi-ness—have been shown to slow the late acceleration phase of reaching. The principal effect of weight appears to be to alter the rate of grip force increase only once the object is grasped (Johansson & Westling, 1984). Thus the order in which a variable is incorporated into action appears to recapitulate the order in which it is incorporated into planning.

An alternative influence on the time course of planning is the perceptual salience of the variable that is planned for. In particular, in the present studies (and likely in general), texture was more salient than weight, and it appeared to enter the forward model earlier. Weight was manipulated between subjects in part to compensate for the difficulty of discriminating different levels. Subjects could then rely on memory for the experienced weight level; however, the retrieval of memory information about weight may be slower than the percep-tion of texture from obvious surface cues. It would be useful to conduct experiments in which the perceptual salience of a variable was specifically manipulated, in order to determine its influence on the time course of motor preparation. However, it is worth noting that the required action (grasp, post, or lift) took effect as early as initiation time, whether it was blocked—i.e., retrieved from memory—or randomized—signalled by an arbitrarily associated auditory cue. In neither case would the required action be signalled by a perceptually salient cue, which argues against the idea that perceptual salience is necessary in order for a variable to have an impact early in the preparation process.

In terms of the framework of Wolpert and Ghahramani (2000), the action constraints and object attributes that were manipulated here are enduring contextual variables that alter predictions of the forward dynamic model about the more continuously changing states of the system. They also should alter predictions of the forward sensory model about the sensory consequences of action, for example, the anticipated pressure on the skin from contact with a heavy vs light object or the visual and kinesthetic inputs resulting from pre-shaping the hand for the required grasp. Context alone does not govern movement; ongoing sensory feedback is used to revise the predictive models and adjust performance as the movement unfolds. Nonetheless, context plays a critical role in specifying the predicted states.

Our data indicate how pre-contact initiation and movement time, along with postcontact errors, respond to different levels of a contextual parameter. How are we to interpret these effects? An effect on initiation time can be attributed to the differential demands on planning for the different levels of a variable, for example, longer time to make predictions about a slippery object than an uncoated one. The possibility must be acknowledged that a parameter could be incorporated into the forward models during the initiation period, but fail to have an effect on initiation time, because planning time is constant across the different levels of the parameter. However, we attempted to minimize this possibility, by selecting the different levels of a parameter so that they differed widely in their demands on the eventual manipulatory act and hence should make very different predictions of states within a forward model.

An effect of parameter variation on movement time is more ambiguous, as was noted earlier when discussing the effects of the required action: It could reflect either planning time during the movement or consequences of planning for movement *per se*. For example, a slippery object should slow the movement time not solely because it is slower to plan for, but because its slipperiness means that lower terminal speed is required in order to reduce the force when the object is contacted. When the effect of a variable arises during movement but not initiation time, one can infer that it reflects planning during the movement interval, although alteration of reaching can play a role in the effect as well. When the effect of parameter variation arises exclusively in errors, as occurred for the weight variable in Experiment 2, it suggests that planning was deferred until manipulation itself—with negative consequences.

The present data show that not all contextual variables that ultimately affect a simple action are incorporated into planning prior to movement. They do indicate, however, that the early planning process considerably precedes object contact. The overlapping nature of effects across pre-movement and movement periods suggest that the model unfolds relatively continuously in time, with at least some parameters being incorporated well before motor imperatives assert themselves.

REFERENCES

Bootsma, R.J., & Van Wieringen, R.J. (1990). Timing an attacking forehand drive in table tennis. *Journal of Experimental Psychology: Human Perception and Performance, 16*, 21–29.

Fearing, R.S. (1986). Simplified grasping and manipulation with dextrous robot hands. *IEEE Journal of Robotics and Automation, 2*, 188–195.

Fikes, T.G., Klatzky, R.L., & Lederman, S.J. (1994). Effects of object texture on precontact movement time in human prehension. *Journal of Motor Behavior, 26*, 325–332.

Flanagan, J.R., & Wing, A.M. (1995). The stability of precision grip forces during cyclic arm movements with a hand-held load. *Experimental Brain Research, 105*, 455–464.

Johansson, R.S., & Westling, G. (1984). Roles of glabrous skin receptors and sensorimotor memory in automatic control of precision grip when lifting rougher or more slippery objects. *Experimental Brain Research, 56*, 550–564.

Johansson, R.S., & Westling, G. (1988). Programmed and triggered actions to rapid load changes during precision grip. *Experimental Brain Research, 71*, 72–86.

Klatzky, R.L., Fikes, T.G., & Pellegrino, J.W. (1995). Planning for hand shape and arm transport when reaching for objects. *Acta Psychologica, 88*, 209–232.

Marteniuk, R.G., MacKenzie, C.L., Jeannerod, M., Athenes, S., & Dugas, C. (1987). Constraints on human arm movement trajectories. *Canadian Journal of Psychology, 41*, 365–378.

Meegan, D.V., & Tipper, S.P. (1998). Reaching into cluttered visual environments: Spatial and temporal influences of distracting objects. *Quarterly Journal of Experimental Psychology, 51A*(2), 225–249.

Pratt, J., & Abrams, R.A. (1994). Action-centered inhibition: Effects of distractors on movement planning and execution. *Human Movement Science, 13*, 245–254.

Purdy, K.A., Lederman, S.J., & Klatzky, R.L. (1999). Manipulation with no or partial vision. *Journal of Experimental Psychology: Human Perception and Performance, 25*(3), 755–774.

Rosenbaum, D.A. (1980). Human movement initiation: Specification of arm, direction, and extent. *Journal of Experimental Psychology: General, 109*, 444–474.

Sidaway, B. (1991). Motor programming as a function of constraints on movement initiation. *Journal of Motor Behavior, 23*, 120–130.

Spijkers, W.A.C. (1987). Programming of direction and velocity of an aiming movement: The effect of probability and response specificity. *Acta Psychologica, 65*, 285–304.

Weir, P.L., MacKenzie, C.L., Marteniuk, R.G., & Cargoe, S.L. (1991). Is object texture a constraint on human prehension?: Kinematic evidence. *Journal of Motor Behavior, 23*, 205–210.

Weir, P.L., MacKenzie, C.L., Marteniuk, R.G., Cargoe, S.L., & Frazer, M.B. (1991). The effects of object weight on the kinematics of prehension. *Journal of Motor Behavior, 23*(3), 192–204.

Witney, A.G., Goodbody, S.J., & Wolpert, D.M. (1999). Predictive motor learning of temporal delays. *Journal of Neurophysiology, 82*, 2039–2048.

Witney, A.G., Goodbody, S.J., & Wolpert, D.M. (2000). Learning and decay of prediction in object manipulation. *Journal of Neurophysiology, 84*, 334–343.

Wolpert, D.M., & Ghahramani, Z. (2000). Computational principles of movement neuroscience. *Nature Neuroscience, 3*(Suppl.), 1212–1217.

APPENDIX
F TESTS FOR EFFECTS ON ERRORS WITH $p < .10$, BY EXPERIMENT

	Experiment 1	Experiment 2	Experiment 2 (heavy) vs 3
Base move effects			
action	$F(2, 74) = 20.97, p < .0001$	$F(2, 72) = 24.33, p < .0001$	$F(2, 68) = 40.45, p \leq .0001$
texture	$F(1, 74) = 29.16, p < .0001$	$F(1, 36) = 10.58, p = .0025$	$F(1, 34) = 30.31, p < .0001$
weight	n.s.	$F(1, 36) = 51.13, p < .0001$	—
action × texture	$F(2, 74) = 9.58, p = .0002$	$F(2, 72) = 3.10, p = .0509$	$F(2, 68) = 13.33, p < .0001$
action × weight	n.s.	$F(2, 72) = 19.97, p < .0001$	—
texture × weight	n.s.	$F(1, 36) = 4.61, p = .0001$	—
action × texture × weight	n.s.	n.s.	—
expectancy	—		$F(1, 34) = 6.57, p = .0150$
action × expectancy	—		$F(2, 68) = 6.12, p = .0036$
texture × expectancy	—		$F(1, 34) = 10.38, p = .0028$
action × text × expectancy	—		$F(2, 68) = 4.60, p = .0134$
Grasp slip effects			
action	$F(2, 74) = 19.39, p < .0001$	$F(2, 72) = 14.04, p < .0001$	$F(2, 68) = 20.24, p \leq .0001$
texture	$F(1, 37) = 79.06, p < .0001$	$F(1, 36) = 28.44, p < .0001$	$F(1, 34) = 31.72, p < .0001$
weight	$F(1, 37) = 4.78, p = .0352$	$F(1, 36) = 19.84, p < .0001$	—
action × texture	$F(2, 74) = 18.54, p < .0001$	$F(2, 72) = 12.83, p < .0001$	$F(2, 68) = 19.58, p < .0001$
action × weight	$F(2, 74) = 2.74, p = .0708$	$F(1, 36) = 10.11, p < .0001$	—
texture × weight	$F(1, 37) = 5.26, p = .0275$	$F(1, 36) = 21.60, p < .0001$	—
action × texture × weight	$F(2, 74) = 3.32, p = .0417$	$F(2, 72) = 10.94, p < .0001$	—
expectancy	—		n.s.
action × expectancy	—		n.s.
texture × expectancy	—		n.s.
action × text × expectancy	—		n.s.

VISUAL COGNITION, 2002, 9 (4/5), 528–539

Post-response stimulation and the Simon effect: Further evidence of action–effect integration

Marc Grosjean and J. Toby Mordkoff

Department of Psychology, The Pennsylvania State University,
University Park, PA, USA

The recently proposed action-concept view of perceptual-motor behaviour posits that a stimulus which consistently follows a certain response will become associated with that response. Some evidence in favour of this view comes from the finding that the size of the Simon effect can be altered by the inclusion of post-response stimuli. However, only one study has investigated the effects of including *same*-side in addition to *opposite*-side post-response stimuli, as well as a neutral Simon condition, and, possibly because of a failure of random assignment, the results from that study were inconclusive. In light of this limitation, a Simon experiment was performed in which the location of post-response stimulation was manipulated within subjects. The results showed that: (1) the Simon effect can both decrease and increase in the presence of post response stimuli, and (2) the amounts of Simon interference and Simon facilitation are both affected by post-response stimuli, whereas performance on neutral trials is not. These findings provide additional support for the action-concept view and suggest that further research concerning this new approach is warranted.

One of the clearest and most basic differences between the information-processing and ecological approaches to human performance concerns the assumed relationship between perceptual and motoric mechanisms (compare, e.g., Fitts, 1959, or Sternberg, 1969, with Gibson, 1979). According to information-processing accounts, perceptual processes comprise an

Please address all correspondence to M. Grosjean, Max Planck Institute for Psychological Research, Amalienstrasse 33, 80799 München, Germany.
Email: grosjean@mpipf-muenchen.mpg.de
We would like to thank Bernhard Hommel, Robert Ward, and an anonymous reviewer for valuable comments on an earlier draft of this manuscript, and Cara Trout for help with data collection.

© 2002 Psychology Press Ltd
http://www.tandf.co.uk/journals/pp/13506285.html   DOI:10.1080/13506280143000566

autonomous "front-end" system that is relatively unaffected by the assignment of specific stimuli to responses (see, e.g., Kornblum & Lee, 1995). In contrast, according to ecological accounts, perceptual processes are intimately related to motor processes, because people perceive stimuli in terms of the behaviours that they afford (see, e.g., Michaels, 1988). Despite this clear distinction— along with the myriad deeper implications for research and models—neither position may claim a majority of empirical support.

Instead, in the 1990s a new view emerged. This approach, which is known as the action-concept view (e.g., Hommel, 1996, 1997; Prinz, 1990) allows the predictable consequences of a response to become associated with the response itself. This idea would not usually be considered by information-processing theorists, because their models typically "end" at the time of the response. And although the two share some general features, the action-concept view is also very different from the ecological approach. According to Gibsonians, stimuli are perceived in terms of the responses that they afford; according to the action-concept view, responses are represented in terms of their likely consequences (which are—from the position of the actor—additional stimuli). If anything, the one set of previous ideas that overlaps most with the action-concept view are found in some cognitive models of operant conditioning (see, e.g., Rescorla, 1991).

Some of the best evidence for the action-concept view comes from experiments concerning the Simon effect (see Simon, 1990, for a review). In a Simon experiment, non-spatial stimulus features (e.g., red vs green or *H* vs *S*) are mapped onto spatial responses (e.g., left vs right). On critical trials, the reaction stimulus is presented in a task-irrelevant, non-central location that is either consistent or inconsistent with the response that is indicated by the task-relevant feature (for the motivation behind the use of the words *consistent* and *inconsistent*, instead of *compatible* and *incompatible*, see Kornblum & Lee, 1995). For example, if the colour red is assigned to the left-hand response and the colour green is assigned to the right-hand response, then a consistent trial might involve a red stimulus to the left of fixation, whereas an inconsistent trial might involve a red stimulus to the right of fixation. The Simon effect is the difference in mean response time (RT) between inconsistent and consistent trials. The typical advantage for consistent trials is about 30 ms, which is roughly 10% of mean RT.

Information-processing theorists explain the Simon effect in terms of automatic encoding of stimulus location (without reference to the possible responses), followed by automatic priming of whichever response most closely matches the stimulus (see, e.g., Kornblum & Lee, 1995). Gibsonians explain the Simon effect in terms of affordances, with (for example) left-hand responses being faster to left-side stimuli because the location of the stimulus affords this particular response. Note one crucial similarity between these two explanations: The advantage for consistent trials does not depend on the consequences of the available, alternative responses; rather, the advantage comes from some sort of similarity or directly-perceived link between some aspect of the stimulus and one of the possible responses.

In contrast, the more recent, action-concept view (see, e.g., Hommel, 1996, 1997; Prinz, 1990) explains at least part of the Simon effect in terms of an association between using a particular hand to make a response and *subsequent* stimulation on the same side of the body. For example, when a person presses the left-hand button in a Simon experiment, there is often an audible click on the left side of the mid-line, as well as tactile feedback from the left hand. These particular events—which are stimuli, although post-response and task-irrelevant—are perfectly correlated with left-hand responses and, therefore, might become integrated into the cognitive representation of a left-hand response. Once this association has been established, these new attributes of the response may serve as additional pathways or mechanisms of response priming.

One source of evidence in favour of the action-concept view comes from experiments that have broken the (typical) perfect correlation between responding with a particular hand and subsequent stimulation on the same side of the mid-line (Hommel, 1993, 1996). In the most relevant case (Hommel, 1996, Exp. 1), this was done by including (for half of the blocks) task-irrelevant, post-response events that occurred on the opposite side as the button that was pressed; in all other ways, the study was a typical Simon experiment. According to the action-concept view, these post-response events will become integrated into the cognitive representation of each response. Thus, each response will now be represented with a conflicting set of spatial features: Those that are related to the ipsilateral events that typically follow a lateralized response, and those that are related to the experimentally-induced contralateral post-response events. This, in turn, will cause any lateralized stimulus to prime both left and right responses (instead of one or the other), thereby reducing the size of the Simon effect. Consistent with this view, the advantage of consistent trials over inconsistent trials was reduced (from 28 to 18 ms) when post-response events reliably occurred on the opposite side as the response that was made as opposed to the situation where post-response events were absent.

These data are important for several reasons. First, at a basic level, they suggest that post-response events may become associated with the behaviours that evoke them. Going further, the cognitive representations of the post-response stimuli may become integrated with the representations of the responses, themselves. This is an important new development in models of human cognition and performance. Second, at the level of methodology, these findings imply that researchers need to be careful when designing the trial-by-trial feedback that will be provided during experiments, because these post-response events might quickly come to have unwanted effects on performance. As a concrete example: Experimenters would be advised to make sure that all visual feedback occurs at a central location (preferably fixation), in order to avoid introducing a correlation between certain responses and certain locations. Finally, at an applied level, these data suggest that there might be simple ways to reduce the amount of interference that is often observed in real-world tasks that resemble the well-known experiments on stimulus–response compatibility (see, e.g., Alluisi & Warm, 1990).

PURPOSE OF THE PRESENT STUDY

There are several aspects of the published experiments, however, that suggest that further study of the effects of post-response stimuli is required. In particular, as far as we know, there has only been one study that has investigated the effects of including *same*-side post-response stimuli in addition to *opposite*-side post-response stimuli, as well as a neutral Simon condition (Hommel, 1993, Exp. 1). Before turning to the results of this experiment, however, let us first consider why the addition of such conditions is relevant. First, the inclusion of same-side post-response stimuli is important because the action-concept view predicts that they would act to increase the size of the Simon effect. Indeed, the integration of additional ipsilateral post-response events into the representation of each response will provide redundant pathways for response priming to occur, thereby increasing the advantage of consistent trials over inconsistent trials. If such an increase were actually found, then the value of the action-concept view would be greatly enhanced.

Second, with regard to the hypothesis that associations between post-response stimuli and responses develop automatically (Hommel, 1996), the inclusion of a neutral Simon condition is also very important. More detailed information can be extracted from a Simon experiment when a neutral condition is included (i.e., a condition where the stimulus appears equidistant from each of the alternative responses—usually at fixation) because the Simon effect may now be parsed into *Simon interference* and *Simon facilitation*. Simon interference is defined as the difference in mean RT between inconsistent and neutral trials, whereas Simon facilitation is defined as the difference between neutral and consistent trials. If the automatic-integration hypothesis is correct, then the amounts of Simon interference and Simon facilitation should be affected in parallel ways. In particular, both components should be reduced when opposite-side stimuli are included and both should be enlarged when same-side stimuli are included.

Finally, the inclusion of a neutral Simon condition is important with respect to an additional hypothesis of the action-concept view (Hommel, 1997): The integration of features associated with post-response events into the representation of a response should only have an affect on performance when the reaction stimulus shares at least one of those features. Thus, because in the neutral condition the stimulus appears at fixation, no location-based links with either response should be activated and, consequently, no response priming should occur. This leads to the prediction that the inclusion of lateralized post-response stimuli should have no effect on performance in the neutral condition. The alternative—that the inclusion of post-response stimuli has some unspecified, general effect on processing that indirectly alters the size of the Simon effect—needs to be ruled out. An example of an indirect model is one where post-response stimuli alter overall mean RT (regardless of consistency); because Simon effects are known to "fade with time" (e.g., see De Jong, Liang, & Lauber, 1994; Hommel, 1994), the changes in overall mean RT would lead to changes in the Simon effect.

Let us now turn to the results of the only published experiment that has included these critical conditions (Hommel, 1993, Exp. 1). The data are shown in Figure 1, where mean RT is plotted as a function of post-response stimulus condition (opposite side, same side) and Simon condition (consistent, neutral,

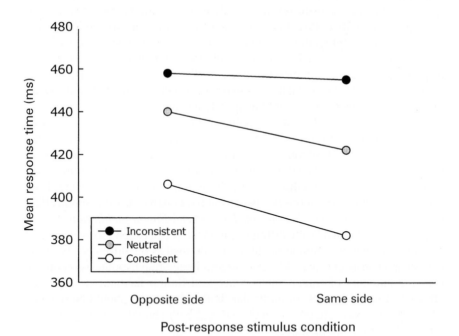

Figure 1.   Mean response time as a function of post-response stimulus condition (opposite side, same side) and Simon condition (consistent, neutral, inconsistent). From Hommel (1993). Inverting the Simon effect by intention: Determinants of direction and extent of effects of irrelevant spatial information. *Psychological Research, 55,* 270–279. Copyright © 1993 by Springer-Verlag. Adapted with permission.

inconsistent). As can be seen, people were faster overall at emitting responses under the same-side than under the opposite-side condition. Moreover, the magnitudes of the Simon effect, Simon interference, and Simon facilitation were all larger when post-response stimuli occurred on the same side than when they occurred on the opposite side as the location of the button press.[1]

Although these data provide an important first step in addressing the previously mentioned issues, there are a number of factors that render the interpretation of Hommel's (1993) results difficult. First, the Simon condition × Post-response stimulus condition interaction did not reach significance. Thus, there is, as yet, no statistical evidence in favour of the idea that the Simon effect can be increased in the presence of same-side post-response stimuli. Second, Hommel employed a between-subjects design, such that his participants only experienced one of the post-response stimulus conditions. This allows for the possibility that the overall difference observed in mean RT between the two post-response stimulus conditions was caused by a failure of random assignment. If this were the case, then one could account for the larger Simon effect in the same-side as opposed to the opposite-side condition by reasoning that the irrelevant spatial code had less time to "fade" over the course of the trial, and was, thus, able to cause more interference/facilitation (e.g., see De Jong et al., 1994; Hommel, 1994). Finally, a failure of random assignment could also account for why mean RT on neutral trials differed between the two post-response stimulus conditions.

In light of these limitations, the purpose of this study was to better address the issues raised earlier, by replicating Hommel's (1993) experiment using a within-subjects design.

Method

In nearly all regards, the present study was typical of published Simon experiments. Participants were asked to make a rapid, two-alternative, forced-choice response to a visual stimulus while ignoring its spatial location. The only change from what is usual was the addition of task-irrelevant, post-response stimuli during two segments of the experimental session. These stimuli occurred either on the opposite side as the produced response or on the same side as the produced response. Between these two critical segments, the present study also included a control condition that did not include any post-response

---

[1]Participants in Hommel's (1993) Experiment 1 were either given instructions in terms of response-button locations (i.e., "press the button") or in terms of post-response stimulus locations (i.e., "produce the light"). Because the present study is only concerned with the former type of instruction, we have only considered the data he obtained under that instruction condition.

stimuli. This latter condition was added to parallel previous experimental designs (e.g., Hommel, 1996, Exp. 1). Because there were two different orders of conditions, all participants began their session in a "baseline" replication of the control condition. This segment provided practice making rapid, accurate responses to (arbitrary) visual stimuli, and also allowed us to conduct a test for successful random assignment.

Participants.   A total of 40 undergraduates (mean age 19.25 years, range 18–23 years) from the Pennsylvania State University participated in return of partial course credit. Twenty participants were assigned to each order group. None reported any uncorrected visual or auditory deficits, and were all unaware of the purpose of the study.

Apparatus.   The experiment was run in a dimly-lit and sound-attenuated booth. The presentation of stimuli and the recording of responses were controlled by an IBM-compatible microcomputer that allowed for millisecond timing resolution. The visual stimuli were presented on a SVGA monitor approximately 60 cm in front of the participant. The auditory (post-response) stimuli were presented using two loud-speakers approximately 90 cm from the participant at angles of 45° to each side. Responses were made by pressing one of two buttons (horizontally separated by about 9 cm) on a custom-made box. Approximately 100 cN of force was required for switch closure.

Procedure.   Each trial began with the presentation of a grey fixation cross (0.48° × 0.48°) on a black background at the centre of the screen. After 350 ms, fixation was removed and the screen remained blank for 150 ms. Finally, the reaction stimulus appeared and remained visible until the participant made a response or 1500 ms had elapsed. The reaction stimuli were the upper-case letters *H* and *S* (0.57° × 0.95°) presented in white on a black background. The reaction stimulus appeared either at fixation or 2.20° to one side of fixation. For half of the participants in each group, the letter *H* was mapped onto the left button and the letter *S* was mapped onto the right button; for the other half, the mapping was reversed. The left and right index fingers were used to press the left and right buttons, respectively. Trials for which the incorrect button was pressed or for which RT exceeded 1500 ms were counted as errors and were followed by written feedback on the computer monitor for 2 s that read "you pressed the wrong button" or "no response was detected," respectively. These trials were followed by a recovery trial (for rationale, see Rabbitt, 1966) and were repeated at a randomly chosen point later in the block.

Participants performed 16 blocks of about 40 pseudo-randomly ordered trials (2 letters × 3 locations × 6 repetitions + practice trials), divided into 4 segments of 4 blocks each. The first and third segments did not include post-response stimuli. For half of the participants, the second segment included same-side stimuli (i.e., the post-response stimuli occurred on the same side as the button that was pressed), whereas the fourth segment included opposite-side stimuli (i.e., the post-response stimuli occurred on the opposite side as the button that was pressed). For the other half of the participants, the second and fourth segments were reversed. The two orders of conditions will be referred to as BSNO (i.e., baseline, same-side, none, opposite-side) and BONS (i.e., baseline, opposite-side, none, same-side).

There was an enforced, 7-s break between adjacent blocks during which participants received summaries of their RTs and accuracies. There was a longer break (30 s minimum) between segments, during which the participants were told whether the following four blocks would contain "some noises and lights between trials". No other explicit instructions regarding the post-response stimuli were given. The entire session lasted about 50 min.

Post-response stimuli.   The post-response stimuli were both visual and auditory. Starting within 14 ms of the response, a small plus-sign (identical to the fixation cross) appeared 4.40° to one side of fixation. The location of the plus-sign depended on the post-response stimulus condition and which button had been pressed. Over the course of 250 ms, the plus-sign expanded from 0.19° × 0.19° to 0.67° × 0.67° of visual angle. Simultaneously, a rising tone (250–950 Hz; approximately 64 dB[A] measured at the participant's ear) was played from the speaker located on the same side as the expanding plus-sign.

Data analysis.   To reduce the possibility of carry-over effects, the first block of each segment was treated as "practice" and these data were not included in any of the reported analyses. The first five trials of all other blocks were "warm-up" and were also omitted, as were error and recovery trials. For the purposes of conducting statistical tests, the first segment (which never included any post-response stimuli) was only used to verify that the two groups of participants produced equal-sized Simon effects prior to the addition of post-response stimuli. (In several, unreported experiments with smaller numbers of participants, we observed a series of reliable failures of random assignment—i.e., significant differences between groups *prior to* any between-subjects manipulation.) The remaining three segments were used as the critical data. In a second preliminary analysis, the possibility of an order effect (or an interaction involving order) was tested. It was planned a priori to exclude order from the main analyses if no main effect nor any interaction involving order was significant. It was also planned to correct for violations of sphericity using the Huynh-Feldt ε and to define significance (after correction) using an α of .05 (to facilitate reading, the uncorrected degrees of freedom are provided).

Results

In the initial check for successful random assignment, the mean RT data from the first segment of the experiment were analysed as a function of order (BSNO, BONS) and Simon condition (consistent, neutral, inconsistent) in a mixed-factor analysis of variance (ANOVA). As expected (or, at least, as hoped), there was neither a main effect of order nor an interaction between order and Simon condition (both Fs < 1). There was, however, a large and significant main effect of Simon condition, $F(2, 76) = 34.41$, $MSe = 494.17$, $\varepsilon = 0.99$. The mean Simon effects were 45 ± 10 and 35 ± 5 ms for the BSNO and BONS groups, respectively.

In the second preliminary analysis, the mean RT data from the three main segments were analysed as a function of order, Simon condition, and post-response stimulus condition (opposite side, none, same side) in a mixed-factor ANOVA. There was no main effect of order, no interaction between order and Simon condition, no interaction between order and post-response stimulus condition (all Fs < 1), and no three-way interaction, $F(4, 152) = 1.58$, $MSe = 294.63$, $\varepsilon = 0.90$. Therefore, all subsequent analyses were collapsed across order.

The main analysis examined mean RT as a function of Simon condition and post-response stimulus condition (see Figure 2) in a repeated-measures ANOVA. As is typical, there was a large main effect of Simon condition, $F(2, 78) = 150.86$, $MSe = 309.28$, $\varepsilon = 0.82$. In contrast, the main effect of post-response stimulus condition was not significant, $F(2, 78) = 2.34$, $MSe = 1138.38$, $\varepsilon = 0.93$. However, the interaction between Simon condition and post-response stimulus condition was significant, $F(4, 156) = 5.72$, $MSe = 299.14$, $\varepsilon = 0.90$.

In a planned follow-up test, a repeated-measures ANOVA showed that mean RT in the neutral Simon condition did not vary as a function of post-response stimulus condition, $F(2, 78) = 2.36$, $MSe = 575.00$, $\varepsilon = 0.88$. In a separate test, the magnitudes of Simon interference and Simon facilitation were computed for each participant and then analysed as a function of component (Simon interference, Simon facilitation) and post-response stimulus condition in a repeated-measures ANOVA. This analysis revealed that the amount of Simon interference was larger than the amount of Simon facilitation, $F(1, 39) = 65.93$, $MSe = 405.15$, and that both changed as a function of post-response stimulus condition, $F(2, 78) = 13.59$, $MSe = 220.97$, $\varepsilon = 1.00$. Equally important, the interaction between component and post-response stimulus condition was not significant ($F < 1$), demonstrating that post-response stimuli altered the size of Simon interference and Simon facilitation by similar amounts. The apparent linear trends in the amounts of Simon interference and Simon facilitation (as a function of post-response stimulus condition; see Figure 2) were also significant, $F(1, 39) = 28.12$, $MSe = 202.64$.

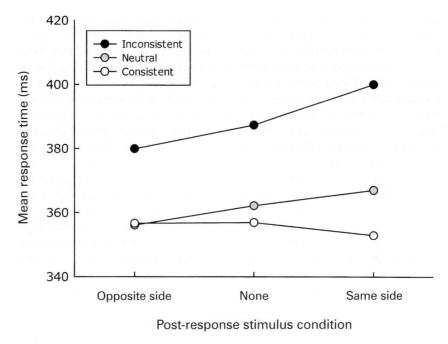

Figure 2.   Mean response time as a function of post-response stimulus condition (opposite side, none, same side) and Simon condition (consistent, neutral, inconsistent).

The participants were very accurate overall, making a mean of 2.37% errors. The pattern of mean error rates essentially paralleled that of mean RT. Collapsing across order, a repeated-measures ANOVA (performed on the arcsine-transformed error rates) yielded a significant main effect of Simon condition, $F(2, 78) = 21.58$, $MSe = 0.01$, $\varepsilon = 0.88$, no main effect of post-response stimulus condition, $F(2, 78) = 1.84$, $MSe = 0.01$, $\varepsilon = 1.00$, and no Simon condition × post-response stimulus condition interaction, $F(4, 156) = 1.18$, $MSe = 0.01$, $\varepsilon = 1.00$.

DISCUSSION

The present results make three empirical points. First, the size of the Simon effect can be altered by the addition of task-irrelevant, post-response stimuli. Replicating the findings of Hommel (1993, 1996), when these stimuli occur on the opposite side from the response, the Simon effect is reduced (from 30 ± 4 to 23 ± 3 ms) as compared to when no post-response stimuli are present. Extending this pattern, when these stimuli occur on the same side as the response, the Simon effect is enlarged (from 30 ± 4 to 47 ± 4 ms). Second, the influences of post-response stimuli on Simon interference and Simon facilitation are similar. This supports the idea that the post-response stimuli are being automatically integrated with their associated responses, such that they have similar effects on all conditions with non-centred stimuli. Third, neutral Simon trials are not affected by the inclusion of post-response stimuli. This supports the idea that the inclusion of post-response events only affects performance when the reaction stimulus shares at least one feature with them, as opposed to altering processing in some general manner (e.g., causing general slowing, such that the Simon effect was given a chance to "fade with time" in the opposite-side condition).

More generally, these findings make it clear that the reliable consequences of responses can be a source of compatibility effects. This is exactly what the action-concept view predicts. Therefore, much more attention should be devoted to this alternative to the traditional information-processing and ecological views. Furthermore, additional attempts to integrate concepts from operant and classical conditioning with modem models of human performance should be undertaken.

REFERENCES

Alluisi, E.A., & Warm, J.S. (1990). Things that go together: A review of stimulus–response compatibility and related effects. In R.W. Proctor & T.G. Reeve (Eds.), *Stimulus–response compatibility: An integrated perspective* (pp. 3–20). Amsterdam: North-Holland.

De Jong, R., Liang, C.-C., & Lauber, E. (1994). Conditional and unconditional automaticity: A dual-process model of effects of spatial stimulus–response correspondence. *Journal of Experimental Psychology: Human Perception and Performance, 20*, 731–750.

Fitts, P.M. (1959). *Human information handling in speeded tasks* (Report No. RC-109). Yorktown Heights, NY: IBM Research Center.

Gibson, J.J. (1979). *The ecological approach to visual perception.* Boston: Houghton Mifflin.

Hommel, B. (1993). Inverting the Simon effect by intention: Determinants of direction and extent of effects of irrelevant spatial information. *Psychological Research, 55*, 270–279.

Hommel, B. (1994). Effects of irrelevant spatial S–R compatibility depends on stimulus complexity. *Psychological Research, 56*, 179–184.

Hommel, B. (1996). The cognitive representation of action: Automatic integration of perceived action effects. *Psychological Research, 59*, 176–186.

Hommel, B. (1997). Toward an action-concept model of stimulus–response compatibility. In B. Hommel & W. Prinz (Eds.), *Theoretical issues in stimulus–response compatibility* (pp. 281–320). Amsterdam: North-Holland.

Kornblum, S., & Lee, J.-W. (1995). Stimulus–response compatibility with relevant and irrelevant stimulus dimensions that do and do not overlap with the response. *Journal of Experimental Psychology: Human Perception and Performance, 21*, 855–875.

Michaels, C.F. (1988). S–R compatibility between response position and destination of apparent motion: Evidence of the detection of affordances. *Journal of Experimental Psychology: Human Perception and Performance, 14*, 231–240.

Prinz, W. (1990). A common coding approach to perception and action. In O. Neumann & W. Prinz (Eds.), *Relationships between perception and action* (pp. 167–201). Berlin: Springer.

Rabbitt, P.M.A. (1966). Errors and error corrections in choice-response tasks. *Journal of Experimental Psychology*, *71*, 264–272.

Rescorla, R.A. (1991). Associative relations in instrumental conditioning: The eighteenth Bartlett memorial lecture. *Quarterly Journal of Experimental Psychology*, *43B*, 1–23.

Simon, J.R. (1990). The effects of an irrelevant directional cue on human information processing. In R.W. Proctor & T.G. Reeve (Eds.), *Stimulus–response compatibility: An integrated perspective* (pp. 31–86). Amsterdam: North-Holland.

Sternberg, S. (1969). The discovery of processing stages: Extensions of Donders' method. *Acta Psychologica*, *30*, 276–315.

VISUAL COGNITION, 2002, 9 (4/5), 540–558

S–R correspondence effects of irrelevant visual affordance: Time course and specificity of response activation

Julian C. Phillips and Robert Ward

University of Wales, Bangor, UK

It has been suggested that representations for action, elicited by an object's visual affordance, serve to potentiate motor components (such as a specific hand) to respond to the most afforded action. In three experiments, participants performed speeded left–right button press responses to an imperative target superimposed onto a prime image of an object suggesting a visual affordance oriented to left or right visual space. The time course of response activation was measured by varying the onset time between the prime and target. Long-lasting and gradually developing correspondence effects were found between the suggested affordance of the prime and the side of response, with little effect of response modality (hands uncrossed, hands crossed, or foot response). We conclude that visual affordances can evoke an abstract spatial response code, potentiating a wide variety of lateralized responses corresponding with the affordance.

Co-ordinated and effective behaviour requires that we perceive and assess the possibilities for action afforded by objects in the environment. Visual affordances of objects support or invite certain types of actions: In this sense, the appearance of a handle affords its grasping. Traditionally, the notion of affordances for action has been linked with the theory of "direct" perception offered by Gibson (1979). Gibson argued that affordances for action were based on intrinsic perceptual properties of objects, registered directly and without the need for intervening processes such as object recognition. Here we use the term "affordance" more broadly, de-coupled from a theory of direct perception. For our purposes, an affordance may best be described purely as a

---

Please address all correspondence to J. Phillips, Centre for Cognitive Neuroscience, University of Wales (Bangor), The Brigantia Building, Penrallt Road, Bangor, Gwynedd, LL57 2AS, UK. Email: j.phillips@bangor.ac.uk

---

© 2002 Psychology Press Ltd

http://www.tandf.co.uk/journals/pp/13506285.html   DOI:10.1080/13506280143000575

feature of an object with the power to elicit some form of mental representation for action within a perceiver.

Previous research has argued that visual affordances are closely linked to action. Studies of patients with anarchic or alien hand (Della Sala, Marchetti, & Spinnler, 1991), have shown that visual properties of objects sometimes evoke associated action or at least gestures (Riddoch, Edwards, Humphreys, West, & Heafield, 1998). One interpretation of utilization behaviour, in which patients with damage to frontal cortex appear unable to inhibit themselves from using objects placed in front of them, is that the objects evoke involuntarily actions that the patients are unable to inhibit.

Studies of stimulus–response (S–R) compatibility have traditionally been used to assess the linkage between systems for perception and those for rapid action. S–R compatibility studies demonstrate that actions compatible with the visual properties of a target object are executed faster and more reliably than incompatible actions (e.g., Craighero, Fadiga, Rizzolatti, & Umiltà, 1998). Compatibility can be defined over a wide range of object and response properties, even for stimulus properties that are irrelevant to current goals. In the Simon effect (Simon, 1969), compatibility is defined by the correspondence between the irrelevant spatial location of the stimulus and the (relevant) location of the response. This spatial correspondence between the location of the target and the responding hand produces very robust facilitation of performance (e.g., Hommel, 1995; Kornblum & Lee, 1995; Simon, 1969); for example, a target located on the left is responded to more quickly with the left than the right hand. Compatibility effects have been generally attributed to the overlap of codes generated by the target stimulus and by the associated response (Kornblum, Hasbroucq, & Osman, 1990; Wallace, 1971).

One way then to assess whether the visual affordances of a target elicit representation for action is to measure compatibility effects between the target and its afforded actions. That is, if objects do tend to elicit their afforded actions, then responses compatible with such affordances should be faster and more accurate than incompatible responses. For example, Michaels (1988) observed that spatial compatibility effects to a looming stimulus were based not on the physical location of the target, but on its apparent destination. For example, a target appearing to move from the far left to the near right would be responded to more quickly with the right hand than with the left. Michaels (1988) argued that these results were consistent with the notion that the looming stimulus preferentially afforded catching or interception by the hand nearest the apparent destination, and that this hand was therefore activated for response (but see Proctor, Van Zandt, Lu, & Weeks, 1993). Studies by Craighero et al. (1998) and Craighero, Fadiga, Umiltà, and Rizzolatti (1996) show evidence to support the operation of what they refer to as a "visuo-motor priming effect" linking the "representation of an object's visual properties with the specific motor programs to act upon it" (Craighero, Fadiga, Rizzolatti, & Umiltà, 1998, 1999).

Of central importance here is an extremely interesting study by Tucker and Ellis (1998; see also Ellis & Tucker, 2000), looking at response activation initiated by specific affordances for action. Tucker and Ellis (1998) presented images of everyday graspable objects with handles (e.g., cups, screwdrivers, teapots). The objects themselves could appear either upright or upside-down, with the handles randomly oriented either to the left or right side of space. The question of interest was whether the affordance suggested by the picture of the handle potentiated any form of action. Participants had to key speeded left- or right-hand responses to indicate whether the target object was upright or upside-down. Tucker and Ellis found a significant correspondence effect based on whether the affording handle appeared on the same side of space as the responding hand, e.g., left responses were faster when the handle appeared on the left side of space. Tucker and Ellis interpreted this effect as lending support for the idea that "certain action related information, in this case, *the hand most suited to grasp the object*, is represented automatically when the object is viewed in peripersonal space" (p. 836; our italics). Such a conclusion promotes an account of *action specificity* from visual affordances: That is, the visual affordances of an object potentiate the specific motor acts that are best suited for manipulating and interacting with the target object.

The findings of Tucker and Ellis (1998) carry interesting and important implications. Do object affordances automatically activate codes for response, even when they are irrelevant? If so, how long do these codes last? And can we define more precisely the nature of the activated response? In this paper, we further explore these issues. First, we develop a methodology that lets us look at the time course of any compatibility effect that may be attributed to object affordance. Second, recall that in the studies of Tucker and Ellis the task was to determine the orientation (upright or upside-down) of the "affording" object. That is, the affording object was always relevant for response. Here we examine whether these same object affordances evoke action even when the objects themselves are irrelevant to current goals. Finally, in Experiments 2 and 3, we examine in more detail at the issue of action specificity from visual affordances. Do the visual affordances of an object potentiate a specific response code for the hand or limb most suited to respond to the affordance; or do they activate more abstract spatial codes, which may potentiate a wide variety of responses to the afforded side of space?

EXPERIMENT 1
Correspondence effects from visual affordance

In our first experiment, we attempt to replicate the compatibility effects found by Tucker and Ellis (1998) using a method that separates presentation of an object affordance from presentation of an imperative target. In this experiment, we present an image of a familiar graspable object as a prime display. This prime has a handle oriented towards the left or right, but is irrelevant for the task. After a variable stimulus onset asynchrony (SOA), the prime is followed by an imperative target requiring a left or right hand keypress. We measure reaction time (RT) to the target as a function of correspondence between the target response side and the orientation of the prime handle, and as a function of stimulus-onset asynchrony (SOA) between prime and target. This method allows us to measure the time course of response activation generated by the irrelevant prime.

Method

Participants.   Eight undergraduate students took part in this experiment; all were registered as major psychology students at the University of Wales, Bangor, UK. All were right handed (self-report), and had normal or corrected to normal vision. Participants were naive to the purpose of the study. Each received one course credit for participation.

Apparatus and stimuli.   On each trial there appeared an image of a "prime" object and a small visual target, symbolising either left "I–IIII" or right "IIII–I" response (counterbalanced across participants). The set of possible primes consisted of four images of a frying pan, each image showing a particular orientation of the handle (Figure 1): The handle could appear either oriented to the left or right, at an apparent depth either towards or away from the viewer. The orientation and depth of the handle simulated an apparent affordance for grasping with either left or right hand. In addition, there was a fifth neutral prime display in which the handle was oriented along the midline. These images subtended 21.7° (horizontal) and 9.2° (vertical) of viewing angle and were presented centrally, in colour upon a white background.

The target appeared in the centre of the display, superimposed over the prime, and subtending a viewing angle of 2.9° (horizontal) and 1.1° (vertical). There were two alternative targets, which differed in their arrangements of horizontal and vertical lines (Figure 2). The mapping of the two targets to left and right response keys was counterbalanced between participants. Analyses showed no main effect of this mapping or interactions with correspondence, and all findings we report collapse over both mappings.

Prior to the prime and target displays, a central fixation display was presented until participants initiated the trial. The fixation display consisted of four vertical segments of the same width and size as those in the target, black on a light screen background. All images were presented on a standard Hi-Res 17-inch Applevision monitor connected to a Power PC 8500/120 Macintosh computer. The experiment was run on PsyScope version 1.2.2 software (Cohen, MacWhinney, Flatt, & Provost, 1993).

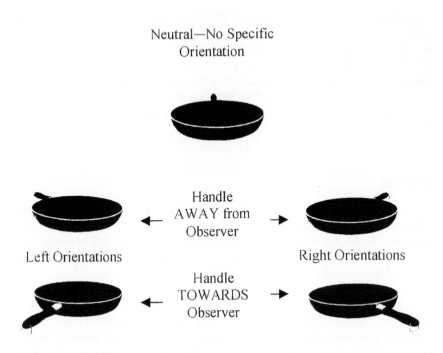

Figure 1. Examples of the five priming images in Experiment 1, showing left and right orientations of handle. These left/right orientations were also either towards (bottom) or away (top) from the observer. The neutral position is at the top of figure. The same images were also used in Experiment 2. A right target would be corresponding with either of the right-oriented objects as would the left orientations with a left target. Courtesy of Michael J. Tarr (Brown University, Providence, RI).

Figure 2. Sequence of events for Experiments 1 and 2. Actual figure shows a corresponding trial for those participants where IIII–I denotes right key response. A case where the handle was pointing away from the participant but still to the right would also be classed as corresponding.

544

Design. The experiment comprised two blocks of 320 trials each in a within-subject four-factor design. The factors consisted of response (the response key indicated by the target; left or right); correspondence (the left/right orientation of the handle in the prime in the same or opposite direction to the target response; either corresponding or non-corresponding); depth (apparent orientation of the handle in the depth plane; either towards or away from the viewer); and SOA between the prime and target presentations (0, 400, 800, or 1200 ms). Within each block we added 80 neutral prime trials, whose presentation was systematically varied by SOA and target response (but not correspondence or depth).

Procedure. Participants were positioned sitting down and facing the computer monitor at a face to screen distance of approximately 50 cm. The keyboard was placed in front of the monitor and participants were asked to place the index fingers of left and right hands over the respective response key while resting arms on the desk that supported the monitor. Left responses were to be made by depressing key "z" with a left-hand finger; and right responses by depressing key "m" with the right-hand finger. Instructions to participants were to fixate on the central fixation marker until it was replaced by a target indicating left or right response; then to respond as quickly as possible by pressing the relevant key. Participants were told to ignore any other screen image and to focus at screen centre where fixation and target would appear.

An experimental trial began when the fixation marker was displayed at screen centre for 1500 ms. This marker would then be replaced by the prime image. The target, indicating either a left- or right-side response would then appear superimposed upon the prime image. The onset of the target would vary between 0, 400, 800, or 1200 ms after prime onset. The target and prime would remain visible until receipt of the speeded keyboard response. Feedback tones were given on incorrect trials. Participants received a short practice block of 30 trials before beginning the actual experiment.

Results and discussion

Response errors accounted for 2.5% of trials. Analysis of response errors showed significantly higher error rates for non-corresponding response mappings than corresponding, $F(1, 7) = 14.67, p < .006$, but there were no other main effects or interactions for error data. Mean reaction times (RTs) were computed for correct trials only. Reaction times greater than 1000 ms were excluded as timeouts as were RTs greater than three standard deviations from the subsequent grand mean. In addition, RTs of less than 200 ms were excluded as anticipations. These exclusions represented 1.9% of all trials.

The remaining RT data was submitted to a three-way repeated measures ANOVA examining correspondence, depth, and SOA; the resulting means are shown in Figure 3. Results from the ANOVA showed a significant main effect of Correspondence, such that corresponding trials were faster than non-corresponding, $F(1, 7) = 8.64$, $p < .022$. A highly significant main effect of SOA was also obtained, such that RTs at 0 ms SOA were slowest, as apparent in Figure 3; $F(3, 21) = 24.45$, $p < .001$. However, of most interest was a significant interaction between correspondence and SOA, $F(3, 21) = 4.53$, $p < .013$, such that the benefit for corresponding over non-corresponding trials increased with SOA. There was no significant main effect or interaction involving depth, that is, whether the handle was apparently towards or away from the observer, and no other significant interactions at an alpha level of .05.

The results (Figure 3) showed a significant benefit of corresponding over non-corresponding mappings between the handle orientation and the responding hand. In this sense, results from the present experiment replicate those found by Tucker and Ellis (1998), even though the prime object was totally irrelevant to the response task. It is tempting to suggest that our findings are consistent with the claims of Tucker and Ellis that objects can evoke specific responses related to their apparent affordances. However, there are several puzzling aspects to the present data that do not fit easily with this notion. First, the benefits of correspondence between the prime's handle and the

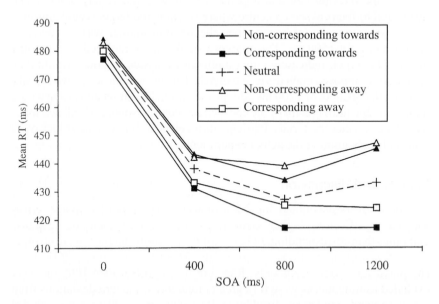

Figure 3.   Mean reaction times for all orientations of prime object in Experiment 1, showing facilitation for corresponding over non-corresponding mappings, grouped by SOA. Those handle orientations towards the observer (both corresponding and non-corresponding trials) are depicted with solid data points, whereas away orientations are shown as outlines only.

responding hand developed gradually over a period of 1200 ms. This pattern of response activation from the irrelevant prime affordance is quite different from irrelevant response activation found in the Simon and Stroop tasks. In Simon-type tasks, response activation from an irrelevant stimulus attribute decays after a much shorter interval of roughly 200, and perhaps around 400 ms in Stroop tasks (Hommel, 1994; Kornblum, Stevens, Whipple, & Requin, 1999). This is not to say that all automatic behaviours must show the same rapid time course; some automatic behaviours may develop only gradually. However, the idea of any adaptive (evolutionary) advantage from the perception of affordances on automatic response would seem to lie in the speed and immediacy of effect. Thus, the idea of a building over time periods of approximately 1 s might not comfortably fit the general idea of a functional automaticity, or "direct route" to action (Eimer, Hommel, & Prinz, 1995).

A second potential puzzle is that, if the compatibility effects here are due to action potentiation for the most afforded hand, then it seems reasonable to expect that the response activation would be strongest where the orientation was towards rather than away from the observer. That is, a handle which is apparently rotated towards the hand would offer greater ease of action than the same handle rotated away from the hand. We therefore might have expected a Depth × Correspondence interaction, such that towards primes would generate both greater benefits in Corresponding trials, and greater interference in non-corresponding trials than away primes. We consider effects of depth in more detail in the General Discussion, but for now we note that, in this experiment, there were no significant effects involving depth, and further, the general trend was simply that towards primes produced slightly faster responses than away, both for corresponding and non-corresponding trials (see Figure 3). We do not suggest that these considerations can be telling by themselves. But they do suggest that we consider and test alternative accounts of the response activation generated by the prime affordance.

One alternative interpretation of the results is that, rather than potentiating a specific motor response, the affordance may be generating some form of abstract spatial coding. This is arguably what happens in Simon tasks, for example. In these tasks it is clearly not the case that an object appearing on the left side of space simply activates the left hand for response. In Simon tasks, it has been found that the location of an object activates a constellation of spatial response codes, including multiple codings based upon the relative positions of other objects (Danziger, Kingstone, & Ward, 2001; Roswarski & Proctor, 1996), body-centred frames of reference (Hommel, 1993b), and codings based on the location of anticipated effects of the response (Hommel, 1993a). Although the time course we observe here suggests that our response activation is not directly analogous to Simon-type activation. it may be similarly abstract. For example, a handle oriented towards the left might evoke a generalized "left" code, facilitating all sorts of responses towards the left side of space. This alternative account to action specificity, that the affordance does not potentiate a specific activation of the hand most suited to response, but instead evokes a more abstract spatial-response code, was previously anticipated by Tucker and Ellis (1998).

In a second experiment to test the relative contributions of abstract coding and action specificity, Tucker & Ellis (1998) asked participants to respond to the target's upright or inverted orientation using two fingers of the same hand, rather than fingers of separate hands as in their first experiment. By an account of action specificity, any effect of action potentiation from the object handle would not differentially activate the fingers of a single hand; however, an abstract spatial code could produce such differential activation (as found, e.g., in variants of the Simon task using fingers of the same hand; Shulman and McConkie, 1973).

In this second experiment, Tucker and Ellis (1998) did not find compatibility effects; i.e., there was no significant interaction of object orientation and side of response. Tucker and Ellis interpreted the elimination of compatibility effects in this experiment as consistent with the idea that the position of the handle activated the ipsilateral hand and not any generalized response code. However, there are several reasons why the results of Tucker and Ellis' Experiment 2 are probably not conclusive.

First, it is a reported absence of abstract coding rather than a positive demonstration of effect. Second, interactions between responding hand and affordance orientation, although not significant, are present as trends that would be consistent with abstract coding: For leftward-oriented objects, left-finger presses were both faster and more accurate than right-finger presses. However, with rightward-oriented objects, the advantage for left-finger over right-finger responses was reduced in the RT measure, and reversed in the error measure. Finally, we have seen in our own results that compatibility effects from object affordances build over time. The prime and target form a single object and so appear simultaneously in Tucker and Ellis (1998); with longer exposure to the prime, larger correspondence effects may have emerged.

Our next experiment investigates further the possibility that response activation from the appearance of a graspable object produces abstract response coding not tied to a specific hand.

EXPERIMENT 2
Responses with crossed hands

The aim of Experiment 2 was to examine further whether the facilitation produced by Correspondence between the irrelevant prime's orientation and the responding hand, was due to action potentiation for a particular hand evoked by an affordance, as per an action specificity account. In Experiment 1, compatibility effects could be attributed either to correspondence between the prime handle and the responding hand, or simply between the prime handle and the side of the response. This difference is theoretically significant. Consider a pan with a handle oriented towards the right. For co-ordinated and effective manipulation of the pan, the handle should preferably be grasped with the right hand, regardless of which hand happens to be initially closer to the handle. If the affordance offered by the right-pointing handle produced an automatic response activation to facilitate functional interaction, this activation should be specific to the right hand. However, if the handle (affordance) produces a more generalized "right" response code, it might then activate the rightmost or closest hand, or any of a number of right spatial codes which would not necessarily promote interaction with the affordance.

In this experiment, we explore these alternatives by asking participants to respond to the target with their hands crossed. If the results of Experiment 1 were due to a specific hand being primed by the appearance of an affordance, then when hands are crossed, that priming effect should follow the hand most suited to dealing with the object in a useful and economical manner. The factor of correspondence is still defined with respect to the response side. As a result of crossing the hands, non-corresponding mappings are therefore responded to with the afforded hand, and corresponding mappings are responded to with the non-afforded hand, as depicted in Figure 4. Therefore, if the response

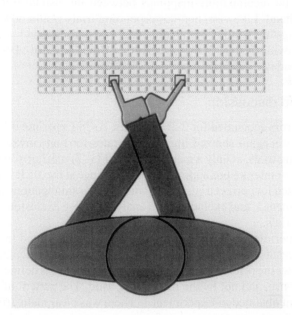

Figure 4.   Making the response in Experiment 2. Responses to stimuli were exactly as in the previous experiment. A left target is still responded to with a left effector button and vice versa. Correspondence of the trial has not been affected by crossing hands, although hand Correspondence has.

activation found in Experiment 1 is due to specific activation of the most appropriate hand, we should now see slower response latencies for corresponding than for non-corresponding trials.

Method

Participants.   A fresh sample of eight undergraduate students took part in this experiment; all were registered as major psychology students at the University of Wales, Bangor, and all received one course credit for their participation. All reported having normal or corrected to normal vision, were right handed, and naive to the purpose of the study.

Apparatus, stimuli, design, and procedure.   The method was identical to Experiment 1, with one exception. Participants now crossed their hands, so that left-key responses were made by depressing the left key with the right index finger, and right-key responses made by depressing the right key with the left index finger. Participants were free to choose whether their right hand crossed over the left, or left crossed over right. The design of this experiment (unlike Experiment 1) allowed that corresponding mappings between orientation of the handle (left or right), and response side (left or right, as indicated by the target), would now be incompatible mappings between the handle orientation and responding hand. Likewise, non-corresponding trials would now be compatible mappings of handle orientation and responding hand (crossed-hand effect), as previously used in Simon tasks (see Bradshaw et al., 1994; Nicoletti, Umiltà, & Ladavas, 1984).

Results and discussion

Response errors accounted for 2.2% of trials. As in Experiment 1, analysis of response errors again showed higher error rates for non-corresponding than corresponding trials, at only a marginal level, $F(1, 7) = 5.3, p < .054$. No other main effects or interactions approached significance at the .05 level. Mean RTs were computed for correct trials only. Timeouts and anticipations were defined as in Experiment 1, and excluded from analysis. These exclusions represented 4.5% of all trials.

As in Experiment 1, the resulting RT data were submitted to a three-way repeated measures ANOVA examining correspondence, depth, and SOA. Figure 5 shows the resulting means when correspondence is defined only by the side of response, and not by the responding hand. The pattern of data is very similar to that obtained in Experiment 1. There was clear main effect of correspondence, showing faster response for corresponding compared to non-corresponding trials, $F(1, 7) = 125.06, p < .001$. A main effect of SOA was also obtained, such that latency was longest at the 0 ms SOA, $F(3, 21) = 10.23$,

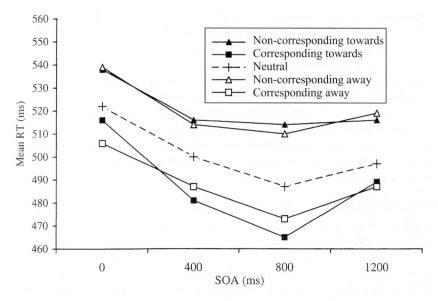

Figure 5.   Hands crossed in Experiment 2. Mean reaction times for all orientations of prime object, showing facilitation for corresponding over non-corresponding mappings, grouped by SOA. Those handle orientations towards the observer (both corresponding and non-corresponding trials) are depicted with solid data points, whereas away orientations are shown as outlines only.

$p < .001$. Again, there was a significant interaction between correspondence and SOA, $F(3, 21) = 3.20$, $p < .044$, so that the benefit for corresponding over non-corresponding trials developed gradually, in this case peaking at an SOA of 800 ms. Despite the crossing of hands, these effects replicate all the significant outcomes found in Experiment 1. The results show clearly that an affordance does not necessarily potentiate responses of the ipsilateral hand.

There were no other main effects or interactions significant at an alpha level of .05. Although the Correspondence × SOA × Depth interaction did not quite reach significance, $F(3, 21) = 2.87$, $p < .060$, the trend was that handles oriented towards the observer produced slightly larger compatibility effects than those pointing away, especially at 800 ms SOA (see Figure 5). Again, we defer detailed consideration of depth effects to the General Discussion.

Other than the position of the hands, Experiments 1 and 2 used identical stimuli and procedures. We have already seen that main effects and interactions that were significant in Experiment 1 were significant in Experiment 2, and vice versa. However, we made a more detailed comparison of results between experiments in a four-factor, between-subjects ANOVA examining Hands (crossed or uncrossed) × Correspondence × Depth × SOA. As expected, effects that were significant in the separate analyses of Experiments 1 and 2 were also significant in this combined analysis: Main effects of correspondence, $F(1, 14)$ = 68.76, $p < .001$, and SOA were found, $F(3, 42) = 33.07$, $p < .001$, as well as a significant interaction of correspondence and SOA, $F(3, 42)$ 4.62, $p < .007$.

There were two other significant interactions, both involving hands. First, the effect of correspondence was larger for crossed than for uncrossed hands, as illustrated in Figure 6 and indicated by the significant interaction of correspondence and hands, $F(1, 14) = 10.60$, $p < .006$. This effect may be best understood in light of a second interaction involving hands. The greater effect of correspondence in the crossed condition was not equivalent across all SOAs, as indicated by the three-way interaction of Hands × Correspondence × SOA, $F(3, 42)$ = 3.22, $p = .032$. Post hoc independent t-tests showed significantly larger effects of correspondence for crossed relative to uncrossed conditions for SOAs of 0, 400, and 800, $t(14) > 2.7$, $p < 017$, but not for SOA 1200, $t(14) = 1.27$, $p = .223$. Most obviously this is seen at the SOA of 0 ms, where there is a significant correspondence effect for crossed hands, $t(7) = 4.56$, $p < .003$, but not uncrossed, $t(7) = 1.09$, $p = .309$. We suggest that the difference in correspondence effects at the SOA of 0 ms may reflect the overall slower RTs in Experiment 2. In both experiments, we have seen that longer delays between presentation of the prime and response tend to produce larger correspondence effects. The slower RTs in Experiment 2 may have allowed more

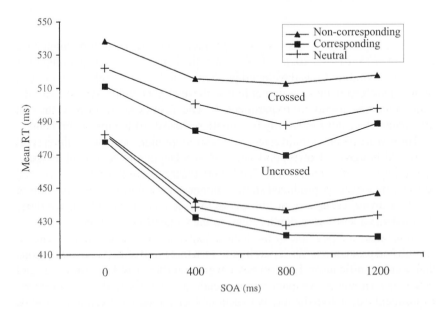

Figure 6. Comparison of mean reaction times for Experiments 1 and 2 showing the generally slower RTs for crossed vs uncrossed hands, and over all factors of correspondence and SOA.

time for the influence of the prime, and therefore produced larger effects of correspondence. If correct, this suggestion may also account for the larger overall correspondence effect found in Experiment 2 compared to Experiment 1. However, at present the influence of slower RTs on correspondence effects is only a tentative suggestion, and in any case these outcomes do not affect our main conclusions. Beyond the effects described here, the between-experiment analysis showed no other significant effects at an alpha level of .05.

The results from this experiment show clearly that a leftward pointing handle does not necessarily activate responses of the left hand. As in other response compatibility paradigms (e.g., Bradshaw et al., 1994; Nicoletti et al., 1983), what seems to be more important is the correspondence between elements of the stimulus set and the actual response location. These results are consistent with the idea of a visual affordance evoking an abstract response code facilitating all kinds of lateralized action, as opposed to potentiating a specific motor response for interacting with the affordance. However, an alternative account of action specificity is possible. We have suggested that, regardless of starting position, the left hand is best suited for grasping a leftward pointing handle. Instead, it could be the case that any affordance effect may be more "location" based, that is to say, the hand situated closest to the object's handle may be the hand most or best afforded the action. The next experiment further examines the distinction between action specificity and abstract response coding accounts of visual affordances.

EXPERIMENT 3
Foot-press responses

In an effort to disambiguate the action specificity account from an abstract coding account, a third experiment was devised. The basic idea was to replicate the results of Experiment 1 with an important alteration in method of response. According to an account of abstract response coding, all sorts of lateralized responses should be affected by the correspondence between the stimulus (in this case, the affordance suggested by the prime) and the response effector. In this experiment, participants no longer responded by pressing keys with their left or right hands, but instead, by pressing switches with their left or right feet. According to an abstract coding account, the form of response is largely immaterial, as long as correspondence between stimulus and response is maintained. If an abstract coding account is correct, we should therefore see similar effects of correspondence as in Experiments 1 and 2, despite the change of response modality. However, by an action specificity account, although the affordance suggested by the prime object might potentiate a specific response from the most proximal or otherwise most afforded hand, it would be unlikely to afford any specific action for a particular (or indeed any) foot. An action specificity account should therefore predict no effect of correspondence in this experiment.

Method

Participants.   A fresh sample of 13 undergraduate students took part in this experiment; all were right handed (self-report), and had normal or corrected to normal vision. Participants were naive to the purpose of the study. Each received two course credits for participation.

Apparatus and stimuli.   The apparatus and stimuli were identical to that used in the previous experiments, with the exception of the introduction of two response effectors in the form of foot switches (placed to left and right feet of participants). These micro-switches were connected and programmed through the PsyScope button box.

Procedure.   The procedure only differed from the previous experiments by way of response effector. Instead of responding to the target by depressing a left or right button with the left or right hand, participants now responded by pressing a left or right footswitch with the left or right foot, respectively. Participants held their hands in a natural position in their lap. All other aspects of the experiment were identical to those of Experiment 1.

Results and discussion

Response errors accounted for 2.7% of trials. As in the two previous experiments, analysis of response errors showed higher error rates for non-corresponding than corresponding responses, $F(1, 12) = 10.06, p = .008$. There were no other main effects or interactions for the error data.

Mean RTs were computed for correct trials and processed as in the two previous experiments. Timeouts and anticipations were excluded from the analysis. These exclusions represented 3.3% of all trials.

The resulting RT data were analysed using a three-way repeated measures ANOVA examining correspondence, depth, and SOA; the resulting means are shown in Figure 7. Results from the ANOVA showed a now familiar pattern, demonstrating a highly significant main effect of correspondence, such that corresponding trials were faster than non-corresponding, $F(1, 12) = 29.8, p < .001$; and a highly significant main effect of SOA, such that RTs at 0 ms SOA were slowest, $F(3, 36) = 24.4, p < .001$. Also in accordance with previous results was a significant interaction between correspondence and SOA, $F(3, 36) = 5.20, p < .005$, such that the benefit for corresponding over non-corresponding trials increased with SOA, in this case peaking at 800 ms. There were no other interactions significant at an alpha level of .05.

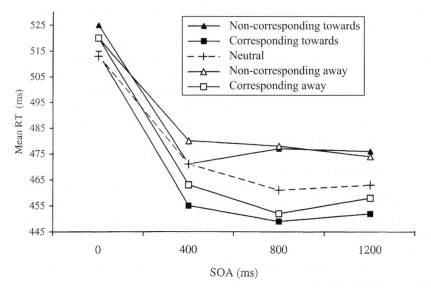

Figure 7.   Mean reaction times for all orientations of prime object in Experiment 3, showing facilitation for corresponding over non-corresponding mappings, grouped by SOA. Those handle orientations towards the observer (both corresponding and non-corresponding trials) are depicted with solid data points, whereas away orientations are shown as outlines only.

These results replicate our previous outcomes from Experiments 1 and 2, and argue that at least some form of the abstract coding account must be correct. They demonstrate that the effects of the prime affordance can be found even on responses unlikely to be specifically activated for manipulation of the affordance.

GENERAL DISCUSSION

We set out to investigate whether the action representation evoked by the presentation of a visual affordance, potentiates a specific motor response bias for the limb most suited to perform the afforded action; or whether it catalyses an interaction between more abstract representational codes generated by the overall S–R set. We investigated these issues by developing a method where the prime object and the orientation of its handle (i.e., the appearance of its affordance for grasping) were irrelevant to the participants' task. By separating the target display from the image of the affording prime, we could examine both whether the appearance of an irrelevant affordance could produce response activation, and the time course of that activation. Results from all three experiments show clearly that visual affordances of objects can potentiate action, even when these objects and affordances are irrelevant to current goals.

Our results also go some way to answering questions about the way that affordances might operate and how they might best be measured. The results of Experiment 1 showed that the orientation of the object's handle did produce correspondence benefits, as in the work of Tucker and Ellis (1998). In this experiment, the effects of correspondence could be attributed either to activation of (1) the "afforded hand", that is, the hand most suited for manipulation of the object depicted in the prime; (2) a more abstract spatial response code tied to the side of response; or (3) some combination of the two.

In Experiment 2, we attempted to separate these possibilities, by using the same procedure as in Experiment 1, but with participants responding with crossed hands. Benefits of correspondence were tied to the side of response, not to the afforded hand. Experiment 3 provided strong evidence that the presence of a visual affordance can activate an abstract response code which facilitates a range of responses corresponding with the affordance location. In this experiment, correspondence benefits from the affordances were found for lateralized foot-press responses.

Across the experiments then, we have found that the same prime affordance can produce correspondence effects for the ipsilateral hand (Experiment 1), the contralateral hand (when positioned to correspond with the affordance location as in Experiment 2), and the ipsilateral foot (Experiment 3). The pattern of results was equivalent in all three experiments, showing a gradually developing and long-lasting effect of correspondence with time. Evidently, the prime affordance in this experiment can potentiate a range of responses which correspond with its orientation, consistent with an account of abstract response coding. Clearly an affordance does not necessarily activate the specific motor commands best suited for manipulation of the affordance. Our analysis of the time course of the correspondence effects evoked by the prime affordance shows that they develop gradually, over about a second. For example, one account of our results, as well as those of Tucker and Ellis (1998), would be that perceptual segmentation results in the handle itself acting as a lateralized stimulus. If so, the handle in the prime image might produce response activation similar to that of lateralized objects in the Simon paradigm. However, we do not think this is a likely account for the correspondence effects we have observed. This time course clearly distinguishes the correspondence effects we observe from those found in the Simon effect (Hommel, 1994; Kornblum et al., 1999). The long-lasting and gradual development of correspondence effects in these experiments is in sharp contrast to the transient response activation found by lateralized stimuli in the Simon paradigm. In none of our three experiments did we find a significant effect of depth; that is, an effect of whether the affordance was presented as facing towards or away from the observer. Although our failure to find depth effects in Experiment 1 did spur us to investigate alternative accounts of action potentiation from affordances, with the luxury of hindsight, we cannot make too much of this null effect.

It could be that perceptually the difference between handles facing towards and away from the participant was too small to affect the strength of evoked action. Perhaps a stronger perceptual manipulation would have produced an influence of depth on the observed correspondence effects. However, it is consistent with both abstract coding and action specificity accounts that the strength of evoked action may be influenced by the salience of the affordance. The difference between the accounts is in the predicted specificity of response activation. The null effect of depth therefore does not affect our conclusions regarding the time-course or generality of responses evoked by affordances. A serious issue in examining action potentiation from real-life objects (or images of these objects) is that object affordances will often be confounded with other perceptual factors. For example, a handle oriented to one side of space not only offers an affordance to one hand or the other, but also creates a perceptual asymmetry in the object's appearance. In fact, many or most artefacts are designed in such a way in order to attract attention to their functional parts and thus offer clues to their interaction possibilities. Handles invariably stick out or are painted different colours or textures. Doorbells and buttons are designed to invite pressing with a finger, and many objects are designed to fit a grip or hand in a specific manner. This is evidence of good design, but from an experimental point of view, it makes the facilitatory or inhibitory elements of any S–R effect in ecologically valid experimental conditions difficult to pin down. Future studies with symmetrical objects that acquire affordances for action through training offer a way forward for future research; perhaps where different participants are trained to respond to the same object but in different ways.

REFERENCES

Bradshaw, J.L., Willmott, C.J., Umiltà, C., Phillips, J.G., Bradshaw, J.A., & Mattingley, J.B. (1994). Handemisphere spatial, compatibility, precueing, and stimulus-onset asynchrony. *Psychological Research, 56*(3), 170–178.

Cohen, J.D., MacWhinney, B., Flatt, M., & Provost, J. (1993). PsyScope: A new graphic interactive environment for designing psychology experiments. *Behavioural Research Methods, Instruments and Computers, 25*(2), 257–271.

Craighero, L., Fadiga, L., Rizzolatti, G., & Umiltà, C. (1998). Visuomotor priming. *Visual Cognition, 5,*109–125.

Craighero, L., Fadiga, L., Rizzolatti, G., & Umiltà, C. (1999). Action for perception: A motor-visual attentional effect. *Journal of Experimental Psychology: Human Perception and Performance, 25*(6), 1673–1692.

Craighero, L., Fadiga, L., Umiltà, C., & Rizzolatti, G. (1996). Evidence for a visuomotor priming effect. *NeuroReport, 8,* 347–349.

Danziger, S., Kingstone, A., & Ward, R. (2001). Environmentally defined frames of reference: Their sensitivity to spatial cues and attention, and their time course. *Journal of Experimental Psychology: Human Perception and Performance, 27,* 494–503.

Della Sala, S., Marchetti, C., & Spinnler, H. (1991). Right-sided anarchic (alien) hand: A longitudinal study. *Neuropsychologia, 29*(11), 1113–1127.

Eimer, M., Hommel, B., & Printz, W. (1995). S–R compatibility and response selection. *Acta Psychologica, 90*, 301–313

Ellis, R., & Tucker, M. (2000). Micro-affordance: The potentiation of components of action by seen objects. *British Journal of Psychology, 91*, 451–471.

Gibson, J.J. (1979). *The ecological approach to visual perception.* Boston: Houghton Mifflin.

Hommel, B. (1993a). Inverting the Simon effect by intention: Determinants of direction and extent of effects of irrelevant spatial information. *Psychological Research, 55*, 270-279.

Hommel, B. (1993b). The role of attention for the Simon effect. *Psychological Research, 56*,179–184.

Hommel, B. (1994). Spontaneous decay of response-code activation. *Psychological Research, 56*, 261–268.

Hommel, B. (1995). Stimulus-response compatibility and the Simon effect: Toward an empirical clarification. *Journal of Experimental Psychology: Human Perception and Performance, 21*, 764–775.

Kornblum, S., Hasbroucq, T., & Osman, A. (1990). Dimensional overlap: Cognitive basis for stimulus–response compatibility—a model and a taxonomy. *Psychological Review, 97*, 253–270.

Kornblum, S., & Lee, J. (1995). Stimulus–response compatibility with relevant and irrelevant stimulus dimensions that do and do not overlap with the response. *Journal of Experimental Psychology: Human Perception and Performance, 21*, 855–875.

Kornblum, S., Stevens, G.T., Whipple., A., & Requin, J. (1999). The effects of irrelevant stimuli: The time-course of stimulus–stimulus and stimulus–response consistency effects with Strooplike stimuli, Simon-like tasks, and their factorial combinations. *Journal of Experimental Psychology: Human Perception and Performance, 25*(3), 688–714.

Michaels, C.F. (1988). SRC between response position and destination of apparent motion: Evidence of the detection of affordances. *Journal of Experimental Psychology: Human Perception and Performance, 14*, 231–240.

Nicoletti, R., Umiltà, C., & Ladavas, E. (1984). Compatibility due to the coding of the relative position of the effectors. *Acta Psychologica, 57*(2), 133–143.

Proctor, R.W., Van Zandt, T., Lu, C.-H., & Weeks, D.J. (1993). Stimulus–response compatibility for moving stimuli: Perception of affordances or directional coding. *Journal of Experimental Psychology: Human Perception and Performance, 19*, 81–91.

Riddoch, M.J., Edwards, M.G., Humphreys, G.W., West, R., & Heafield, T. (1998). Visual affordances direct action: Neuropsychological evidence from manual interference. *Cognitive Neuropsychology, 15*, 645–683.

Roswarski, T.E., & Proctor, R.W. (1996). Multiple spatial codes and temporal overlap in choice-reaction tasks. *Psychological Research, 59*(3), 196–211.

Shulman, H.G., & McConkie, G.M. (1973). S–R compatibility, response discriminability, and response codes in choice reaction time. *Journal of Experimental Psychology, 98*, 375–378.

Simon, J.R. (1969). Reaction toward the source of stimulation. *Journal of Experimental Psychology, 81*, 174–176.

Tucker, M., & Ellis, R. (1998). On the relations between seen objects and components of potential actions. *Journal of Experimental Psychology: Human Perception and Performance, 24*, 830–846.

Wallace, R.J. (1971). S–R compatibility and the idea of a response code. *Journal of Experimental Psychology, 88*, 354–360.

VISUAL COGNITION, 2002, 9 (4/5), 559–590

Action matters: The role of action plans and object affordances in selection for action

Antonella Pavese

Moss Rehabilitation Research Institute, Philadelphia, PA, USA

Laurel J. Buxbaum

*Moss Rehabilitation Research Institute and Thomas Jefferson University,
Philadelphia, PA, USA*

In a series of three experiments requiring selection of real objects for action, we investigated whether characteristics of the planned action and/or the "affordances" of target and distractor objects affected interference caused by distractors. In all of the experiments, the target object was selected on the basis of colour and was presented alone or with a distractor object. We examined the effect of type of response (button press, grasping, or pointing), object affordances (compatibility with the acting hand, affordances for grasping or pointing), and target/distractor positions (left or right) on distractor interference (reaction time differences between trials with and without distractors). Different patterns of distractor interference were associated with different motor responses. In the button-press conditions of each experiment, distractor interference was largely determined by perceptual salience (e.g., proximity to initial visual fixation). In contrast, in tasks requiring action upon the objects in the array, distractors with handles caused greater interference than those without handles, irrespective of whether the intended action was pointing or grasping. Additionally, handled distractors were relatively more salient when their affordances for grasping were strong (handle direction compatible with the acting hand) than when affordances were weak. These data suggest that attentional highlighting of specific target and distractor features is a function of intended actions.

Please address all correspondence to L. Buxbaum, Moss Rehabilitation Research Institute, 1200 W. Tabor Rd., Philadelphia, PA 19141, USA. Email: Lbuxbaum@aehn2.einstein.edu

We are grateful to Myrna Schwartz and John Duncan for their contributions to experimental design and data interpretation. Perdita Permaul, Ivan Kautter, and Adrian Wilson are to be thanked for running subjects and assisting with data analysis. Supported by NIH grants R29 NS36387 and RO1 NS31824.

http://www.tandf.co.uk/journals/pp/13506285.html   DOI:10.1080/13506280143000584

Cognitive processes involved in selection of objects for action have been widely and successfully investigated in experimental psychology (Allport, 1987). For the most part, the strategy has been to limit the range of object features and action features that are experimentally manipulated and to use artificial (usually two-dimensional) environments that permit control over experimental variables and precise measurement of dependent variables (usually reaction times or errors). In many instances, as in studies of visual search processes, for example, this strategy is effective and appropriate in reducing computational complexity of the problem and permitting isolation of the variables that influence visual selection. In studies involving attentional selection for action, however, such experimental simplification necessarily depends upon specific assumptions about which factors are relevant for object and action selection and which are not. In turn, the choice of variables that are investigated influences experimental results and the theories based on these results.

An instructive example comes from the debate on stimulus–response (S–R) compatibility effects. The influential coding theory of S–R compatibility (Kornblum, Hasbroucq, & Osman, 1990; Proctor & Reeve, 1990) states that S–R compatibility effects arise from the consistency of stimulus and response codes. This approach proposes that both the stimulus and the response are represented as abstract mental codes and that the appropriate response is selected via a process of S–R translation of these codes (Proctor, Van Zandt, Lu, & Weeks, 1993). Therefore, specific and concrete parameters of action (such as the type and extent of movement required to access the target) are unimportant in the coding theory. In keeping with this view (and reinforcing it), S–R compatibility has traditionally been studied by using button-press responses to demonstrate compatibility between location of stimulus and location of response (Proctor & Reeve, 1990).

Ecological approaches, in contrast, hold that S–R compatibility phenomena reflect the extent to which available information can guide action. On this approach, a situation is "compatible" if the information inherent in an object or array is appropriate to the needs of the physical programming of a co-ordinated action (Michaels & Stins, 1997). Objects directly afford a number of possible actions as a joint function of object characteristics (e.g., shape, size, weight, texture, and location) and organism attributes (e.g., size and type of effectors, type of movements, motivation; Gibson, 1979). Because the influence of affordances emerges in tasks that require direct action upon objects in the array, the ecological perspective holds that such tasks are necessary if the relationships between objects, goals, and actions are to be well understood.

In the next section, we will discuss several recent results that suggest that the relationship between action parameters, affordances, and object features influences selection for action.

EFFECT OF AFFORDANCES AND ACTION PARAMETERS ON SELECTION

Three characteristics of traditional selective attention paradigms limit their relevance for the study of attention and action. First, the stimuli to be selected are frequently symbolic or simple visual elements, which do not have affordances for action. Second, participants locate or identify target objects presented in a visual display, but respond by performing an unrelated action directed to locations other than the targets. For example, they may select a red shape on the computer monitor, and respond by pressing a key on the computer keyboard. Third, the mapping of this action is arbitrary and does not correspond in any natural way to features present in the object. All three factors minimize the possibility of observing relationships between affordances and action parameters in selective attention tasks.

Recently, there has been increased interest in studying selection for action in more naturalistic contexts (e.g., Castiello, 1996). Under such circumstances, the influence of affordances may begin to emerge. For example, Tucker and Ellis (1998) showed that subjects' responses to the orientation of an object were influenced by task-irrelevant affordances of the object. Subjects viewed photographs of upright and inverted objects which had handles on the left or right. On one experimental trial, for example, subjects viewed a frying pan, oriented upside-down, whose handle was on the right of the photograph. Subjects responded by a button press with one hand if the photographed object was upright, and with the other hand if it was inverted. The task-irrelevant feature (handle direction) resulted in significant compatibility effects: Left-hand responses were faster when handles were on the left, and right-hand responses were faster when handles were on the right. In contrast, this effect was not observed when participants used left and right fingers of a single hand. This suggests that the photograph of the object activated the hand appropriate to object grasping. In this experiment, the response did not require reaching for the target object, and the mapping between target feature (object orientation) and response (left or right button press) was arbitrary. However, the use of photographs of complex, real objects (rather than, say, abstract shapes) revealed the presence of automatic activation of responses based on object affordances.

Similar conclusions emerged from an interesting study by Riddoch, Edwards, Humphreys, West, and Heafield (1998) that examined action on objects in a patient with impairment of hand control associated with corticobasal degeneration. In one experiment, the task requirement was to grasp cups presented on the left of the array with the left hand and cups presented on the right with the right hand. The position of the cup handle was the crucial variable. In half of the trials the position of the cup and the position of the handle were compatible (e.g., the cup was on the right, requiring a right-hand response, and the handle faced right), and in half of the trials they were incompatible (e.g., the cup was on the right and the handle faced left). The patient's performance was strongly influenced by handle compatibility. She responded with the correct hand on 98% of the trials in the compatible condition, but only 10% of the trials in the incompatible condition. The studies of Riddoch et al. (1998) and Tucker and Ellis (1998) provide converging evidence that the presence of a handle in the target object activates responses with the ipsilateral hand.

Compelling evidence for the importance of action parameters (e.g., type of manual response) in selection for action comes from experiments that require reaching and pointing to a target stimulus rather than pressing an unrelated key. A seminal series of studies by Tipper and colleagues (Meegan & Tipper, 1998, 1999; Tipper, Howard, & Jackson, 1997; Tipper, Lortie, & Baylis, 1992) revealed that distractor interference is influenced by the position of the distractor relative to the effector. Stimuli were pairs of LEDs of different colours, and participants were asked to reach to and touch the target stimulus (red LED), ignoring the distractor stimulus (yellow LED). They demonstrated four important effects. First, distractors close to the acting hand yielded more interference than distractors further from the acting hand, even when they were not on the reaching path (Meegan & Tipper, 1998; Tipper et al., 1992). Second, when distance was controlled, distractors on the same side of the array as the acting hand yielded more interference than distractors on the opposite side. Third, the trajectory of the reaching movement was influenced by the presence of distractors even when they did not represent a physical obstacle to the movement. Fourth, the interfering potential of a distractor depended on the relative ease of programming a movement toward that distractor as compared to the target. Interference from distractors that were covered by a transparent obstacle was reduced, whereas when the *target* was covered by a transparent obstacle, interference from distractors was increased (Meegan & Tipper, 1999). These effects were only observed when a reaching response was required, and not when the response was verbal (Meegan & Tipper, 1999).

Tipper et al. (1992) proposed that attention to the array (and hence, object selection) is action-centred (rather than retinotopic or body-centred) when responses require action upon objects in the array. This proposal assumes that perception and action are inter-dependent (Gibson, 1979; Shaw & Turvey, 1981), and that what is attended and perceived depends on the action to be performed.

Two important conclusions emerge from the literature cited. First, the effect of affordances can be observed when familiar objects, rather than symbols or simplified shapes, are used as stimuli. Second, the effects of action parameters (e.g., effector side, distance between effector and stimuli, type of response) can be observed when the task requires reaching for the target stimulus, rather than pressing a button associated with the target feature by an arbitrary rule.

OVERVIEW

In this study, our goal was to examine the influence of affordances and action parameters on selection for action. To maximize the possibility that we would observe affordance effects, we used familiar objects (cups with and without handles in Experiments 1 and 2; drawer handles, doorbells, and light-switches in Experiment 3) associated naturalistically with grasping and pointing responses. To examine the effect of action parameters, we varied the type of motor response required. Each experiment had a button-press version and a reaching version; in Experiments 2 and 3, the reaching version called for both pointing and grasping responses. In all three experiments, the dependent variable was interference (reaction time differences between a distractor present condition and a distractor absent condition).

In Experiment 1, we tested a naturalistic extension of the proposal by Meegan and Tipper (1999) that the interference caused by distractors is a function of the relative ease of programming an action to the distractors versus the targets. We assessed the hypothesis that in a task requiring reaching to and grasping a target cup, the interference caused by distractors with handles would be modulated by the position of the handle relative to the responding hand. In Experiment 2, we tested the hypothesis that the *type* of reaching response to target cups (pointing vs grasping) may influence the interference caused by distractor cups with and without handles. In Experiment 3, we assessed whether affordance-related interference effects are enhanced when objects (handles and buttons) strongly afford their associated actions (grasping and pointing, respectively) and when these actions can be pre-programmed.

GENERAL METHODS

Apparatus

The display apparatus was a wooden structure (dimensions: 21" height × 23" width × 8" depth) with four platforms (Figure 1). The display platforms were 4" wide × 4" deep and were fitted with touch-sensitive microswitches. Only the two lower platforms, which were mounted 2 inches from the base of the apparatus and 6 inches apart from each other, were used in the present study. Portable visual occlusion spectacles (PLATO, Translucent Technologies, Inc.) were used to control stimulus presentation time. The lenses of these goggles can rapidly (about 5 ms) switch from their light scattering, occluding state to their transparent state, during which 90% of incident light is transmitted. The display platform, goggles, and a start button were all connected to a PC. The computer was controlled by a custom program that timed the trials, played auditory stimuli, and recorded responses.

Figure 1. The apparatus used for stimulus presentation. The photograph also shows the start key used to control for the starting position of the hand and to record initiation times. The start key is positioned in front of the right platform.

To control the start position in each trial and to obtain a measure of movement initiation time, participants started each trial by pressing a button on a keypad. In the reaching conditions, the start button was a single round button in the centre of a square keypad. In the button-press conditions, the keypad had two response keys. The start button was a square button in the centre of the pad and the two response buttons were placed to the right of the start button, 2 cm above and 2 cm below the start button position.

A description of the objects used as stimuli is provided in the Methods sections of the individual experiments.

Participants

Participants in these experiments were right-handed older adults. Some individuals participated in more than one experiment. All had normal or corrected to normal vision and normal colour vision. Fourteen individuals (ten women) participated in Experiment 1. Their average age was 59.2 years (range 45–76) and the average education was 13.4 years. Fourteen individuals (seven women) participated in Experiment 2. Their average age was 56.5 (range 39–81) and the average education was 13.2 years. Finally, 18 individuals participated in Experiment 3 (11 women). Their average age was 64.1 (range 29–83) and the average education was 13.7 years.[1]

Procedure

Participants were seated directly in front of the display platform with the centre of the platform at midline. This placed the two lower platforms approximately 11 inches away from the body wall, approximately 10 inches below eye level (when the subjects looked straight ahead), and at 20° and 70° from the body midline. Before each trial, with the goggles in the occluded state, the experimenter placed the stimulus objects on the platforms. To begin each trial, the participants pushed the start button, which was placed to the right of midline, directly in front of the right platform.[2] The experimenter started the trial after determining that the participant was ready, was seated with head and body midline, and was pushing the start button. A tone was played and, after 500 ms, the goggles cleared. Participants were asked to respond to the target stimulus, selected by colour (blue). In the button-press task, participants were asked to press one of two buttons corresponding to a target feature (e.g., press the top button if the handle of the blue cup faces right and press the bottom button if the handle faces left). To avoid stimulus–response compatibility effects, the two response keys were organized vertically and the key assignment was

---

[1]The subjects run in these experiments are, on average, older than those commonly used in the experimental literature, and their ages span a greater range. Investigations in our laboratory frequently centre on patients aged 30–80 who have suffered strokes. To leave open the option of studies comparing healthy and brain-damaged subjects, we often recruit healthy, active subjects from a population that is age-matched to our stroke population.

[2]We chose this right-of-midline start position to maximize the possibility of observing proximity-to-hand distractor interference effects.

switched in the middle of each experiment. In grasping tasks, participants were asked to reach to and grasp the target object. In pointing tasks, participants were asked to reach and point to the target objects, perturbing them slightly with a light touch. The instructions specified that responses were to be executed as quickly as possible. Initiation time was recorded as the latency between goggles clearing and the point at which the hand was lifted from the keypad. Movement time was recorded as the latency between the hand lifting from the keypad and the point at which an object on one of the platforms was perturbed. When the subject made the correct response, a short (100 ms) beep-tone was played. If the subject responded to the distractor object, an external buzzer was played for 500 ms. If the subject failed to respond within 10 s, initiation and movement times were not recorded, and a different long tone was played.

Dependent variable and experimental design

Interference scores served as dependent variable in the three experiments. After discarding trials with RTs longer than 2000 ms, mean RTs were computed for the distractor present and distractor absent conditions for each subject and each condition. The 2000 ms cut-off led to the elimination of 115 trials out of 21,120 total trials (0.5%). Interference scores were computed by subtracting the no-distractor condition from the corresponding distractor condition. This procedure allowed us to subtract out variability in RTs due to differences in reaching to the two target positions (left or right) or differences in motor response (e.g., grasping vs pointing). For example, we would expect faster responses to targets on the right, because the starting position was closer to the right than left stimulus pad. However, any observed differences in interference with right versus left distractors would not be attributable to the different trajectories required to reach the target.

We chose to use interference scores computed from total RT (from clearing of the goggles to contact with stimuli) rather than from initiation RT because the moment at which participants released the start button could be influenced by strategy. Because there were no catch trials in which participants were asked to withhold responses, there was no motivation for participants to delay release of the start button until object selection was complete. Indeed, it has been reported that in such conditions, participants often release the start button before the selection process is completed (see Meegan & Tipper, 1998, for a detailed discussion of this issue).

The experimental design was similar for the three experiments. Each study had four within-subjects factors: response type, target compatibility, distractor compatibility, and distractor position. The levels of each variable were different in the three experiments, and they are specified in the Methods sections of each experiment.

EXPERIMENT 1
Effects of handle-hand compatibility

The first experiment examined whether the affordances of distractor objects affect responses to target objects. The findings by Riddoch et al. (1998) and Tucker and Ellis (1998), discussed earlier, demonstrated that affordances of the target stimulus influence responses even when irrelevant. In particular, these studies have shown that (1) the presence of a handle in a target object automatically activates responses with the hand, and (2) responses with the hand are particularly facilitated when the handle is oriented toward the hand as compared to when the handle is oriented in the opposite direction.

These results suggest the possibility that the interference caused by distractor objects may be modulated by the degree to which the distractors afford actions by the responding hand. In particular, interference caused by distractors with handles may be a function of the position of the handles relative to the acting hand. We expect distractor cups to be more interfering when their handles are oriented toward the responding hand as compared to when their handles are oriented away from the responding hand. Furthermore, this effect should be found when the task requires participants to grasp the cup handle, but not when participants are asked to press a button arbitrarily associated with the handle attribute of the target cup. We also expect to observe the proximity-to-hand effect found by Tipper et al. (1992); that is, to find greater interference from distractors close to the acting hand as compared to distractors farther from the acting hand. In the button-press task, we do not expect affordance-related or action-centred interference effects. Instead, we expect that other variables (for example, perceptual salience) should influence interference.

To test these hypotheses, we asked participants to respond with their right hands to target cups selected on the basis of colour. In most trials, a distractor cup of a different colour was also presented. Both target and distractor cups could have their handles facing right (good affordance for grasping) or left (bad affordance for grasping). In both the grasp and button-press tasks, the details of the response were a function of stimulus attributes. In the grasping task, participants had to grasp the handle of the target cup, and parameters of the grasp (e.g., degree of wrist flexion) were influenced by whether the handle faced right or left. In the button-press task, participants had to press one button if the target handle faced right and another button if it faced left.

Methods

Stimuli.   The stimuli were ceramic cups 5 inches high and with a diameter of 4 inches (Figure 2). Cup handles protruded 2 inches horizontally and had a vertical opening of about 2 inches. The cups were painted dark blue and dark purple. Colours were piloted to insure that selection on the basis of colour was not unduly easy.

Figure 2.   Cups used as stimuli in Experiments 1 and 2. A (cups with handle facing left) and B (cups with handle facing right), were the two stimulus configurations used in Experiment 1. B (cups with handle facing right) and C (cups without handle) were the two stimulus configurations used in Experiment 2.

Procedure.   The target cup (blue) was presented either on the left or on the right lower pad of the display apparatus, with the handle facing right (compatible condition) or left (incompatible condition). Participants always responded with the right hand. There were three distractor compatibility conditions: No-distractor, distractor with handle facing right (compatible distractor), and distractor with handle facing left (incompatible distractor). The no-distractor condition was used as a baseline to compute interference. Therefore, there were 12 cells for each response type (grasp and button press): 2 Positions × 2 Target compatibilities × 3 Distractor compatibilities.

The experimental session was divided in four 96-trial blocks, two grasping blocks and two button-press blocks. The two blocks for each task were run consecutively. The order of the two tasks (grasp first vs button press first) was counterbalanced across subjects. A short block of practice trials was presented before each task. During the entire session, participants completed 384 experimental trials, 16 for each of the 24 cells in the design.

Results

Table 1 shows the mean response latencies in distractor and no-distractor conditions in this experiment. The results of Experiment 1 were analysed in a four-way repeated measures ANOVA that included the following factors: (1) Response type (button press vs grasping), (2) target compatibility (compatible and incompatible), (3) distractor compatibility (compatible and incompatible), and (4) distractor position (left and right). The dependent variable was interference (total RT in each of the distractor-present conditions minus total RT in the equivalent distractor-absent condition). Significance values of post hoc comparisons were calculated using two-tailed paired *t*-tests.

TABLE 1a

Mean response latencies in distractor and no-distractor conditions of Experiment 1

	Button press					
	Right			Left		
Target type	Compatible	Incompatible	No distractor	Compatible	Incompatible	No distractor
Target compatible	995	1073	928	970	976	878
Target incompatible	1012	1044	941	1041	995	911

TABLE 1b

	Grasp					
	Right			Left		
Target type	Compatible	Incompatible	No distractor	Compatible	Incompatible	No distractor
Target compatible	1003	989	952	954	925	908
Target incompatible	1093	1079	1050	958	933	894

Compatible = handle on the right; incompatible = handle on the left.

The analysis showed a significant effect of response type, $F(1, 13) = 18.72$, $MSe = 10024.33$, $p < .001$. Interference was greater in the button-press task than in the grasping task (99 and 41 ms, respectively).

Response type interacted with distractor compatibility, $F(1, 13) = 16.24$, $MSe = 11230.77$, $p < .002$. In the grasping task, interference was greater in the compatible distractor condition than in the incompatible distractor condition (51 and 31 ms, respectively, $p < .005$). In the button-press task, the opposite pattern was observed: Interference was smaller in the compatible distractor condition than in the incompatible distractor condition (90 and 108 ms, respectively, $p < .05$).

Two three-way interactions involving response type were also significant: Response type × Distractor compatibility × Target compatibility, $F(1, 13) = 6.59$, $MSe = 1342.99$, $p < .025$, and Response type × Distractor compatibility × Distractor position, $F(1, 13) = 5.12$, $MSe = 2751.65$, $p < .05$. To explore the Response type × Distractor compatibility × Distractor position interaction, two separate ANOVAs were carried out on the button-press and grasping data, revealing that the Target compatibility × Distractor compatibility interaction was significant in the button-press task, $F(1, 13) = 5.72, p < .03$, but not in the grasping task ($F < 1, p > .8$). In the grasping task, compatible distractors yielded more interference than incompatible distractors, regardless of the type of target: For compatible targets: 49 vs 27 ms, $t(13) = 2.1, p = .05$; for incompatible targets: 54 vs 34 ms, $t(13) = 2.8, p = .01$. In contrast, in the button-press task, incompatible distractors were relatively more interfering than compatible distractors (122 vs 80 ms) when the target was compatible, $t(13) = 2.8\ p = .01$; and compatible distractors were slightly, though not significantly, more interfering when the target was incompatible (101 vs 94 ms, $t(13) = 0.7, p = .4$) (Figures 3 and 4).

To further explore the Response type × Distractor compatibility × Distractor position interaction, we performed two separate ANOVAs on the button-press and grasping data. These revealed that the target compatibility × distractor position interaction was significant in the button press task, $F(1, 13) = 12.40$, $p < .005$, but not in the grasping task ($F < 1, p > .35$). In the button-press task, compatible distractors were more interfering when presented on the left, $t(13) = -4.67, p < .0005$, and incompatible distractors tended to be more interfering when presented on the right, although not significantly so, $t(13) = 1.53, p = .1$. In the grasping task this trend was arguably still present but dramatically reduced (Figures 5 and 6).

The Target compatibility × Distractor position interaction approached significance, $F(1, 13) = 4.26$, $MSe = 2861.05$, $p < .06$. This interaction

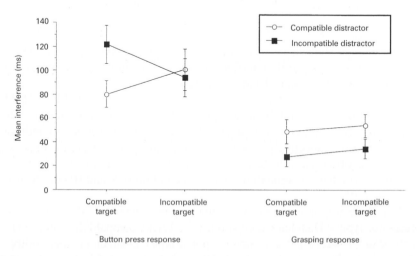

Figure 3.   Interference in ms (and standard error) as a function of response type (button press and grasping), distractor compatibility (compatible and incompatible), and target compatibility (compatible and incompatible) in Experiment 1.

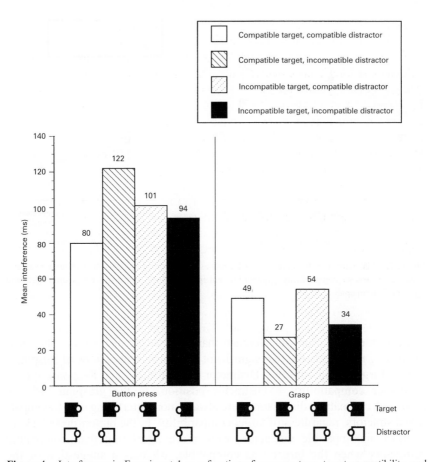

Figure 4. Interference in Experiment 1 as a function of response type, target compatibility, and distractor compatibility, shown with graphic representations of stimulus configurations in each condition.

indicated that compatible targets tended to receive more interference from right distractors than left distractors (75 vs 64 ms), whereas the opposite was true for incompatible targets (62 vs 79 ms).

Discussion

Experiment 1 showed that button-press and grasping tasks differ in the pattern of interference caused by distractors. First, interference effects were generally greater in the button-press task than in the grasping task. More importantly, in the grasping task compatible distractors yielded more interference than incompatible distractors, whereas in the button-press task, incompatible

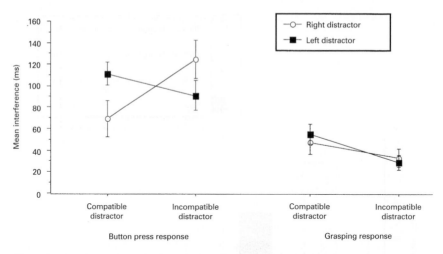

Figure 5.   Interference in ms (and standard error) as a function of response type (button press and grasping), distractor compatibility (compatible and incompatible), and distractor position (left and right) in Experiment 1.

distractors caused more interference than compatible distractors. The most interesting results are the two significant three-way interactions of Response type × Target compatibility × Distractor compatibility, and Response type × Distractor compatibility × Distractor position. In the grasping task, as predicted, compatible distractors were always more interfering than incompatible distractors, regardless of target compatibility. In the button-press task, in contrast, incompatible distractors were more interfering than compatible distractors when the target was compatible, whereas a suggestion of the opposite tendency (compatible distractors slightly more interfering than incompatible distractors) was observed when the target was incompatible. The pattern of interference effects found in the button-press task can be interpreted as consistent with a response congruency effect: Greater interference when target and distractors are associated with different button-press responses than when they are associated with the same button-press response. Thus, it is easier to programme an abstract button-press response when both stimuli in the array call for the same response than when they call for conflicting responses (Eriksen & Eriksen, 1974).

The second three-way interaction indicated that in the button-press task, compatible distractors (handle on the right) yielded more interference when they were presented in the left position than in the right position. Incompatible distractors (handle on the left) tended to yield more interference when they were presented in the right position than in the left position. This effect can be explained as a perceptual salience effect. In the compatible condition,

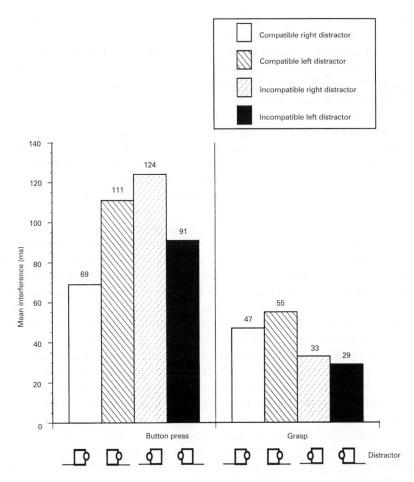

Figure 6. Interference in Experiment 1 as a function of response type, distractor compatibility, and distractor position, shown with graphic representations of stimulus configurations in each condition.

distractor handles are facing right. In this condition, left distractors will have right-facing handles close to the centre of the display, that is, close to fixation, whereas right distractors will have handles on the extreme right, far from fixation. In the incompatible condition, handles are facing left. In this case, it is the right distractors that are more interfering. This is the condition in which the handle is again in the centre. For incompatible left distractors, handles are on the extreme left of the display, and are less interfering.

To summarize, in the button-press task, response congruency and perceptual salience effects guide the pattern of interference, whereas in the grasping task only affordance variables in the distractors (compatibility between handle position and acting hand) modulate interference effects. Thus, selection for action is influenced by the nature of the action, i.e., attention to objects in the array is allocated as a function of the actions intended. When the action plan calls for actual interaction with objects, the features of all objects in the array affording the intended action are highlighted by attention.

Surprisingly, in this experiment we did not find an effect of distractor position in the grasping task. We expected right distractors to be more interfering than left distractors, especially (or solely) in the grasping task. However, the only effect of position was in the button-press task. Here, distractor position interacted with distractor compatibility, indicating differential perceptual salience of distractor handles as a function of their position in the display. In the grasping task, none of the effects involving position were significant ($p > .15$).

A possible effect of distractor position is suggested by the Target compatibility × Distractor position interaction, which only approached significance, $p = .06$. This effect indicated a trend toward greater interference from right distractors when the target handle faced right and greater interference from left distractors when the target handle faced left. This result suggests that distractors on the same side as the target handle yielded more interference than distractors that are on the opposite side. This effect is likely to arise after target selection, because it depends on the position of the target handle, but not on the position of distractor handle, $p > .9$, and is independent of response type, $p > .9$. Thus, it is possible that after target selection and before response execution, objects that are close to the relevant response attribute (in this case, the target handle) become particularly salient and yield more interference than objects that are far from the response attribute.

Methodological differences may explain the discrepancy between the results of this experiment and those reported by Tipper et al. (1992). First, Tipper and colleagues used a pointing response in their study, whereas in the present experiment we used a grasping response. There is evidence that grasping and pointing responses differ in their degree of pre-programming, with grasping relying more on on-line control than pointing (Carnahan, Goodale, & Marteniuk, 1993), and it is possible that such differences may affect the pattern of interference observed. Second, the stimuli used in the two studies were quite different: Tipper and colleagues used simple buttons arranged in a two-dimensional array, whereas we used more complex, three-dimensional stimuli. We will pursue the implications of this point later. Third, in this experiment participants were asked to respond to either the left or the right side of the target object, depending on the position of the handle, whereas in Tipper et al.'s study the reaching always terminated at the centre of the target stimulus. It is possible that one or more of these factors are responsible for the absence of a distractor position effect in this experiment, but further investigation is required to address these issues.

EXPERIMENT 2
Effects of presence of handles

In Experiment 1, we showed that distractors with good affordances for grasping yielded more interference than distractors with bad affordances, but that this was true only when the task required reaching to and grasping the handle of the target, and not when it required pressing a button on a keypad. There were two main differences between the button-press and the grasping response in Experiment 1. First, the grasping response required reaching for the target object, whereas the button-press response required pushing a button close to the hand, in the absence of any reaching movement. Second, grasping required acting on the target handle, whereas button pressing required participants to map the position of the target handle onto the two response keys following an arbitrary rule. Therefore, differences in distractor interference could have been caused by (1) the presence/absence of the reaching movement, (2) the presence/absence of manipulation of the handle attribute of the target object, or (3) both.

In Experiment 2, participants were asked to use three different motor responses: Button press, reaching and grasping, and reaching and pointing. If affordance-based interference is associated with the presence of a reaching movement but not with the type of distal manipulation, we should find differ-ences in distractor interference between button press and the two reaching responses (grasping and pointing), but not between the two reaching responses. If affordance-based interference is associated with manipulation of the handle rather than with the reaching component, we should find a difference between button press and pointing, on the one hand, versus grasping, on the other. If both proximal and distal component of the movement influence distractor interfer-ence, we should find that all three responses are associated with different inter-ference patterns.

Methods

In Experiment 2 we used the same stimuli and target selection criterion (blue colour) as in Experiment 1. The target object was a blue cup and the distractor a purple cup. In the handle present condition, the cups were presented with the handle facing right. In the handle absent condition, the cups were presented with the handle in the back, invisible to the subject. The three distractor condi-tions were handle present, handle absent, and no-distractor. The no-distractor condition was used as a baseline to compute interference scores. Two different responses were used: Reaching (pointing and grasping) and button press. In the reaching tasks, participants were asked to grasp the handle if the blue target cup had a handle or to point to the body of the cup if the blue cup did not have a handle. In the button-press task, participants were asked to press a button if the blue target cup had a handle and a different button if the blue cup did not have a handle. The button-press task was thus analogous to the grasp task with respect to the selection of a response based on the presence or absence of a critical feature in the target.

Half the participants began the experiment by responding to handled targets with the upper button and half started by responding to handled targets with the lower button; this mapping was switched half-way through the experiment.

The design included four factors: Response type (button press and reaching), target type (cup with handle and cup without handle), distractor type (cup with handle, cup without handle, and no distractor), and distractor position (left and right). Therefore, the design included 24 cells, 12 for each response type.

The experimental session was divided in four 96-trial blocks—two reaching blocks and two button-press blocks. The two blocks for each task were run consecutively and the order of the two tasks (reaching first vs button press first) was counterbalanced across subjects. A short block of practice was presented before each task.

Results

Table 2 shows the mean response latencies in distractor and no-distractor conditions in this experiment. Two comparisons are relevant. The first is between the button-press vs reaching tasks, and the second is the comparison between pointing and grasping responses within the reaching task. Therefore, we carried out two different ANOVAs. The first analysis compared reaching versus button press, and the second analysis included only the reaching task and examined differences in grasping versus pointing. Significance values of post hoc comparisons were calculated using two-tailed paired t-tests.

Button press versus reaching. We carried out a four-way repeated measures ANOVA with interference scores that included the following factors: (1) Response type (button press vs reaching), (2) target type (handle vs no-handle cup), (3) distractor type (handle vs no-handle cup), and (4) distractor position (left and right).

The main effect of response type was significant, $F(1, 13) = 9.73$, $MSe = 3404.83$, $p < .01$, indicating greater interference in the button-press than in the reaching task (72 and 47 ms, respectively). Distractor type was also significant, $F(1, 13) = 12.52$, $MSe = 1779.77$, $p < .005$. Handle distractors were more interfering than no-handle distractors (69 and 49 ms, respectively). The Target type × Distractor type interaction was highly significant, $F(1, 13) = 23.16$, $MSe = 1663.80$, $p < .0005$. This interaction indicates that handle distractors were more interfering when the target had no handle than when the target had a handle

TABLE 2a

Mean response latencies in distractor and no-distractor conditions of Experiment 2

| | Button press | | | | | |
| | Right | | | Left | | |
Target type	Handle	No handle	No distractor	Handle	No handle	No distractor
Handle target	829	856	767	947	912	865
No handle target	940	894	830	957	899	868

TABLE 2b

| | Grasp | | | | | |
| | Right | | | Left | | |
Target type	Handle	No handle	No distractor	Handle	No handle	No distractor
Handle target	925	943	879	893	907	862
No handle target	969	927	885	893	853	839

(84 and 55 ms, respectively), $t(13) = -2.11$, $p = .05$, whereas no-handle distractors were more interfering when the target had a handle than when the target had no handle (61 and 38 ms, respectively), $t(13) = 2.29$, $p < .05$.

Both the two-way interaction Distractor position × Distractor type, $F(1, 13) = 8.69$, $MSe = 583.84$, $p < .02$, and the three-way interaction Response type × Distractor position × Distractor type, $F(1, 13) = 4.90$, $MSe = 897.33$, $p < .05$, were significant (Figures 7 and 8).

In the button-press task, handle distractors were much more interfering than no-handle distractors when they were on the left (85 and 39 ms, respectively), $t(13) = 4.19$, $p = .001$, but they yielded comparable interference when they were on the right (86 and 77 ms, respectively), $t(13) = 1.047$, $p > .3$. In the reaching task, handled distractors were always more interfering than no-handle distractors, $t(13) = 2.22$, $p < .05$, and there was a tendency for right distractors to interfere more than left distractors, $t(13) = 1.85$, $p = .09$. These two variables did not interact ($F < 1$).

Pointing vs grasping.   To examine whether handled distractors were more interfering when participants had to grasp than when they had to point, a separate analysis of the reaching task was carried out. An affordance-related

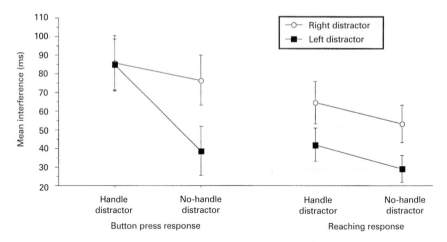

Figure 7. Interference in ms (and standard error) as a function of response type (button press and reaching), distractor type (handle and no-handle), and distractor position (left and right) in Experiment 2.

interference effect would manifest as an interaction between target type and distractor type. In particular, we expected that when the target had a handle, and thus the response required grasping the handle, we would find more interference from handle distractors than when the target did not have a handle and the task required pointing to the cup.

The Target type × Distractor type interaction was indeed significant in this analysis, $F(1, 13) = 21.21$, $MSe = 1086.96$, $p = .0005$, but the pattern of interference was different than predicted (Figure 9). The interaction indicates a strong response congruency effect, similar to what was observed in the previous analysis, in which handle distractors were more interfering than no-handle distractors when the targets had no handles, and thus the required response was pointing (69 and 28 ms, respectively), $t(13) = 4.15$, $p = .0025$, and no-handle distractors were more interfering than handle distractors when the target had handles, and the required response was grasping (54 and 38 ms, respectively), $t(13) = -2.62$, $p < .025$. This is opposite to what we had predicted.

Discussion

In Experiment 2, we again found differences in the pattern of distractor interference as a function of response type. In particular, when the task required participants to reach for the target, handle distractors were more interfering than no-handle distractors and there was a tendency for right distractors to be more interfering; there was no interaction between these two variables. When the

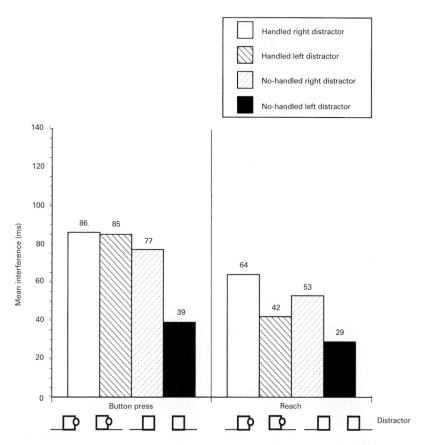

Figure 8.   Interference in Experiment 2 as a function of response type, distractor type, and distractor position, shown with graphic representations of stimulus configurations in each condition.

task required participants to press a button, right distractors yielded a similar amount of interference whether or not they had handles (86 and 77 ms, respectively), whereas left distractors were much more interfering when they had handles than when they did not have handles (85 and 39 ms, respectively). This is likely a perceptual effect similar to what we observed in Experiment 1. When the distractor handle is central and close to fixation (cup in left position with handle facing right) it yields greater interference.

This pattern of results confirms that different variables influence distractor interference depending on whether the task requires reaching for the target or pressing a button associated arbitrarily with the target attribute. In the reaching task, affordance and action-centred effects predominated: Handle distractors were always more interfering than no-handle distractors, and right distractors

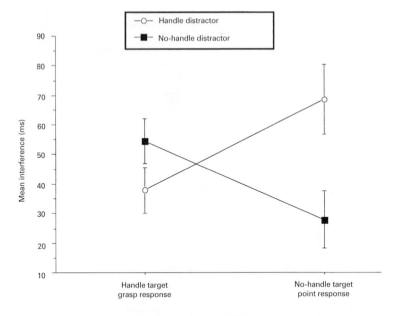

Figure 9.   Interference in ms (and standard error) as a function of target type (handle and no-handle) and distractor type (handle and no-handle) in the reaching condition of Experiment 2.

tended to cause greater interference than left distractors. In the button-press task, perceptual elements (such as salience of a handle presented at fixation) were more influential in modulating interference.

We expected to find a differential effect of handle distractors depending on the type of reaching response (grasping vs pointing), but this was not the case. The results of Experiment 2 suggest that affordances influence distractor interference any time participants must reach for the target object, regardless of the distal component of the action. However, before accepting this conclusion, we must consider two factors that may have reduced the possibility of observing differential effects of pointing and grasping in this experiment.

First, the experiment required selection of an appropriate action (pointing or grasping) subsequent to target identification and contingent upon the features of the target. This means that although participants knew in advance that they had to reach for the target object, they did not know whether they had to grasp or point to the target until the target object was selected. If it is the case that an action plan must first be selected to influence target selection processes, it would then not be surprising that, under the present conditions, we would observe a difference in patterns of interference as a function of the presence or absence of the reaching component, but not with changes in the manipulation component.

Second, cups are not likely to afford pointing and grasping equivalently. Cups afford grasping, regardless of whether handles are present or absent, in part because of their physical features (e.g., hand-sized curvature), and in part because of the over-learned response of grasping cups. On the other hand, neither learned use nor object shape suggest an association between cups and the action of pointing. Therefore, although grasping may receive automatic activation from the cup's features as well as from task instructions ("grasp the target if it has a handle"), pointing receives activation only from the task instruction ("point to the target if it does not have a handle").

This observation suggests that when the target has a handle, selecting the grasping response should be relatively easy, and a no handle distractor should yield minimal interference. Thus, with handle targets we should find interference to be similar whether the distractor is associated with the same response (handle distractor) or opposite response (no-handle distractor). On the contrary, when the target has no handles, selecting the pointing response should be relatively difficult in the presence of a handle distractor that activates a grasping response. The results of the Target type × Distractor type interaction, described previously in terms of a response congruency effect, follow this pattern. In the handle target/grasp response condition, no handle distractors caused 16 ms more interference than handle distractors. In the no-handle target/point condition, in comparison, the relative interference caused by handle distractors as compared to no-handle distractors was much greater (41 ms). This difference between the two conditions is significant, $t(13) = -2.22$, $p < .05$ (Figure 9). In other words, the response congruency effect is largely "driven" by the no handle target/handle distractor condition.

To maximize the chances of finding differences in distractor interference in pointing versus grasping responses, we reasoned that the experimental paradigm must be changed in two ways. First, the type of motor response should be blocked, so that the appropriate distal action is selected before target selection and can influence distractor processing. Second, we should use two types of objects: Objects that have good affordances for grasping, and objects that have good affordances for pointing. The aim of this manipulation would be to allow equivalent activation of grasping and pointing actions by different objects in the array.

EXPERIMENT 3
Button interference versus handle interference

Experiment 3 had the same purpose as Experiment 2, but we made some modifications to maximize the possibility of finding a differential effect of distractor affordances as a function of reaching response (pointing vs grasping). The first modification was to block the motor response required so that target selection occurred *after* action selection. The second was to use objects with clear affordances: Button-switches affording pointing but not grasping, and drawer and door handles affording grasping but not pointing (Figure 10).

To ensure that affordances and not visual similarity were influencing interference, in each affordance set we used two perceptually different objects. The two objects that afforded pointing were a round button (doorbell) and a long button (light-switch), and the two objects that afforded grasping were a round handle and a long handle. In each trial, the target afforded either grasping or pointing, the distractor afforded either grasping or pointing, and the two objects were always perceptually dissimilar. For example, if the target was a long handle, the distractor could be a round button or a round handle.

Our predictions were that in the grasping blocks, distractors that afforded grasping would be more interfering than distractors that afforded pointing. In the pointing blocks, distractors affording pointing should interfere more than distractors affording grasping. As in the prior experiments, a button-press task served as a non-reaching control.

Methods

In this experiment, the target could be one of four objects created by the crossing of two factors: Shape (round and long) and affordance (buttons affording pressing and handles affording grasping; see Figure 7). Each object

Figure 10.   Stimuli used in Experiment 3. On the left are shown the two long stimuli and on the right the two round stimuli. The upper row shows the two handles and the lower row the two buttons.

was mounted on a wooden block of $3\frac{1}{2}$ by $3\frac{1}{2}$ by $6\frac{1}{2}$ inches. The long handle was $4\frac{3}{8}$ inches long, $\frac{3}{4}$ inches wide, and protruded from the block $\frac{7}{8}$ inches. The round handle had a diameter of $1\frac{1}{2}$ inches and protruded from the block $\frac{3}{4}$ inch. The long button was $2\frac{9}{12}$ inches long, $1\frac{1}{4}$ inches wide, and protruded from the block $\frac{1}{4}$ inch. The round button had a diameter of $\frac{5}{8}$ inches and sat in a base of $2\frac{1}{4}$ inches in diameter; the button-and-base ensemble protruded from the block $\frac{1}{2}$ inch.

Three distractor conditions were used in this experiment: Button distractor, handle distractor, and no distractor. The no-distractor condition served as a baseline to compute interference. The experiment was run in two experimental sessions over two different days. In each session, three blocks of trials were run: A button-press block, a pointing block, and a grasping block. Each block comprised 96 trials. The order of the blocks was counterbalanced across subjects. As in prior experiments, the target object was selected on the basis of colour (blue). In the reaching conditions, participants were instructed to grasp or point to the blue target object, depending upon the block. Thus, for example, in the grasp blocks, subjects were required to grasp blue handles and blue buttons, and the buttons had a relatively poor affordance for grasping. In the button-press condition, the task required participants to press the key corresponding to the position (left or right) of the blue target object. As in previous experiments, the button-press condition was analogous in some respects to the reach conditions. In this experiment, both button-press and reaching conditions had blocked action parameters, and response selection concerned indication of the location of the target object.

Results

Table 3 shows the mean response latencies in distractor and no-distractor conditions in this experiment. Two repeated measures ANOVAs were carried out on the interference data. The first analysis examined interference data from the three response types (button press, grasping, and pointing). The goal of this analysis was to examine whether there was any difference in interference as a function of the type of response. Because the aim of this experiment was to investigate whether different patterns of interference would be observed for reaching responses with different distal components (point vs grasp), the second ANOVA analysed interference data in pointing and grasping conditions. Significance values of post hoc comparisons were calculated using paired t-tests.

All response types. Interference scores were analysed in a four-way ANOVA comprising response type (button press, grasping, and pointing), target type (button and handle), distractor type (button and handle), and distractor position (left and right). Only one effect reached significance. The

TABLE 3a

Mean response latencies in distractor and no-distractor conditions of Experiment 3

| | Button press | | | | | |
| | Right | | | Left | | |
Target type	Button	Handle	No distractor	Button	Handle	No distractor
Button target	970	1002	919	974	924	871
Handle target	980	978	935	1001	939	865

TABLE 3b

| | Grasp | | | | | |
| | Right | | | Left | | |
Target type	Button	Handle	No distractor	Button	Handle	No distractor
Button target	1147	1188	1105	1082	1096	1014
Handle target	1098	1106	1042	1019	1028	931

TABLE 3c

| | Point | | | | | |
| | Right | | | Left | | |
Target type	Button	Handle	No distractor	Button	Handle	No distractor
Button target	1148	1164	1079	1063	1077	991
Handle target	1103	1122	1043	1034	1031	953

Response type $\times$ Distractor type interaction was highly significant, $F(1, 17) = 17.09$, $MSe = 8887.33$, $p < .0001$ (Figure 11). In the button-press task, button distractors were more interfering than handle distractors (83 and 63 ms for button interference and handle interference, respectively), $t(18) = 2.84$, $p < .02$), whereas the opposite pattern was observed in the two reaching tasks: Handle distractors were more interfering than button distractors for the grasping response (81 and 64 ms, respectively), $t(18) = -2.22$, $p < .05$, and showed a strong tendency in the same direction for the pointing response (82 and 70 ms, respectively), $t(18) = -1.90$. $p = .07$.

Pointing vs grasping. We carried out a second four-way ANOVA in which task (pointing and grasping), target type (handle and button), distractor

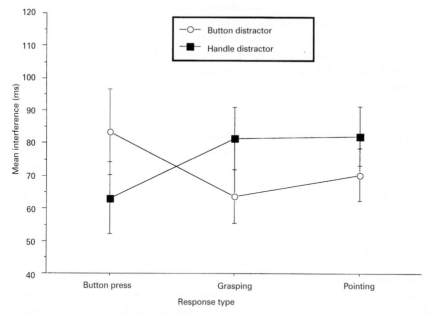

Figure 11. Interference (in ms) as a function of response type (button press, grasping, and pointing) and distractor type (button and handle).

type (handle and button), and distractor position (left and right) were factors. The only significant effect in this analysis was distractor type, $F(1, 17) = 5.23$, $MSe = 3027.18$, $p < .04$, indicating that handle distractors were more interfering than button distractors (82 and 67 ms, respectively) in both the pointing and grasping tasks. Distractor type did not interact with response type ($F < 1$, $p < .3$).

Discussion

In Experiment 3 we examined interference effects in three tasks: Button press, reaching and pointing, and reaching and grasping. Button press and pointing have a similar distal component, but button press lacks the reaching component that the pointing task requires. Pointing and grasping both have a reaching component, but differ in the final hand shape used to interact with the object.

The interpretation of Experiment 3 is relatively straightforward. The highly significant interaction between response type and distractor type indicates that button distractors yielded greater interference than handle distractors in the button-press task, whereas handle distractors yielded more interference in the two tasks that required reaching for the target (grasping and pointing). A direct comparison between pointing and grasping confirmed that in both tasks, handle distractors were more interfering than button distractors, but did not reveal any differences between the two response types.

Three points are worth discussing. First, the results of Experiment 3 closely replicated those of Experiment 2, indicating that reaching for an object produces a different pattern of distractor interference than pressing a button close to the hand, but that the type of distal manipulation of the target (pointing or grasping) does not influence distractor interference. This replication is particularly striking because in Experiment 3 we used different stimuli and modified the experimental procedure to maximize the chances of finding differential affordance-related interference effects associated with pointing and grasping responses. It is possible to account for these results by assuming that reaching actions, regardless of the distal component, always increase the salience of objects that afford grasping. We will pursue this further in the General Discussion.

Second, in Experiment 3 we found relatively greater interference from button as compared to handle distractors in the button-press task. Because the distal movements used in button presses and in pointing to door bells or switches are similar, it is possible that this constitutes an affordance-related effect. It is interesting to note that this is the only experiment in which we used objects that afford pointing, and the only experiments in which we found putative affordance effects for button-press responses. Thus, even with responses not requiring participants to reach and act on the target object, it may be possible to observe affordance-related effects. As discussed earlier, findings potentially relevant to this notion have been reported previously (Tucker & Ellis, 1998).

Third, it is of note that in this experiment we did not observe the "action-centred" interference effects reported by Tipper and colleagues (1992). The effect of distractor position approached significance in the overall analysis, $F(1, 17) = 3.94$, $p = .063$, but the trend was in the opposite direction: Distractors close to the acting hand tended to be *less* interfering than distractors far from the acting hand (63 and 85 ms, respectively). Furthermore, there was no hint of an interaction between distractor position and response type ($F < 1$, $p > .4$).

As already mentioned, it is possible that differences in the motor responses and stimuli used in these studies are responsible for this discrepancy. It is particularly interesting that we did not observe the distractor position effect in the pointing blocks of our reaching task, in which the motor response was similar to that used by Tipper and colleagues. One possible explanation is based on the notion that it is the ease of response to a stimulus, relative to other stimuli in the array, that determines its salience as a distractor. The relative potency of distractors close to the hand (the "action-centred" effect) may be observed only when targets and distractors are two-dimensional shapes of no naturalistic relevance to the actor (e.g., coloured lights). Under such circumstances, potential actions to all objects are similar, and location is a relatively salient feature of the stimuli. In contrast, when familiar objects are used, other object features such as affordances or pragmatic characteristics of the objects (Jeannerod, 1994) may determine the ease of response to the objects, and thus have relatively stronger effects on the pattern of distractor interference. In this case, the degree to which object affordances match planned actions, rather than relative location, may become dominant in determining interference effects, and spatial effects concerning the relationship of the responding hand and objects in the array will be difficult to observe. This is a speculative proposal, but it may be useful in informing future research.

GENERAL DISCUSSION

In this study, our goal was to examine the influence of affordances and action parameters on selection for action. To maximize the possibility that we would observe affordance effects, we used familiar objects (cups with and without handles in Experiments 1 and 2; drawer handles, doorbells, and light-switches in Experiment 3) associated naturalistically with grasping and pointing responses. To examine the effect of action parameters, we varied the type of motor response required. In Experiment 1, we assessed the hypothesis that in a task requiring reaching to and grasping a target cup, the interference caused by distractors with handles would be modulated by the position of the handle relative to the responding hand. In Experiment 2, we tested the hypothesis that the *type* of reaching response to target cups (pointing vs grasping) may influence the interference caused by distractor cups with and without handles. In Experiment 3, we assessed whether affordance-related interference effects are enhanced when objects strongly afford their associated actions and when these actions can be pre-programmed.

In all three experiments we found task effects: Button press and reaching actions produced different pattern of interference. In Experiments 1 and 2, we used objects that afford grasping (cups), and found that button-press actions were associated with perceptual effects (greater interference when critical features were presented close to fixation) and response congruence effects (greater interference by distractors associated with different responses than targets). In contrast, reaching and grasping was associated with affordance-interference effects (greater interference by compatible distractors in Experiment 1; greater interference by handled distractors in Experiment 2). In Experiment 3, we used objects that afford grasping (handles) and objects that afford pointing (door bells and light-switches), and found that reaching actions were associated with affordance-interference effects (greater interference from handled distractors). In contrast, button-press actions were more vulnerable to interference from distractors affording pointing than from distractors affording grasping. Thus, selection for action is influenced by the nature of the action, that is, attention to objects in the array is allocated as a function of the actions intended. When the action plan calls for actual interaction with objects, the features of all objects in the array affording action are highlighted by attention. The handles of target and distractor cups are attended differently depending upon whether one intends to reach to or merely locate the target.

Contrary to our predictions, we failed to find a difference in interference as a function of the precise hand posture required (grasping vs pointing). Instead, in all tasks requiring reaching to objects in the array, distractors affording grasping (handle distractors) generally caused more interference than distractors not affording grasping, regardless of the hand posture afforded by the target (Experiments 2 and 3) or required by the blocked nature of response instructions (Experiment 3). One possibility is that the asymmetric affordance-interference effects observed (strong interference by distractors affording grasping and weak interference by distractors affording pointing in both grasping and pointing tasks) may reflect differences in the processing or representation of objects affording grasping as compared to pointing actions. Given that relatively large portions of the dorsal visual processing stream in monkey and man (e.g., areas AIP and F5 and F6 in the monkey) are devoted to processing various kinds of grasp actions (e.g., precision grip, power grip), it is possible that the grasping response is dominant over other types of manual responses, and that objects affording grasping, in part because of the sheer magnitude of their neural representation, are strong competitors for the control of action irrespective of the manual response required (e.g., Grafton, Arbib, Fadiga, & Rizzolatti, 1996; MacKay, 1992; Rizzolatti et al., 1988; Sakata & Taira, 1994; Stein, 1992).

Additionally of interest are the data from Experiment 3, which revealed that button distractors in the array were highly interfering when the response was a button press on the table-top. We suggest that the emergence of this effect may have been possible because of differences between this experiment and the previous experiments. In this experiment, it was not possible to observe "response congruency" effects as in Experiments 1 and 2, because subjects responded on the basis of the location of the target (left or right), and there was never a case in which both the target and distractor called for the same response. Second, unlike in previous experiments, the stimuli were symmetrical (i.e., without handles on the left or right), so it was not possible to observe perceptual salience effects (e.g., handles close to initial fixation at midline). Finally, this was the only experiment in which we used stimuli that had a strong affordance for pointing. It is not clear which of these factors are instrumental in revealing the strong interference by buttons in the button-press task; this will be an interesting question for future investigations.

Several investigators (Castiello, 1998, 1999; Tucker & Ellis, 1998) have suggested that objects in the array automatically activate responses associated with them, even in the absence of the subject's intention to act. This phenomenon has been termed a "visuomotor priming" effect (Craighero, Fadiga, Rizzolatti, & Umiltà, 1999). Our data speak to a phenomenon that is in some respects opposite to this; namely, whether preparation and planning of an action affects the features of objects highlighted by attention. Our data suggest that object affordances are indeed attended (and hence, activate their associated responses) differently depending upon the intentions and plans of the actor. This notion accords well with the "premotor theory of attention" proposed by Rizzolatti and colleagues (Rizzolatti & Camarda, 1977; Rizzolatti, Riggio, Dascola, & Umiltà, 1987). On this theory, activity of neural circuits programming motor plans produces a shift of attention to the spatial regions where the action is to be executed. In other words, visual attention to a particular location comprises facilitation of neurons involved in preparing and directing actions to that part of space. The present data suggest an extension of the premotor account: That the preparation of an action influences the particular *features* of objects that are attended. Thus, in tasks requiring action upon objects in the array, it is the relationship between objects and potential actions that guide interference effects. In contrast, if no actions upon the objects are planned, as is the case in many traditional distractor interference studies, it is the relationship between target and distractor objects (e.g., relative locations, relative discriminability; Duncan & Humphreys, 1989) that influences the pattern of interference.

REFERENCES

Allport, D.A. (1987). Selection for action: Some behavioral and neuropsychological considerations of attention and action. In H. Heuer & A.F. Sanders (Eds.), *Perspectives on perception and action* (pp. 395–419). Hillsdale, NJ: Lawrence Erlbaum Associates, Inc.

Carnahan, H., Goodale, M.A., & Marteniuk, R.G. (1993). Grasping versus pointing and the differential use of visual feedback. *Human Movement Science, 12*(3), 219–234.

Castiello, U. (1996). Grasping a fruit: Selection for action. *Journal of Experimental Psychology: Human Perception and Performance, 22*, 582-603.

Castiello, U. (1998). Attentional coding for three-dimensional objects and two-dimensional shapes: Differential interference effects. *Experimental Brain Research, 123*(3), 289–297.

Castiello, U. (1999). Mechanisms of selection for the control of hand action. *Trends in Cognitive Sciences, 3*(7), 264–271.

Craighero, L., Fadiga, L., Rizzolatti, G., & Umiltà, C. (1999). Action for perception: A motor-visual attentional effect. *Journal of Experimental Psychology: Human Perception and Performance, 25*(6), 1673–1692.

Duncan, J., & Humphreys, G.W. (1989). Visual search and stimulus similarity. *Psychological Review, 96*, 433–458.

Eriksen, B.A., & Eriksen, C.W. (1974). Effects of noise letters upon the identification of a target letter in a nonsearch task. *Perception and Psychophysics, 16*, 143–149.

Gibson, J.J. (1979). *The ecological approach to visual perception.* Boston: Houghton-Mifflin.

Grafton, S.T., Arbib, M.A., Fadiga, L., & Rizzolatti, G. (1996). Localization of grasp representations in humans by positron emission tomography: 2. Observation compared with imagination. *Experimental Brain Research, 112*(1), 103–111.

Jeannerod, M. (1994). Object oriented action. In K.M.B. Bennet & U. Castiello (Eds.), *Insights into the reach and grasp movement* (pp. 3–15). Amsterdam: Elsevier.

Kornblum, S., Hasbroucq, T., & Osman, A. (1990). Dimensional overlap: Cognitive basis for stimulus–response compatibility—a model and taxonomy. *Psychological Review, 97*, 253–270.

MacKay, W.A. (1992). Properties of reach-related neuronal activity in cortical area 7A. *Journal of Neurophysiology, 67*(5), 1335–1345.

Meegan, D.V., & Tipper, S.P. (1998). Reaching into cluttered visual environments: Spatial and temporal influences of distracting objects. *Quarterly Journal of Experimental Psychology, 51A*, 225-249.

Meegan, D.V., & Tipper, S.P. (1999). Visual search and target-directed action. *Journal of Experimental Psychology: Human Perception and Performance, 25*(5), 1347–1362.

Michaels, C.F., & Stins, J.F. (1997). An ecological approach to stimulus–response compatibility. In B. Hommel & W. Prinz (Eds.), *Theoretical issues in stimulus–response compatibility* (pp. 333–360). Amsterdam: Elsevier.

Proctor, R.W., & Reeve, T.G. (Eds.). (1990). *Stimulus–response compatibility: An integrated perspective*. Amsterdam: North-Holland.

Proctor, R.W., Van Zandt, T., Lu, C.H., & Weeks, D.J. (1993). Stimulus–response compatibility for moving stimuli: Perception of affordances or directional coding? *Journal of Experimental Psychology: Human Perception and Performance, 19*(1), 81–91.

Riddoch, J.M., Edwards, M.G., Humphreys, G.W., West, R., & Heafield, T. (1998). Visual affordances direct action: Neuropsychological evidence from manual interference. *Cognitive Neuropsychology, 5*, 645–683.

Rizzolatti, G., & Camarda, R. (1977). Influence of the presentation of remote visual stimuli on visual responses of cat area 17 and lateral suprasylvian area. *Experimental Brain Research, 29*(1), 107–122.

Rizzolatti, G., Camarda, R., Fogassi, L., Gentilucci, M., Luppino, G., & Matelli, M. (1988). Functional organization of inferior area 6 in the macaque monkey: II. Area F5 and the control of distal movements. *Experimental Brain Research, 71*(3), 491–507.

Rizzolatti, G., Riggio, L., Dascola, I., & Umiltà, C. (1987). Reorienting attention across the horizontal and vertical meridians: Evidence in favor of a premotor theory of attention. *Neuropsychologia, 25*(1A), 31–40.

Sakata, H., & Taira, M. (1994). Parietal control of hand action. *Current Opinions in Neurobiology, 4*(6), 847–56.

Shaw, R., & Turvey, M.T. (1981). Coalitions as models of eco-systems: A realist perspective on perceptual organization. In M. Kubovy & J.R. Pomerantz (Eds.), *Perceptual organization*. Hillsdale, NJ: Lawrence Erlbaum Associates, Inc.

Stein, J.F. (1992). The representation of egocentric space in the posterior parietal cortex. *Behavioral and Brain Sciences, 15*, 691–700.

Tipper, S.P., Howard, L.A., & Jackson, S.R. (1997). Selective reaching to grasp: Evidence for distractor interference effects. *Visual Cognition, 4*, 1–38.

Tipper, S.P., Lortie, C., & Baylis, G.C. (1992). Selective reaching: Evidence for action-centered attention. *Journal of Experimental Psychology: Human Perception and Performance, 18*, 891–905.

Tucker, M., & Ellis, R. (1998). On the relations between seen objects and components of potential actions. *Journal of Experimental Psychology: Human Perception and Performance, 24*(3), 830–846.

VISUAL COGNITION, 2002, 9 (4/5), 591–614

Action-centred negative priming: Evidence for reactive inhibition

Steven P. Tipper

University of Wales, Bangor, UK

Daniel Meegan

McMaster University, Hamilton, Ontario, Canada

Louise A. Howard

University of Wales, Bangor, UK

Experiments are described in which the spatial relationship between a stimulus and respondent is held constant in terms of visual and body-centred coordinates, while the complexity of the response is manipulated. It is demonstrated that the degree of complexity of an action directed to the same spatial location determines the level of negative priming observed. This result supports the notions that (1) inhibitory selection mechanisms act on action-centred representations, and (2) the level of inhibition is reactive to the relative potency of the evoked action. The results are also discussed in terms of alternative explanations of negative priming. It is concluded that the results are inconsistent with theories that do not involve inhibitory selection mechanisms.

For mammals to be able to survive in complex and often dangerous environments, it has been necessary for very efficient visuomotor processes to evolve. That is, visual systems have to very rapidly extract from the visual array information capable of guiding suitable actions, whether these be the pursuit of

Please address all correspondence to S.P. Tipper, Centre for Cognitive Neuroscience, School of Psychology, University of Wales, Bangor, Gwynedd, LL57 2DG, UK.
Email: s.tipper@bangor.ac.uk

This research was supported by NSERC graduate student award to the second author and BBSRC research grant reference S07727. We would like to thank Steve Lindsay, Bruce Milliken, and Bruce Weaver for their constructive comments on an earlier version of this paper.

http://www.tandf.co.uk/journals/pp/13506285.html   DOI:10.1080/13506280143000593

prey, avoidance of a predator, the leap to a branch, or the grasp of a ripe fruit. The enormous efficiency of such visuomotor translations can be appreciated by the fact that there is now substantial evidence that visual information can activate action systems without the conscious intention to act. For example, Tucker and Ellis (1998) have shown that the complex grasp evoked by an object becomes active even when grasp type is irrelevant to current task demands. Similarly, the actions of some individuals with frontal lobe lesions are automatically activated by objects within range of a reach, even when these individuals are explicitly told not to act on the object, and they are consciously aware of this restriction (e.g., Lhermitte, 1983). Even stimuli that are being ignored, while attention is directed to a different object, can activate actions in parallel and compete for the control of behaviour (e.g., Eriksen & Eriksen, 1974).

Given that vision-to-action can be so fluently processed, independently of an individual's intention, a critical question is how normal humans are so efficient at selectively responding to the appropriate object at the appropriate time. Clearly selection mechanisms linking parallel perception to serial action have had to evolve in tandem with efficient visuomotor systems. To exercise free choice and control, it is essential that the strongest action, which will vary from moment to moment, can be appropriately inhibited. However, although it is possible to study such inhibitory selection mechanisms directly in single unit recording experiments with monkeys (e.g., Moran & Desimone, 1985; Schall & Hanes, 1993), indirect measures, such as priming, have to be developed to study such selection inhibition in intact humans.

Negative priming refers to the apparent disruption (usually slowing) of the response to an item if it has previously been ignored. Negative priming effects have been extensively studied (see for example, Fox, 1995; May, Kane, & Hasher, 1995; Neill, Valdes, & Terry, 1995, for reviews). The theoretical stance behind the procedure when used as a tool to study selection processes is as follows: If the internal representations of competing distractors are inhibited during selection of a target in a prime display, then processing of a subsequent probe stimulus accessing these inhibited representations will be impaired. For example, if a to-be-ignored distracting picture of a dog is inhibited in the prime, when the same or a similar stimulus is presented shortly afterwards in the probe, the previously inhibited representations will be accessed. This inhibition will slow down retrieval of the representations necessary to identify the picture of dog.

Tipper, Weaver, and Houghton (1994) argued that inhibitory mechanisms acting on competing inputs are determined by the behavioural goals of the task. That is, not all properties of a distractor are necessarily inhibited, but rather, the stimulus dimension required to control overt behaviour can be selectively inhibited. Thus, in tasks requiring analysis of low level percep- tual information, as when matching meaningless shapes, it is the perceptual properties of a distractor that compete and have to be inhibited (e.g., DeSchepper & Treisman, 1996). In contrast, in a task requiring report of more abstract semantic properties of a stimulus, as when reporting the semantic category of a drawing or word, it is the semantic property of the distractor that competes for the control of action and has to be inhibited, whereas other properties of the distractor, such as perceptual features, are not inhibited. In this case, equivalent negative priming is found when there is complete overlap of features (the same picture is presented in prime and probe displays), as when there are no features in common (a picture is presented in the prime, and a word in the probe) (e.g., Tipper & Driver, 1988). Other tasks have shown that the spatial location of a distractor can be inhibited, while its identity remains uninhibited, when report of target location is the behavioural goal (e.g., Tipper et al., 1994).

As with almost all studies of visual attention, the responses in negative priming experiments are arbitrary. Thus, although prior work has shown that behavioural goals influence the function of inhibition mechanisms, the actions required in these experiments do not have a direct relationship with the stimulus. For example, in studies reporting the spatial position of target, a key-press has been utilized (e.g., Tipper, Brehaut, & Driver, 1990) or a joy stick movement (Tipper et al., 1994). However, these actions are spatially displaced from the stimulus, and are quite arbitrary; indeed a foot response could also be used in such tasks. Other studies, however, have begun to consider the ecological validity of such procedures (e.g., Tipper, Lortie, & Baylis, 1992b). Clearly our visuomotor systems have evolved to provide very rapid analysis of the visual environment to enable fast and accurate actions. These actions are rarely arbitrary, but contain a direct and invariant relationship with the selected object. Thus, when grasping a glass full of milk, a very specific non-arbitrary action is required.

In real life contexts we propose that the mechanisms of selection, such as inhibition, are acting on action-centred frames of reference. More specifically, if the task requires directing the hand to an object, the frame of reference is hand-centred, meaning that stimuli are encoded in terms of the spatial relationship between them and the responding hand (e.g., Meegan & Tipper 1998, 1999; Tipper, Lortie, & Baylis, 1992b). For example, consider a table containing two coffee cups. When the goal is to reach for one of them, the fluent visuomotor processes can begin to activate reaching responses to both cups in parallel. In such situations inhibitory control processes are necessary to ensure action is directed to the appropriate object at the appropriate time, and the inhibitory control will also be hand-centred.

Previous work has indeed demonstrated that negative priming, which we assume to reflect inhibition of competing distractors, is action-centred in tasks requiring direct reaches to objects. Thus distractors closer to the hand evoke more rapid and fluent actions than those further from the hand. Because near distractors win the race for the control of action, they interfere more, and hence require greater levels of inhibition. Such predictions of greater negative priming from more potent distractors actually emerge from the model of selective attention proposed by Houghton and Tipper (1994).

The Houghton and Tipper model describes a neural network in which an internal template is created against which perceptual inputs are compared. The template contains stimulus features that specify which object is the target for action. For example, if participants are told to name the red object in each stimulus array, the template would be red (Tipper & Cranston, 1985). Other potential templates include location (Tipper, MacQueen, & Brehaut, 1988), shape (Tipper et al., 1990), size (Tipper, Weaver, & Milliken, 1995), or any other feature, such as place in a temporal sequence (e.g., Milliken, Joordens, Merikle, & Seiffert, 1998), that distinguishes target from distractor. Any inputs matching this template receive excitatory feedback, whereas those of the distractor which mismatch the template receive inhibitory feedback. For example, in the studies of Tipper (1985) subjects were presented with red and green pictures. They were required to name the red picture as fast as possible. Via this instruction an internal model of the selection feature "red" was created, and maintained throughout the experiment, and all perceptual inputs were matched against this template.

The second property of the Houghton and Tipper model that is of central relevance to the ideas presented in this paper is the notion that the inhibition that feeds back to the distractor is reactive. That is, the level of inhibition is determined by the activation state of the distractor. Distractors that are highly salient and intrude into the control of action receive greater inhibitory feedback than less salient distractors (see Grison & Strayer, 2001; Houghton, Tipper, Weaver, & Shore, 1996, for evidence to support notions of reactive inhibition). An important point to note, that will be returned to in later discussions, is that the potency/salience of a stimulus is completely determined by context. Thus a specific stimulus may be very salient because it wins the race for the control of action relative to other stimuli in the scene. On the other hand, exactly the same stimulus becomes less salient if the other stimuli in the scene win the race for the control of action. This property of the model is very important for our current arguments.

A crucial feature of this type of formal model is that they can be used to make a priori predictions. In other work we have examined the trajectories taken by the reaching hand when distractors are present. Linking our neural network model with the known physiology of the motor cortex where population coding represents reach direction (e.g., Georgopoulos, 1990; Georgopoulos, De Long, & Crutcher, 1983; Kalaska, 1988; Kalaska, Caminiti, & Georgopoulos, 1983) has led to the prediction that the more salient the distractor, the greater will be the deviation of the hand away from it. Empirical research has indeed supported this model (see Howard & Tipper, 1997; Tipper, Howard, & Jackson, 1997).

Such direct measures of behaviour are easily integrated into theories of selection proposing inhibitory mechanisms, whereas alternative accounts that do not involve inhibitory mechanisms do not address such findings.

Although, as described previously, previous work on reaching has suggested that selection mechanisms are accessing hand-centred frames, alternative explanations have to be considered. For example, in the studies of Tipper et al. (1992b) it was observed that distractors closer to the hand produced greater interference and greater negative priming than those further from the hand. Such a pattern of results shows that the spatial relationship between hand and visual stimulus is critical, but need not necessarily imply that selection mechanisms are interacting with hand-centred frames. For example, it is not possible to know where covert spatial visual attention is oriented. Perhaps it is the case that the "spotlight" of spatial attention is directed to the hand in such reaching tasks. If so, distractors that are closer to the hand are also closer to the focus of covert attention, hence they receive greater levels of analysis, produce more interference, and receive greater reactive inhibitory feedback.

Therefore further studies are necessary to show that the pattern of negative priming is determined by the action properties of a stimulus, rather than the spatial relationship between a stimulus and the responding hand. This is possible in experiments in which all spatial frames, such as visual- (e.g., retinotopic) and body-centred (e.g., head, shoulder, hand), are held constant, while the ease of action is varied. For example, even though the starting point of the reaching hand and the location of a visual stimulus remain constant, by use of a physical obstacle to increase the relative complexity of an action, the negative priming associated with the complex action should be reduced. Such an observation would imply that reactive inhibition mechanisms are indeed accessing action-based frames, as the results would not easily be interpretable in terms of spatial frames of reference.

The proposed experiment also has implications for alternative accounts of negative priming. In recent years there have been a number of papers that argue that negative priming does not reflect reactive inhibitory mechanisms of attention. It is necessary to mention two of these at this point, and a third alternative will be discussed later. (Further discussion of anti-inhibition accounts of negative priming can be found in Tipper, 2001.)

Park and Kanwisher (1994) have argued that negative priming effects in spatial tasks reflect perceptual mismatching, not distractor inhibition. In these tasks (e.g., Tipper et al., 1990) subjects report the location of a target specified by identity (e.g., O) while ignoring a distractor with a different identity (X). When a subsequent probe was presented in the same location as the previous distractor, the response was impaired. It was assumed by Tipper and colleagues that inhibition of action towards the competing distractor in the prime display impaired response to the subsequent probe presented in the same location.

In contrast, according to Park and Kanwisher (1994) negative priming in these tasks is caused by a change in the bindings of symbol identities associated with objects which appear in the same location in prime and probe displays. In other words, there is a perceptual mismatch when the probe target (O) appears in the location of the prime distractor (X), as it does in the critical "ignored repetition" condition. Or, as Kahneman, Treisman, and Gibbs (1992) might describe it, the same object file is associated with different identities (O and X). This mismatch does not occur in the baseline (or control) condition. We shall refer to this as the "perceptual mismatching" account.

A clear prediction from the perceptual mismatching theory is that if such mismatching is held constant, then the level of negative priming should also remain constant. For example, if a prime is yellow, and a subsequent probe appearing in the same location is red, the mismatch of the perceptual features of colour should produce negative priming, and this should be independent of other properties of the task, such as type of action. In sharp contrast, the action-based reactive inhibition account predicts that perceptual mismatching is not the critical variable. Rather, the form of action evoked by the stimulus will determine levels of reactive inhibition, and hence negative priming.

A further interpretation of negative priming effects that apparently challenges inhibition accounts needs to be discussed. This work places less emphasis on the highly complex selection processes that enable subjects to make fast and accurate responses to a target stimulus when it is in the presence of a distractor, and instead concentrates on retrospective processes triggered by the probe. Milliken et al. (1998) argue that when a stimulus is processed, there is analysis of whether it is old (recently encountered), which allows automatic retrieval of the stimulus, or whether it is new (not recently encountered), which requires further perceptual processing. They explain negative priming as slowed categorization of whether an item is old or new. That is, partial activation via the ignored prime leads to ambiguity as to whether the item is old (evoking automatic retrieval from memory), or whether it is new (requiring perceptual analysis).

The temporal discrimination of a probe item from those seen recently takes different amounts of time in various priming conditions. For example, in attended repetition conditions (the same item is attended in the prime and probe) the decision that the probe item is old can be made rapidly, and hence retrieval from memory is initiated quickly. Similarly, in the control condition (items in the prime display are different from those of the probe) the decision that the probe is new/novel can be taken rapidly, and hence the further perceptual analysis necessary for identification is undertaken immediately. However, in ignored repetition conditions (the ignored prime and subsequent probe are identical) there is greater ambiguity in temporal discrimination. The low level of activity produced by the ignored prime suggests that the probe is old, but this is not clear-cut. Therefore the ambiguity as to whether retrieval from memory or further perceptual encoding is necessary, slows down processing of the probe. This account has been termed "temporal discrimination".

It is not clear that the temporal discrimination account can explain negative priming in selective reaching tasks that use a small sample of stimuli. For one thing, all the stimuli are regularly repeated, and familiar, which will make temporal discrimination a difficult strategy for subjects to adopt in this type of task. Furthermore, in the first experiment to be described here, an obstacle is used to manipulate response competition while holding constant the visual and temporal discriminability between prime and probe. The temporal discrimination account of Milliken et al. (1998) would predict no change in the amount of negative priming with this manipulation, whereas the reactive inhibition model of Houghton and Tipper (1994) predicts clear differences, determined by the race for the control of action.

EXPERIMENT 1

Consider Figure 1. Subjects are required to reach out and depress the key adjacent to a red light while ignoring a yellow distractor light adjacent to one of the other keys. Previous work (e.g., Meegan & Tipper, 1998; Tipper et al., 1992b) has clearly shown that the distractor slows down the response to the target (i.e., the interference effect). These interference effects are best explained by a race model within an action-based frame of reference. That is, distractors interfere most when they are close (e.g., Meegan & Tipper, 1998; Tipper et al., 1992b), and/or ipsilateral (Fisk & Goodale, 1985; Ivry, Cohen, & Danziger, 1997; Meegan & Tipper, 1998; Prablanc, Echallier, Komilis, & Jeannerod, 1979; Tipper, Lortie, & Baylis, 1992b) to the responding hand, independently of visual frames of reference. This is because actions to objects close and/or ipsilateral to the responding hand can be programmed faster than to those of more distant or contralateral distractors. These close or ipsilateral distractors are therefore more salient and hence generally win the race for the control of action.

The inhibition model described earlier predicts the level of inhibition that is associated with a distractor. Recall that inhibition is reactive, being determined by the *relative* salience of the distractor in a particular experimental context. Therefore, distractors that evoke more rapid responses than other stimuli in the task will receive greater levels of inhibitory feedback. This pattern of results was confirmed by Tipper et al. (1992b). Furthermore, it is important to note that the model can also comfortably account for individual differences in reaching performance. Although global analysis of experiments shows that stimuli near and/or ipsilateral to the responding hand are more easily responded to, not all subjects show this pattern. This is because there are an infinite number of ways actions can be directed through 3D space, and this variability is an example of

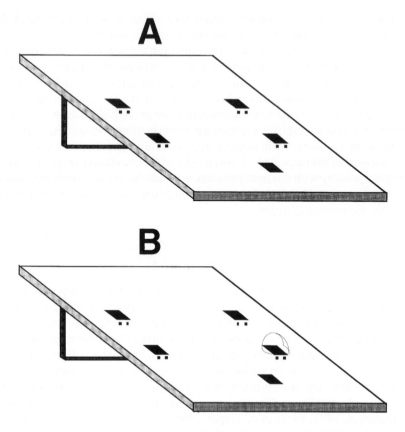

Figure 1.   Diagram of the stimulus board showing the start key and four target/distractor locations as response keys with small lights. In B, the transparent obstacle is shown in front of the near-right response key.

the degrees of freedom problem (Bernstein, 1967).[1] Nevertheless, the model simply predicts that stimuli that are most easily responded to for a particular subject, will interfere more when they are to be ignored, and hence will receive greater inhibitory feedback. The ability to predict patterns of inhibition for each individual subject is one of the advantages of the model, and this idea will be discussed further after Experiment 2.

---

[1] When a subject is reaching through 3D space to press a key with the index finger, and they are free to rotate the wrist, elbow, and shoulder, it is possible to reach this point with an infinite number of postures. This is because the degrees of freedom for the effector (including shoulder, elbow, and wrist) is much larger than the point in space where the reach terminates.

The critical condition in the current experiment is the near-right location. In Figure 1A it can be seen that this key is the same as the others in the response apparatus. Actions toward this stimulus are relatively fast and hence significant interference is produced when it is a to-be-ignored distractor (Meegan & Tipper, 1998, 1999; Tipper, Lortie, & Baylis, 1992b). By contrast, in Figure 1B a transparent obstacle is placed between the hand and the to-be-depressed target key. Although the critical visual information (key and lights) is virtually the same in Figure 1A and Figure 1B, the complexity of the action is very different. In the obstacle condition of Figure 1B the hand has to deviate around the transparent surface. Therefore this action is far more complex, and hence will tend to lose the race for the control of action. The logic of this is based on a considerable body of evidence that has shown that the time to prepare a motor programme is a direct reflection of the complexity of the action to be produced, both in simple (see Keele, 1981, for review) and choice (see Klapp, 1978, for review), reaction time tasks (see also Henry & Rogers, 1960; and Sternberg, Monsell, Knoll, & Wright, 1978, for other "response complexity" effects). Other research (e.g., Meegan & Tipper, 1999) has indeed confirmed that the obstacle produces significantly less interference than the response key alone.

What do the alternative accounts of negative priming predict? The inhibition account derived from the Houghton and Tipper (1994) model predicts a dramatic difference in the level of inhibition associated with the near-right distractor both without (Figure 1A) and with (Figure 1B) the obstacle. The former is a relatively more potent stimulus that wins the race for the control of action, and hence greater levels of inhibition will feed back to this representation. The obstructed key is much more slowly processed relative to the other stimuli in the task, and hence minimal amounts of inhibition will feed back on to this internal representation. Therefore negative priming will be significantly larger in the no-obstacle condition than in the obstacle condition.

The alternative explanations of negative priming predict quite different results. For example, Park and Kanwisher (1994) argued that negative priming in such target localization tasks was caused entirely by perceptual mismatches between prime and probe stimuli. Thus, in the experiment to be described here, on the critical ignored repetition trials the ignored distractor prime is yellow, and the subsequent probe target appearing in the same location is red. This mismatch in colour between prime and probe is what causes increased RTs, according to Park and Kanwisher (1994). Interestingly, in both the obstacle and no-obstacle conditions such colour mismatching is held constant, and hence the same level of negative priming should be observed. This predicted pattern of results contrasts quite clearly with those predicted by the inhibition model.

Similarly, the temporal discrimination account (Milliken et al., 1998) would not predict that the addition of a transparent obstacle would alter the speed with which a probe stimulus could be classified as old or new. The physical relationship between prime and probe, in terms of salience and temporal distance, is held constant. One would assume then, that the temporal discrimination of these two events is equivalent, and changes in negative priming are not predicted. However, perhaps a prediction that is opposite to that of the inhibition account can be made. That is, negative priming may be greater in the obstacle condition. One of the motivations for the temporal discrimination strategy is the avoidance of responses that correspond to the probe distractor rather than to the probe target. Thus, given that the possibility of responding to the probe distractor increases when it is an easily activated no-obstacle response relative to the slowly activated target obstacle response, even greater reliance on temporal discrimination may be predicted: Hence greater negative priming in the obstacle condition could result.

Method

Subjects.   Twenty-four undergraduate student (nineteen females and five males) from McMaster University participated in the experiment for course credit. All subjects were right-handed, had normal colour vision, and had normal or corrected-to-normal visual acuity.

Reaching apparatus.   Figures 1A and 1B represent the stimulus displays used in the experiment. For both displays, the board (area = 51 cm^2) was raised to an angle of approximately 30° from the horizontal and placed on a table 14 cm from the front edge. On the board were four 1.7 cm × 1.7 cm buttons, with a distance of 13.5 cm separating front and back buttons, and 29 cm separating left and right buttons. Two small light-emitting diodes (LEDs), one red and one yellow, were positioned beside each other directly below each button. The start button was located 13.3 cm before the centre of an imaginary line connecting the two front row buttons. The board was interfaced to an Apple IIe computer, which controlled stimulus lights, and recorded response times and errors.

Half of the subjects performed the experiment with a transparent plastic obstacle in front of the near-right button (see Figure 1B). The obstacle was 5.4 cm high from the surface of the board at its peak above the key, by 3.3 cm wide nearest the front of the board, fanning out to 7 cm wide towards the back of the board. The obstacle was placed in a position such that it was in front of the button but not the target and distractor lights below it. It was completely transparent and vision of the button and lights was not obstructed.

Design.   Excluding practice trials, there were 288 probe trials: 24 ignored repetition (IR) trials and 24 control trials for each of the 4 target locations, and 96 filler trials. In IR trials the probe target was at the same location as the prime distractor, and in control trials no probe targets or distractors were at the same locations as the preceding prime targets or distractors. Without filler trials, the probe target location was predicted by the prime distractor location on 50% of trials, so filler trials were included in which the prime target predicted the probe distractor.[2]

Response time was measured from the time the stimulus lights appeared until the time the target button was pressed. Half of the subjects performed the experiment with the obstacle at the near-right location (obstacle condition). All subjects used their right hand for the experiment.

Procedure.   The subjects sat in front of the stimulus board under dim illumination and were told to get into a position from which they could comfortably reach all four buttons with their right hand. They were asked to maintain a body posture such that the body midline was in line with the start button and the shoulder line was parallel to the front edge of the board. As in the Tipper, Lortie, and Baylis (1992a) experiments, no chin rest was employed because arm movements can be disrupted when the head is restricted (e.g., Biguer, Jeannerod, & Prablanc, 1985). Subjects were instructed to press the start and target buttons with the tip(s) of the index and/or middle finger. They were instructed that on each trial a red light would appear at one of the four buttons and a yellow light would appear at a different location. They were instructed to press the button above the red light as quickly as possible while ignoring the yellow light. The only special instruction given to subjects in the obstacle condition was that they were to avoid hitting the obstacle by going over the top of it. Each trial began with the subject pressing and holding the start key with the right hand. A pause (approximately 600 ms) occurred between start key depression and stimulus onset. After the pause, the target and distractor appeared and remained on until the subject completed the response. After the response, the subject could initiate the next trial at any time. After a five prime–probe trial demonstration from the experimenter, the subjects completed ten prime–probe practice trials which were chosen randomly from the prime–probe pairs used in the experiment.

---

[2] It should be noted that not every prime–probe stimulus relationship is included in this study. There are 144 uniquely different prime–probe pairs in such a design, which would result in a number of hours of testing for each subject. Therefore the majority of studies of negative priming have employed the reduced design to enable testing to be completed within 1 hour. Fortunately, Frame, Klein, and Christie (1993) have thoroughly investigated this issue of balanced versus unbalanced designs. Although this can influence how some priming conditions behave, critically for the current and previous work, negative priming is uninfluenced by probability of prime–probe relationships. They say, "Negative priming was observed using a full design and the effect did *not* change when the degraded design normally used in studies of inhibitory priming, was implemented. Thus subject expectancies of what occurs on the probe trial did not appear to influence inhibitory effects in selective attention tasks." Furthermore, "the negative priming effect does not attenuate with practice." (p. 17, our emphasis added).

Results

Mean of median response times and percent errors for control and IR trials are shown in Table 1. It is obviously of fundamental importance that we demonstrate that the obstacle affected the ease with which actions are evoked, before observing the associated changes in priming. The success of the obstacle manipulation in determining reach difficulty is demonstrated by the performance of near reaches which are of equal distance from the reaching hand. Eleven out of twelve subjects reaching without an obstacle showed the predicted pattern, in which the near-right ipsilateral reach is faster than the near-left control condition. The one participant who did not show this pattern was excluded at this stage of the analysis (but see later discussions), and the resultant group means were 609 ms and 674 ms for the near-right and near-left reaches respectively (cf., Fisk & Goodale, 1985). In sharp contrast, when a reach over the obstacle is necessary during reaches to the near-right location, responses to the near-right are slower than to the near-left (858 > 685 ms) for all subjects.

The inhibition model (Houghton & Tipper, 1994) predicted that negative priming for the near-right target would be reduced in the obstacle condition. To test this prediction, median response times were entered into a mixed $2 \times 4 \times 2$ ANOVA with obstacle condition as a between-groups factor, and target location (near-right, near-left, far-right, and far-left) and priming condition (IR vs control) as two repeated factors.

Significant negative priming was obtained overall, the control (704 ms) conditions being quicker than the IR conditions (718 ms), $F(1, 21) = 18.03$,

TABLE 1
Mean and standard deviation (SD) of median response times (in ms), and percentage errors, with and without the obstacle for Experiment 1; control (C) and ignored repetition (IR) conditions are shown separately for each of the four target locations

	Near-right		Near-left		Far-right		Far-left	
	IR	*C*	*IR*	*C*	*IR*	*C*	*IR*	*C*
No obstacle ($n = 11$)								
Mean	633	609	682	674	677	650	731	713
SD	61	49	78	73	57	52	71	72
% errors	2.67	3.04	3.04	2.65	3.42	2.64	1.52	0.76
Obstacle present ($n = 12$)								
Mean	843	858	700	685	719	706	749	725
SD	116	120	72	79	74	83	82	76
% errors	1.05	0.00	0.00	0.35	1.74	1.04	1.75	0.69

$MSe = 518.77$, $p < .0005$. Also, the group with the obstacle (748 ms) were significantly slower than those without (671 ms), $F(1, 21) = 6.47$, $MSe = 41846.81$, $p < .05$. As we have seen repeatedly before, response time was affected by target location, $F(3, 63) = 16.31$, $MSe = 2025.15$, $p < .0001$. And as might be expected, target location also interacted with obstacle condition, $F(3, 63) = 60.01$, $MSe = 2025.15$, $p < .0001$. In accordance with the hypothesis, the three-way interaction, in which target location interacted with priming condition and obstacle condition, was significant, $F(3, 63) = 3.90$, $MSe = 366.01$, $p < .01$. Planned contrasts of reaches to the important near-right location confirmed predictions. Thus, when no obstacle was present significant negative priming was observed ($p < .005$); in dramatic contrast, when an obstacle was present a marginally significant positive priming effect was produced ($p = .07$).

Table 1 shows a tendency for errors to increase in the no-obstacle condition compared with the obstacle, whereas the RTs decrease. An arcsine transformation was conducted on the proportion of errors in each condition and these were analysed with ANOVA, using the same factors as the RT data. Errors were significantly less common when the obstacle was present, $F(1, 22) = 5.73$, $MSe = .107$, $p < .05$, but there were no other significant main effects and no interactions. To make absolutely certain that a speed–accuracy tradeoff could not account for the RT differences found in the priming effects, errors were analysed in the critical near-right reaches separately. Again, there was no evidence for a negative priming effect, nor did it interact with obstacle condition.

Discussion

The results obtained here are predicted a priori by the inhibition account developed by Houghton and Tipper (1994), Houghton et al. (1996) and Tipper et al. (1994). This inhibition mechanism is reactive, being determined by the potency of the distractor relative to the target. Thus, when the reach evoked by the distractor is very complex relative to other possible reaches, as in the obstacle condition, the distractor tends to lose the race for the control of action, and hence evokes very little inhibition.

In sharp contrast, the perceptual mismatch account of Park and Kanwisher (1991) is severely challenged by the pattern of priming effects. Recall that this account would argue that negative priming is caused because a yellow light in the prime display is replaced by a red light in the probe display. This colour mismatch slows down the response. Hence, as this mismatch takes place in both obstacle and no obstacle conditions, negative priming must, by necessity, be equivalent in these conditions. The results obtained are dramatically different. Therefore, taken together with other work (Baylis, Tipper, & Houghton, 1997; Milliken, Tipper, & Weaver, 1994; Tipper et al., 1994, 1995) it appears that detection of perceptual mismatches generally does not mediate negative priming.

Similarly, we consider that the dramatic contrast in priming effects when a distractor evokes a rapid response (no obstacle) as compared to when slower complex responses are evoked (obstacle) is not easily explained by the Milliken et al. (1998) prime–probe discrimination account. That is, the perceptual discriminability between the ignored prime and the subsequent probe is held constant in terms of interval between the events, and physical distinctiveness (yellow vs red). Thus selection of the current response to the probe from past responses to the prime is the same in both obstacle and no obstacle conditions. However, like the episodic account to be discussed, these are new ideas, and hence future development of this temporal discrimination account may be better able to explain these data.

When interpreting these results there is yet another theory of negative priming that must be considered. Neill, Valdes, Terry, and Gorfein (1992) have argued that negative priming reflects a retrieval process, so that during processing of the probe prior processing in the prime is retrieved. A central notion in this theory is that similarity between prime and probe is crucial for retrieval of prime processing to succeed. The more similar prime and probe events are, the better is the retrieval, and hence larger negative priming is observed. Properties such as the temporal discriminability of the prime (Neill & Valdes, 1992; but see Conway, 1999, and Hasher, Zacks, Stoltzfus, Kane, & Connelly, 1996, for failures to replicate), or the contextual overlap between prime and probe (Fox & de Fockert, 1998; Lowe, 1998; Neill, 1997) have been shown to be important.

For example, concerning prime–probe similarity, completely false conclusions concerning levels of inhibition in particular selection tasks may be drawn from failures to observe a negative priming effect. A lack of negative priming may occur not because inhibition levels were very low, but rather, because the probe failed to cue retrieval of the prime processing episode. A situation in which this may have taken place was in a study reported by Tipper and Cranston (1985). When a probe stimulus was presented alone, without a competing distractor, no negative priming was observed. Tipper and Cranston suggested that inhibition may have rapidly decayed when selection was not required in the probe. However, an alternative account is that inhibition remained at the same level, but the change in context between prime (select red target from green distractor) and probe (no selection of a black stimulus) prevented the probe from cueing retrieval of the prime.

The similarity between prime and probe is therefore a critical dimension that has to be considered carefully when interpreting changes in negative priming effects in various conditions. Therefore it is necessary to examine one of the possible retrieval explanations for the lack of negative priming in the obstacle condition. Thus, in the presence of the obstacle the action to the probe in the near-right location is very different from the action previously produced in the prime display to one of the other three unobstructed keys. This difference between evoked actions in the prime and probe displays might have impaired retrieval of the prime processing episode, hence there is no evidence for negative priming.

In Experiment 2 we designed a task that directly compares this version of the retrieval theory with the inhibition account of negative priming within our reaching task. In this version of the reaching task obstacles are placed in three loci (near-right, near-left, and far-right). The episodic account just described predicts no negative priming when subjects respond to a probe at the unobstructed far-left location. This is because this action is quite different from that produced in the previous prime trial in which a reach to one of the obstructed locations must have been produced.

However, in direct opposition to this episodic view, the inhibition account predicts that negative priming will be observed in the non-obstacle far-left location, because it will be, compared to the three obstacle stimuli in the experiment, relatively easier to reach. In particular, since inhibition is reactive to the potency of the distractor, the far-left non-obstacle distractor will require a higher level of inhibition than the occluded far-right distractor, for example. Thus, the inhibition account actually predicts a trend for increased negative priming in reaches to the far-left target when obstacles are present at the other three loci, as compared to when there are no obstacles.

EXPERIMENT 2

Method

The experiment was based on Experiment 1, but was conducted in a different laboratory. Changes to the experimental set-up enabled confirmation of the generality of the inhibition theory.

Subjects. Thirty-eight people took part in the experiment (twenty-four females, fourteen males). They were either undergraduate students of the University of Wales and gained course credit, or were members of the community subject panel and were paid a small fee. All subjects were right handed, had normal colour vision, and had normal or corrected-to-normal acuity.

Reaching apparatus. The layout of the stimulus board was based on that shown in Figure 1, with the following differences: The board was not placed at an angle, but was raised on a box to 9 cm above the table surface. The transparent keys were each 2.2 × 1.4 cm and LEDs were placed inside rather than in front. Each LED could light up either red or green. An Apple Macintosh

PowerPC 8100/100 programmed with LabView 4.0 was used to control the stimulus lights and record response times and errors.

Three plastic obstacles were constructed out of semi-circles of acetate with a 5.4 cm radius, and were glued on to the board in front of the near-right, near-left, and far-right stimulus lights for the participants in the obstacle condition. The obstacles were fixed in a semi-circular shape such that the back of the obstacle was approximately level with the back of the obstructed key. Obstacles were completely transparent and vision of the keys was not obstructed.

Design.   Nineteen of the participants did the experiment with the three obstacles present, and nineteen other participants did the no-obstacle condition without any obstacles present.

Procedure.   The procedure was similar to that of Experiment 1. Subjects were instructed to press the key that lit up green and to ignore the one that lit up red on each trial. A break was incorporated into the procedure in the middle of the experiment.

Results

Two subjects from the obstacle condition were excluded from analyses. During routine de-briefing one reported that they had noticed the ignored repetition condition, which is known to abolish negative priming effects (Tipper, 1985; Tipper, Eissenberg, & Weaver, 1992a). The other failed to follow instructions correctly, consistently colliding into the obstacles rather than reaching over them. The remaining subjects in either group made no errors.

Preliminary analyses were used to confirm that the speed of reaches conformed to the required pattern in the two groups of subjects. Some participants were excluded from this stage of the analysis. It is important to point out again that such exclusions could not artificially lead to favourable results, but were used to ensure that the manipulation used in the experiment (that obstacles would slow reaches to obstructed targets) was successful. In the no-obstacle condition all but four of the nineteen subjects were faster at reaching to the far-right than to the equidistant far-left location showing the anticipated advantage of ipsilateral over contralateral reaches. Those who did not conform to this pattern were excluded at this stage of the analyses, resulting in group means of 763 ms and 802 ms for the far-right and far-left reaches respectively. A further analysis confirmed the success of the obstacle manipulation, showing that responses were faster to the far-left non-obstacle than to the far-right obstacle target in this group of subjects. This pattern held true for 14 of the 17 subjects; the 3 non-conformers were excluded from this stage of the analysis. The resultant means were 859 ms (far-right) and 804 ms (far-left). Means and standard deviations of median response times are shown in Table 2.

TABLE 2
Mean and standard deviation (SD) of median response times (in ms) for groups with
and without obstacles for Experiment 2; control (C) and ignored repetition (IR)
conditions are shown separately for each of the four target locations

	Near-right		Near-left		Far-right		Far-left	
	IR	C	IR	C	IR	C	IR	C
No obstacle (n = 15)								
Mean	667	648	715	697	777	763	813	802
SD	72	79	81	85	91	82	96	90
Obstacles present (n = 14)								
Mean	749	730	774	768	869	859	819	804
SD	80	89	86	88	100	88	86	76

There were no errors.

Significant negative priming was obtained overall, the control (758 ms) conditions being quicker than the IR conditions (772 ms), $F(1, 27) = 27.12$, $MSe = 405.80$, $p < .0001$. Also, the group with the obstacles (796 ms) were marginally slower than those without (735 ms), $F(1, 27) = 4.03$, $MSe = 53802.51$, $p < .06$. As we have seen repeatedly before, response time was affected by target location, $F(3, 81) = 144.40$, $MSe = 1305.47$, $p < .0001$. And as might be expected, target location also interacted with obstacle condition, $F(3, 81) = 17.80$, $MSe = 1305.47$, $p < .0001$. No other interactions were significant: Negative priming × Obstacle, $F(1, 27) = 0.28$, $MSe = 405.80$; Target × Negative priming, $F(3, 81) = 0.52$, $MSe = 139.01$; Target × Negative priming × Obstacle, $F(3, 81) = 0.58$, $MSe = 265.15$.

The critical measure in this study is whether negative priming is observed at the far-left location when obstacles are presented at the other three loci. Recall that retrieval-failure explanations of the results of Experiment 1 predict no negative priming at the far-left location, whereas the inhibition account predicts significant negative priming. The result of a planned contrast on ignored repetition versus control reaches to the far-left location clearly distinguishes between these alternative theories, and supports the inhibition view, as negative priming *was* significant at the far-left location in the three-obstacle condition, $F(1) = 5.18$, $p < .03$.

Further planned contrasts at the critical far locations also revealed trends in the data predicted by the inhibition account. Thus, at the far-right location negative priming was significant when there was no obstacle, $F(1) = 6.002$, $p < .02$, but non-significant when an obstacle was present, $F(1) = 2.33$, n.s. This implies that the presence of the obstacle reduced response encoding speed and hence, reduced competition for the control of action during prime trials. In the far-left location the opposite trend was revealed, in that negative priming was marginally significant when there were no obstacles present at the other three loci, $F(1) = 3.82$, $p < .06$; but as noted previously, it was clearly significant when obstacles were positioned at the other three loci.

Furthermore, the data were also in the expected direction at the near-left location, where negative priming was significant without an obstacle, $F(1) = 10.056$, $p < .003$, but was not significant when an obstacle was present at that location, $F(1) = .94$, n.s. Finally, the predicted decline in negative priming when an obstacle was presented at the near-right location was not observed. Thus, negative priming was of an equivalent size in obstacle, $F(1) = 7.91$, $p < .01$, and no-obstacle conditions, $F(1) = 10.83$, $p < .003$. However, it should be noted that even though responses to the near-right location are slowed when an obstacle is present, this stimulus evokes the fastest response in the context of this experiment, and hence is relatively the most potent distractor. This issue of relative salience is discussed further next

Discussion

The results of Experiment 2 provide a data pattern predicted by the inhibition account. In the obstacle condition, even though the reach to the far-left unob-structed probe is qualitatively different from the reach directed to the previous obstructed prime, significant negative priming was obtained among those subjects for whom the former was a relatively easier reach. Therefore, an expla-nation of the results from Experiment 1 solely in terms of episodic retrieval, in which qualitatively different reaches to prime and probe disrupt retrieval, and hence abolish or reduce negative priming effects, is not possible. Rather, the significant negative priming at the far-left location is predicted by an inhibition account.

Other patterns of data, although not as strong as we would have liked, also generally support the inhibition model. For example, in three out of the four target loci the expected pattern of negative priming was observed. Thus, when an obstacle was present in a location, negative priming generally declined, whereas at the far-left location, which never contained an obstacle, there was an increase in negative priming when obstacles were placed at the other three loci, which we interpret as being due to an increase in response encoding *relative* to the slowed encoding of the obstructed keys.

As we have tried to make clear, in our model inhibition is determined by the *relative* salience of a stimulus. In these selective reaching tasks we now have extensive evidence for hand-centred frames of reference (see Tipper, Howard, & Houghton, 1998). That is, target and distractor stimuli are encoded in terms of the actions they evoke, and there is competition between these action-based representations. The inhibition mechanism resolves this conflict by suppres-sing the representations of the distractor. The level of inhibition required to suppress the distractor representation is determined by the salience of the distractor relative to other stimuli in the display: Those that evoke actions more easily receive greater levels of inhibitory feedback.

At this point it seems to be necessary to emphasize the notion of *relative* salience. A number of reviewers have asked questions like the following: If the occluded obstacle at the near-right location is similar in both Experiments 1 and 2, why aren't the negative priming effects the same? Such questions reveal a common misunderstanding about how the external world is internally represented in the brain. Absolute stimulus properties cannot be represented. Take the simple textbook example of the representation of a light bulb. The absolute property of this stimulus is that it emits a particular intensity of light. However, the perceived intensity is totally determined by context. The light in a very dark room is an extremely salient/potent stimulus, but the same light in a room filled with sunlight is hardly noticed.

The same logic applies in the current studies. The occluded near-right location in Experiment 1 is quite different from the same stimulus in Experiment 2, because its potency is relative to the other stimuli in the experiment. Thus, the occluded near-right location in Experiment 1 evokes the slowest response in the task. Therefore in the context of that experiment it was a relatively weak distractor. In sharp contrast, because other stimuli were also occluded in Experiment 2, the near-right occluded stimulus was not the slowest stimulus. In fact, even though occluded, in the context of Experiment 2, the near-right stimulus remained the fastest response, hence its relatively high level of negative priming.

Further analysis

In these experiments we have attempted to manipulate relative ease of action. That is, we have attempted to manipulate speed of response to specific keys via the obstacle manipulation. Broadly speaking, these techniques have been successful. However, as mentioned previously, a complication in the study of reaching behaviour involves the degrees of freedom with which movements can be made. There are an infinite number of ways in which a subject can move the hand from one location to another through three-dimensional space, which might affect the relative speed of their responses.

Importantly, however, the reactive inhibition model can easily accommodate variability in reaching behaviour. The model simply predicts that for each subject, the *relative* speed of response evoked by a stimulus determines the level of reactive inhibition triggered by the stimulus when it is to-be-ignored. Thus, within any particular experimental context, stimuli evoking fast reaches will be associated with greater inhibition than stimuli evoking slow reaches.

A further analysis of all the data from Experiments 1 and 2 confirmed the basic prediction that stimuli evoking fast responses receive greater reactive inhibition. In this analysis, the position of the stimulus, and whether or not it was obstructed, was not considered. Rather, we simply ordered the data in terms of speed of response of the control conditions to each target location. That is, each subject's median response to each of the four keys was ordered in terms of fastest to slowest. All subjects from Experiments 1 and 2 were included in this analysis except for two from Experiment 2: One who noticed the ignored repetition manipulation, and one who knocked into the obstacles. No other subject selection criteria were employed.

A two way ANOVA on all the data from Experiments 1 and 2 compared speed of response to a key (fastest to slowest) with negative priming. The main effect of negative priming was highly significant, $F(1, 59) = 47.79$, MSe 436.00, $p < .0001$. Most importantly, negative priming interacted with speed of response to depress a key, $F(3, 177) = 7.01$, $MSe = 304.08$, $p < .0002$. Thus, the amount of negative priming associated with the fastest to slowest responses was 24 ms, 16 ms, 8 ms, and 5 ms respectively (see Figure 2).[3]

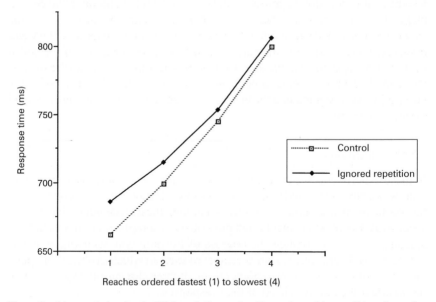

Figure 2.   Line graph showing the RT (in ms) of control and ignored repetition conditions for reaches ranked fastest to slowest by individual subject.

---

[3] This analysis reveals an interesting contrast between negative priming and inhibition of return (IOR; Posner & Cohen, 1984). Although these two inhibitory mechanisms are considered by some to have very similar underlying processes (e.g., Houghton & Tipper, 1994), they differ in terms of their frame of reference as measured by temporal properties such as reaction time and movement time. That is, in a very similar key pressing task, Howard, Lupiáñez, and Tipper (1999) did not find any difference in IOR when ordering uncued trials from fastest to slowest.

Finally, this experiment highlights the research strategy that is required when studying selective attention via priming procedures. It is necessary to consider both retrieval and encoding processes. In this case, it was not sufficient to interpret the data of Experiment 1 in terms of the model proposing hand-centred reactive inhibition mechanisms. Clearly, careful consideration of alternative accounts based on retrieval processes was necessary. Such consideration of how retrieval processes triggered by the probe could increase or decrease the size of negative priming effects must always be undertaken to ensure correct interpretation of data.

CONCLUSION

These experiments have investigated the nature of action-centred inhibitory mechanisms. Previous work had shown that the distance between a stimulus and responding hand influenced the level of interference and the level of negative priming associated with the stimulus. However, for unequivocal claims that distractors activate competing actions, and that inhibition acts on the competing actions to enable selection of a target, manipulating spatial relationships between hand and stimulus is insufficient. Therefore, we have shown here that the nature of action towards a particular spatial location determines the level of inhibition associated with a distractor. That is, actions that are rapidly encoded receive greater inhibitory feedback than those with complex slower actions.

A further aim of this study was to examine how alternative accounts deal with the negative priming obtained in such selective reaching experiments. Three theories were examined. Perceptual mismatching argued that negative priming is produced when perceptual properties of prime and probe differ. This account cannot explain why negative priming was so dramatically different at the near-right location in Experiment 1 when exactly the same perceptual mismatch existed. Similarly, the temporal discrimination theory, which argues that the ability to decide whether a stimulus was recently presented or is new is critical for response speed, also does not obviously explain the data of Experiment 1. One would imagine that the nature of the motor response does not affect whether a particular stimulus is viewed as recent or new. But perhaps this relatively new idea may be developed to encompass such data.

Finally, Experiment 2 was necessary to rule out yet a third theory of negative priming. This account argues that the relationship between prime and probe determines whether the prior prime processing (e.g., inhibitory states) is retrieved during processing of the probe. The idea is that the more similar the prime and probe, the greater the chance of retrieval. In Experiment 1 reaches to the occluded near-right probe were very different from the reach made immediately before to a non-occluded prime. This change of action could disrupt retrieval, hence failing to access prior inhibitory episodes. However,

Experiment 2 showed that change of action did not disrupt negative priming. That is, when a prime response required obstacle avoidance, and a subsequent probe response (to the far-left key) did not avoid an obstacle, negative priming was nevertheless obtained. Therefore we feel that these results are best explained within a framework describing inhibitory mechanisms acting on action-centred representations. As Figure 2 clearly reveals, ease/speed of response to a stimulus determines the level of reactive inhibition acting on that stimulus.

REFERENCES

Baylis, G.C., Tipper, S.P., & Houghton, G. (1997). Externally cued and internally generated selection: Differences in distractor analysis and inhibition. *Journal of Experimental Psychology: Human Perception and Performance, 23,* 1617–1630.

Bernstein, N. (1967). *The coordination and regulation of movement.* London: Pergamon.

Biguer, B., Jeannerod, M., & Prablanc, C. (1985). The role of position gaze in movement accuracy. In M.I. Posner & O.S.M. Marin (Eds.), *Attention and performance XI: Mechanisms of attention* (pp. 407–424). Hillsdale, NJ: Lawrence Erlbaum Associates Inc.

Conway, A.R.A. (1999). The time-course of negative priming: Little evidence for episodic trace retrieval. *Memory and Cognition, 27,* 575–583.

DeSchepper, B., & Treisman, A. (1996). Visual memory for novel shapes: Implicit coding without attention. *Journal of Experimental Psychology: Learning, Memory, and Cognition, 22,* 27–47.

Eriksen, B.A., & Eriksen, C.W. (1974). Effects of noise letters upon the identification of a target letter in a non-search task. *Perception and Psychophysics, 16,* 143–449.

Fisk, J.D., & Goodale, M.A. (1985). The organization of eye and limb movements during unrestricted reaching to targets in contralateral and ipsilateral visual space. *Experimental Brain Research, 60,* 150–178.

Fox, E. (1995). Negative priming from ignored distractors in visual selection: A review. *Psychonomic Bulletin and Review, 2,* 145–173.

Fox, E., & de Fockert, J.W. (1998). Negative priming depends on prime–probe similarity: Evidence for episodic retrieval. *Psychonomic Bulletin and Review, 5,* 107–113.

Frame, K.A., Klein, R.M., & Christie, J.J. (1993). *Negative priming of spatial location: An empirical puzzle and methodological critique* (p. 21). Washington, DC: The Psychonomic Society.

Georgopoulos, A.P. (1990). Neurophysiology of reaching. In M. Jeannerod (Ed.), *Attention and performance XIII: Motor representation and control.* Hillsdale, NJ: Lawrence Erlbaum Associates Inc.

Georgopoulos, A.P., De Long, M.R., & Crutcher, M.D. (1983). Relations between the parameters of step-tracking movements and single cell discharge in the globus pallidus and subthalamic nucleus of the behaving monkey. *Journal of Neuroscience, 3,* 1586–1598.

Grison, S., & Strayer, D.L. (2001). Negative priming and perceptual fluency: More than what meets the eye. *Perception and Psychophysics, 63,* 1063–1071.

Hasher, L., Zacks, R.T., Stoltzfus, E.R., Kane, M.J., & Connelly, S.L. (1996). On the time course of negative priming: Another look. *Psychonomic Bulletin Review, 3,* 231–237.

Henry, F.M., & Rogers, C.E. (1960). Increased response latency for complicated movements in a "memory drum" theory of neuromotor reaction. *Research Quarterly, 31,* 448–458.

Houghton, G., & Tipper, S.P. (1994). A model of inhibitory mechanisms in selective attention. In D. Dagenbach & T.H. Carr (Eds.), *Inhibitory processes in attention, memory, and language* (pp. 53-112). San Diego, CA: Academic Press.

Houghton, G., Tipper, S.P., Weaver, B., & Shore, D.I. (1996). Inhibition and interference in selective attention: Some tests of a neural network model. *Visual Cognition*, *3*, 119–164.

Howard, L.A., Lupiáñez, J., & Tipper, S.P. (1999). Inhibition of return in a selective reaching task: An investigation of reference frames. *Journal of General Psychology*, *126*(Whole no.), 421–442.

Howard, L.A., & Tipper, S.P. (1997). Hand deviations away from visual cues: Indirect evidence for inhibition. *Experimental Brain Research*, *113*, 144–152.

Ivry, R., Cohen, A., & Danziger, S. (1997). *Flanker interference is primarily from the distractor ipsilateral to the response side*. Paper presented at the Psychonomic Society meeting, Chicago, USA.

Kahneman, D., Treisman, A., & Gibbs, B.J. (1992). The reviewing of object files: Object-specific integration of information. *Cognitive Psychology*, *2*, 175–219.

Kalaska, J.F. (1988). The representation of arm movements in postcentral and parietal cortex. *Canadian Journal of Physiological Pharmacology*, *66*, 455–463.

Kalaska, J.F., Caminiti, R., & Georgopoulos, A.P. (1983). Cortical mechanisms related to the direction of two-dimensional arm movements: Relations in parietal area 5 and comparison with motor cortex. *Experimental Brain Research*, *51*, 247–260.

Keele, S.W. (1981). Behavioural analysis of movement. In V.B. Brooks (Ed.), *Handbook of physiology* (Section 1, Vol.II, Pt. 2, pp. 1391–1414). Baltimore: American Physiological Society.

Klapp, S.T. (1978). Reaction time analysis of programmed control. In R. Hutton (Ed.), *Exercise and sport sciences reviews* (Vol. 5, pp. 231–253). Santa Barbara, CA: Journal Publishing Affiliates.

Lhermitte, F. (1983). "Utilization behaviour" and its relation to lesions of the frontal lobes. *Brain*, *106*, 237–255.

Lowe, D. (1998). Long term positive and negative identity priming: Evidence for episodic retrieval. *Memory and Cognition*, *26*, 435–443.

May, C.P., Kane, M.J., & Hasher, L. (1995). Determinants of negative priming. *Psychological Bulletin*, *118*, 35–54.

Meegan, D.V., & Tipper, S.P. (1998). Reaching into cluttered visual environments: Spatial and temporal influences of distracting objects. *Quarterly Journal of Experimental Psychology*, *51A*, 225–249

Meegan, D.V., & Tipper, S.P. (1999). Visual search and target-directed action. *Journal of Experimental Psychology: Human Perception and Performance*, *25*, 1347–1362.

Milliken, B., Joordens, S., Merikle, P.A., & Seiffert, A.E. (1998). Selective attention: A reevaluation of the implications of negative priming. *Psychological Review*, *105*, 203–229.

Milliken, B., Tipper, S.P., & Weaver, B. (1994). Negative priming in a spatial localization task: Feature mismatching and distractor inhibition. *Journal of Experimental Psychology: Human Perception and Performance*, *20*, 624–646.

Moran, J., & Desimone, R. (1985). Selective attention gates visual processing within extrastriate cortex. *Science*, *229*, 782–784.

Neill, W.T. (1997). Episodic retrieval in negative priming and repetition priming. *Journal of Experimental Psychology: Learning, Memory, and Cognition*, *3*, 1291–1305.

Neill, W.T., & Valdes, L.A. (1992). The persistence of negative priming: Steady-state or decay? *Journal of Experimental Psychology: Learning, Memory, and Cognition*, *18*, 565–576.

Neill, W.T., Valdes, C.A., & Terry, K.M. (1995). Selective attention and the inhibitory control of cognition. In F.N. Dempster & C.J. Brainerd (Eds.), *Interference and inhibition in cognition* (pp. 207–261). San Diego, CA: Academic Press.

Neill, W.T., Valdes, L.A., Terry, K.M., & Gorfein, D.S. (1992). Persistence of negative priming: II. Evidence for episodic trace retrieval. *Journal of Experimental Psychology: Learning, Memory, and Cognition*, *18*, 993–1000.

Park, J., & Kanwisher, N. (1994). Negative priming for spatial locations: Identity mismatching, not distractor inhibition. *Journal of Experimental Psychology: Human Perception and Performance, 20*, 613–623.

Posner, M.I., & Cohen, Y. (1984). Components of visual orienting. In H. Bouma & D.J. Bouwhuis (Eds.), *Attention and performance X: Control of language processes*. Hove, UK: Lawrence Erlbaum Associates Ltd.

Prablanc, C., Echallier, J.R., Komilis, E., & Jeannerod, M. (1979). Optimal response of eye and hand motor systems in pointing at a visual target: 1. Spatio-temporal characteristics of eye and hand movements and their relationships when varying the amount of visual information. *Biological Cybernetics, 35*, 113–124.

Schall, J.D., & Hanes, D.P. (1993). Neural basis of saccade target selection in frontal eye fields during visual search. *Nature, 366*, 467–469.

Sternberg, S., Monsell, S., Knoll, R., & Wright, C.E. (1978). The latency and duration of rapid movement sequence: Comparisons of speech and typewriting. In G. Stelmach (Ed.), *Information processing in motor control and learning* (pp. 117–152). New York: Academic Press.

Tipper, S.P. (1985). The negative priming effect: Inhibitory priming by ignored objects. *Quarterly Journal of Experimental Psychology: Human Experimental Psychology, 37A*, 571–590.

Tipper, S.P. (2001). Does negative priming reflect inhibitory mechanisms? A review and integration of conflicting views. *Quarterly Journal of Experimental Psychology, 54A*, 321–343.

Tipper, S.P., Brehaut, J.C., & Driver, J. (1990). Selection of moving and static objects for the control of spatially directed action. *Journal of Experimental Psychology: Human Perception and Performance, 16*, 492–504.

Tipper, S.P., & Cranston, M. (1985). Selective attention and priming: Inhibitory a facilitatory effects of ignored primes. *Quarterly Journal of Experimental Psychology: Human Experimental Psychology, 37A*, 591-611.

Tipper, S.P., & Driver, J. (1988). Negative priming between pictures and words in a selective attention task: Evidence for semantic processing of ignored stimuli. *Memory and Cognition, 16*, 64–70.

Tipper, S.P., Eissenberg, T., & Weaver, B. (1992a). The effects of practice on mechanisms of attention. *Bulletin of the Psychonomic Society, 30*, 77–80.

Tipper, S.P., Howard, L.A., & Houghton, G. (1998). Action-based mechanisms of attention. *Philosophical Transactions of the Royal Society of London, Series B, 353*, 1385–1393.

Tipper, S.P., Howard, L.A., & Jackson, S.R. (1997). Selective reaching to grasp: Evidence for distractor interference effects. *Visual Cognition, 4*, 1–38.

Tipper, S.P., Lortie, C., & Baylis, G.C. (1992b). Selective reaching: Evidence for action-entered attention. *Journal of Experimental Psychology: Human Perception and Performance, 18*, 891–905.

Tipper, S.P., MacQueen, C.M., & Brehaut, J.C. (1988). Negative priming between response modalities: Evidence for the central locus of inhibition in selective attention. *Perception and Psychophysics, 43*, 45–52.

Tipper, S.P., Weaver, B., & Houghton, G. (1994). Behavioural goals determine inhibitory mechanisms of selective attention. *Quarterly Journal of Experimental Psychology, 47A*, 809–840.

Tipper, S.P., Weaver, B., & Milliken, B. (1995). Spatial negative priming without mismatching: Comment on Park and Kanwisher (1994). *Journal of Experimental Psychology: Human Perception and Performance, 21*, 1220–1229.

Tucker, M., & Ellis, R. (1998). On the relations between seen objects and components of potential actions. *Journal of Experimental Psychology: Human Perception and Performance, 24*, 830–846.

VISUAL COGNITION, 2002, 9 (4/5), 615–661

Modelling direct perceptual constraints on action selection: The Naming and Action Model (NAM)

Eun Young Yoon, Dietmar Heinke, and Glyn W. Humphreys

*Behavioural and Brain Sciences, School of Psychology,
University of Birmingham, UK*

There is increasing experimental and neuropsychological evidence that action selection is directly constrained by perceptual information from objects as well as by more abstract semantic knowledge. To capture this evidence, we develop a new connectionist model of action and name selection from objects—NAM (Naming and Action Model), based on the idea that action selection is determined by convergent input from both visual structural descriptions and abstract semantic knowledge. We show that NAM is able to simulate evidence for a direct route to action selection from both normal subjects (Experiments 1 and 2) and neuropsychological patients (Experiments 3–6). The model provides a useful framework for understanding how perceptual knowledge influences action selection.

SEMANTICALLY MEDIATED ACTION SELECTION

What are the mental operations involved when we select an action to an object, when we make a cutting action with a knife? Traditional cognitive models have emphasized that this process involves the retrieval of semantic knowledge about the object, with the semantic knowledge then being used to guide retrieval of the action (e.g., Roy & Square, 1985, for one example). For instance, for the knife, this may involve accessing knowledge that it is a utensil frequently found in the kitchen, that it is used in the preparation and eating of food, that it is employed along with a fork, and so forth. This semantic information, based on contextual and associative knowledge, is then used to "look up" a

Please address all correspondence to E.Y. Yoon, Behavioural and Brain Sciences, School of Psychology, University of Birmingham, Birmingham B15 2TT, UK.
Email: eyy844@bham.ac.uk

This work was supported by grants from the Medical Research Council and the Wellcome Trust.

http://www.tandf.co.uk/journals/pp/13506285.html   DOI:10.1080/13506280143000601

learned action that would normally be made with that utensil. Visual information may be used directly to "parameterize" the specific motor response (e.g.,
so that the grip aperture is scaled correctly; see Marr, 1982; Milner & Goodale,
1995), but the selection of "cutting", as opposed to any other class of action, is
semantically mediated. Furthermore, many models assume that the same
semantic knowledge is accessed irrespective of the modality in which the
object is presented—whether presentation involves sight of the actual object,
hearing its sound, reading its name, or touch (see Caramazza, Hillis, Rapp, &
Romani, 1990; Humphreys, Lamote, & Lloyd-Jones, 1995, for examples).
Hence, according to such models, actions will be selected in the same manner
from visual, verbal, and tactile input, with modality differences emerging only
in how easily semantic information itself is accessed in the first place—for
example, there may be "privileged" access to semantics from vision since the
physical properties of objects may covary with their semantic category (see
Hillis & Caramazza, 1991). For such models, selection of an action to an object
involves a similar set of processes to selecting a name for speech production,
which is also thought to be contingent on access to semantic knowledge (e.g.,
see Humphreys, Price, & Riddoch, 1999; Levelt, Roelofs, & Meyer, 1999).
Action and name retrieval from objects are often thought to contrast with tasks
such as word naming, which, in addition to being semantically mediated, may
also involve direct associations between input and output representations (e.g.,
orthographic representations and phonology for either the whole word or for
sub-parts; see Coltheart, Curtis, Atkins, & Haller, 1993; Plaut, McClelland,
Seidenberg, & Patterson, 1996).

A DIRECT VISUAL ROUTE IN ACTION SELECTION

The proposal that we select actions on the basis of semantic knowledge has had
some success in accounting for disturbances of action found in neurologically
damaged patients. For example, some patients have what appears to be a central
disturbance in their conceptual knowledge of particular objects, so that not only
do they use the objects incorrectly but they also can fail to judge when the
objects are used correctly (Rothi, Mack, & Heilman, 1986). In such cases,
the problem in selection of action can be tied to a deficit in action recognition,
consistent with a core semantic disturbance. In other patients, though, the
deficit in action seems more related to retrieving the associated motor plan;
thus, objects and actions may both be recognized (even named), but actions
cannot be effected normally (e.g., in the syndrome of ideomotor apraxia; see
DeRenzi & Faglioni, 1999). This pattern can be attributed to impaired access to
learned knowledge of action after semantic access is achieved.

However, other evidence is less easy to reconcile with the semantic account.
We list next five main findings that suggest that actions are selected not only on

the basis of semantic knowledge (an indirect route, for visually presented objects), but also directly from the visual information present in the environment. We use this evidence to motivate a "dual-route" model of object action and naming (the Action and Naming Model; NAM), which, we show, can simulate pieces of evidence that are difficult for pure semantic accounts. According to NAM, there is a close coupling between the visual properties of objects and actions, which determines not only prehensile movements to objects (reaching and grasping) but also the selection of which class of action to perform with a given stimulus. Perception and action are coupled in the selection as well as the parameterization of action.

Before presenting NAM, we first present the evidence favouring a direct route from vision to the processes mediating action selection. We begin with two sets of experimental findings before discussing three pieces of neuro-psychological evidence.

Action slips

Reason (1984) used diary studies to document "action slips" that occur in everyday life, when we perform incorrect actions on objects. These slips can include omissions and perseverations of action (e.g., stirring three rather than two spoonfuls of coffee into a cup), that may not be informative about the kinds of cues that are used in the selection of action. Other slips, however, can include actions that seem to be based on the visual properties of objects—an example being using an air freshener as a hairspray. In such instances, the action seems to be selected according to the shape of the object, without our necessarily taking account of the context where the object is found (e.g., along with cleaning material in a bathroom).

One problem with action slips, documented in diary studies, is that it is difficult to judge how frequently they occur, or even whether their report reflects a selective memory bias on the part of the subject (only certain kinds of errors being remembered). Action errors can be found in laboratory conditions, however, if subjects are required to respond to an unusually fast deadline. Rumiati and Humphreys (1998) had subjects make gesture or naming responses to objects and words under deadline conditions. They found that, in both gesturing and naming, some errors could be classified as being visually related to target objects (e.g., making a "hammering" gesture to a razor, presumably because these objects have similar shapes), whereas others were classed as semantically related (e.g., making a gesture to the razor as though it were a shaving brush, with a loose rather than a firm wrist action). When pictures of objects were presented and gesture responses required of subjects, visual errors were proportionately greater in number than errors that were "purely" semantic or judged as both semantically *and* visually related to targets. In contrast, when naming responses were required, visual errors were less frequent than semantic and semantic/visual errors. Rumiati and Humphreys proposed that this cross-over result was consistent with actions tending to be selected directly from the visual properties of objects without mediation by semantic knowledge. Object naming, on the other hand, tended to be driven by semantic knowledge, leading to relatively higher proportions of semantic and semantic/visual errors (see also Vitkovtich & Humphreys, 1991; Vitkovitch, Humphreys, & Lloyd-Jones, 1993, for similar evidence from naming to deadline).

Rumiati and Humphreys also had subjects make gestures-to-deadline to written words corresponding to objects. In this case they found that visual gesture errors were minimal, although semantic and semantic/visual errors still occurred. This indicates that visual gesture errors are not generated on the basis of the similarity of the actions for different objects, but only when prompted by the visual properties of objects. With words, semantic and semantic/visual errors predominate because actions are then semantically mediated.

Rumiati and Humphreys' study provides the first documentation of the relative proportion of visual to other types of action errors made by normal subjects, and it suggests that actions are selected directly from visual representations.

Response priming

Tucker and Ellis (1998, 2001) had subjects make left- or right-hand responses according to whether objects were depicted as upright or inverted in pictures. They found that responses were affected by the position of the handle of the objects with respect to the hand used for the response, even though the horizontal orientation of the object was irrelevant for the task. Thus a right hand response (e.g., for "upright") was faster if the object's handle was oriented to the right, and vice versa for a left hand response (e.g., for "inverted"). They propose that visuo-motor relations between objects and actions are coded automatically, even when these are not necessary for the task.

Similar effects of compatibility between the orientation of the object and the hand used for response has been reported by Craighero, Fadiga, Rizzolatti, and Umiltà (1998, 1999). They had subjects make a simple reaction time (RT) response by reaching and grasping an oriented bar stimulus. The initiation of the response was cued by a picture of a bar in the same or different orientation to the response bar. Although the orientation of the initiation cue was irrelevant, Craighero et al. found that RTs were faster when the cue and the response bar had the same orientation than when they had different orientations. They suggest that there was automatic activation of the oriented grasp action by the orientation of the cue.

Optic aphasia

Neuropsychological evidence for direct linkages between visual information and action comes from the syndrome of optic aphasia. The term optic aphasia is applied to patients who seem to have a problem in naming objects that is specific to the visual modality. Such patients will fail to name an object when shown to them visually (e.g., a hammer), but will name it when given a verbal definition (what do you use to knock a nail into wood?), indicating that there is not a general problem in naming. However, and in contrast to their impaired naming from vision, the patients will often make appropriate gestures to the objects (e.g., moving a hand up and down in a gesture of "striking", when shown a hammer; e.g., Lhermitte & Beauvois, 1973; see Riddoch, 1999, for a recent summary). The presence of good gesturing has often been taken to indicate that the patients can retrieve semantic information from objects, but then fail to find the associated name (e.g., Beauvois, 1982). Against this, patients have been shown to be impaired when required to make semantic matches to visually presented objects (see Hillis & Caramazza, 1995; Riddoch & Humphreys, 1987; Sirigu, Duhamel, & Poncet, 1991). For example, patient JB documented by Riddoch and Humphreys (1987) was asked to judge which two of the following three objects were used together: "hammer, chisel, screw". From vision alone he made around 30% errors. When presented with the names for the objects, though, he performed at ceiling. JB's good performance when given the names of the objects indicates that he had reasonably intact semantic knowledge, but that he had difficulty in accessing this from vision. From this it follows that the gestures he made were not necessarily based on semantic knowledge but rather were accessed directly from vision. Interestingly some of the gestures made by JB were highly specific. For instance, he gestured with his left hand to a fork and his right to a knife. The specificity of these gestures suggests that they were contingent on access to stored knowledge about the objects. Riddoch and Humphreys thus proposed that there were direct links between stored knowledge of the structural properties of objects (represented in a stored "structural description system") and learned actions. This direct route by-passed semantic (associative, contextual) knowledge about objects, and so could be used in optic aphasia even when visual access to semantic knowledge was impaired.

A similar dissociation, involving the relative preservation of action compared with impaired object recognition, has also been reported in patients with semantic dementia. Hodges, Spatt, and Patterson (1999), Lauro-Grotto, Piccini, and Shallice (1997), and Riddoch, Humphreys, Heslop, and Castermans (in press), for instance, have documented cases where the patients showed poor matching based on inter-object associations. The patients reported by Lauro-Grotto et al. and Riddoch et al. remained able to perform well-learned everyday tasks. The patient of Hodges et al. made accurate functional judgements about how objects could be used. Such deficits can be accounted for if a direct route to action is left undisturbed when semantic knowledge deteriorates.

Modality-specific apraxias

The term apraxia is used to describe disorders of motor performance that are not contingent on impaired intellect, object recognition, or motor responses (e.g., hemiplegia; see DeRenzi & Faglioni, 1999). As we have noted earlier, at least some apraxic disorders seem to reflect a central problem in retrieving stored knowledge about actions, whereas others seem contingent on impaired production, though comprehension of actions is intact. More relevant to our present purposes, some patients also manifest modality-specific deficits in action. Most frequently, patients may be impaired at making gestures to verbal input ("show me how to use a hammer") but are rather better at gesturing to the presence of a visually presented object (when the hammer is actually present). In other instances, however, an opposite pattern is apparent. Patients are worse at gesturing to visually presented objects than they are at gesturing to verbal input (e.g., DeRenzi, Faglioni, & Sorgato, 1982; Pilgrim & Humphreys, 1991; Riddoch, Humphreys, & Price, 1989). This last pattern, which may be labelled "visual apraxia", seems to comprise the opposite form of impairment to optic aphasia. In optic aphasia, patients can make actions to but are impaired at naming visually presented objects. In visual apraxia, patients are impaired at making actions to visually presented objects, but this can be in the presence of preserved naming and comprehension of the objects concerned (see Riddoch et al., 1989). To account for such a disorder, Riddoch et al. proposed that there was damage to a direct route to action from vision, which was sufficient to block actions to visually presented objects despite a semantic route to action being intact (there is good gesturing to object names), and despite good visual access to semantic knowledge (e.g., object naming being relatively preserved). In patients showing impaired gesturing to verbal input, and an improvement with visually presented objects, it can be argued that preservation of a visual route to action supports performance even when the semantic route is damaged. The double dissociations, between visual apraxia and optic aphasia and between the different modality-specific apraxias, are difficult to account for in terms of a single semantic route to action.

Utilization behaviour

Following damage to the frontal lobes, patients can manifest so-called utilization behaviour, in which they appear to act in a very environmentally driven manner. For example, Lhermitte (1983) first described cases in which patients placed successive pairs of spectacles on their faces, even when others were still present, if given the objects to hold. There is recent evidence that such behaviours are strongly cued by the visual properties of the objects present. Riddoch and colleagues (e.g., Riddoch, Edwards, Humphreys, West, & Heafield, 1998; Riddoch, Humphreys, & Edwards, 2000) had patients carry out a novel task in the face of conflicting visual cues to make over-learned responses. The stimuli were cups placed either on the left or right side of the patient's body, and the task was to pick up each cup using the hand on the side of space matching the position of the cup (left hand to left-side cup, right to right-side cup). The handles of the cups could face left or right, but this was irrelevant to the task. Although patients were able to explain the rules to the task, Riddoch et al. found that many errors were made by patients responding with the hand congruent with the handle of the cup, even though this could contradict the task rule (e.g., using the right hand to reach to the right-side handle of a cup placed on the left of the patient's body). Interestingly, these utilization-like behaviours were modulated by the visual properties of the objects. For example, the action errors reduced if the cups were inverted. Now, since access to semantic knowledge about objects is relatively indifferent to the left–right orientation of objects (see Biederman & Cooper, 1991), the strong effects of left-sight orientation observed by Riddoch et al. indicate direct visual constraints on the activation of the overlearned actions. This is also suggested by the effects of object inversion, which reduces the visual familiarity of stimuli.

Humphreys, Forde, and Francis (2000) demonstrated similar effects in multi-object tasks. They presented a patient with frontal lobe damage with an array of objects and instructed him to use them in relatively novel ways—for example, to place a saucer on a cup. They found that the patient frequently made an over-learned action rather than the action as instructed (e.g., putting the cup on the saucer), even though he could often recall the instruction when asked. Here the over-learned response overrode control from a verbal memory representation. The likelihood of this occurring was much reduced, though, if the objects were replaced by cards (then the patient might place the card saying "saucer" on the card saying "cup"), even though the words could be recognized and should cue a semantic route to action. Again it appears that utilization-like behaviours are most likely to be generated by visually familiar objects, which may directly cue visually associated actions.

THE NAMING AND ACTION MODEL (NAM)

The experimental and neuropsychological evidence cited in the previous section is consistent with the existence of a direct, visual route to action in addition to a route to action through semantic (associative and contextual) knowledge. There appear to be dynamic constraints on action selection from the visual properties of objects, so that visually related actions are activated rapidly and emerge under deadline conditions (Rumiati & Humphreys, 1998). These visually activated actions may subsequently be integrated with semantic knowledge, so that, usually, an action is selected that is consistent with both the visual and semantic properties of objects. In patients, one or other route may be damaged, giving rise to different modality-specific apraxias, although impaired visual access to semantic knowledge can still leave a visual route to action able to support gestures, in optic aphasia. Utilization behaviours may also be contingent on fast-access to action through the visual route, which may be activated by the presence of objects even when this activation contravenes a representation of the task held in verbal working memory (Humphreys et al., 2000). A framework illustrating a "dual-route" model of action selection, first proposed by Riddoch et al. (1989), is presented in Figure 1.

The "boxes and arrows" framework given in Figure 1 is useful in accounting for the functional dissociations in action and naming found in brain-lesioned patients discussed in the previous section. However, it provides a less satisfactory account of dynamic aspects of action selection. For example, it is not clear how actions activated by the visual properties of objects can be integrated with

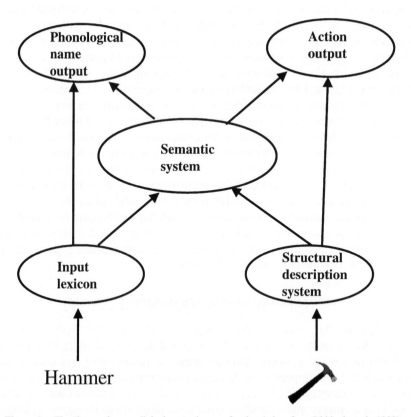

Figure 1.   The "box and arrows" dual-route theory of action (taken from Riddoch et al., 1989).

semantic knowledge during the normal action process, and why this process may lead to a "blocking" of the semantically generated response in cases of visual apraxia (see Pilgrim & Humphreys, 1991; Riddoch et al., 1989). It is also unclear how interactions between "acting" and "naming" could take place. For instance, in cases of optic aphasia it has been noted that misnaming an object can sometimes induce action errors (where patients make an action that matches the name they produce; Lhermitte & Beauvois, 1973). However, it can also be noted that, quite often, such patients may only name an object after having retrieved the associated action (Riddoch & Humphreys, 1987). What is needed here is a more explicit account of the dynamic properties of semantic and visual routes to action that can account for the time course and interactions in naming and acting, but that is nevertheless able to capture the patterns of dissociation that occur. This is the aim of the present paper. We present the Action and Naming Model (NAM), which uses a "quasi-modular" connection-ist framework to simulate action selection in normality and pathology (after brain lesions). NAM provides a dynamic account of action and name selection from objects and words. We use the model to simulate evidence on action slips in normal observers, and both optic aphasia and modality-specific apraxias (see earlier). Since NAM is applied to just action and name selection from known objects, it cannot currently simulate orientation decision tasks (cf.,Tucker & Ellis, 1998) or tasks involving actions based on the locations of objects (cf., Riddoch et al., 1998). Nevertheless, we show that it can capture evidence on a visual route to action that is difficult for a traditional, semantic approach to account for. It can also simulate interactions between acting and naming, consistent with prior neuropsychological evidence. The model provides a framework for understanding how perception directly constrains action to objects.

The architecture of NAM is presented in Figure 2. The mathematical func-tions determining the operation of the model are given in Appendix A. The model can accept two forms of input, corresponding respectively to written words and objects, and it can generate two forms of output corresponding to actions and phonological names. The model is based around a quasi-modular set of representations for the different inputs and outputs and for three main forms of stored knowledge—a visual lexicon and a structural description system, concerned respectively with the visual properties of words and objects, and semantic knowledge. Semantic knowledge is further segregated according to whether units represent superordinate information (e.g., tool, kitchen utensil, clothing) or item-specific information (hammer, spoon, tie). The input and output representations can be thought to stand for lexica for objects, words, and actions. The action lexicon contains stored representations of classes of action (e.g., twist, pour, drink), which may be specified in relatively abstract terms and even independently of the particular effectors used for the action. The operation of the model is based on an interactive activation and competition network

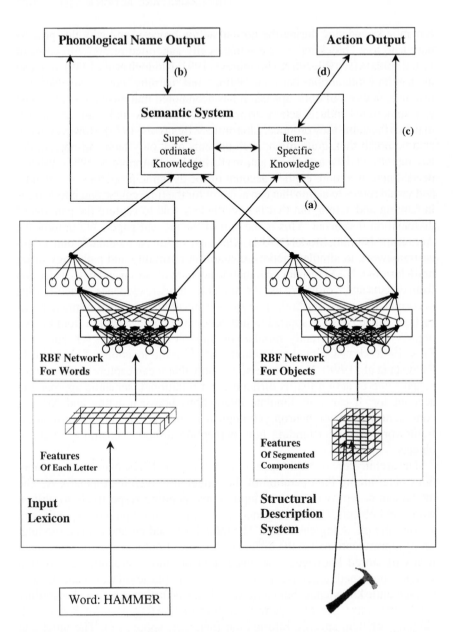

Figure 2. The architecture of NAM. (a) corresponds to the pathway from the structural description system to the item-specific semantic knowledge; (b) corresponds to the pathway from the semantic system to the phonological name output; (c) corresponds to the pathway from the structural description system to the action output; (d) corresponds to the pathway from the item-specific semantic knowledge to the action output. These pathways were lesioned to produce the neuropsychological disorders discussed in the text.

(Humphreys et al., 1995; Rumelhart & McClelland, 1982). Activation is transmitted continuously between units at the different levels, with units being competitive with one another within a given level. The time taken for convergence to be reached for a given response is taken as the RT for the model.

NAM primarily uses local representations, though words and objects produce a distributed pattern of activation across the local units in the input lexicon and in the structural description system, respectively—the source of feature similarity effects in naming and action selection for objects. Local representations are useful for understanding the functional operation of models, and they may fractionate in an appropriate way when lesioned (see Young & Burton, 1999). Furthermore, the interactive activation framework used in NAM gives rises to emergent interactions between separate processing routes, which help to capture some of the behaviours observed in optic aphasia and disorders such as visual apraxia. These emergent interactions extend our understanding beyond that offered by traditional "box and arrow" models, and they lead to effects that cannot be predicted purely on the basis of the architecture of the model.

Input descriptions

For objects, input to the structural description system is based on the activation of input units that capture plausible visual features within each nameable part of an object, with the parts arranged in the appropriate spatial location with respect to one another. There was one feature unit for each of the following features: The number of straight lines in the part, the number of curved lines, the number of vertices, and the length and width of the part. The feature units took a particular value, depending on the number and type of features present (see Table 1 for one example—a hammer). The feature units were also replicated across a two-dimensional visual field of size 5 × 5, creating a three-dimensional feature matrix (5x values × 5y values × 5 feature types). Objects were positioned so that what was judged their main functional component was placed at the centre of the field (location 3,3), and other components activated units in appropriate locations with respect to this main component. Figure 3

TABLE 1
Measurements for the feature vector of the object "hammer"

Features/components	Head of a hammer	Handle of a hammer
Width	16	3
Length	3	9
Number of vertices	12	11
Number of curved lines	3	6
Number of straight lines	7	3

gives an example of a hammer, which was segmented into two parts (the handle and the head), with the head being judged the main functional part (placed at the centre of the field). The representation captured in the matrix represents the spatial relations between the parts of objects implicitly, according to which relative locations are activated. The representation is "centred" on the main component part of the object, as would be the case if the description were activated after attention had been drawn to this main component. One realization of

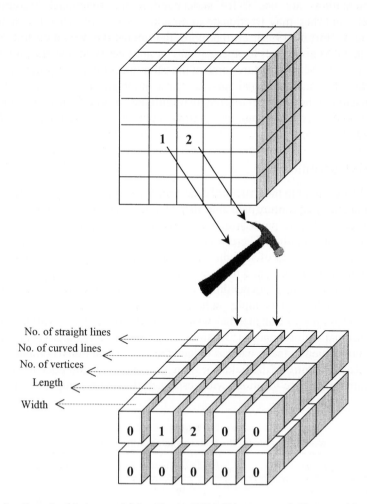

Figure 3.   Example of the input coded for objects in NAM. Objects were coded in terms of the values of each part along five feature dimensions: Width, length, number of vertices, number of curved lines, and number of straight lines. Descriptions were centred on the major functional part in each object (which was assigned to the central sets of units in the input matrix).

this is the SAIM model of visual selection (Selective Attention for Identification Model) proposed by Humphreys and Heinke (1998; Heinke & Humphreys, in press), which fixes an attentional window onto a central part of an object. Stored representations are then activated according to the positions of object features with respect to this part. The unit that responds to the object parts being in the appropriate spatial locations corresponds to the structural description of an object.

Features are mapped through to the structural description system by means of a radial basis function (RBF) network. Units in the structural description system are local, and each corresponds to one object (32 units in total). However, the profile of activation in the structural description system, given by the RBF network, is distributed across the objects, and this provides a similarity measure across the object set. Each unit in the structural description system is positively connected to units that are features of the particular object. However, given that features appear in more than one object, several structural descriptions can be activated by any given object input. The activation profile in the structural description system, then, indicates the degree of match between all known objects and the input object. Units in all other layers of the model are also local, each corresponding to one object. This allows for tractable analysis of the model (see Young & Burton, 1999).

At the level of the input lexicon for words, there is also a distributed activation of input across the local units corresponding to each word, generated in a similar way to the structural description for objects (see Table 2 for the example of a hammer). In this case, just three visual features were used to represent the visual features making up each letter. These were: The number of straight lines, the number of curved lines, and the number of vertices. On a more abstract level, the input could also be taken to be the auditory description for words, with the features corresponding to something like the phonemic properties of words. An example is presented in Figure 4. Each feature unit took a particular value according to the features presented, and this was coded in a two-dimensional vector, where the letters within a word were positioned from left to right in a feature matrix. As with the structural description for objects, the vector coded in the input lexicon was mapped through to the semantic layer by means of a radial basis function (RBF) network.

TABLE 2
Measurements for the feature vector of the word "hammer"

Features/components	H	A	M	M	E	R
Number of vertices	2	3	3	3	3	2
Number of curved lines	0	0	0	0	0	1
Number of straight lines	3	3	4	4	4	2

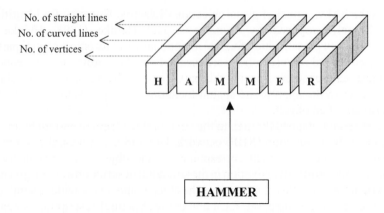

Figure 4.   Example of the input coded for words in NAM. Words were coded in terms of the values of each part along three feature dimensions: Number of vertices, number of curved lines, and number of straight lines. Descriptions were centred on the letters within a word, assigned from left to right in the two-dimensional input matrix.

The semantic system and mapping to output

Both words and objects, as inputs, can be mapped through to the semantic system. In addition, each input type has a direct route to particular output units (to phonological names, for words as input, and to actions, for objects as input). The mapping is in all cases one-to-one, from each input system respectively to the semantic system and to the two different output representations (phonological names and actions). However, words can only be mapped to actions through the semantic system, and objects can only be mapped to names through this same system. This provides a dual-route architecture, for both words and objects (for naming in the one case, and for action in the other). Units in the input lexicon (for words) and the structural description system (for objects) are mapped through independently to both superordinate and item-specific semantic representations, and units at the semantic level are only competitive within the respective sub-systems (for superordinate and item-specific knowledge). There were six superordinate units (corresponding to accessories, tools, toys/sports, household objects, food, and office items), and 32 item-specific semantic units. Units at the semantic level draw together activation from stimuli in different modalities (words and objects), and they also capture categorical relations between visually different stimuli (via the superordinate units). At the output level, names can also correspond to superordinate or to item-specific representations, but these were all competitive with one another since only one name should be selected for a given input (38 phonological name units). A control unit was used to modulate the transmission of activation from the semantic to the name output units, so that naming could be biased either to superordinates or to item-specific names (see Cohen, Dunbar, & McClelland, 1990, for an example of a similar approach in modelling the Stroop effect). Action units were item-specific (32 units), since a common action cannot be made to all objects belonging within a common category. The parameters for the model are provided in Appendix C, and the full list of objects in Appendix D.

The dual semantic and non-semantic routes from orthography to phonology are motivated by both normal experimental and neuropsychological evidence—including findings of phonological interference on semantic classification decisions to words (e.g., see Van Orden, 1987) and double dissociations between surface dyslexia, on the one hand, and phonological and deep dyslexia on the other (e.g., see Patterson & Morton, 1985). We have discussed the evidence for dual semantic and non-semantic routes to action from objects, and NAM stands as an existence proof of whether such an approach can accommodate the data on action and naming responses to objects and words.

EXPERIMENT 1
Basic times for action, naming, and categorization

Before going on to simulate evidence that favours the idea of a direct route from vision to action selection, we sought to apply NAM to basic data on naming, categorization, and action from words and objects. There is a substantial literature demonstrating that words can be named faster than objects, whereas, in contrast, objects seem to gain faster access to semantic knowledge, as measured in categorization times (e.g., see Glaser, 1994; Potter & Faulconer, 1975). Few studies have measured naming and semantic categorization times in relation to the time to access action knowledge. However, Chainay and Humphreys (in press) compared naming, superordinate classification, and action decisions to words and pictures of objects (action decisions required subjects to decide whether a given object would be used to make a "twisting" or a "pouring" action). They too found that words were named faster than objects. There was some advantage for objects over words when stimuli had to be assigned to categories for "use indoors" and "use outdoors". The advantage for objects over words was increased further, though, for action decisions. These fast decisions for actions are again consistent with either a direct route to action for objects or with a semantic system organized so that visual information more heavily connects to action than does word input. Indeed there was little advantage for action decisions over superordinate classification for words, so the fast action decisions for objects cannot simply be because these decisions can be based on less semantic knowledge. NAM needs to be able to capture this qualitative pattern of effects to provide a plausible account of object and word processing.

Method

There were 32 objects used in the simulation (see Appendix D for a full list). The items corresponded to common everyday objects, each of which can be associated with a specific manual response (hammer, fork, pen), and each of which could be coded in terms of the set of visual features allocated to the model. There were thus 32 input units in each of the structural description and input word representations, 32 units for item-specific semantic knowledge, 32 item-specific name units, and 32 action units. The 32 objects divided into 6 categories, with different numbers of members. There were six superordinate units at the semantic level, and the same number of superordinate name units. The threshold for activation in the (name and action) output units was set to 0.9. Naming and action decision times were based on the number of cycles for units to reach threshold at the phonological name and action output layers. Figures 5 and 6 illustrate the mean activation at each network cycle over the 32 visual objects and words respectively, specifying the threshold and the mean reaction times (RTs) for naming and action decisions for objects and words. The times

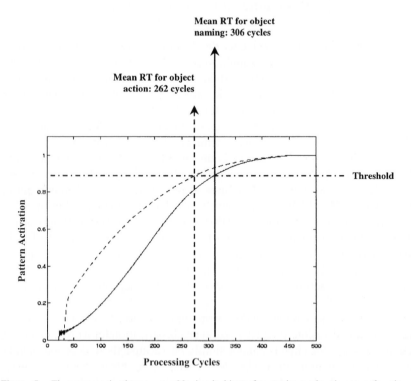

Figure 5. The mean activations across 32 visual objects for naming and action as a function of network cycles: The dotted line is for action and the solid for naming.

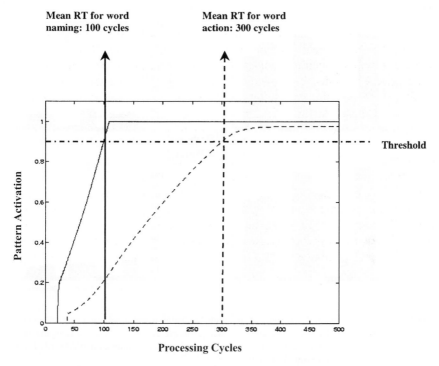

Figure 6. The mean activations across 32 words for naming and action as a function of network cycles: The dotted line is for action and the solid line for naming.

for superordinate classification were derived from the units corresponding to the superordinate phonological names, whereas naming times for individual objects were based on the item-specific units at the phonological name level. Word inputs were always for specific items (hammer, spoon) rather than for superordinate terms (tool, kitchen utensil), to prevent fast superordinate classification responses being based on the direct route to phonological names for words.

Results and discussion

The mean RTs for naming, superordinate classification, and action decisions for NAM are given in Figure 7(a). Figure 7(b) presents data from human subjects collected by Chainay and Humphreys (in press). Error proportions are given in Figures 7(c) (NAM) and 7(d) (humans). For NAM the error proportions are based on the residual, summed activity in output units for non-targets (those units not corresponding to the item presented on a trial), when the

(a)   (c)

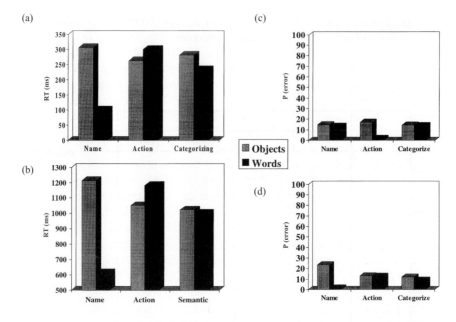

Figure 7. (a) Simulation of RTs (in network iterations) for naming, action selection, and categorization tasks. (b) Data from human participants performing naming, action decision, and categorization tasks (from Chainay & Humphreys, in press). (c) Residual error probabilities in NAM. (d) Error probabilities in human participants.

target's threshold is passed. This provides an estimate of the likelihood of response errors occurring in the model.[1]

The RT data from NAM were analysed in a repeated measures ANOVA, with two factors: Input type (object, word) and response (individual name, superordinate classification and action decision). Objects were treated as a random factor. This showed significant effects of input type, $F(1, 31) = 38.78$, $p < .001$ and response, $F(2, 30) = 96.48, p < .001$. The interaction was highly reliable, $F(2, 30) = 229.86, p < .001$.

Naming times to words were considerably faster than naming times to objects, consistent with the literature on word and object naming (e.g., Glaser,

---

[1]This would be the case if the model operated stochastically rather than in a deterministic fashion. In its normal state, the model was deterministic. However, with some degree of internal noise, activation in non-target units that is on average less than that in target units, would nevertheless sometimes give rise to errors if set higher than the target unit (by noise) on a given trial. The probability that this occurs is predicted by the average activation levels in the units, even when the model is run in deterministic mode.

1994; Potter & Faulconer, 1975). In NAM this word naming advantage comes about because words can be mapped directly through to individual phonological names, whereas objects can only be mapped through to names via sets of intermediary semantic units (i.e., words alone have a direct route to phonology). For words, actions are accessed slowly, now because activation must be transmitted through the semantic system. This means not only that a further set of connections must be passed through (when compared with the direct naming route), but also that there is added competition in selection. In particular, activation of superordinate units at the semantic level generates activation in a number of action units (for all objects within a given category), creating competition for action selection. Indeed, actions for words are selected somewhat more slowly than superordinate categorization responses, even though superordinate responses to word inputs must also be recovered through the semantic system, $t(31) = 85.38$, $p < .001$. For superordinate responses, however, activation from both superordinate and item-specific semantic units converges on a common response, ensuring little competition in superordinate name selection. In contrast, as we have noted, there is some competition for action selection.

For objects, actions are accessed faster than both superordinate and item-specific names, with the differences being greatest relative to item-specific names, $t(31) = 8.61$, $p < .001$; the advantage for action selection over superordinate classification was not reliable, $t(31) = -1.3$, $p > .05$. Actions are also selected faster from objects than from words, $t(31) = -2.49$, $p < .025$. The advantage in action selection for objects over words (due to the direct route from objects to action) is somewhat less than the advantage in naming for words over objects (due to the direct route from spelling to sound). This asymmetry occurs because action selection from objects requires more time in order to overcome competition created by the distributed representation of objects at the structural description level, relative to the competition created when input words are mapped through to their names. Interestingly, RTs for action selection and superordinate classification also go in opposite directions for objects and words. Objects are more advantaged over words for action than for superordinate classification, a result that matches our own psychological data (Chainay & Humphreys, in press). Indeed, in our simulations, words were categorized faster on average than objects, $t(31) = 3.48$, $p < .01$. For NAM, the differences in superordinate classification time reflect the contrast in the distributed representations between words and objects, and the fact that the categories here were comprised of items with heterogeneous perceptual structures. This heterogeneity, at a category level, means that overlap in structural descriptions is somewhat disruptive. In our own study examining human superordinate classification, when subjects were asked to decide whether or not a stimulus was a kitchen utensil, we have also found that RTs were faster to words as input (Chainay & Humphreys, in press; Figure 7b). It is possible that

the shared structural properties of objects cue several categories, slowing classification at a relatively fine-grained level. Note that studies that have shown a
categorization advantage for objects over words have tended to high-level classifications, such as living vs non-living, when correlated visual features can be
used to facilitate object classification (e.g., Job, Rumiati, & Lotto, 1992; Potter
& Faulconer, 1975).

Overall, then, NAM can generate data that approximate existing findings on
human naming, action decision, and classification, albeit with highly simplified input.

EXPERIMENT 2
Naming and acting to deadlines

When human subjects have to make appropriate actions, or name objects, to
unusually fast deadlines, they generate different error profiles for each task
(Rumiati & Humphreys, 1998). For actions, proportionately higher numbers of
visual errors are made than semantic and semantic/visual errors; for naming,
this pattern is reversed. The relatively high numbers of visual errors in action
are difficult to explain if actions are derived solely through a semantic system
used for both naming and action. We attempted to simulate this result in NAM,
by setting response deadlines that were faster than the thresholds normally used
for convergence. We contrasted action errors to deadline with objects and
words as input, since the proportion of visual errors is higher for objects, and,
for words (unlike for objects), more semantic plus semantic/visual errors than
visual errors are made to words (Rumiati & Humphreys, 1998). This differential error pattern fits with a direct route to action for objects but not words.

Method

For the simulations of naming and action slips, a response deadline of 100
network cycles was chosen; under these conditions the residual error variance
in non-target units increased considerably (see later). The naming control unit
was set so that item-specific naming responses were favoured. In all other
respects, the method followed that in Experiment 1.

For each object taken as a target, the other objects in the set were classified as
being visually related, semantically related, both semantically and visually
related or not related, using an error classification scheme used to label errors
generated in neuropsychological studies of object naming (Hodges, Salmon, &
Butters, 1991). Visual errors were defined as being responses corresponding
to objects that shared visual properties with the target but they belonged to
a different category and they were not associated with the target. Semantic
errors were responses corresponding to objects that do not share visual
properties with targets, but which do belong to the same category and/or are

associated with targets. Semantic/visual errors were responses corresponding to objects that are both semantically and visually related to targets; unrelated errors were for objects that were neither visually nor semantically related to targets. For a target "knife", a visual error would be "pen", a semantic error would be "jug", a semantic/visual error would be "fork", and an unrelated error would be "spinning top". Two independent judges labelled each of the possible item-specific outputs as being a visual, semantic, semantic/visual, or unrelated error, for each target. Then, for each target input, the activation in outputs units corresponding to visual, semantic, semantic/visual, and unrelated errors was summed, to provide a measure of the probability that each error type could arise under the deadline condition. Judge 1 classified 176 comparisons of target input and non-target outputs as visually related, 140 as semantic, and 36 as semantic/visual. The equivalent scores for judge 2 were 172, 138, and 38 (out of 32 input × 31 output comparisons). The same classifications were made for 89% of the comparisons by the two judges (880 out of 992 combinations). The data were analysed taking "judge" as a factor (to assess effects of the small differences in error classification across judges).

Objects and words were presented to the model. Outputs were derived from item-specific representations for names, for actions for objects, and for actions for words.

Results and discussion

The probabilities of visual and semantic (semantic + visual) errors are presented in Figure 8.

The data were analysed by taking the activation levels across the phonological name and action units for objects, and summing those for non-target units that were assigned to common error types by each judge (specifically for visual, semantic, and semantic/visual errors). These activation levels were subjected to a three-way analysis of variance with the within-item factors being task (naming objects, actions to objects, and actions to words), error type (visual vs summed semantic and semantic/visual errors[2]) , and judge (activation assigned according to the error classifications performed by each judge). This analysis revealed a reliable main effect of task, $F(2, 30) = 14.05, p < .001$, and a Task × Error interaction, $F(2, 30) = 8.66, p < .01$. There was no effect of judge, and no interactions with this factor. Accordingly, the data shown in Figure 8 are averaged across the two judges.

---

[2]In analysing their data, Rumiati and Humphreys (1998) summed semantic and semantic/visual errors as a conservative way of testing whether "pure" visual errors were more frequent than all possible semantic errors (noting that semantic/visual errors could be "pure" visual errors too).

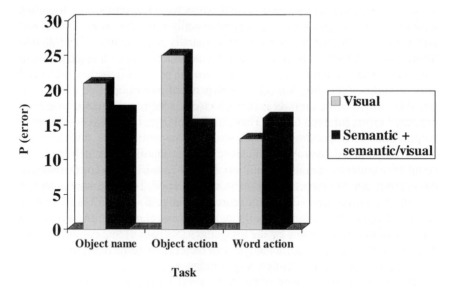

Figure 8. Simulation of responses to a fast deadline in NAM. Residual error probabilities are separated for "visual" and "semantic" (semantic + semantic/visual) error types.

The data are broadly consistent with the patterns of errors reported by Rumiati and Humphreys (1998). For action, there was considerably higher chance of making a visual action error than an action error that was semantically related to the target (the combined semantic and semantic/visual error rate). This increase in visual relative to semantic errors was less marked for naming responses (hence the interaction between task and error type). Unlike the human data, visual errors remained more prevalent, however, even in naming. This may in part reflect the constraints of the limited set of items we used, which curtail the errors across broad sets of category members (since each category was limited in size). More important, is the qualitative shift in the probabilities of the two types of error, when action and naming were compared. In addition, like Rumiati and Humphreys, we find a pattern in which more semantic plus semantic/visual errors than visual errors arose for action selection to words. Thus the high prevalence of visual errors in the same task with objects is not simply caused by interactions in the action selection system. Rather the contrast is due to the different ways in which actions are selected from objects when compared with both name selection from objects and action selection from words, with a direct visual route contributing to the proportionately high numbers of visual errors found when actions are selected to objects. For NAM, the distributed representation, generated across the structural description units, exerts a strong influence on action selection, and the spread of activation across actions to objects that have similar structures leads to the occurrence of visual errors in action. For object naming, the distributed activity at the structural description level is cleaned up to some degree by the local semantic units, prior to high levels of activation being passed on to the phonological name system. This reduces the relative frequency of visual errors. Likewise, for action selection from words, the occurrence of visual errors in action diminishes as the distributed activity at the input lexicon is "filtered" through the semantic system prior to being passed to the action output system.

One disparity with the human data is that Rumiati and Humphreys (1998) reported essentially no visual errors when subjects made gestures to deadline with words. There are some visual errors found in NAM, even with words, because the convergence procedure allows some small levels of activation to remain in units of all nontarget items; this generates a residual probability for each error type irrespective of the stimulus presented. Over and above this, though, NAM produces stimulus-specific changes in error probabilities that mimic those found when humans respond to fast deadlines.

EXPERIMENT 3
Optic aphasia

In the subsequent experiments with NAM, we evaluated whether the model could simulate patterns of performance in naming and action selection found in neuropsychological patients. Experiment 3 tested whether NAM could capture important aspects of the neuropsychological syndrome of optic aphasia. As we noted in the introductory sections, optic aphasic patients can make relatively precise actions to objects despite showing impaired object naming (e.g., Lhermitte & Beauvois, 1973). In some cases where it has been tested, visual access to detailed semantic knowledge about objects has also been shown to be impaired (e.g., Hillis & Caramazza, 1995; Riddoch & Humphreys, 1987), though the patients may still access general (superordinate) knowledge. We tested whether these deficits associated arose when the model suffered damage to the route mapping visual input descriptions of objects into the semantic system (and in particular, when damage affected mapping into item-specific semantic knowledge). In some cases of optic aphasia, the naming responses of patients seems contingent on their generating an appropriate action, though on other occasions the generation of an incorrect name can elicit an erroneous gesture (based on the name rather than the object; see Lhermitte & Beauvois, 1973). This suggests that the performance of these patients can be influenced by complex, dynamic interactions between the processes involved in name and action retrieval. We were interested in whether instances of these dynamic interactions would be apparent in NAM's performance.

Method

Lesions were simulated by adding randomly distributed noise to the pathway from the structural description system to item-specific semantic knowledge and by reducing the magnitude of the input values being transmitted at this level to 60% of the values used in the unlesioned model (see Appendix B for details). The patients studied by Hillis and Caramazza (1995) and Riddoch and Humphreys (1987) were both able to make accurate discrimination judgements between real objects and nonsense objects constructed by combining the parts of different objects. These authors suggested that the deficits in the patients occurred after intact access to stored knowledge of object form had taken place (enabling the patients to discriminate familiar, real from unfamiliar, novel objects). Hence our lesioning operated post access to the structural description units. Noise values varied between 0 and 1.5, and these values were applied to the weights shown in Figure 2, location (a). Thirty simulations were conducted, with the noise values varying across simulations but with it being constant across objects, for one given lesion example. Previous attempts to simulate neuropsychological data in connectionist models have demonstrated variable results, according to the precise lesion conducted (see Hinton & Shallice, 1991, for one example). By carrying out 30 simulations, we ensured that any results were generally true for lesions applied to this location in the model, irrespective of the particular values of noise added on one occasion. The different lesion replications can be considered to correspond to tests with different patients with damage to the same neural locus. Performance was assessed using four tasks: Object naming, object action, object categorization, and word action. Word naming and categorization were not included, as these tasks have not been critical to the neuropsychological studies.

Results and discussion

In Figures 9 and 10 we present the mean RTs and error rates for name and action selection, and for selection of the appropriate superordinate category name, with objects as input, and also the RTs and error rates for action selection to words.[3] RTs overall were slowed by lesioning, relative to the unlesioned version of the model (Figure 9). This slowing was most pronounced for object naming relative to action selection from objects. For example there was an interaction between model version (intact vs lesioned) and task (object naming, object action, object categorization, word action), in a comparison of the RTs in Experiment 1 and the RTs for each object averaged across the 30 exemplars

---

[3]Word naming was preserved under all of the present lesion conditions, since all lesions left intact the direct route from word inputs to phonological name outputs.

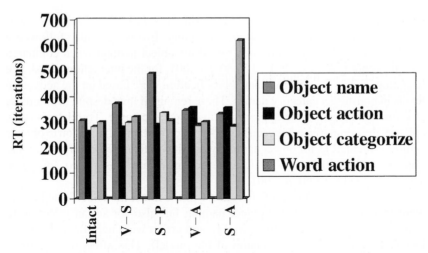

Figure 9. Simulation of RTs for object naming, object action decisions, object categorization, and word action decisions following different lesions to NAM. V–S corresponds to a lesion affecting the mapping from the structural description system to the semantic system. S–P corresponds to a lesion affecting mapping from the semantic system to the phonological name system. V–A corresponds to a lesion to the connections from the structural description system to the action lexicon. S–A corresponds to a lesion from the semantic system to the action lexicon.

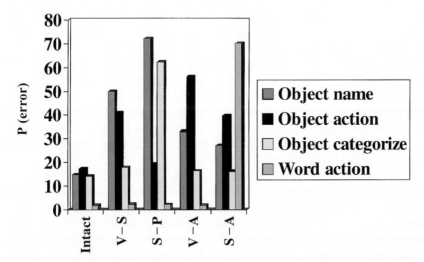

Figure 10. Simulation of the residual error probabilities for object naming, object action decision, object categorization, and word action decisions after lesioning. V–S corresponds to a lesion affecting the mapping from the structural description system to the semantic system. S–P corresponds to a lesion affecting mapping from the semantic system to the phonological name system. V–A corresponds to a lesion to the connections from the structural description system to the action lexicon. S–A corresponds to a lesion from the semantic system to the action lexicon.

with varying degrees of lesioning in Experiment 3, $F(3, 93) = 22.35, p < .001$, for the interaction between task and lesioning. Errors generally followed a similar pattern. The error rate was raised for object naming when compared with the other tasks, $F(3, 93) = 125.80, p < .001$, for the interaction of task and lesioning. Errors for superordinate classification were based on the activation levels in non-target category names. These remained low, despite the increase in errors for selecting the appropriate item-specific name. To relate to optic aphasia, the comparison between name selection and action selection to objects is most critical. RTs for object naming were slower than for action selection to objects, $t(31) = 10.56$, $p < .001$, and the error rate was raised for name selection, $t(31) = 12.60, p < 001$.

It is also of some interest that, relative to the intact model, RTs and errors were increased not only for object naming but also for action selection to objects. In the other tasks, though, RTs and errors were not affected (for the lesioned vs the unlesioned version of the model). This affect on actions to objects arises in NAM because activation from the semantic as well as the direct visual route converges on the stage of action selection. Disruption to semantic access from objects impairs the contribution of the semantic route to action. However, this in turn has a linked disruptive effect on visually mediated selection of action (via the direct visual route). The speed of action selection in optic aphasia has not been examined, so it is difficult to judge whether this account fits with the neuropsychological data. What is the case is that the accuracy to gesture from vision is relatively preserved when compared with object naming, as simulated here on the accuracy data (Figure 10). Nevertheless, gestures in such patients are often not perfect (Hillis & Caramazza, 1995; Riddoch & Humphreys, 1987). Partial preservation is predicted by NAM, with the magnitude of any deficits dependent on the precision of the required gestures. Note that, in the neuropsychological studies, less precise responses can be required for gesturing than for naming (e.g., axe and hammer would be given the same gesture but not the same name; see Funnell, 1987), and so gesturing may be scored more liberally. NAM simulates performance on tasks that require item-specific gesture responses.

We also examined whether correct naming in the model was sometimes contingent on the appropriate action being selected, and, contrariwise, whether retrieval of the wrong name sometimes led to the wrong action being selected. Figure 11 gives an example in which correct naming appeared to be contingent on retrieval of the appropriate example. Here the structure description for the object "pen" was presented. Activity in the action lexicon was rapidly generated and the appropriate output unit was activated above threshold (dotted line). Activity in the phonological output lexicon was generated more slowly, and initially the unit most activated did not correspond to the target ("pen") (solid lines). However, once the action unit for "pen" reached threshold, so support was provided (via the semantic system, see Figure 2) for the correct name,

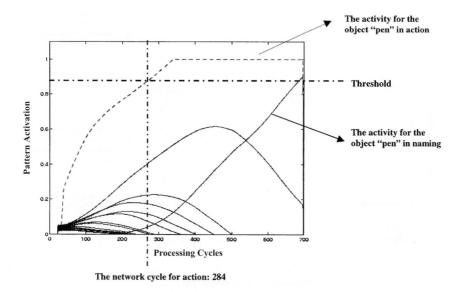

Figure 11. The effect of action retrieval on naming. The dotted line corresponds to the activation of the object "pen" in the action output lexicon. The solid lines indicate activation in the phonological output lexicon.

enabling the name unit for "pen" to gain in activation so that it eventually reached threshold. Action retrieval facilitated naming.

On some occasions, the opposite also occurred. In the example in Figure 12, the structural description for the object "ring" was presented. Although there was greater activation in the action output lexicon (dotted lines) than in the phonological lexicon (solid line), there was competition for action selection between the responses appropriate for "ring" and "bracelet". This delayed action selection and enabled a name unit to reach the threshold first (for the incorrect name, "bracelet"). The selected name then provided support for a matching action (through the semantic system), driving the action for "bracelet" to threshold. Here an incorrect action was produced, due to retrieval of the inappropriate name.

Figures 11 and 12 illustrate that action and name selection interact in NAM, with the direction of the effects dependent on whether action or name information is dominant first. Generally action retrieval is faster (Figure 9), so that, on average, actions support naming.

In addition to showing more errors in naming than in action selection, optic aphasic patients also make a variety of errors in object naming, including both visual and semantic (and semantic/visual) errors (see Hillis & Caramazza, 1995; Lhermitte & Beauvois, 1983; Riddoch & Humphreys, 1987). The

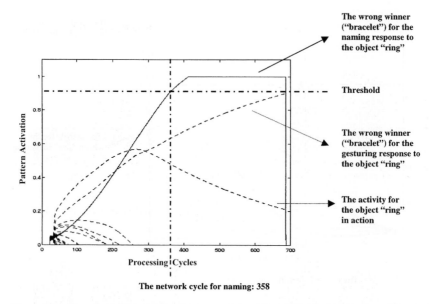

Figure 12.   The effect of (incorrect) naming on gesturing. The solid line is the activation of the name "bracelet", though the object "ring" was presented to NAM. The dotted lines indicate activation in the action output lexicon.

proportions of these contrasting error types can differ across patients (see Davidoff & de Bleser, 1993; see also Riddoch, 1999, for further discussion). We assessed error types by breaking down the error scores in the model according to whether the non-targets had visual or semantic + semantic/visual relationships with target objects, using the scoring criteria applied by judge 1 (Experiment 2).[4] The percentages of the error scores that were due to visual or semantic + semantic/visual errors are given in Figure 13, for object naming and action retrieval. Both visual and semantic errors (semantic + semantic/visual) occurred. Nevertheless, relative to normal performance under response deadline conditions (Figure 8), there was a disproportionate increase in semantic relative to visual errors, for both naming and action retrieval.

It is interesting that semantic + semantic/visual errors tended to increase disproportionately after a lesion that disrupts input into the semantic system. In a prior simulation of optic aphasia, Plaut and Shallice (1993) similarly found that a pattern of semantic and semantic/visual errors emerged even when there was a pre-semantic lesion. For both their model and ours, such errors occur

---

[4]Note that there were very few differences between the judges, and judge did not interact with any of the factors influencing the performance of the lesion model.

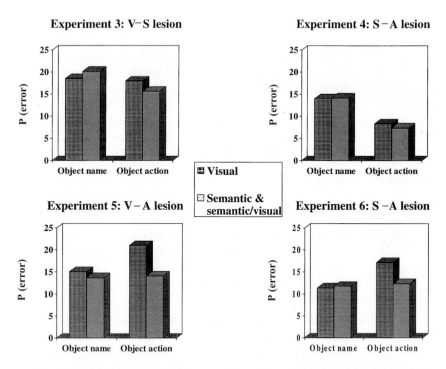

Figure 13.   The proportions of the residual error that corresponds to visual and semantic (semantic + semantic/visual) errors after lesioning NAM.

because visual input vectors were directed by the lesion into the wrong part of semantic space. The simulations provide an existence proof that we should not conclude that a patient has a deficit at a semantic level simply due to relatively high proportions of semantic and semantic/visual errors being made.

In sum, a lesion that affects mapping from the structural description system to item-specific knowledge in the semantic system can generate patterns of deficit resembling those found in optic aphasia. Following the lesion, the overall performance for both naming and action to seen objects was disturbed. Nevertheless, NAM was more likely to make errors in selecting object names than in selecting actions, although the retrieval of super-ordinate names was relatively preserved. In addition, semantic + semantic/visual errors tended to increase relative to pure visual errors. The relative preservation of action retrieval over name retrieval occurs because, in NAM, action retrieval is supported by a direct route from visual to action. Semantic errors occur because the noise added to the mappings into semantics leads to stimuli being represented incorrectly within the semantic system.

EXPERIMENT 4
Anomia

In Experiment 4 we examined the effects of introducing a lesion to the mappings between the semantic system and phonological name output units. In the neuropsychological syndrome of anomia, patients can have preserved access to semantic knowledge about objects, and they can produce appropriate actions to objects, but they showed selectively impaired naming (e.g., Kay & Ellis, 1987). For NAM, this pattern should emerge after lesioning the "output route" from semantics to the phonological names of objects.

Method

Lesioning and testing was performed in the same way as for Experiment 3, except that noise was introduced to the mappings between the semantic system and the phonological name system (locus (b), Figure 2). We also reduced input from the semantic system to the phonological output system to 60% of its normal value.

Results and discussion

The mean RTs and error rates across items are illustrated in Figures 9 and 10. RTs were increased and error rates raised relative to the unlesioned version of the model, with this effect being particularly large for object naming (there was a significant interaction between task and lesioning for both RTs and errors, $F(3, 93) = 135.81$ and 1084.51, both $p < .001$, for RTs and errors respectively). RTs were faster and error rates lower for action selection than for name selection; for RTs, $t(31) = 10.68$, $p < .001$, and for errors, $t(31) = 44.87$, $p < .001$. In contrast to when there was lesioning of input from objects to semantics, there was also some difficulty for the model in retrieving the superordinate names of the objects presented; thus, RTs were increased and error rates raised for superordinate as well as for item-specific naming, relative to action retrieval: for RTs, $t(31) = -2.37$, $p < .025$, and for errors, $t(31) = -27.59$, both $p < .001$. In anomia, patients may often provide high-level category information about objects (e.g., describing a dog as an animal), but to our knowledge studies have not tested whether such patients are impaired at retrieving "intermediate level" category information (e.g., discriminating between accessories, household objects, and stationery items), which is tested here. NAM predicts that such patients should encounter some difficulties with such intermediate level categories.

In contrast to Experiment 3, there was only a small increase in the error rate in the action retrieval tasks. Note that, here, both the semantic and the direct route to action were left undamaged, whereas there was damage to the semantic route to action in Experiment 3. The relative lack of an effect of the present lesion on action retrieval demonstrates that action retrieval for the model is not affected by changes in the efficiency of name retrieval, when the processes that lead to action retrieval are undamaged.

Figure 13 gives the relative proportions of the errors that could be classified as either visually or semantically (semantic + semantic/visual) related to targets. There were proportionately fewer visual and semantic errors here than in Experiment 3, due to an increase in "other" (unrelated) errors. The pattern of visual to semantic errors, however, did not differ greatly. Studies of anomic patients with deficits at this late stage of name retrieval reveal that the patients typically make no response rather than either visual or semantic errors (Kay & Ellis, 1987).

EXPERIMENT 5
Visual apraxia

In Experiment 5 we present data on the effects of lesioning the direct route from structural descriptions of objects to action (locus (c), Figure 2). In contrast to Experiments 3 and 4, this should disrupt action rather than name selection, so generating a form of apraxia. In particular, the damage may generate a modality-specific visual apraxia, in which action selection to visually presented objects is worse than action selection to object names (see DeRenzi, Faglioni, & Sorgato, 1982; Pilgrim & Humphreys, 1991; Riddoch et al., 1989). Note that this pattern, if apparent, would stem from NAM's adoption of an interactive framework, in which action retrieval is dependent on convergent activation from the visual and semantic routes. In this case, damage to the visual route could "block" retrieval via a semantic route. This would not follow from a more standard dual-route framework, where the visual and semantic routes would operate independently.

Method

The only difference relative to the prior lesion studies was that noise was added to the mappings between the structural description system and the action selection system, leaving other parts of the model intact. Input from the structural description system to the action selection system was also reduced to 60% of its normal value.

Results and discussion

The mean RTs and error rates are given in Figures 9 and 10. The data contrast with those reported in Experiments 3 and 4. Whereas name selection to objects was previously more likely to generate errors than action selection, the opposite results were found here. Comparing performance of the lesioned model to the intact version, there were interactions of Task × Lesioning for both RTs and errors, $F(3, 93) = 30.04$ and 164.56, both $p < .001$. Whereas, in the intact version, action selection from objects tended to be faster than object categorization (Figure 9), here action selection from objects was slowed relative to object categorization, $t(31) = 3.91$, $p < .001$. Although RTs and errors increased for object naming as well as action retrieval, the increase was particularly large for action retrieval. Error rates were also increased for action selection to objects, relative to both object naming and object categorization, $t(31) = 17.41$ and 19.87, both $p < .001$. There can be selective damage to the procedures more involved much greater in action retrieval than in name retrieval for objects. In addition, action selection to words remained relatively fast and accurate (Figure 10).

Figure 13 presents the proportions of visual and semantic (semantic + semantic/visual) errors made in object and action selection in this lesioned version of NAM. There tended to be proportionately fewer visual and semantic errors in object naming than in action retrieval. For action retrieval there were more visual than semantic errors, but this did not differ drastically from the effects of the other lesions.

NAM here mimics data showing that relatively good object recognition can occur in patients with visual apraxia (i.e., there should be good object categorization in patients who are impaired at retrieving actions for visually presented objects; Riddoch et al., 1989). In addition, the retrieval of action from words is relatively spared, in both patients and the model. The model is able to capture the qualitative patterns of spared and impaired processes in this syndrome. It is of some interest that a model such as NAM, with a dual-route architecture, produces a deficit in retrieving output even though access to that output can be achieved through an undamaged route—here the semantic route, which continued to operate relatively well (e.g., for action selection from words). For NAM, access to actions from the semantic route is disrupted by the damaged visual route when objects are presented. This blocking effect occurs because action selection in the model is contingent on the convergence of activity from both the visual and the semantic routes. Here the noise within the visual route was sufficiently high to override activation generated semantically, which would otherwise be sufficient for actions to be selected successfully. Indeed, due to input from the direct visual route (albeit noisy), there can be faster convergence of activation in the action selection system than in the semantic system, minimizing the impact of intact semantic information on action retrieval. In essence damage to the fast direct route "pushes" activation away from the correct unit in the action output lexicon, and this is not overcome by correct semantic input. One other point to note is that object naming was also disrupted to some degree by the lesion (albeit to a larger extent than action retrieval; see Figures 9 and 10). This occurred because early activation in the action output lexicon was fed back to influence semantic activation, which in turn affected object naming. NAM predicts that naming should not be completely intact in visual apraxia.

EXPERIMENT 6
Apraxia due to a damaged semantic route
to action

Many patients with apraxia are more impaired when required to gesture to a name than when asked to gesture with the object present (see DeRenzi et al., 1982). This need not be a semantic problem, since object recognition can be intact. Within the framework of NAM, this pattern could follow from damage to a semantic route to action (affecting action selection to words) along with a preserved visual route. This was evaluated in Experiment 6.

Method

The mappings from the semantic system to the action selection system were lesioned (using the same lesioning procedure as before, with both noise added and input from the semantic to the action system reduced to 60% of normal). NAM was tested as in Experiments 3–5.

Results and discussion

Figures 9 and 10 reveal the mean RTs and error rates. Now a quite different pattern of results emerged compared with those found in Experiment 5. Responses were particularly slow and error prone for action selection to words. When compared with the unlesioned version of the model there were interactions between task and lesioning, for both RTs and errors, $F(3, 93) = 183.70$ and 498.74, both $p < .001$. For action selection from words, RTs were slower and there were more errors than for action selection from objects, $t(31) = -11.13$ and -13.0, both $p < .001$, for RTs and errors respectively. Action selection from words was also worse than object naming, $t(31) = -13.67$ and -18.32, both $p < .001$, for RTs and errors respectively. Thus, there was selective disruption of action selection for words, even though actions could be selected to objects and objects could be named. This mimics the pattern found in many apraxic patients (DeRenzi et al., 1982).

Interestingly, as we observed in Experiment 3, damage to the semantic route to action again had some impact on action selection for objects, even though the direct visual route was preserved here. For example, the error rate in action selection to objects was raised when compared to when lesioning affecting the mappings from semantics to names (i.e., relative to when a comparable "output" lesion was made, in Experiment 4; see Figure 10). NAM makes the quantitative prediction that some deficit in action selection to objects should still be found in patients with all forms of apraxia, when compared with normal subjects.

The relative percentages of visual and semantic (semantic + semantic/ visual) errors were relatively low, as found with the other lesion of output from the semantic system (Experiment 4; see Figure 13). Damage to output from the semantic system can lead to unrelated errors rather than necessary increases in visual and semantically related errors.

GENERAL DISCUSSION

NAM is a dual-route model of action selection, incorporating a direct visual route to action along with an indirect semantic route. In its normal state, NAM is able to simulate patterns of performance found with normal human subjects. For the task of action selection, RTs are faster to objects than to words, and action selection for objects is faster than name selection and even classification of objects into superordinate groups (Experiment 1). Chainay and Humphreys (in press) reported similar effects when subjects had to decide whether objects were found in a kitchen, in the classification task. When an artificially fast response deadline was used, then NAM has an increased probability of making an error and, with action selection to objects, there are proportionately more errors that are visually related to targets than errors that are semantically related. With words, this trend for more visual than semantic errors was reversed (Experiment 2; see Figure 8). This matches the data reported by Rumiati and Humphreys (1998).

NAM also breaks down in a manner that simulates findings from the human neuropsychological literature. When noise was added to the mappings between the structural description system and the semantic system, performance was similar to that found in the syndrome of optic aphasia (Experiment 3). The model was impaired at object naming but superordinate classification and action selection were both relatively spared. In addition there was a relative increase in the proportion of semantic to visual errors made in object naming (Figure 13), consistent with the neuropsychological data. When the lesion affected the output mappings from the semantic system to the phonological output system, there was again difficulty in object naming, though this now affected the retrieval of superordinate names as well as the retrieval of specific names. There were also fewer errors on action selection than when the lesion affected input from objects into the semantic system (Experiment 4; see Figure 13). The pattern of impaired naming and preserved action matches that found in anomia (e.g., Kay & Ellis, 1987). The increased errors in action selection after a lesion into the semantic system (in Experiments 3 and 6) also illustrates that action selection in NAM is dependent on convergent input from the indirect (semantic) as well as the direct (visual) route. For instance, in Experiment 3 the semantic route to action was disrupted by the lesion affecting input into the semantic system, although the direct visual route was preserved. Nevertheless, errors were increased in action selection relative to when input into the semantic system was intact (though action selection errors remained less than object naming errors with the input lesion; see earlier).

In Experiments 5 and 6, lesions were applied specifically to the processes mediating action selection. Lesions to the direct visual pathway primarily affected action selection to visual objects; action selection to words was less affected (Experiment 5). In contrast, lesions affecting the mapping between semantics and the action lexicon impaired action selection to words more than to objects (Experiment 6). The opposite effects of these lesions is congruent with the double dissociation between apraxic patients who, in one case, are better at acting to words than to objects, and, in the other, are better at acting to objects than words (e.g., DeRenzi et al., 1982; Pilgrim & Humphreys, 1991; Riddoch et al., 1989).

The lesioning data provide an existence proof that a model with a dual-route architecture can generate the patterns of deficit present in the human neuropsychological literature. Particularly interesting is that finding that, despite the dual-route architecture, damage to one route affected action retrieval through the other. For NAM, the visual route to action may be thought relatively dominant, since actions are activated more rapidly via this route (extra connections must be passed through for objects to activate actions through the semantic system; see Figure 5).[5] Despite this, damage to the semantic route to action (Experiments 3 and 6) disrupted visual action retrieval to some degree. In addition, damage to the visual route itself led to impairments in the retrieval of actions to objects through the semantic system, so that the deficits associated with visual apraxia were produced (Experiment 5). This pattern emerges in NAM because the model depends on convergence across routes for outputs to be selected. The model incorporates both a modular architecture and functional interactivity, and this contribution is necessary to account for the full set of results. This is clearly useful in order to capture neuropsychological data. The modular architecture allows processes to be lesioned selectively, so generating overall dissociations between different patients (or different lesion sites, in the model), whereas functional interactivity between routes leads to "blocking" effects even when one route is undamaged. If a modular, dual-route architecture was used without the kind of functional interactivity apparent in NAM, then disorders such as visual apraxia become difficult to explain.

The functional interactivity within NAM is also helpful in accounting for some of the qualitative patterns of performance found in disorders such as optic aphasia. For example, such patients can sometimes use gesturing to prompt name retrieval; on other occasions, however, they may pronounce an incorrect name and produce an action in accordance with that (Lhermitte & Beauvois,

---

[5]Indeed the data from Experiment 2, where more visual than semantic errors were produced when actions were made to a deadline, are a consequence of this.

1973; Riddoch & Humphreys, 1987). These interactions were evident too in NAM, where activation within one route could be influenced by the emergence of a winning item along the other route (even if the winner was incorrect, leading to erroneous responses action and name responses; see Figures 11 and 12). Whichever route is more influential depends upon the dynamics of activation; for objects, activation tended to rise fastest for action responses, making performance biases to favour action over naming (see Figure 5).

New predictions

As well as accounting for a broad set of data from both normal observers and neuropsychological patients, several new predictions can be derived from NAM's performance. These are: (1) In optic aphasia (V → S lesion) there should be some slowing and increase in errors when actions are made to objects, relative to normal subjects (Figures 11 and 12). This effect should vary according to the specificity of the required action; more errors are predicted when more specific responses must be made; (2) in anomia (S → P lesion) there may be an impairment in fine-grained object categorization, as well as in object naming; (3) in visual apraxia (V → A lesion), object naming is unlikely to be perfect; and (4) in other forms of apraxia (S → A lesion), there should be deficits on acting to objects as well as to words, and there may be a somewhat weaker impairment on object naming.

To the best of our knowledge, these predictions have not been evaluated in detail in the neuropsychological literature (e.g., due to generic rather than item-specific gestures being examined), and we look forward to the predictions being put to the test. Note also that, for the most part, the predictions concern associated deficits that may occur in patients in addition to their primary deficit (e.g., a deficit in object categorization as well as naming, in anomia). Associated deficits are often difficult to interpret in neuropsychology, since they can be caused by anatomical damage to separable neural subsystems (see Humphreys & Price, 2001, for one recent account). An explicit computational model, such as NAM, gives a principled framework for explaining such data patterns. Even in this framework, though, the degree of association will depend on the magnitude of the lesion. With smaller lesions, only the primary deficit will tend to occur (an object naming impairment, in anomia).

Extending the model to account for other data

In this paper NAM has been applied to account for RT patterns in normal action and name selection to objects and words, error patterns when normal subjects respond to a fast deadline, and patterns of impairment found in brain-lesioned patients. However, the model has not simulated the effects of action priming in tasks such as deciding whether objects are in an appropriate orientation (e.g.,

Tucker & Ellis, 1998, 2001; see also Craighero et al., 1998, 1999), or the visually driven utilization behaviours found in tasks where patients have to respond to the location of a stimulus whilst suppressing a more familiar response (e.g., see Riddoch et al., 1998, 2000). In order to capture these additional results, we would need to extend NAM to include not only action and name selection, but also information about the orientation and locations of objects (e.g., to enable responses to be made to the locations of objects). In principle it should not be too difficult to do this. For example, we could incorporate output units that could represent occupied locations in the environment, so that activation of these locations would dictate where an action of a particular class (determined by the action selection system) should be made. Utilization behaviours, of the type noted by Riddoch et al., would arise when the familiar action, linked with an object in one location, is activated more than an action to the location determined by the task set. Current work is underway to extend the model in this way.

Neural substrates of action retrieval

There is considerable neurophysiological and neuropsychological evidence implicating the role of the dorsal visual system in the control of prehensile actions to objects (e.g., see reviews by Jeannerod, 1997; Milner & Goodale, 1995). However, we have been concerned not with the guidance of prehensile actions but with the selection of which articulated action to perform on an object—to lift a jug to pour rather than to drink out of—once a reach and grasp have been effected. The data on the neural substrates of this process of action selection are less comprehensive than the data on prehensile actions, and there is evidence that action selection is mediated by ventral as well as dorsal visual streams. Studies using functional brain imaging, for example, have shown that there is activation of regions in ventral cortex, particularly the left medial temporal and the inferior frontal lobes, across a range of tasks that putatively involve action retrieval; these include: Naming tools, naming the action performed tools, identifying and imagining gestures with objects (e.g., Decety et al., 1997; Grabowski, Damasio, & Damasio, 1998; Grafton, Fadiga, Arbib, & Rizzolatti, 1997; Martin, Haxby, Lalonde, Wiggs, & Ungerleider, 1995). There is also, however, some indication of activation in areas linked to the dorsal visual stream, such as area MT, in similar tasks (Chao, Haxby, & Martin, 1999; Martin et al., 1995). However, these studies have typically not compared action retrieval across different modalities of input, to attempt to isolate a direct visual route from a supramodal semantic route to action. Thus the areas implicated could be important solely for action selection based on semantic knowledge.

One imaging study that has attempted to distinguish between direct and indirect routes to action was conducted by Phillips, Humphreys, Noppeney, and Price (this issue). They had subjects make action decisions (would you make a pouring or twisting action with this object?) to either words or pictures of objects, comparing activation in these tasks with that found when physical size decisions were made to the same stimuli. Action and size decisions were also made to pictures of non-objects. They found that both the middle temporal and inferior frontal regions of the left hemisphere were activated in the action compared with the size decision tasks, but this was equally the case for objects and words. Thus, these regions seem to mediate action selection irrespective of the input modality, and they serve as good candidates for a semantic route to action. In contrast, regions of the left inferior, posterior temporal lobe were more activated to objects and non-objects relative to words, for action relative to size decisions. These regions are implicated in high-level visual processing of stimuli (e.g., Ungerleider & Haxby, 1994). The data suggest that there is increased high-level visual processing of objects and object parts in ventral visual areas in order to sustain action selection to objects. Activation in this region may subsequently project to more anterior brain regions to provide a direct visual route to action. It is interesting to note that, in NAM, the direct visual route is based on a distributed pattern of activation that reflects the parts that are common to several objects. This could lead to parts-based activation of actions to non-objects as well as to objects. The direct visual route may be said to "afford" action even when objects may not be recognized as known exemplars.

Phillips et al. (this issue) failed to find any evidence for a dorsal route to action selection. Nevertheless, there is neurophysiological evidence for cells in inferior parietal cortex firing when a particular action is performed with an object (Taira, Mine, Georgopoulos, Murata, & Sakata, 1991). In addition, Sakata and colleagues (1998) have reported that cells in this region are sensitive to the orientation of objects in three dimensions, suggesting that they can support articulated actions to objects and not just prehensile movements to particular locations. It remains possible, then, that a direct route to action is supported also through more dorsal visual areas. A question for future research to examine is whether dorsal and ventral areas differ in the types of action retrieval process they support (e.g., "afforded" actions to object parts vs retrieved actions to known objects).

Perception and action

NAM holds that perceptual processes directly constrain the selection of actions to objects. These processes can operate in parallel with action retrieval processes based on the activation of semantic knowledge about stimuli. The question of the relations between action and visual object perception is currently undergoing some debate (e.g., Rossetti, in press). There is consider-able evidence indicating that prehensile actions can be dissociated from conscious perception, coded within the ventral visual stream (e.g., Milner & Goodale, 1995; Pisella et al., 2000). Nevertheless, there are circumstances too in which prehensile actions are affected by perceptual information likely to be coded by ventral brain areas—such as actions determined by the colour of stimuli (Pisella et al., 2000). Stored knowledge can also influence simple reach and grasp movements (Jeannerod, Decety, & Michel, 1994; Riddoch et al., 1998). Several accounts can be put forward to explain both the dissociations and the interactions between perception and action. Thus, Rossetti has argued that the timing of the actions is crucial. Fast prehensile actions are based on a dorsal visual route, whereas slow actions may be governed by a ventral visual pathway. NAM does not simulate prehensile actions for reaching and grasping, but rather the selection of a category of action that may be performed once a grasp has been completed. The model assumes that the process of action selection is contingent on the activation of stored object knowledge, though this is distributed across exemplars and may not correspond to any one known object in particular. Now it is possible that information about the category of action (e.g., to drink or pour) is retrieved in parallel with the initiation of a grasp to an object, but operates over a longer time course and so is influenced by stored knowledge. The inter-relations between reaching and grasping on the one hand, and action selection on the other, have hitherto been little studied, but the development of an explicit model of the selection process invites an analysis of how selection, reaching, and grasping interface. For now, NAM shows how psychological and neuropsychological evidence can be captured if visual information is allowed not only to affect the reach-and-grasp component but also the action selection process.

REFERENCES

Beauvois, M.F. (1982). Optic aphasia: A process of interaction between vision and language. *Philosophical Transactions of the Royal Society*, *B298*, 35–47.

Biederman, I., & Cooper, E.E. (1991). Object recognition and laterality: Null effects. *Neuropsychologica*, *29*, 685–694.

Caramazza, A., Hillis, A.E., Rapp, B.C., & Romani, C. (1990). The multiple semantics hypothesis: Multiple confusions? *Cognitive Neuropsychology*, *7*, 161–189.

Chainay, H., & Humphreys, G.W. (in press). Privileged access to action for objects. *Psychonomic Bulletin & Review*.

Chao, L.L., Haxby, J.V., & Martin, A. (1999). Attribute-based neural substrates in temporal cortex for perceiving and knowing about objects. *Nature Neuroscience*, *2*, 913–919.

Cohen, J.D., Dunbar, K., & McClelland, J.L. (1990). On the control of automatic processes: A parallel distributed processing account of the Stroop effect. *Psychological Review*, *97*, 332–361.

Coltheart, M., Curtis, B., Atkins, P., & Haller, M. (1993). Models of reading aloud: Dual-route and parallel-distributed-processing approaches. *Psychological Review*, *100*, 589–608.

Craighero, L., Fadiga, L., Rizzolatti, G., & Umiltà, C. (1998). Visuomotor priming. *Visual Cognition*, *5*, 109–126.

Craighero, L., Fadiga, L., Rizzolatti, G., & Umiltà, C. (1999). Action for perception: A motor-visual attentional effect. *Journal of Experimental Psychology: Human Perception and Performance*, *25*, 1673–1692.

Davidoff, J., & De Bleser, R. (1993). Optic aphasia: A review of past studies and a reappraisal. *Aphasiology*, *7*, 135–154.

Decety, J., Grezes, J., Costes, N., Perani, D., Jeannerod, M., & Procyk, E. (1997). Brain activity during observation of actions: Influence of action content and subject's strategy. *Brain*, *120*, 1763–1777.

DeRenzi, E., & Faglioni, P. (1999). Apraxia. In G. Denes & L. Pizzamiglio (Eds.), *Handbook of clinical and experimental psychology* (pp. 421–440). Hove, UK: Psychology Press.

DeRenzi, E., Faglioni, P., & Sorgato, P. (1982). Modality-specific and supramodal mechanisms of apraxia. *Brain*, *105*, 301–312.

Funnell, E. (1987). Object concepts and object names: Some deductions from acquired disorders of word processing. In G.W Humphreys & M.J. Riddoch (Eds.), *Visual object processing: A cognitive neuropsychological approach* (pp. 233–264). Hove, UK: Lawrence Erlbaum Associates Ltd.

Glaser, W. (1994). Picture naming. *Cognition*, *42*, 61–105.

Grabowski, T.J., Damasio, H., & Damasio, A.R. (1998). Premotor and prefrontal correlates of category-related lexical retrieval. *Neuroimage*, *7*, 232–243.

Grafton, S.T., Fadiga, L., Arbib, M.A., & Rizzolatti, G. (1997). Premotor cortex activation during observation and naming of familiar tools. *Neuroimage*, *6*, 231–236.

Heinke, D., & Humphreys, G.W. (in press). Attention, spatial representation and visual neglect: Simulating emergent attention and spatial memory in the Selective Attention for Identification Model (SAIM). *Psychological Review*.

Hillis, A.E., & Caramazza, A. (1991). Constraining claims about theories of semantic memory: More on unitary versus multiple semantics. *Cognitive Neuropsychology*, *12*, 175–186.

Hillis, A., & Caramazza, A. (1995). Cognitive and neural mechanisms underlying visual and semantic processing: Implication from "optic aphasia". *Journal of Cognitive Neuroscience*, *7*, 457–478.

Hinton, G., & Shallice, T. (1991). Lesioning an attractor network: Investigations of acquired dyslexia. *Psychological Review*, *98*, 74–96.

Hodges, J.R., Salmon, D.P., & Butters, N. (1991). The nature of the naming deficit in Alzheimer's and Huntington's diseases. *Brain*, *114*, 1547–1558.

Hodges, J.R., Spatt, J., & Patterson, K. (1999). "What" and "how": Evidence for the dissociation of object knowledge and mechanical problem-solving skills in the human brain. *Proceedings of the National Academy of Sciences*, *96*, 9444–9448.

Humphreys, G.W., Forde, E.M.E., & Francis, D. (2000). The sequential organization of actions. In S. Monsell & J. Driver (Eds.), *Attention and performance XVIII: Control of cognitive processes*. Cambridge, MA: MIT Press.

Humphreys, G.W., & Heinke, D. (1998). Spatial representation and selection in the brain: Neuropsychological and computational constraints. *Visual Cognition*, *5*, 9–47,

Humphreys, G.W., Lamote, G., & Lloyd-Jones, T.J. (1995). An interactive activation approach to object processing: Effects of structural similarity, name and frequency and task in normality and pathology. *Memory*, *3*, 535–586.

Humphreys, G.W., & Price, C.J. (2001). Cognitive neuropsychology and functional brain imaging: Implications for functional and anatomical models of cognition. *Acta Psychologica*, *107*, 119–153.

Humphreys, G.W., Price, C.J., & Riddoch, M.J. (1999). From objects to names: A cognitive neuroscience approach. *Psychological Research*, *62*, 118–130.

Jeannerod, M. (1997). *The cognitive neuroscience of action*. Oxford, UK: Blackwells.

Jeannerod, M., Decety, J., & Michel, F. (1994). Impairment of grasping movements following a bilateral posterior parietal lesion. *Neuropsychologia, 32,* 369–380.

Job, R., Rumiati, R., & Loto, L. (1992). The picture superiority effect in categorization: Visual or semantic? *Journal of Experimental Psychology: Learning, Memory, and Cognition, 18,* 1019–1028.

Kay, J., & Ellis, A.W. (1987). A cognitive neuropsychological case study of anomia: Implications for psychological models of word retrieval. *Brain, 110,* 613–629.

Lauro-Grotto, R., Piccini, C., & Shallice, T. (1997). Modality-specific operations in semantic dementia. *Cortex, 33,* 593–622.

Levelt, W.J.M., Roelofs, A., & Meyer, A.S. (1999). A theory of lexical access in language production. *Behavioral and Brain Sciences, 22,* 1–38.

Lhermitte, F. (1983). Utilisation behaviour and its relation to lesions of the frontal lobes. *Brain, 106,* 237–255.

Lhermitte, F., & Beauvois, M.F. (1973). A visual-speech disconnection syndrome: Report of a case with optic aphasia. *Brain, 96,* 695–714.

Marr, D. (1982). *Vision.* San Francisco: W.H. Freeman.

Martin, A., Haxby, J.V., Lalonde, F.M., Wiggs, C.L., & Underleider, L.G. (1995). Discrete cortical regions associated with knowledge of color and knowledge of action. *Science, 270,* 102–105.

Milner, A.D., & Goodale, M. (1995). *The visual brain in action.* London: Academic Press.

Mjolsness, E., & Garrett, C. (1990). Algebraic transformations of objective functions. *Neural Networks, 3,* 651–669.

Patterson, K., & Morton, J. (1985). From orthography to phonology: An attempt at an old interpretation. In K.E. Patterson, J.C. Marshall, & M. Coltheart (Eds.), *Surface dyslexia* (pp. 333–360). Hove, UK: Lawrence Erlbaum Associates Ltd.

Phillips, J., Humphreys, G.W., Noppeney, S., & Price, C.J. (this issue). The neural substrates of action retrieval: An examination of semantic and visual routes to action. *Visual Cognition, 9*(4/5), 662–684.

Pilgrim, E., & Humphreys, G.W. (1991). Impairment of action to visual objects in a case of ideomotor apraxia. *Cognitive Neuropsychology, 8,* 459–473.

Pisella, L., Grea, H., Tilikete, C., Vighetto, A., Desmurget, M., Rode, G., Boisson, D., & Rossetti, Y. (2000). An "automatic pilot" for the hand in human posterior parietal cortex: Toward reinterpreting optic ataxia. *Nature Neuroscience, 3,* 729–736.

Plaut, D.C., McClelland, J.L., Seidenberg, M.S., & Patterson, K. (1996). Understanding normal and impaired word reading: Computational principles in quasi-regular domains. *Psychological Review, 103,* 56–115.

Plaut, D.C., & Shallice, T. (1993). Perseverative and semantic influences on visual object naming errors in optic aphasia: A connectionist account. *Journal of Cognitive Neuroscience, 5,* 89–117.

Poggio, T., & Edelman, S. (1990). A network that learns to recognize three-dimensional objects. *Nature, 343,* 263–266.

Potter, M., & Faulconer, B.A. (1975). Time to understand pictures and words. *Nature, 253,* 437–438.

Reason, J.T. (1984). Lapses of attention in everyday life. In W. Parasuraman & R. Davies (Eds.), *Varieties of attention* (pp. 515–549). Orlando, FL: Academic Press.

Riddoch, M.J. (1999). Optic aphasia. In G.W. Humphreys (Ed.), *Case studies in the neuropsychology of vision* (pp. 133–160). Hove, UK: Psychology Press.

Riddoch, M.J., Edwards, M.G., Humphreys, G.W., West, R., & Heafield, T. (1998). Visual affordances direct action: Neuropsychological evidence from manual interference. *Cognitive Neuropsychology, 15,* 645–684.

Riddoch, M.J., & Humphreys, G.W. (1987). Visual object processing in a case of optic aphasia: A case of semantic access agnosia. *Cognitive Neuropsychology, 4,* 131–185.

Riddoch, M.J., Humphreys, G.W., & Edwards, M.G. (2000). Visual affordance and object selection. In S. Monsell & J. Driver (Eds.), *Attention and performance XVIII: Control of cognitive processes*. Cambridge, MA: MIT Press.

Riddoch, M.J., Humphreys, G.W., Heslop, J., & Castermans, E. (in press). Dissociations between object knowledge and everyday action. *Neurocase*.

Riddoch, M.J., Humphreys, G.W., & Price, C.J. (1989). Routes to action: Evidence from apraxia. *Cognitive Neuropsychology*, *6*, 437–454.

Rosetti, Y. (in press). Several different "vision for action" systems: A guide to dissociating and integrating dorsal and ventral functions. In W. Prinz & B. Hommel (Eds.), *Attention and performance XIX: Common mechanisms in perception and action*. Oxford, UK: Oxford University Press.

Rothi, L.J.G., Mack, L., & Heilman, K.M. (1986). Pantomine agnosia. *Journal of Neurology, Neurosurgery and Psychiatry*, *49*, 451–454.

Roy, E.A., & Square, P.A. (1985). Common considerations in the study of limb, verbal, and oral apraxia. In E.A. Roy (Ed.), *Neuropsychological studies of apraxia and related disorders* (pp. 111–162). Amsterdam: North-Holland.

Rumelhart, D.E., & McClelland, J.L. (1982). An interactive activation model of context effects in letter perception: Part 2. The contextual enhancement effect and some tests and extensions of the model. *Psychological Review*, *89*, 60–94.

Rumiati, R.I., & Humphreys, G.W. (1998). Recognition by action: Dissociating visual and semantic routes to actions in normal observers. *Journal of Experimental Psychology: Human Perception and Performance*, *24*, 631–647.

Sakata, H., Taira, M., Kusunoki, M., Murata, M., Tanaka, Y., & Tsutsui, K. (1998). Neural coding of 3D features of objects for hand action in the parietal cortex of the monkey. *Philosophical Transactions of the Royal Society*, *B353*, 1363–1373.

Sirigu, A., Duhamel, J.-R., & Poncet, M. (1991). The role of sensorimotor experience in object recognition, *Brain*, *114*, 2555–2573.

Taira, M., Mine, G., Georgopoulos, A.P., Murata, A., & Sakata, H. (1991). Parietal cortex neurons of the monkey related to the visual guidance of hand movements. *Experimental Brain Research*, *83*, 29–36.

Tikhonov, A.N., & Arsenin, V.Y. (1977). *Solutions of ill-posed problems*. Chichester, UK: J. Wiley & Sons.

Tucker, M., & Ellis, R. (1998). On the relations between seen objects and components of potential actions. *Journal of Experimental Psychology: Human Perception and Performance*, *24*, 830–846.

Tucker, M., & Ellis, R. (2001). The potentiation of grasp types during visual object categorization. *Visual Cognition*, *8*, 769–800.

Ungerleider, L.G., & Haxby, J.V. (1994). "What" and "where" in the human brain? *Current Opinion in Biology*, *4*, 157–164.

Van Orden, G.C. (1987). A ROWS is a ROSE: Spelling, sound and reading. *Memory and Cognition*, *15*, 181–198.

Vitkovitch, M., & Humphreys, G.W. (1991). Perseverative responding in speeded naming to pictures: It's in the links. *Journal of Experimental Psychology: Learning, Memory, and Cognition*, *17*, 664–680.

Vitkovitch, M., Humphreys, G.W., & Lloyd-Jones, T.J. (1993). On naming a giraffe a zebra: Picture naming errors across different categories. *Journal of Experimental Psychology: Learning, Memory, and Cognition*, *19*, 243–259.

Young, A.W., & Burton, A.M. (1999). Simulating face recognition: Implications for modelling cognition. *Cognitive Neuropsychology*, *16*, 1–48.

APPENDICES

Appendix A. NAM

Radial basis function (RBF) network

The structural description system of NAM contained two radial basis function (RBF) networks. One RBF network transformed the input description of objects into a distributed representation of objects and object categories, and the other network did the same for input descriptions of words.

An RBF network is a two-layered network (Poggio & Edelman, 1990) whose hidden layer uses a Gaussian output function:

$$y_i^{h\_rbf} = f\left(\left\|x - w_i^h\right\|\right) \qquad (1)$$

$$\text{with } f(x) = e^{-\frac{x^2}{2 \cdot \sigma^2}}$$

Where $\left\|x - w_i^h\right\|$ is the Euclidian distance between the input (x) and the weights of the i-th unit $\left(w_i^h\right)$. $f(x)$ is the Gaussian output function with σ as standard deviation. The units in the output layer combine the activations from the units in the hidden layers by a weighted sum:

$$y_j^{o\_rbf} = \sum_{i=1}^{n} w_{ji}^o \cdot y_i^{h\_rbf} \qquad (2)$$

Where w_{ji}^o are the n weights for the j-th output unit.

For objects, the inputs (x) into the RBF network were the feature values of the input object. The number of units in the hidden layer was equal to the number of objects known to NAM. The weights of each unit in the hidden layer $\left(w_i^h\right)$ were set to the feature values of the known objects, so that each hidden unit was linked to exactly one object and each unit had the maximum value of one when the object it represents is the input. The resulting output activation at the hidden layer level was a distributed representation of the input object, which captured the similarity between this object and all other known objects. To ensure this distributed representation, the standard deviation was set to 13. This value represented a compromise between two constraints: A distributed representation (large σ) and a sufficient contrast between activations (smaller σ). The second constraint resulted from the fact that the "winner takes all" (WTA) layers, which receive the activations as input (see the following section), need a reasonable contrast between activations, in order to converge successfully into a state with a clear winner.

For words as input a second RBF network followed an analogous approach. Here, the inputs (x) were the feature values of the input word. The number of units in the hidden layer was equal to the number of words and the weights of each unit encoded the feature values of the known words. The resulting output activation at the hidden layer level was a distributed representation of the input word. For the hidden layer of this RBF network the standard deviation had to be chosen so that the likelihood of a visual error for words was small and so σ was set to 1.0. The relationship between visual errors and σ results from an important property of the WTA mechanism used here (see later). The speed of convergence for inhibited units depends on their input activations. If the input activations are high, the convergence is delayed, whereas for low input activations the speed of convergence is increased. To determine the visual error, the output activations of WTA layers at a defined point of time were used. The point of time could be defined by either NAM's reaction time or a set deadline (see main text for details). So, if output activations were still high at this point of time, a large visual error was recorded. A faster convergence thus led to a smaller visual error, whereas a slower convergence resulted in a larger visual error. As mentioned earlier, a small σ leads to small output activations feeding into WTA layers and vice versa. Consequently, a small σ led to a fast convergence and a low visual error.

In NAM the output units of the RBF networks encoded the superordinate representation of objects and words. The weights to the output units $\left(w_{ji}^o\right)$ were set with the help of a widely used interpolation method (Tikhonov & Arsenin, 1977). Let us assume for now that we aimed at a local representation of superordinate representations. For this assumption to hold, the weights of the output layer $\left(w_{ji}^o\right)$ had to fulfill the following equation for an object k:

$$(0,0,\ldots,1,0,\ldots,0) = \sum_{i=1}^{n} w_{ji}^o \cdot f\left(\left\|x_k - w_i^h\right\|\right)$$

where $(0,0,\ldots,1,0,\ldots,0)$ denotes the targeted superordinate representation of the k-th object, given the feature values (x_k) as input for the k-th object. In the case of n objects, n of these equations have to be fulfilled:

$$\begin{pmatrix} 1 & 0 & \cdots \\ 1 & 0 & \cdots \\ \cdot & \cdot & \cdot \\ 0 & \cdots & 1 \end{pmatrix} = \begin{pmatrix} w_{00}^o & w_{0i}^o & \cdots & w_{0n}^o \\ w_{10}^o & w_{1i}^o & \cdots & w_{1n}^o \\ \cdot & \cdot & & \cdot \\ w_{n0}^o & w_{ni}^o & \cdots & w_{nn}^o \end{pmatrix} \cdot \begin{pmatrix} f\left(\left\|x_0 - w_0^h\right\|\right) & f\left(\left\|x_1 - w_i^h\right\|\right) & \cdots & f\left(\left\|x_n - w_0^h\right\|\right) \\ f\left(\left\|x_0 - w_i^h\right\|\right) & f\left(\left\|x_1 - w_i^h\right\|\right) & \cdots & f\left(\left\|x_n - w_i^h\right\|\right) \\ & & & \\ f\left(\left\|x_0 - w_n^h\right\|\right) & f\left(\left\|x_1 - w_n^h\right\|\right) & \cdots & f\left(\left\|x_n - w_n^h\right\|\right) \end{pmatrix}$$

In order to shorten this expression the previous equation is rewritten as:

$$Y^{o\_rbf} = W^o \cdot H$$

where H are the activations of the hidden layer for all the objects. W^o are the weights to the output layer and Y^{o_rbf} are the superordinate representations for all the objects. Now the process of finding the weights to the output layer (W^o) turns into a simple matrix inversion:

$$W^o = Y^{0\_rbf} \cdot H^{-1}$$

Note that this approach is only applicable when the number of units in the hidden layer are the same as the number of training patterns. However, this exact interpolation leads to a strictly local representation of object categories. In order to reach a distributed representation, an additional parameter λ was introduced, turning the equation for the weights into:

$$W^o = Y^{o\_rbf} \cdot (H + \lambda \cdot I)^{-1}$$

where I is the identity matrix. λ makes the interpolation less precise and lets the RBF network generate a distributed representation at the output layer. In order to maintain the fact that the correct category unit for each object generates the largest activation, λ should be smaller than one. Here it was set 0.2 for both RBF networks.

Interactive activation within NAM

The core of the interactive activation system is based on winner take all (WTA) layers, which interact with each other. There are four separate WTA networks for (1) item-specific semantic knowledge (*ITEM*), (2) superordinate semantic knowledge (*SUP*), (3) the action output system (*ACT*), (4) the phonological name output system (*OUT*). For the WTA layer a mechanism suggested by Mjolsness and Garrett (1990) was used. The following equations denote this mechanism for an arbitrary layer *LA*.

$$x_y^{la}(t) = x^{la}(t-1) + \tau^{la} \cdot \left(-x_i^{la}(t-1) - a^{la} \cdot \left(\sum_{i=1}^{n_{la}} f\left(x_i^{la}(t-1)\right) - 1 \right) + I_i(t-1) \right) \tag{3}$$

with an approximation of a sigmoid function:

$$f(x) = \begin{cases} 0 & 4 \cdot m^{la} \cdot \left(x - s^{la}\right) + 0.5 < 0 \\ 4 \cdot m^{la} \cdot \left(x - s^{la}\right) + 0.5 & 0 \le 4 \cdot m^{la} \cdot \left(x - s^{la}\right) + 0.5 \le 0 \\ 1 & 4 \cdot m^{la} \cdot \left(x - s^{la}\right) + 0.5 > 0 \end{cases}$$

The output of the WTA was derived from: $y_i(t) = f(x_i(t))$.

In order to shorten the documentation of NAM a shorthand notation for the WTA layer LA is used here:

$$y^{la}(t) = LA(I(t))$$

Note that this notation implicitly comprises the parameters of this particular layer, where n^{la} corresponds to the number units in the WTA layer, a^{la} as the strength of inhibition τ^{la} the speed of activation changes in the layer, m^{la} the slope of the sigmoid function, and finally, s^{la} the "threshold" of the sigmoid function.

With a visually presented object, activation at the action output layer (ACT) was given by:

$$y^{act}(t) = ACT\left(a^{a1} \cdot y^{h\_rbf} + y^{item}(t)\right) \tag{4}$$

Where $a^{a1} \cdot y^{h\_rbf}$ is the direct path from the structural description system to the action output layer and y^{item} is the indirect pathway from the semantic system. For words as input the direct path was omitted:

$$y^{act}(t) = ACT\left(y^{item}(t)\right) \tag{5}$$

Activation of the superordinate units (SUP) was based on:

$$y^{cat}(t) = SUP\left(y^{input2}(t) + y^{o\_sup}(t) + a^{ci} \cdot W^{sup\_item} \cdot y^{item}(t)\right) \tag{6}$$

y^{input2} can be either y^{o_rbf} for visually presented objects of y^{c_word} for words as input. y^{o_sup} is the feedback from the phonological name output. $W^{sup\_item} \cdot y^{item}$ denotes a weighted sum of the output activation from the item-specific knowledge layer. The weighted sum transforms the item-specific activation into superordinate activation by summing the activation of all items belonging to the same category. Furthermore the weights were set in a way that the sum of activities was normalized, by dividing them by the number of items in a category.

The activation in the item-specific knowledge layer ($ITEM$) was given by:

$$y^{item}(t) = ITEM\left(y^{input1} + y^{o\_item}(t) + a^{ci} \cdot w^{sup\_item^T} \cdot y^{sup}(t) + a^{a1} \cdot y^{act}(t)\right) \tag{7}$$

y^{input1} can be either y^{h_rbf} for objects or word for words. y^{o_item} is the feedback from the phonological name output layer. $W^{sup\_item^T} \cdot y^{sup}(t)$ denotes the feedback from the superordinate knowledge layer. The weighted sum in this term results in support for all items which are members of the same category in the layer.

The phonological name output layer (OUT) received input from the category layer and the item-specific layer:

$$\left[y^{o\_item}(t), y^{o\_sup}(t)\right] = OUT\left(\left[y^{item}(t) + y^{word} + c_1, y^{sup}(t) + c_2\right]\right) \tag{8}$$

The notation [., .] states the fact that two sets of units are combined to be part of one WTA layer. y^{word} was set to zero, if objects were used. c_1 and c_2 were the two control units. Their values determined, if naming operated at a superordinate level ($c_1 = 0$ and $c_2 = 1$) or an item-specific level ($c_1 = 1$ and $c_2 = 0$). The control results from modulating the competition between units in the phonological name output layer. So setting c_1 to one results in mainly superordinate output units (y^{o_sup}) winning the competition, whereas setting c_2 to one gives the item-specific units (y^{o_item}) an advantage, forcing NAM to operate on an item-specific level in naming.

Appendix B: Lesioning

NAM was "lesioned" by inserting noise into a specific pathway. The noise was based on a uniformly distributed random variable η which produced values in the range of 0 to 1.

$$y^{lesion} = a^{lesion} \cdot y^{pathway} + (b^{lesion} - a^{lesion}) \cdot \eta \tag{9}$$

The equation of y^{lesion} was chosen in a way that the parameter b^{lesion} determined the possible maximum value of y^{lesion}. This is possible because the maximum activation of every $y^{pathway}$ is one. This limitation aims at maintaining a correct working of the WTAs. Furthermore, $a^{lesoin1}$ weights the amplitude of noise against the amplitude of pathway activation ($y^{pathway}$), where a small a^{lesion} gives rise to a large influence of noise whereas a large a^{lesion} reduces the influence of noise. Throughout this paper the parameter of the lesion was kept constant with $b^{lesion} = 1.5$ and $a^{lesion} = 0.6$.

Four different pathways were lesioned. The first lesion affected the pathway between the structural description system and the item-specific semantic knowledge layer. Here, equation (7) turned into:

$$y^{lesion1} = a^{lesion} \cdot y^{input} + (b^{lesion} - a^{lesion}) \cdot \eta$$
$$y^{item}(t) = ITEM\left(y^{lesion1} + y^{o\_item}(t) + a^{ci} \cdot w^{sup\_item^T} \cdot y^{sup}(t) + a^{a1} \cdot y^{act}(t) \right) \tag{10}$$

The second lesion affected the pathway between the semantic and the phonological output layer and turned equation (8) into:

$$y^{lesion2}(t) = a^{lesion} \cdot \left[y^{item}(t) + y^{word} + c_1, y^{sup}(t) + c_2 \right] + (b^{lesion} - a^{lesion}) \cdot \eta$$
$$\left[y^{o\_item}(t), y^{o\_sup}(t) \right] = OUT\left(y^{lesion2}(t) \right) \tag{11}$$

The third lesioned pathway was the direct pathway between the structural description system and the action output layer. With this lesion equation (4) turned into:

$$y^{lesion3} = a^{lesion} \cdot y^{h\_rbf} + (b^{lesion} - a^{lesion}) \cdot \eta$$
$$y^{act}(t) = ACT\left(y^{lesion3} + a^{a1} \cdot y^{item}(t) \right) \tag{12}$$

Finally, the fourth and last lesion affected the pathway between the item-specific knowledge layer and the action output layer. The equations were:

$$y^{lesion4} = a^{lesion} \cdot y^{item}(t) + (b^{lesion} - a^{lesion}) \cdot \eta$$
$$y^{act}(t) = ACT\left(a^{a1} \cdot y^{h\_rbf} + y^{lesion4}(t) \right) \tag{13}$$

Appendix C: Parameters

The choice of parameters is an important aspect of NAM. However, as with other models of this type, there is a concern that any data pattern could be captured, if there are sufficient parameters. In order to minimize this concern, we aimed to keep the parameters as parsimonious as possible by keeping them the same in every WTA and by maintaining the strength of interactions between the layers at a value of one. However, this was not always possible as the following discussion shows.

The parameters of all layers, apart from the speed of the action output layer and the inhibition of the superordinate layer, were the same: $m^{sup} = m^{item} = m^{out} = 0.5$, $a^{sup} = a^{out} = 8$, $s^{sup} = s^{item} = s^{out} = 0.95$, $\tau^{sup} = \tau^{item} = \tau^{out} = 0.0038$.

The speed of the action output layer was set $\tau^{act} = 0.025$. The speed was set to a value different from that used within the other layers in order to slow down the selection of a winning node. This was necessary because the action output layer received two inputs which would otherwise speed up the selection process beyond that justified by an experimental data. The parameter for the interaction between the superordinate layer and the item-specific layer (a^{ci}) was increased from 1 to 2 to inflate the influence of the superordinate layer. This was necessary, because with $a^{ci} = 1.0$, simulations for word inputs showed a similar proportion of semantic errors and visual errors in action, contrary to the empirical data. With the increase of a^{ci} the difference between semantic and visual errors was increased and provided a better fit to experimental data.

The influence of the direct route on the action output layer (a^{a1}) was set to 1.5. With $a^{a1} = 1.0$, gesturing to word stimuli was faster than gesturing to objects. This contradicts the experimental data, where gesturing to objects is faster than gesturing to words (see the main text for details). With an increase of a^{a1} to 1.5, NAM's simulation results matched the experimental data, because the higher influence of the direct pathway speeds up the WTA of the action output layer. As a consequence of increasing a^{a1} and a^{ci}, the item-specific layer received higher activation than before. To ensure convergence of this layer into a state with only winner (see Mjolsness & Garrett, 1990), the inhibition (a^{item}) was increased to 13. This alteration influenced the dynamics of NAM only marginally. It should be noted, however, that once set, the parameters for NAM were maintained across simulations (e.g., for both the "normal" and lesioned versions of the model).

Appendix D

The list of objects used

1.	Aerosol can	17.	Nail
2.	Axe	18.	Nut
3.	Banana	19.	Opener
4.	Bat	20.	Peg
5.	Boomerang	21.	Pen
6.	Bottle	22.	Pliers
7.	Bracelet	23.	Ring
8.	Doorknob	24.	Ruler
9.	Drill	25.	Saw
10.	Fork	26.	Screw
11.	Hair clip	27.	Screwdriver
12.	Hammer	28.	Spinning top
13.	Ice-cream	29.	Spoon
14.	Jug	30.	Stapler
15.	Knife	31.	Toothbrush
16.	Lighter	32.	Tweezers

Object categorizations for the 32 items used

1. Accessories: Aerosol-can, bracelet, hair-clip, ring, toothbrush, tweezers
2. Tool: Axe, doorknob, drill, hammer, nail, pliers, saw, screw, screwdriver
3. Play/Sports: Bat, boomerang, spinning top
4. Household: Bottle, fork, knife, jug, lighter, opener, peg, spoon
5. Food: Banana, Ice-cream, nut
6. Stationery: Pen, ruler, stapler

VISUAL COGNITION, 2002, 9 (4/5), 662–684

The neural substrates of action retrieval: An examination of semantic and visual routes to action

Jacqueline A. Phillips

*The Wellcome Department of Cognitive Neurology,
Institute of Neurology, London, UK*

Glyn W. Humphreys

*Behavioural Brain Sciences, School of Psychology,
University of Birmingham, UK*

Uta Noppeney and Cathy J. Price

*The Wellcome Department of Cognitive Neurology,
Institute of Neurology, London, UK*

We report three PET experiments that examine the neural substrates of the conceptual components of action retrieval. In all three experiments, subjects made action or screen-size decisions to familiar objects presented either as pictures or written words (the names of the objects). In Experiment 1, a third task was included, requiring a decision on the real-life size of the stimuli. In Experiment 2, a third stimulus type was included, with action and size decisions also performed on pictures of meaningless novel objects. Finally, in Experiment 3, we changed the response mode from a button press to a more explicit movement made with a "manipulandum". Based on neuropsychological findings, we predicted that when action responses were made to pictures of familiar or novel objects, relative to words, there would be less activation in semantic regions but greater activation in visual, motor, and perhaps parietal cortices. We found that,

---

Please address all correspondence to Dr C. Price, Wellcome Department of Cognitive Neurology, Institute of Neurology, 12 Queen Square, London WC1N 3BG, UK.
Email: c.price@fil.ion.ucl.ac.uk
This work was supported by the Wellcome Trust. We thank Mark Georgeson and Dawn Francis for help with creating the spatial-frequency scrambled images for the baseline condition in Experiment 3.

---

http://www.tandf.co.uk/journals/pp/13506285.html   DOI:10.1080/13506280143000610

action relative to screen-size decisions on both pictures and words activated the left hemisphere temporo-frontal semantic system with activation in the left posterior middle temporal cortex specific to action retrieval (Experiment 1). In addition, action retrieval elicited more activation for (1) words than pictures in areas associated with semantics; and (2) novel objects than words or familiar objects in areas associated with pre-semantic object processing. These results are discussed in the context of semantic and visual routes to action retrieval.

Neuropsychological studies suggest that there are separate cognitive and neural systems for retrieving the names or actions associated with objects. This inference is based on studies of patients with visual apraxia and optic aphasia, and the types of errors made by normal subjects.

VISUAL APRAXIA

Patients with visual apraxia are impaired at using objects in a meaningful way when they are presented visually, but are able to describe the function of objects and indicate their use in non-verbal matching tasks (Pilgrim & Humphreys, 1991; Riddoch, Humphreys, & Price, 1989). They are also able to mime the appropriate action when provided with object names (Assal & Regli, 1980; DeRenzi, Faglioni, & Sorgato, 1982; Motomura & Yamadori, 1994; Pilgrim & Humphreys, 1991; Riddoch et al., 1989; Rothi, Mack, & Heilman, 1986). This pattern of performance suggests that the semantic system remains intact and that actions can be retrieved via semantic associations. The problems in accessing actions from visual input are therefore consistent with damage to a direct (non-semantic) route in which visual representations of objects are associated with actions. Damage to this route appears to block action retrieval operating within an apparently intact semantic route (see Yoon, Heinke, & Humphreys, this issue, for an explicit account of this).

OPTIC APHASIA

A contrasting pattern of performance is found in patients with optic aphasia. These patients are able to use visually presented objects appropriately but can be impaired at accessing semantic information about objects. For example, when the patient reported by Riddoch and Humphreys (1987) was shown a knife and fork and asked to demonstrate their use, he was able to gesture with the left hand for a fork and with the right hand for a knife. However, he could not name the objects, or match which two of three objects (knife, fork, chisel) might be used together. This problem is not due to a general deficit in name retrieval, since optic aphasic patients can name to a definition. Rather, the problem appears to reflect poor visual access to semantic information for naming, although visual access to action remains relatively intact (see Hillis &

Caramazza, 1995; Hodges, Spatt, & Patterson, 1999; Riddoch & Humphreys, 1987; Sirigu, Duhamel, & Poncet, 1991).

The dissociation of deficits seen in optic aphasia and visual apraxia suggests that two different procedures can be used to access actions, a visual procedure and a semantic procedure. This is illustrated by the framework shown in Figure 1. The visual route to action involves links between visual analysis of the parts of objects (handles and spouts) and stereotyped actions (e.g., a handle

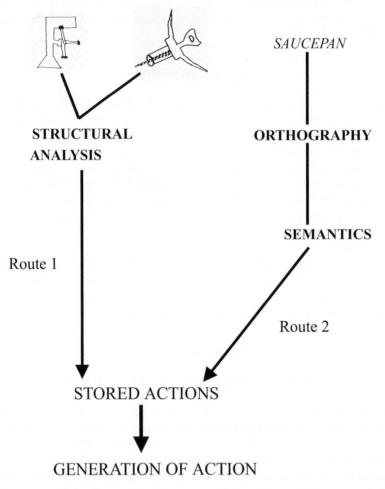

Figure 1.   Suggested framework for learned actions to objects. Route "1" involves linking the structural properties of visually presented objects directly to actions. Route "2" involves accessing stored actions via semantic knowledge (available for pictures of objects or their written names). Taken from Rumiati and Humphreys (1998).

being linked to grasping, pulling, or lifting). Parts of an object therefore "afford" actions without the need to retrieve the object's identity (cf., Gibson, 1979). Words have no such "affordances" to cue an action. In order to retrieve an action associated with a word, access to the semantic representation of the whole object is required (route 2 in Figure 1). Thus, our model includes (1) pre-semantic structural processing of the parts of objects, (2) semantic associations to whole objects, and (3) action specific responses.

ERRORS MADE BY NORMAL SUBJECTS

This dual-route account of action retrieval is also supported by the work of Rumiati and Humphreys (1998). They studied action errors made by normal subjects when responding to a deadline with either a gesture or a naming response to pictures of objects, or to their written names (words). They found that action errors tended to be visually related to pictures, and semantically related to words. An example of a visual error is when a hammering response is made to a picture of a razor (the long handle and head of the razor resemble that of a hammer). An example of a semantic error is when a shaving brush action is made to the word "razor" (shaving brush and razor being semantically related). Rumiati and Humphreys (1998) suggest that action errors to objects reflect partial activation of an action selection system based on a fast "direct route" that circumvents semantics. The semantic errors made when gesturing to a word, or naming an object, reflect activation from a slower semantic route.

NEURO-ANATOMICAL MODELS

On the basis of lesion studies, Liepmann (1900/1977, 1920/1980) and later Geschwind (1965; Figure 2a) hypothesized that actions and gestures are synthesised as a result of interactions between sensory and motor cortices that are relayed via the arcuate fasciculus. They proposed that modality specific apraxias may be caused by disconnection of modality specific regions from motor association and motor cortices, and furthermore, that the disconnection may result from damage to discrete fibre tracts within the arcuate fasciculus. Damage to the arcuate fasciculus often includes overlying parietal cortex, but neither Geschwind nor Liepman explicitly hypothesized a role for this region in mediating praxis. In contrast Heilman et al. (1982; Figure 2b) regards the dominant anterior inferior parietal cortex (AIP), especially the supramarginal gyrus (Brodman's area, BA40), as a supramodal centre for gesture retrieval, containing "visuokineasthetic motor engrams". In Heilman et al.'s model, modality specific apraxias result from disconnection of the dominant parietal cortex from visual and verbal regions (see later), and modality independent apraxia results from damage to the parietal cortex itself. Both models propose that verbal cues (e.g., the written name of an object) for action are processed in

(a)   (b)

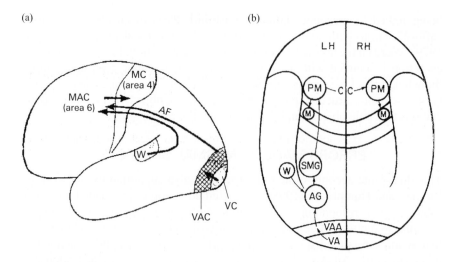

Figure 2. Anatomical models. (a) Geschwind's schema. VC, visual cortex; VAC, visual association cortex; W, Wernicke's area; AF, arcuate fasciculus; MAC, motor association cortex; MC, motor cortex. Taken from Heilman, Rothi, and Valenstein (1982). (b) Heilman et al. schema. LH, left hemisphere; RH, right hemisphere; CC, corpus callosum; VA, visual area; VAA, visual association area; AG, angular gyrus; W, Wernicke's area; SMG, supramarginal gyrus; PM, premotor area; M, motor area. Taken from Heilman et al. (1982).

temporal cortex ("Wernicke's area") of the dominant hemisphere, and visuo-perceptual cues (pictures of objects) for action are processed in occipito-temporal "visual association cortex".

Liepmann (1920/1988) classified apraxia into ideational (conceptual) and ideomotor (production) disorders. Following on from this, Roy and Square (1985) proposed that the production component involved "sensorimotor" knowledge, whereas the conceptual component included three types of knowledge, (1) knowledge of the functions of tools and objects, (2) knowledge of actions independent of tools, and (3) knowledge of the serial organization of actions into sequences. Thus, conceptual knowledge was conceived of both in terms of visual action images (cf., "extra-kinetic engrams"; Liepmann, 1920/1988) and "linguistic referents", i.e., similar to the concept of stored functional semantic knowledge promoted by Warrington and Shallice (1984). Patients with ideational apraxia (damage to the conceptual action system) often have diffuse bilateral posterior cerebral damage (Rapcsak, Ochipa, Anderson, & Poizner, 1995), but have also been reported with focal damage to the posterior left hemisphere, including the parietal areas (DeRenzi & Lucchelli, 1988; Liepmann, 1920/1988). On the basis of autopsy findings, Liepmann localized the conceptual (ideational praxis) system to the level of the dominant occipito-parietal cortex, as did Hécaen (Hécaen & Sauguet, 1972) and Morlaas (1928).

NEURO-IMAGING

The contrast between action retrieval from objects and from words has not been studied in prior experiments using functional brain imaging. Some of the most relevant studies have examined how stored actions are retrieved in response to the written or auditory names of objects (Martin, Haxby, Lalonde, Wiggs, & Ungerleider, 1995; Petersen, Fox, Posner, Mintun, & Raichle, 1988; Warburton et al., 1996). Other studies have examined stored action retrieval (as spoken verb generation) to pictures of objects (Grabowski, Damasio, & Damasio, 1998; Grafton, Fadiga, Arbib, & Rizzolatti, 1997; Martin et al., 1995). Grabowski et al. (1998) and Grafton et al. (1997) constrained their region of interest to the frontal cortex only, whereas Martin et al. (1995) investigated the whole brain. This latter study suggested that verb generation in response to words and objects engages similar brain regions; however, the two modalities were not contrasted in the same experiment.

Several neuroimaging studies have also investigated the observation of gestures (Bonda, Petrides, Ostry, & Evans, 1996; Decety et al., 1994, 1997; Grafton, Arbib, Fadiga, & Rizzolatti, 1996; Grezes, Costas, & Decety, 1998, 1999). These experiments suggest a segregation of the neural correlates for the conceptual (ideational) and production (ideomotor) components of action. The left frontal and temporal regions appear to be involved in a conceptual action system, since they are preferentially activated when the observed gestures have meaning as compared to no meaning (Decety et al., 1994, 1997; Grezes et al., 1998). In contrast, the anterior inferior parietal region (AIP; BA40) may be involved in the production of manual actions. For example, functional neuroimaging experiments have shown AIP to be activated by:

(1) observing manual gestures relative to observing whole body gestures (Bonda et al., 1996)
(2) observing manual gestures with intent to imitate or memorize for future recognition (Decety et al., 1994, 1997; Grezes et al., 1998)
(3) reaching and grasping an object, relative to a non-prehensile manual gesture performed in response to the same object (Passingham, Toni, Schluter, & Rushworth, 1998).

However, no significant differences in AIP have been reported when observation of meaningful gestures is compared to observation of meaningless gestures (Decety et al., 1994, 1997; Grezes et al., 1998). These neuroimaging experiments suggest that AIP is involved in the preparation and execution of learned manual actions, and/or co-ordination of those actions in space (reaching and prehension). It may be less involved in discriminating between actions or discerning their meaning.

In the present study, we used PET to examine the neural substrates of the conceptual rather than production components of action retrieval from objects and words. Rather than using verb generation (cf., Martin et al., 1995), which is both unconstrained and verbally mediated, we asked subjects to perform an "action decision" task. More specifically, subjects had to indicate whether they would make a twisting or pouring action to a given stimulus. Our overall aim was to assess whether different neural systems for action were activated when cued by visual structure (an object's parts, handles, and spouts) or cued by established semantic associations about the whole object (retrieved by words). There were three experiments, each of which manipulated task (action relative to perceptual decisions) and stimuli (pictures of objects or their written names). In Experiment 1, a third task was introduced (real-life size decision) to disentangle action-specific areas from the more general semantic retrieval processes. In Experiment 2, a third stimulus type was introduced (pictures of novel, meaningless objects), to emphasize the non-semantic route to action retrieval. In Experiment 3, we (1) changed the response mode—instead of pressing a key, twist and pour responses were executed manually using a manipulandum (see Methods section) and (2) presented colour photographs of objects rather than line drawings to make the pictures more realistic. The manipulandum and addition of depth and texture cues in photographs were intended to strengthen the non-semantic "affordances" that cue actions.

Our predictions were based on the cognitive model presented in Figure 1 and the results of previous imaging. We propose that retrieval of the appropriate action to a word must first proceed through semantic associations to the word concept. This process is likely to draw upon the neural systems previously described as active in semantic tasks: Extra-sylvian temporal regions, posterior inferior parietal, and ventral inferior frontal cortices (see Mummery, Patterson, Hodges, & Price, 1998; Vandenberghe, Price, Wise, Josephs, & Frackowiak, 1996, for examples). In addition, Martin et al. (1995) have shown that retrieving action words relative to colour words enhances activations in the left middle temporal cortex, an area not necessarily activated in other semantic tasks. We expect additional activation of this region in the action-retrieval task relative to tasks requiring retrieval of other forms of semantic knowledge (Experiment 1).

Objects can also be recognized and acted upon via the semantic system. However, we hypothesize that, in addition, their visual structures can provide cues for action (see Figure 1). A direct route between visual and motor processing (available for objects and non-objects only) may enhance activation in visual and motor areas (including the anterior inferior parietal cortex) while reducing activation in the semantic system. Although we predict minimum semantic activation when action selection is cued by non-objects, this conflicts with previous findings that novel stimuli can sometimes activate semantic processing regions more than familiar words or objects (Moore & Price, 1999; Price, Wise, & Frackowiak, 1996). We suggest that during unconstrained tasks (such as object viewing), semantic activation reflects a more extensive semantic search that attempts to eliminate all possible solutions. In contrast, action decisions may be cued by an object's structure (e.g., as a visual-motor association), in which case semantic search is not necessary.

METHODS

Design

There were three experiments with three different groups of subjects. Each experiment had six conditions, four of which involved "action" and "screen size" judgements on either pictures of objects or their written names (2 task × 2 stimuli). The other two conditions varied across experiment. In Experiment 1, a third task was introduced with subjects making real-life size decisions on words and pictures (3 task × 2 stimuli). In Experiment 2, a third stimulus was introduced with subjects performing action and screen-size decisions on pictures of novel, meaningless objects as well as familiar objects and written words (2 task × 3 stimuli). In Experiment 3, two additional baselines were included. The baseline stimuli for pictures were obtained by scrambling the spatial frequency components of each picture so that all object-like structure was removed while the baselines for words were consonant letter strings. The baseline stimuli in Experiment 3 were included to (1) ensure that any effects of action were not specific to the contrast with screen size (which would imply a deactivation for screen size), and (2) look for common activations for action and screen-size judgements. These effects are not reported in this paper but there were no parietal activations for action and screen-size judgements on either pictures or words.

Tasks

In Experiment 1, the action task involved deciding whether object usage would require a twisting motion and the real-life size task required a decision on the relative size of the object (e.g., Is the object "longer than a fork?"). The screen-size task involved deciding whether the picture or word presented was wider or narrower than the length of a horizontal line drawn beneath it. To control for visual input, the same reference line was present during all conditions, but subjects attended to it only during screen-size judgements. Subjects were trained to make these judgements prior to scanning. Responses were indicated ("yes" or "no") by pressing a key (e.g., right-hand index finger for "yes" and middle finger for "no", or vice versa, counterbalanced across subjects). In each task, there were four "yes" responses and eight "no" responses. Reaction times and accuracy were recorded in all conditions.

In Experiment 2, the action task also involved keypress responses to indicate whether an object was twisted but this time rather than make a "yes" or "no" response, subjects made a "twist" or "pour" response (e.g., right-hand index finger for "twist" and middle finger for "pour", or vice versa). Half the stimuli cued "twist" responses and half cued "pour" responses. The screen-size task involved deciding whether the picture or word presented was a large or small image/font (with right-hand index finger for "large" and middle finger for "small", or vice versa). Half the stimuli cued "small" responses and half cued "large" responses. Reaction times and accuracy of responses were recorded in all conditions.

In Experiment 3, the action task was the same as in Experiment 2 except that the twist or pour responses were gestured with the right hand using a manipulandum (see Figure 3). The manipulandum had the appearance of a hammer-type structure, the top of which could either be bent down by a leftward wrist movement (akin to pouring a milk bottle), or twisted by a right-turning wrist movement (akin to twisting the lid of a jar). It was also used to make responses in the screen-size decisions. Subjects were either trained to make a twisting action to small stimuli and a pouring action to large stimuli, or vice versa. Thus, motor movements were controlled over condition and the difference between action and screen-size decision was limited to semantic retrieval of action. Screen-size decisions on words involved deciding whether the font size was "large" or "small", as in Experiment 2, but the size control task for familiar pictures was made easier by including a vertical reference line displayed adjacent to the stimuli. This allowed subjects to judge the height of the image ("large" or "small" relative to the reference line). As in Experiment 1, visual input was controlled by presenting the same reference line next to each stimulus irrespective of condition. For the baseline task, subjects had to decide

(a) "Pour"   (b) "Twist"

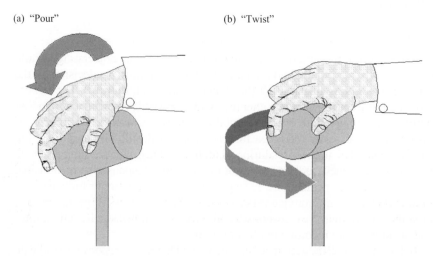

Figure 3.   Manipulandum used to respond to stimuli in Experiment 2. (a) Head of manipulandum is tipped to simulate pouring motion. (b) Head of manipulandum is rotated to simulate twisting motion.

whether the line appeared on the left or the right of the scrambled pictures or consonants. Again, left and right responses were arbitarily linked to twisting and pouring movements on the manipulandum. In all conditions, half the responses involved twisting movements and half the responses involved pouring movements.

Stimuli

In all experiments, the picture and word stimuli appeared on the screen in two sizes: The smaller pictures extended 2.9–8.6°, the larger pictures 17.1–22.6° (overall mean 12.8°). The words were presented in Times New Roman, font size 25 or 35, extending a visual angle of 8.6° and 25.4° respectively (mean of 14.7°).

For Experiment 1, 24 manipulable objects were selected from the Snodgrass and Vanderwart (1980) picture set (see Appendix) and divided into 2 sets of 12 matched for frequency, word length, and number of syllables. Each set was presented to half the subjects as words and to the other half as line drawings. Therefore, the modality an object was presented in was controlled over subjects. Over the experiment, there were three replications of each stimulus, one for each task (action, real-life size, and screen size). This was to ensure that task differences were not due to stimulus confounds. Any effects of stimulus priming over task were reduced by (1) counterbalancing the order of replication across subjects and (2) asking subjects to name the drawings and read the words of all stimuli immediately prior to scanning in order to saturate priming effects. There were a total of six conditions (each presenting twelve stimuli) and no replications.

For Experiment 2, stimuli were chosen on the basis of a prior screening study in which 40 participants (not involved in the PET experiments) were given a list of 100 object names and asked to decide whether they would make a twisting or a pouring action to the object. The same group of participants were also asked to make twist or pour decisions to line drawings of 60 non-objects. These were drawn (black on a white background) by an artist and not derived from any particular objects although they were structurally plausible and had approximately the same visual complexity as the objects.

The objects and non-objects selected for the experiment were those to which actions were agreed by 80% or more of the participants. Forty objects and twenty non-objects were selected, half were associated with twisting and half were associated with pouring (see Appendix). They were divided into four sets of objects and two sets of non-objects with ten stimuli in each set, half associated with twisting and half with pouring. Subjects saw two sets of objects as pictures and the other two as words, counterbalanced across subjects. Thus, per subject there were two sets of pictures, two sets of words, and two sets of non-objects, with different stimuli presented in the word and picture conditions. Each set was presented twice (once for the action task and once for the size task) with the screen size of the stimuli (large or small) reversed on the second presentation. Thus, as in Experiment 1, the same stimuli were presented for each task but words and pictures were counterbalanced over subject.

For Experiment 3, the stimuli were the same as in Experiment 2, except that pictures were photographs rather than line drawings and non-objects were replaced with scrambled photographs (control for pictures) and consonant letter strings (control for words).

Procedure

In all three experiments, stimuli were presented (on a Macintosh computer screen) for 1 s each starting 10 s before data acquisition. There were 12 stimuli and a 4.5 s SOA (stimulus onset asynchony) in Experiment 1 and 10 stimuli with a 6 s SOA in Experiments 2 and 3. Presentation of stimuli with "yes" and "no" or "twist" and "pour" responses were randomized within a set. Before each scan, subjects were told which kinds of stimuli would be presented and what kind of response to make. Condition order was counterbalanced within and between subjects.

Subjects

There was a total of 26 subjects. Twelve (age range 21–45) in Experiment 1, eight (age range 21–57) in Experiment 2, and six (age range 20–65) in Experiment 3. Although there were more subjects in Experiment 1, it should be noted that in this experiment, there was only one scan for each of the six conditions, whereas in Experiments 2 and 3, there were two scans per condition. All subjects were right handed and native English speakers, healthy, on no medication, and free from any history of neurological illness. Consent was obtained according to the declaration of Helsinki, and the study was approved by the local hospital ethics committee and the Administration of Radioactive Substances Advisory Committee (UK) (ARSAC).

Data acquisition

Each subject underwent 12 PET relative perfusion scans over a 2 hour period (in Experiment 1, only six of the scans collected corresponded to the conditions reported in this paper). All scans were acquired using a SIEMENS/CPS ECAT EXACT HR+ (model 962) PET scanner (Siemens/CTI, Knoxville, TN, USA) with collimating septa retracted. Participants received a 20 s intravenous bolus of $H_2^{15}O$ at a concentration of 55 Mbq ml^{-1} and at a flow rate of 10 ml min^{-1} through a forearm cannula. For each subject, a T1-weighted structural magnetic resonance (MR) image was obtained with a 2 Tesla Magnetom VISION scanner (Siemens, Erlangen, Germany).

(a) **Action system for words and pictures**
    Red   = Experiments 1, 2, 3: Words
    Green   = Experiments 1, 2, 3: Pictures
    Yellow   = Overlap of red and green

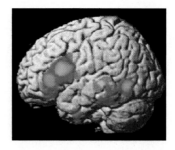

(b) **Action for words > pictures**
    Red   = Experiments 1, 2, 3: Words > pictures
    Blue   = Experiment 2: Words > non-objects
    Green   = Experiment 3: Words > pictures

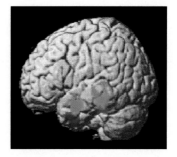

(c) **Action for pictures > words**
    Red   = Experiments 1, 2, 3: Words (all tasks)
    Green   = Experiment 2: Non-objects > words
    Yellow   = Overlap of red and green

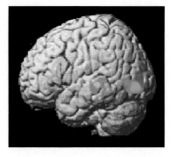

Plate 1.   Neuroimaging results. PET activations for action relative to size decision for (a) words and pictures at $p < .001$, (b) for words more than pictures of real objects, $p < .01$, and (c) words more than pictures of non-objects, $p < .001$. Activations are rendered onto brain templates in Talairach and Tournoux space.

Data analysis

The data were analysed with statistical parametric mapping (using SPM99 software from the Wellcome Department of Cognitive Neurology, London, UK; http//www.fil.ion.ucl.ac.uk/spm) implemented in Matlab (Mathworks Inc. Sherborn, MA, USA) using standardized procedures (Friston et al., 1995a, b). The smoothing kernel was a 3D Gaussian filter of 16 mm. Data from all three experiments were combined in a single design matrix specifying three groups (one per experiment) and six conditions per subject. Condition and subject effects were estimated according to the general linear model at each voxel. To test hypotheses about regionally specific condition effects, these estimates were compared using linear compounds or contrasts (balanced within subject). The resulting set of voxel values for each contrast is an SPM of the t statistic, which was then converted to a z statistic. The significance level was corrected for multiple comparisons, $z > 4.4$, $p < .05$ corrected, for main and simple main effects, and we used $p < .001$ uncorrected ($z > 3.1$) for interactions.

Linear contrasts

(1) The effect of action retrieval (AR)–screen size (SS) was computed for words and pictures separately in each experiment (six contrasts). Conjunction analyses (see Price & Friston, 1997) were then used to identify effects that were common for all experiments as opposed to summed over experiment. The conjunction of AR–SS for words and pictures (six contrasts), words only (three contrasts), and pictures only (three contrasts) are reported in Table 3.

(2) The interaction of task (AR–SS) and stimulus type (words < or > pictures) was computed for each experiment. Conjunction analysis was then used to find the common interactions across experiments.

(3) For Experiment 2 only, there were two additional contrasts: (1) AR–SS for non-objects, and (2) the interaction of task (AR–SS) and stimulus (non-objects > or < words/pictures).

(4) For Experiment 1 only, we also computed (1) the effect of real-life size retrieval (SR) relative to screen size (SR–SS), and (2) AR–SR.

Post hoc contrasts.   The effect of AR–SS for non-objects revealed an area that has previously been associated with presemantic structural object processing (Kanwisher, Woods, Iacoboni, & Mazziotta, 1997; Malach et al., 1995). This effect could not be attributed to differences in perceptual input, which was the same in the AR and SS conditions. The result suggested that action decision on non-objects (in contrast to screen-size decision on non-objects) increased the demands on pre-semantic structural processing. To confirm this hypothesis, we identified the structural processing area as that which was activated for pictures relative to words irrespective of condition and experiment (i.e., the conjunction of six contrasts comparing pictures to words for AR and SS in each of the three experiments). This enabled us to make an independent comparison between the object processing area (identified by pictures relative to words) with the effect of AR–SS for non-objects only.

RESULTS

Behavioural data

The mean error rates and reaction times (RT) over all subjects, for each task (in Experiments 1 and 2, respectively) are shown in Tables 1 and 2.

RTs were analysed with a within-subjects ANOVA to test for significant differences between the conditions. In Experiment 1, the only significant effect pertained to an interaction between task and modality, $F(2, 20) = 4.3$, $p < .0285$, with RTs faster for the baseline task on words than pictures. Similarly, in Experiment 2, the baseline task was faster for words and non-objects than for all other conditions. There were no significant differences between the action tasks: Scheffé test, $p < .05$. This is likely to be due to the small sample size of both participants and items here. In other studies we have found a consistent

TABLE 1
Mean reaction times (ms), standard deviation, and error rates (as a mean percentage) for Experiment 1

Condition	Mean RT (ms)	Standard deviation	Accuracy (% correct)
Words (action)	904	287	88
Words (real-life size)	867	295	94
Words (screen size)	774	112	98
Objects (action)	892	258	90
Objects (real-life size)	813	126	94
Objects (screen size)	1024	437	87

TABLE 2
Mean reaction times (ms), standard error, and error rates (as a mean percentage) for Experiment 2

Condition	Mean RT (ms)	Standard error	Accuracy (% correct)
Words (action)	1402	59.9	95
Words (screen size)	761	47.9	96
Objects (action)	1198	49.3	94
Objects (screen size)	1064	53.7	84
Non-objects (action)	1158	42.3	92
Non-objects (screen size)	876	33.9	91

advantage for action decisions to objects over those to words (Chainay & Humphreys, in press).

In Experiment 1, accuracy for action was 90% for pictures and 88% for words; for real-life size 94% on both pictures and words; and for screen size 87% on pictures and 98% on words. In Experiment 2, accuracy on the action was 92% for pictures of novel objects, 94% for pictures of real objects, and 95% for words. Accuracy on the screen-size judgement task was 91% for pictures of novel objects, 84% for pictures of real objects, and 96% for words. Apparently screen-size judgements were somewhat more difficult for pictures of real objects than for other stimuli.

Imaging data

We focus on activations due to action tasks only, with the screen-size task used to control for sensory and perceptual differences and for activations linked to motor response. The effects of action relative to screen size in all three experiments are summarized in Tables 3–6 (below) and illustrated in Plate 1 (situated between pages 672 and 673).

Common action system for words and pictures. The conjunction of action decision (AR)–screen-size decision (SS) for words and pictures in each experiment (six contrasts) revealed significant activation in the left inferior frontal (BA45), left posterior middle temporal (BA21/37), and left anterior temporal (BA38) cortices, see Table 3, and Plate 1 (situated between pages 672 and 673).

TABLE 3
Location, coordinates of activation, and z scores for action relative to screen size for
Experiments 1–3

Regions	Coordinates	Words and pictures	Words	Pictures	Words > pictures
1. Left inferior frontal	−48 18 16	**6.3**	**7.1**	3.7	3.5
(BA45)	−44 34 4	**6.5**	**6.1**	3.9	n.s.
2. Left middle temporal	−56 −62 −2	**5.3**	**5.0**	3.5	n.s.
(BA21/37)	−52 −38 −10	**5.5**	4.0	3.8	n.s.
3. Left anterior temporal	−42 −8 −36	**4.6**	4.3	2.5	n.s.
(BA38)					
4. Left anterior fusiform	−46 −36 −22	n.s.	**4.7**	n.s.	3.9
(BA20)					

z scores in BOLD were corrected for multiple comparisons.
BA = Brodmann's area.

TABLE 4
Location, coordinates of activation, and z scores for action relative to screen size
for Experiment 3—words > pictures

Regions	Coordinates	Words	Words > pictures
Left anterior temporal (BA38)	−62 −2 −26	3.4	3.2
Left anterior fusiform (BA20)	−64 −36 −16	3.7	3.7

BA = Brodmann's area.

TABLE 5
Location, coordinates of activation, and z scores for action relative to screen size
for Experiment 2—words > non-objects

Regions	Coordinates	Words	Words > pictures
Left anterior temporal (BA38)	−32 −2 −36	4.2	3.3

BA = Brodmann's area.

TABLE 6
Location, coordinates of activation, and z scores for action relative to screen size
for Experiment 2—non-objects > words

Regions	Coordinates	Non-objects	Novel objects > words & pictures	Novel objects > words	Novel objects > pictures
Left middle occipital (BA19)	−46 −74 −4	4.0	3.2	3.1	2.8
Left anterior medial fusiform	−18 −56 −16	4.1	3.4	3.7	2.2

BA = Brodmann's area.

The left inferior frontal and left anterior temporal areas appear to be part of the generalized semantic system. These areas were also activated by the "real-life size " task (SR–SS) in Experiment 1: for words and pictures combined, $z = 3.6$ at −42, +10, 12, and $z = 3.5$ at $x = −36$, 2, −42, $p < .001$. Likewise these areas were activated for associative and real-life size relative to screen-size decisions in the study by Vandenberghe et al. (1996: peak coordinates −42, +22, +20 and −44, −10, −28). In contrast, the left posterior middle temporal cortex (BA21/37) appears to be specific to action. It was not activated for the real-life size decision in Experiment 1 of our study ($p > .05$), nor in the study by Vandenberghe et al. (1996), but there was significantly more activation for action than size decision, $z = 3.8$, $p < .001$, in Experiment 1 of our study and for generation of action relative to colour words, in the study by Martin et al. (1995).

Word-specific action responses. Within the common action retrieval system activated by words and pictures, the left inferior frontal area was more activated for words than for pictures. Words, but not pictures, also activated a left anterior fusiform area and the task (AR–SS) by stimulus (words–pictures) interaction here reached significance (see Table 3). This left anterior fusiform area has also been associated with a generalized semantic system by Vandenberghe et al. (1996; peak coordinates: –46, –46, –20) and was more active for the real-life size than screen-size task (SR–SS) in Experiment 1 of our study, with small but equivocal effects for words and pictures, $z = 2.4$ for words and $z = 2.5$ for pictures. Nevertheless, activation was enhanced further by action decisions on words, $z = 3.2$, $p < .001$ for AR–SR, and this effect was not seen for pictures ($p > .05$). There is no evidence that the difference between words and pictures reflect differences in task difficulty because there were no significant differences in the RTs or accuracy to action and size retrieval tasks for either words or pictures (see Table 1). We conclude that semantic processing is increased for action decision on words more than pictures. This led to increased activation for parts of a common system and recruitment of additional parts of the semantic system for words.

We predicted that, in Experiment 3, action decisions to pictures would reduce semantic activation further because visuo-motor affordances were enhanced (coloured photographs of objects and explicit twist and pour responses with the manipulandum). Indeed, the difference between action decision to words and pictures in Experiment 3 included the left anterior temporal lobe as well as the left anterior fusiform, see Table 4 (on page 676) and Plate 1 (situated between pages 672 and 673). We also expected that actions to novel objects would place least demands on the semantic system (Experiment 2). This was again confirmed with interactions showing greater action related activation for words than novel objects in left anterior temporal cortex (Table 5 and Plate 1) with a trend for words relative to pictures of real objects ($z = 2.7$). There was no significant difference in this area between real and novel objects. In summary, there was more activation for words than pictures in the left anterior fusiform (all three experiments) and in the left anterior temporal cortex both in (1) Experiment 3, when visuo-motor affordances were enhanced, and (2) Experiment 2 when the pictures were of novel objects (Plate 1, situated between pages 672 and 673).

Object-specific activations. The top row of Plate 1 illustrates the areas activated for AR–SS when words and pictures were stimuli. Although activation was more extensive for words than pictures, there were no areas that were more active for action decisions on pictures than words even in Experiment 3 when visuo-motor affordances offered by the picture stimuli were maximized. We did however find, in Experiment 2, that action decisions on pictures of non-objects, relative to objects or words, increased activation in the left occipital temporal cortex and left anterior medial fusiform. Activation in the left occipito-temporal cortex (–46 –74 –4) is close to both area V5 (the visual motion region, average coordinates: $x = -41 \pm 5.6$ mm, $y = -70 \pm 6.0$ mm, $z = +2 \pm 5.3$; Watson et al., 1993) and the lateral occipital object region (LO), which responds to object-like structures (Malach et al., 1995; average coordinates at $x = -42.8 \pm 2.7$ mm, $y = -72.7 \pm 8$ mm, $z = -18.2 \pm 9.8$ mm). Indeed, in our study, the same left occipito-temporal region was more active for pictures than words irrespective of task, $z = 6.3$ at –44, –74, –4; and $z = 8.8$ at –42, –82, 4, and +44, –84, –4, see Post hoc analysis in the Methods section. Since the visual input was the same for action and screen-size judgements, these results suggest that top-down modulation of perceptual processing was required for action decision on non-objects (see Plate 1, situated between pages 672 and 673).

DISCUSSION

In these experiments we investigated the differences in action retrieval to objects and words. More specifically, we tested the prediction, from neuropsychological data, that semantic processing is necessary for action retrieval from verbal cues, but not from objects or pictures of objects. All effects of action were observed in the left hemisphere. This is noteworthy because neuropsychological research suggests that lesions commonly respon-sible for apraxia in right-handed individuals are typically localized to the left hemisphere. Right hemisphere lesions are rarely known to induce apraxia in right-handed patients (Geschwind, 1965; Hécaen & Sauguet, 1972).

A semantic–action route

In all experiments, activations common to retrieving actions from words and pictures were identified in the left inferior frontal, left posterior middle temporal and left anterior temporal cortices. For words, action decision also engaged the left anterior fusiform relative to screen-size and real-life size tasks. With the exception of the left posterior middle temporal cortex, these regions are compo-nents of a general semantic system (Vandenberghe et al., 1996). Our results are therefore consistent with common semantic procedures mediating the retrieval of different types of stored knowledge about objects, including action knowl-edge. The only action specific area (relative to real-life size decisions in Experi-ment 1) was the left posterior middle temporal cortex (LPMT). This area was also reported to be more active for actions than colours (Martin et al., 1995), when human actions are observed (Decety et al., 1994, 1997; Grezes et al., 1998, 1999) or implied (Kourtzi & Kanwisher, 2000; Senior et al., 2000), and for tools more than animals (Cappa, Perani, Schnur, Tettamanti, & Fazio, 1998; Chao, Haxby, & Martin, 1999; Damasio, Grabowski, Tranel, Hichwa, & Damasio, 1996; Martin, Wiggs, Ungerleider, & Haxby, 1996; Moore & Price,

1999; Mummery, Patterson, Hodges, & Price, 1998; Mummery, Patterson, Hodges, & Wise, 1996; Perani et al., 1999). Critically this area was involved in action decisions on words, pictures of real objects, and pictures of non-objects. Therefore, it appears to be involved in all routes to action. This area may correspond to the conceptual or ideational region hypothesized to be located in the parieto-temporo-occipital cortex (Hécaen & Sauguet, 1972; Liepmann, 1920/1988; Morlaas, 1928).

In addition, our results indicate that semantic processing for action is modulated by stimulus demands. This is illustrated by decreased activation in the left anterior fusiform area (a semantic retrieval region) for pictures of real objects (all experiments), and in the left anterior temporal cortex for pictures of non-objects (Experiment 2) and pictures of real objects when visuo-motor affordances were enhanced (Experiment 3). These results indicate that action retrieval from object-like stimuli places less demand on semantic processing and they confirm our prediction that differences would be greater when visuo-motor affordances for pictures were enhanced.

A direct vision–action route

Riddoch et al. (1989) and Rumiati and Humphreys (1998) suggest that, for objects but not for words, there is a "direct route" to action selection that relies on access to structural descriptions of objects, reducing the need for access to semantic descriptions for action retrieval. We found no areas that were more active for pictures of real objects than words. However, actions to novel objects activated an occipital-temporal region (BA19) that was not observed for action decisions on words or pictures of real objects. Peak activation was not only close to previous studies of pre-semantic object processing (as defined by Malach et al., 1995; see also Bly & Kosslyn, 1997; Kanwisher et al., 1997; Moore & Price, 1999), it also overlapped with activation in this study for pictures relative to words irrespective of task (see the third row of Plate 1, situated between pages 672 and 673). Since visual input was the same for action and size decisions on non-objects, these results suggest that performing actions to non-objects enhances the demand for structural processing.

These results are consistent with actions to non-objects requiring more structural processing than words when an action decision rather than a size decision must be made. Enhanced structural processing of objects may enable them to be associated directly with actions, thereby lessening the need for semantically based retrieval processes (see earlier).

A parietal route to action

We also predicted that we might find enhanced activation of the dominant parietal cortex (e.g., the anterior inferior parietal cortex; AIP; BA39/40), when object–action associations were made. This area is thought to "store" "visuo-kinesthetic motor engrams" (Heilman, Rothi, & Valenstein, 1982). However, there was no evidence to indicate that the dominant parietal cortex is involved in retrieving conceptual object–action associations when motor production was controlled. The lack of significant activation in AIP in our experiments, and the reported behaviour of this region in the research of others, suggests that AIP is not specialized to express the conceptual (non-executed) relationship between an object and a manual action, but instead may store "motor engrams" that are not context specific. That is to say, AIP may be part of the "production system" specified in Roy and Square's model (1985), whereas our paradigm selected brain systems involved in the "conceptual" praxis system. As the results of Passingham (1998) suggest, AIP may be more concerned with negotiating an action response in three-dimensional space. The absence of significant parietal activation in our experiments does not permit comment on the proposed role played by the dominant parietal cortex in the models of Geschwind and Heilman. However, Heilman et al. have later refined this theory (Clark et al., 1994; Poizner, Mack, Verfaellie, Rothi, & Heilman, 1990; Poizner et al., 1995), reporting that apraxic patients with dominant parietal lesions commit largely spatial and temporal errors when pantomiming actions. Indeed, the parietal patient reported by Hodges et al. (1999) was impaired with spatial transformation tasks with non-objects. This suggests that the role of the parietal cortex is in contributing to the spatial and temporal information needed to execute learned actions. These aspects of movement production were controlled in the tasks used in our experiments.

Consistency with previous studies of action retrieval

Most previous studies of action retrieval have focused on verb generation (see the introductory sections) and usually report activation in the left posterior temporal lobe (e.g., Fiez, Raichle, Balota, Tallal, & Petersen, 1996; Martin et al., 1995; Warburton et al., 1996). However, they do not typically report left anterior temporal activation. There are three reasons why left anterior temporal activation might previously have been missed: (1) Many of the PET and fMRI studies excluded the anterior temporal cortex because the field of view was less than brain size; (2) fMRI signals in this area are weak due to susceptability artifacts (see Devlin et al., 2000); and (3) when rest is used as the baseline, activation in semantic areas is reduced because semantic processing can occur implicitly during rest (see Binder et al., 1999).

Finally, the absence of action specific ventral and dorsal premotor activation may be surprising given that these areas are sometimes more active for observing tools (Chao & Martin, 2000; Grabowski, Damasio, & Damasio, 1998; Grafton et al., 1996, 1997) The lack of any premotor activation in all three of our experiments suggests that, like the anterior parietal cortex, the left premotor cortex is concerned with movement production, which was fully controlled in all our experimental conditions and not a variable of interest.

CONCLUSIONS

In conclusion, our experiments indicate that action retrieval in response to words activates a set of semantic areas that may relate to the conceptual system for praxis (as proposed by Roy & Square, 1985). However, action retrieval from object-like stimuli results in less activation in the semantic system than words, possibly because the parts of objects can afford motor associations more directly. Indeed, actions to non-objects enhanced processing in brain regions associated with processing the structural properties of objects, suggesting that actions can be made directly from object structure. Further experiments are required to investigate under which circumstances actions to pictures of real objects engage the structural processing route. Nevertheless, the dissociation we report between activation elicited by action retrieval to words and objects is consistent with the cognitive model developed by Riddoch et al. (1989) and Rumiati and Humphreys (1998), which suggests a separation between semantic and non-semantic routes to action.

REFERENCES

Assal, G., & Regli, F. (1980). Syndrome de disconnexion visuo-verbal et visuo-gestuelle. [A syndrome of visuo-verbal and visuo-gestural disconnection. Optic aphasia and optic apraxia]. *Revue de Neurologie (Paris)*, *136*, 365–376.

Binder, J.R., Frost, J.A., Hammeke, T.A., Bellgowan, P.S., Rao, S.M., & Cox, R.W. (1999). Conceptual processing during the conscious resting state: A functional MRI study. *Journal of Cognitive Neuroscience*, *11*(1), 80–95.

Bly, B.M., & Kosslyn, S.M. (1997). Functional anatomy of object recognition in humans: Evidence from positron emission tomography and functional magnetic resonance imaging. *Current Opinion in Neurology*, *10*, 5–9.

Bonda, E., Petrides, M., Ostry, D., & Evans, A. (1996). Specific involvement of human parietal systems and the amygdala in the perception of biological motion. *Journal of Neuroscience*, *16*, 3737–3744.

Cappa, S.F., Perani, D., Schnur, T., Tettamanti, M., & Fazio, F. (1998). The effects of semantic category and knowledge type on lexical-semantic access: A PET study. *NeuroImage*, *8*, 350–359.

Chainay, H., & Humphreys, G.W. (in press). Privileged access to action for objects relative to words. *Psychonomic Bulletin and Review*.

Chao, L.L., Haxby, J.V., & Martin, A. (1999). Attribute-based neural substrates in temporal cortex for perceiving and knowing objects. *Nature Neuroscience*, *2*, 913–919.

Chao, L.L., & Martin, A. (2000). Representation of manipulable man-made objects in the dorsal stream. *NeuroImage*, *12*, 478–484.

Clark, M.A., Merians, A.S., Kothari, A., Poizner, H., Macauley, B., Gonzalez Rothi, L.J., & Heilman, K.M. (1994). Spatial planning deficits in limb apraxia. *Brain*, *117*, 1093–1106.

Damasio, H., Grabowski, T.J., Tranel, D., Hichwa, R.D., & Damasio, A.R. (1996). A neural basis for lexical retrieval. *Nature*, *380*, 499–505.

Decety, J., Grezes, J., Costes, N., Perani, D., Jeannerod, M., Procyk, E., et al. (1997). Brain activity during observation of actions: Influence of action content and subject's strategy. *Brain*, *120*, 1763–1777.

Decety, J., Perani, D., Jeannerod, M., Bettinardi, V., Tadary, B., Woods, R., Mazziotta, J.C., & Fazio, F. (1994). Mapping motor representations with positron emission tomography. *Nature*, *371*, 600–602.

DeRenzi, E., Faglioni, P., & Sorgato, P. (1982). Modality-specific and supramodal mechanisms of apraxia. *Brain*, *105*, 301–12.

DeRenzi, E., & Lucchelli, F. (1988). Ideational apraxia. *Brain*, *111*(Pt. 5), 1173–1185.

Devlin, J.T., Russell, R.P., Davis, M.H., Price, C.J., Wilson, J., Moss, H.E., Matthews, P., & Tyler, L. (2000). Susceptability induced loss of signal: Comparing PET and fMRI on a semantic task. *NeuroImage*, *11*, 588–600.

Fiez, J.A., Raichle, M.E., Balota, D.A., Tallal, P., & Petersen, S.E. (1996). PET studies of posterior temporal regions during passive auditory word presentation and verb generation. *Cerebral Cortex*, *6*, 1–10.

Friston, K., Ashburner, J., Frith, C., Poline, J.-B., Heather, J.D., & Frackowiak, R.S.J. (1995a). Spatial registration and normalisation. *Human Brain Mapping*, *2*, 56–78.

Friston, K., Holmes, A.P., Worsley, K.J., Frith, C., Poline, J.-B., & Frackowiak, R.S.J. (1995b). Statistical parametric maps in functional imaging: A general linear approach. *Human Brain Mapping*, *2*, 189–210.

Geschwind, N. (1965). Disconnexion syndromes in animals and man: II. *Brain*, *88*, 585–644.

Gibson, J.J. (1979). *The ecological approach to visual perception.* Boston: Houghton Mifflin.

Grabowski, T.J., Damasio, H., & Damasio, A.R. (1998). Premotor and prefrontal correlates of category-related lexical retrieval. *NeuroImage*, *7*, 232–243.

Grafton, S.T., Arbib, M.A., Fadiga, L., & Rizzolatti, G. (1996). Localization of grasp representations in humans by positron emission tomography: 2. Observation compared with imagination. *Experimental Brain Research*, *112*, 103–111.

Grafton, S.T., Fadiga, L., Arbib, M.A., & Rizzolatti, G. (1997). Premotor cortex activation during observation and naming of familiar tools. *NeuroImage*, *6*, 241–246.

Grezes, J., Costes, N., & Decety, J. (1998). Top-down effect of strategy on the perception of human biological motion: A PET investigation. *Cognitive Neuropsychology*, *15*, 553–582.

Grezes, J., Costes, N., & Decety, J. (1999). The effects of learning and intention on the neural network involved in the perception of meaningless actions. *Brain*, *122*, 1875–1887.

Hécaen, H., & Sauguet, J. (1972). Cerebral dominance in left-handed subjects. *Cortex*, *7*, 19–48.

Heilman, K.M., Rothi, L.J., & Valenstein, E. (1982). Two forms of ideomotor apraxia. *Neurology*, *32*, 342–346.

Hillis, A.E., & Caramazza, A. (1995). Cognitive and neural mechanisms underlying visual and semantic processing: Implications from "optic aphasia". *Journal of Cognitive Neuroscience*, *7*, 457–478.

Hodges, J.R., Spatt, J., & Patterson, K. (1999). "What" and "how": Evidence for the dissociation of object knowledge and mechanical problem-solving skills in the human brain. *Proceedings of the National Academy Sciences*, *96*, 9444–9448.

Kanwisher, N., Woods, R.P., Iacoboni, M., & Mazziotta, J.C. (1997). A locus in the human extrastriate cortex for visual shape analysis. *Journal of Cognitive Neuroscience*, *9*, 133–142.

Kourtzi, Z., & Kanwisher, N. (2000). Activation in human MT/MST by static images with implied motion. *Journal of Cognitive Neuroscience*, *12*, 48–55.

Liepmann, H. (1977). The syndrome of apraxia (motor asymboly) based on a case of unilateral apraxia. In D. Hockberg (Ed.), *Neurological classics in modern translation.* New York: Macmillan. (Original work published 1900, in German.)

Liepmann, H. (1988). Apraxia. In J.W. Brown (Ed.), *Agnosia and apraxia, selected papers of Liepmann, Lange, and Potzl* (pp. 3–39). Hillsdale, NJ: Lawrence Erlbaum Associates Inc.

Malach, R., Reppas, J.B., Benson, R.R., Kwong, K.K., Jiang, H., Kennedy, W.A., et al. (1995). Object-related activity revealed by functional magnetic resonance imaging in human occipital cortex. *Proceedings of the National Academy of Sciences, 92*, 8135–8139.

Martin, A., Haxby, J.V., Lalonde, F.M., Wiggs, C.L., & Ungerleider, L.G. (1995). Discrete cortical regions associated with knowledge of color and knowledge of action. *Science, 270*, 102–105.

Martin, A. Wiggs, C.L., Ungerleider, L.G., & Haxby, J.V. (1996). Neural correlates of category-specific knowledge. *Nature, 379*, 649–652.

Moore, C.J., & Price, C.J. (1999). A functional neuroimaging study of the variables that generate category-specific object processing differences. *Brain, 122*, 943–962.

Morlaas, J. (1928). *Contribution a l'etude de l'apraxie*. Paris, France: Legrand.

Motomura, N., & Yamadori, A. (1994). A case of ideational apraxia with impairment of object use and preservation of object pantomime. *Cortex, 30*, 167–170.

Mummery, C.J., Patterson, K., Hodges, J.R., & Price, C.J. (1998). Functional neuroanatomy of the semantic system: Divisible by what? *Journal of Cognitive Neuroscience, 10*, 766–777.

Mummery, C.J., Patterson, K., Hodges, J.R., & Wise, R.J.S. (1996). Generating 'tiger' as an animal or a word beginning with T: Differences in brain activation. *Proceedings of the Royal Society London, Biological Sciences, 263*, 989–995.

Passingham, R.E., Toni, I., Schluter, N., & Rushworth, M.F. (1998), How do visual instructions influence the motor system? *Novartis Foundation Symposium, 218*, 129–141, 141–146.

Perani, D., Schnur, T., Tettamanti, M., Gorno-Tempini, M.L., Cappa, S.F., & Fazio, F. (1999). Word and picture matching: A PET study of semantic category effects. *Neuropsychologia, 37*, 293–306.

Petersen, S.E., Fox, P.T., Posner, M.I., Mintun, M., & Raichle, M.E. (1988), Positron emission tomographic studies of the cortical anatomy of single-word processing. *Nature, 331*, 585–589.

Pilgrim, E., & Humphreys, G.W. (1991). Impairment of action to visual objects in a case of ideomotor apraxia. *Cognitive Neuropsychology, 8*, 459–473.

Poizner, H., Clark, M.A., Merians, A.S., Macauley, B., Gonzalez Rothi, L.J., & Heilman, K.M. (1995). Joint coordination deficits in limb apraxia. *Brain, 118*, 227–242.

Poizner, H., Mack, L., Verfaellie, M., Rothi, L.J., & Heilman, K.M. (1990). Three-dimensional computergraphic analysis of apraxia: Neural representations of learned movement. *Brain, 113*, 85–101.

Price, C.J., & Friston, K.J. (1997). Cognitive conjunction: A new approach to brain activation experiments. *NeuroImage, 5*, 261–270.

Price, C.J., Wise, R.J., & Frackowiak, R.S. (1996). Demonstrating the implicit processing of visually presented words and pseudowords. *Cerebral Cortex, 6*, 62–70.

Rapcsak, S.Z., Ochipa, C., Anderson, K.C., & Poizner, H. (1995). Progressive ideomotor apraxia: Evidence for a selective impairment of the action production system. *Brain and Cognition, 27*, 213–216.

Riddoch, M.J., & Humphreys, G.W. (1987). Visual object processing in a case of optic aphasia: A case of semantic access agnosia. *Cognitive Neuropsychology, 4*, 131–185.

Riddoch, M.J., Humphreys, G.W., & Price, C.J. (1989). Routes to action. *Cognitive Neuropsychology, 6*, 437–454.

Rothi, L.J., Mack, L., & Heilman, K.M. (1986). Pantomime agnosia. *Journal of Neurology, Neurosurgery and Psychiatry, 49*, 451–454.

Roy, E.A., & Square, P.A. (1985). Common considerations in the study of limb, verbal, and oral apraxia. In E.A. Roy (Ed.), *Neuropsychological studies of apraxia and related disorders* (pp. 111–161). Amsterdam: North-Holland.

Rumiati, R.I., & Humphreys, G.W. (1998). Recognition by action: Dissociating visual and semantic routes to action in normal observers. *Journal of Experimental Psychology: Human Perception and Performance, 24*, 631–647.

Senior, C., Barnes, J., Giampietro, V., Simmons, A., Bullmore, E.T., Brammer, M., & David, A.S. (2000). The functional neuroanatomy of implicit-motion perception or representational momentum. *Current Biology*, *10*, 16–22.

Sirigu, A., Duhamel, J.R., & Poncet, M. (1991). The role of sensorimotor experience in object recognition: A case of multimodal agnosia. *Brain*, *114*, 2555–2573. [Published erratum appears in *Brain*, 1992, *115*(2), 645.]

Snodgrass, J.G., & Vanderwart, M.A. (1980). Standardised set of 260 pictures: Norms of name agreement, usage agreement, familiarity and visual complexity. *Journal of Experimental Psychology: Human Learning and Memory*, *6*, 174–215.

Vandenberghe, R., Price, C., Wise, R., Josephs, O., & Frackowiak, R.S.J. (1996). Functional anatomy of a common semantic system for words and pictures [see comments]. *Nature*, *383*, 254–256.

Warburton, E., Wise, R.J., Price, C.J., Weiller, C., Hadar, U., Ramsay, S., & Frackowiak, R.S. (1996). Noun and verb retrieval by normal subjects: Studies with PET. *Brain*, *119*, 159–179.

Warrington, E.K., & Shallice, T. (1984). Category specific impairments. *Brain*, *107*, 829–853.

Watson, J.D., Myers, R., Frackowiak, R.S.J., Hajnal, J.V., Woods, R.P., Mazziotta, J.C., Shipp, S., & Zeki, S. (1993). Area V5 of the human brain: Evidence from a combined study using positron emission tomography and magnetic resonance imaging. *Cerebral Cortex*, *3*, 79–94.

Yoon, E.Y., Heinke, D., & Humphreys, G.W. (this issue). Modelling direct perceptual constraints on action selection: The Naming and Action Model (NAM). *Visual Cognition*, *9*, 615–661.

APPENDIX

Experiment 1

Non-twisters	Twisters
Pencil	Doorknob
Kettle	Spanner
Broom	Bulb
Clothespin	Screwdriver
Scissors	Pliers
Saucepan	Button
Thimble	
Hammer	
Needle	
Toothbrush	
Comb	
Fork	
Paintbrush	
Ruler	
Nail	
Saltshaker	
Spoon	
Chisel	

Experiments 2 and 3

Pourers	Twisters
Orange squeezer	Office chair
Spoon	Pen
Teapot	Spanner
Test tube	Toilet handle
Wine bottle	Whisk
Watering can	Meat grinder
Frying pan	Rope
Bowl	Fishing rod
Carafe	Light bulb
Saucepan	Fan
Bucket	Corkscrew
Coffee pot	Wood drill
Decanter	Egg beater
Gravy boat	Hook
Kettle	Key
Ladle	Screw
Mug	Steering Wheel
Wine glass	Watch
Milk bottle	Telephone
Jug	Nut

Subject index